犬夜叉

INUYASHA™

ANI-MANGA™ Vol. 2

CREATED BY
RUMIKO TAKAHASHI

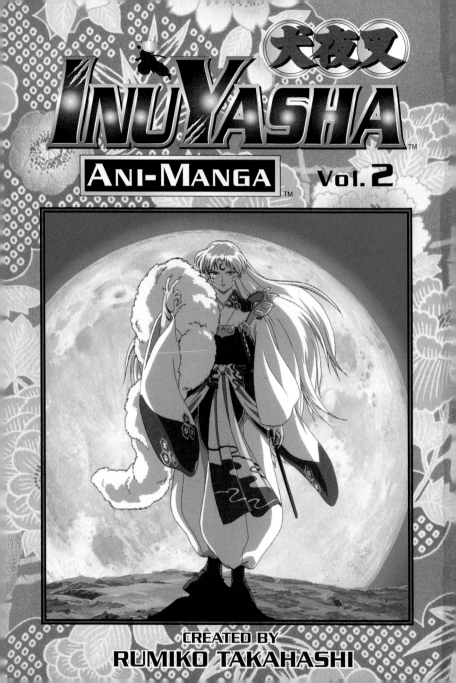

Inuyasha Ani-Manga™
Vol. #2

Created by
Rumiko Takahashi

Translation based on the VIZ anime TV series
Translation Assistance/Katy Bridges
Lettering/John Clark
Cover Design & Graphics/Hidemi Sahara
Editor/Ian Robertson

Managing Editor/Annette Roman
Editorial Director/Elizabeth Kawasaki
Editor in Chief/Alvin Lu
Sr. Director of Acquisitions/Rika Inouye
Sr. VP of Marketing/Liza Coppola
Exec. VP of Sales & Marketing/John Easum
Publisher/Hyoe Narita

Published by VIZ Media, LLC
P.O. Box 77010
San Francisco, CA 94107

10 9 8 7 6 5 4
First printing, March 2004
Fourth printing, October 2006

PARENTAL ADVISORY
INUYASHA ANI-MANGA is rated T+ for Older Teen
and is recommended for ages 16 and up. This volume
contains realistic and fantasy violence.

www.viz.com
store.viz.com

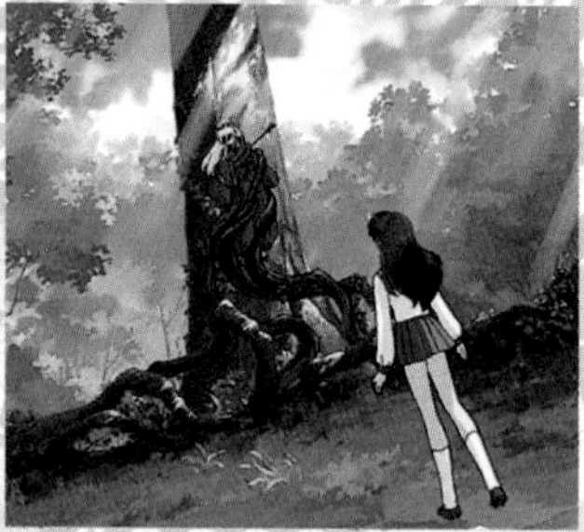

Story thus far

The typical high school girl, Kagome, has been transported into a mythical version of Japan's ancient past. This past is filled with incredible magic and terrifying demons. Who would have thought that the stories her superstitious grandfather told her could ever really be true!?

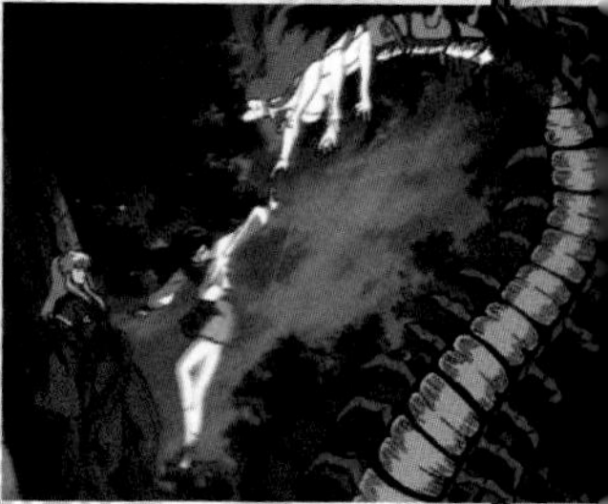

Kagome seems to be the reincarnation of the great warrior, Lady Kikyo.

Fifty years earlier Lady Kikyo had secured Inuyasha to a tree with a magical arrow while defending the Jewel of the Four Souls.

Kagome removed the arrow in a desperate attempt to save herself from the deadly centipede that dragged her into this new world. The Jewel of the Four Souls is released from Kagome's body and Inuyasha vows to steal it. Luckily, a magical necklace is placed around Inuyasha's neck, which allows Kagome to make him "sit" on command. The jewel is soon stolen by a Carrion Crow and then shattered by one of Kagome's arrows. Kagome and Inuyasha must now search for all the shards of the Jewel of the Four Souls.

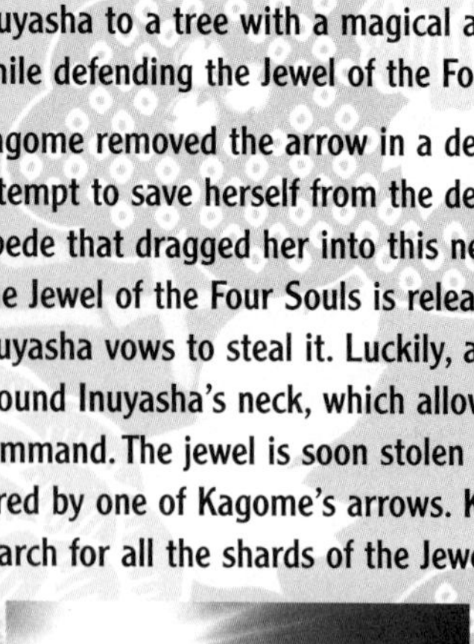

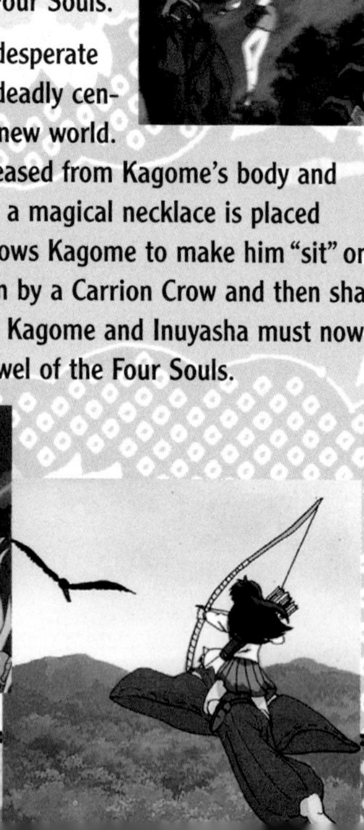

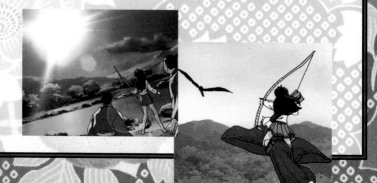

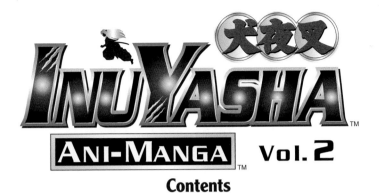

INUYASHA™

ANI-MANGA™ VOL. 2

Contents

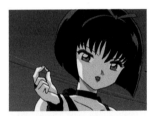

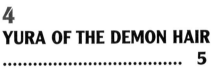

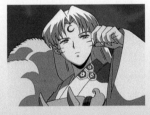

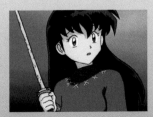

4
YURA OF THE DEMON HAIR

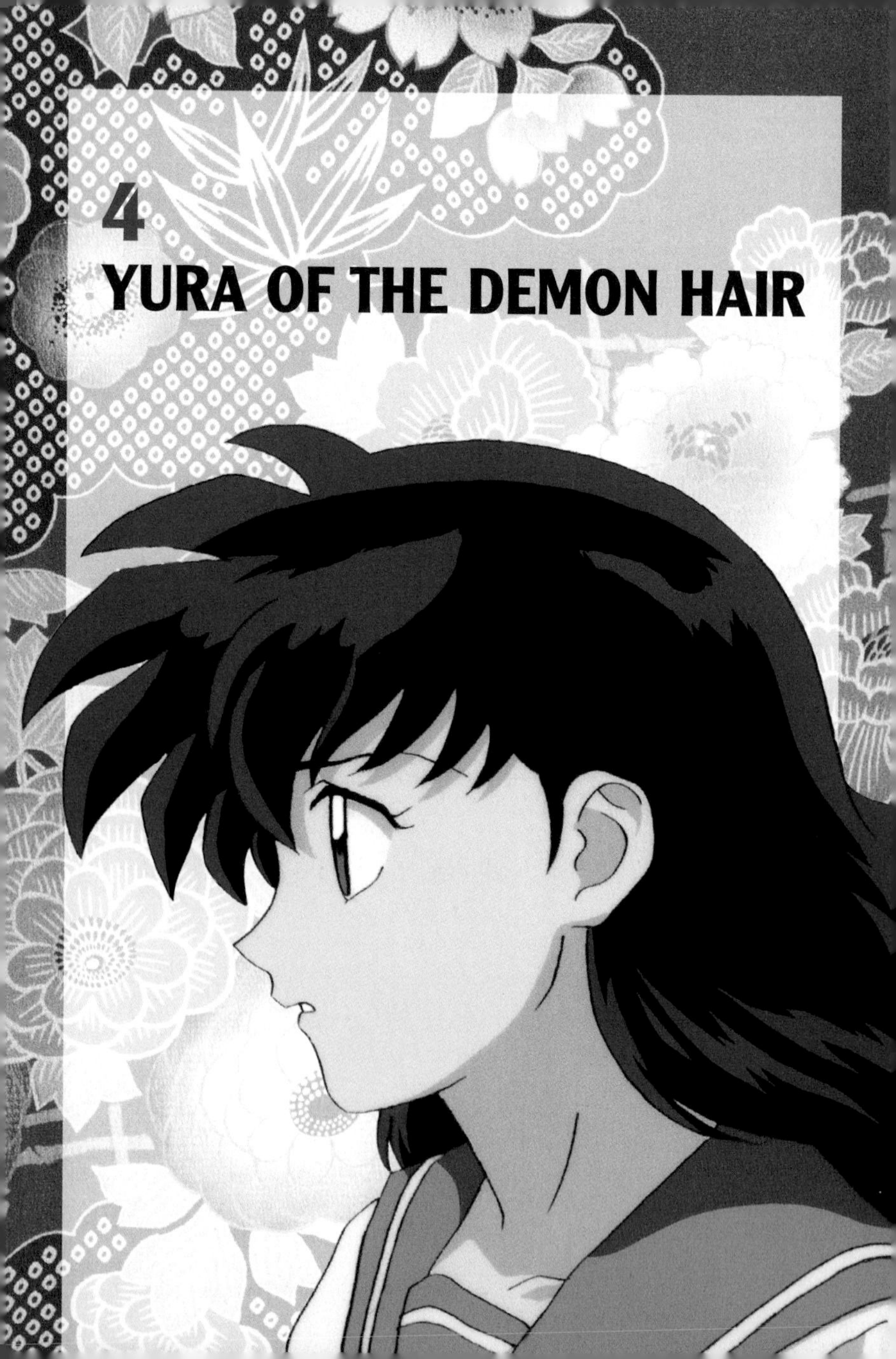

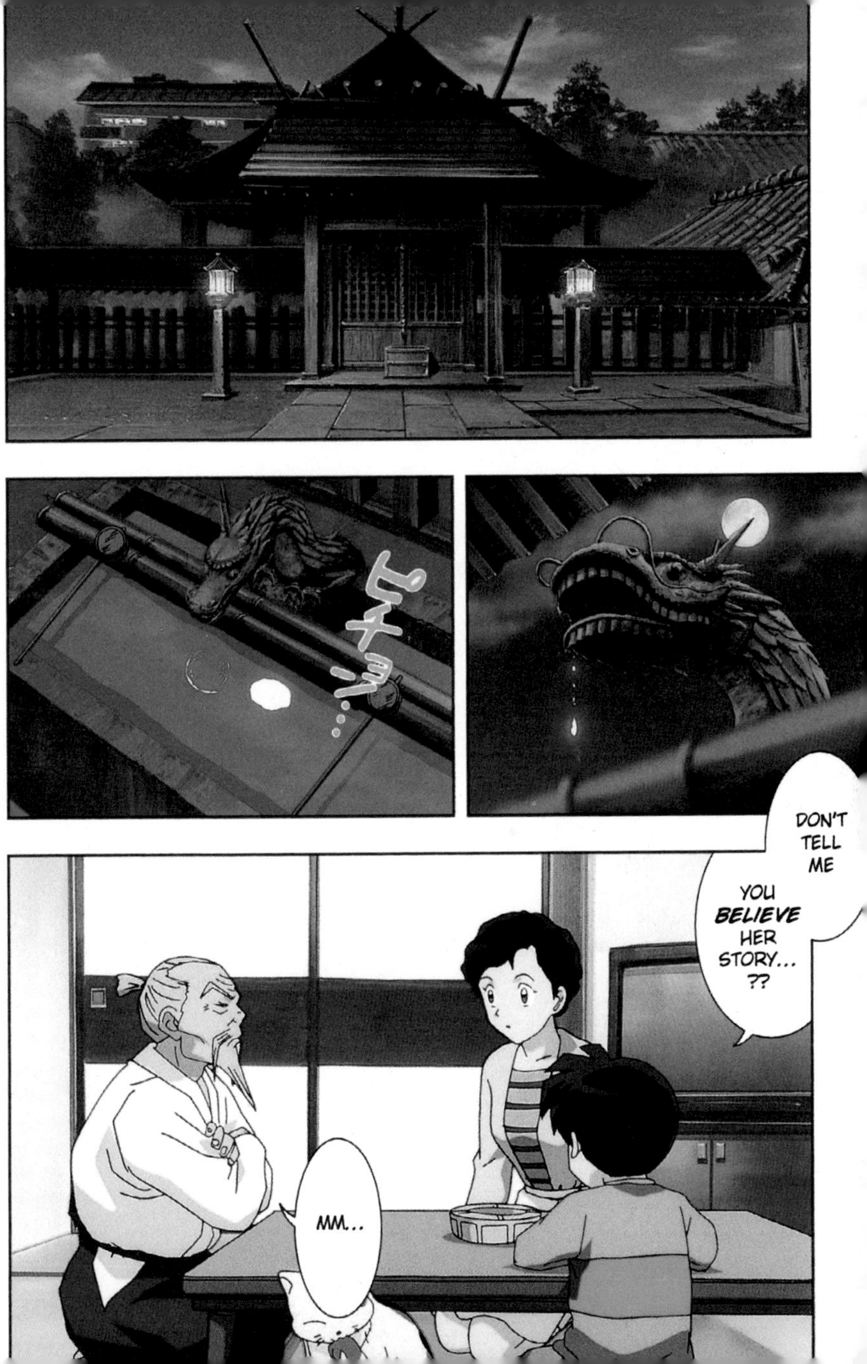
ピチョン…
DON'T TELL ME
YOU **BELIEVE** HER STORY…??
MM…

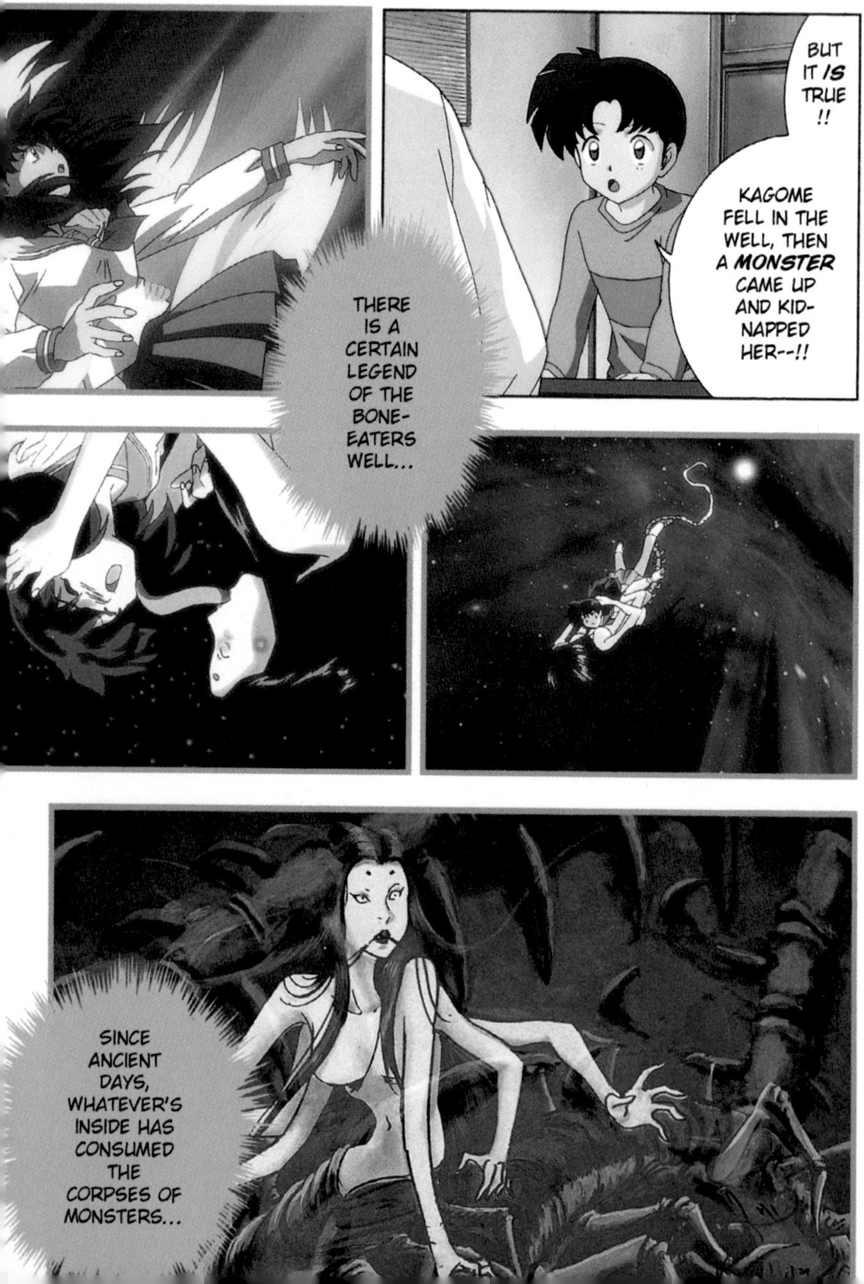
BUT IT IS TRUE!!
KAGOME FELL IN THE WELL, THEN A MONSTER CAME UP AND KID-NAPPED HER--!!
THERE IS A CERTAIN LEGEND OF THE BONE-EATERS WELL...
SINCE ANCIENT DAYS, WHATEVER'S INSIDE HAS CONSUMED THE CORPSES OF MONSTERS...

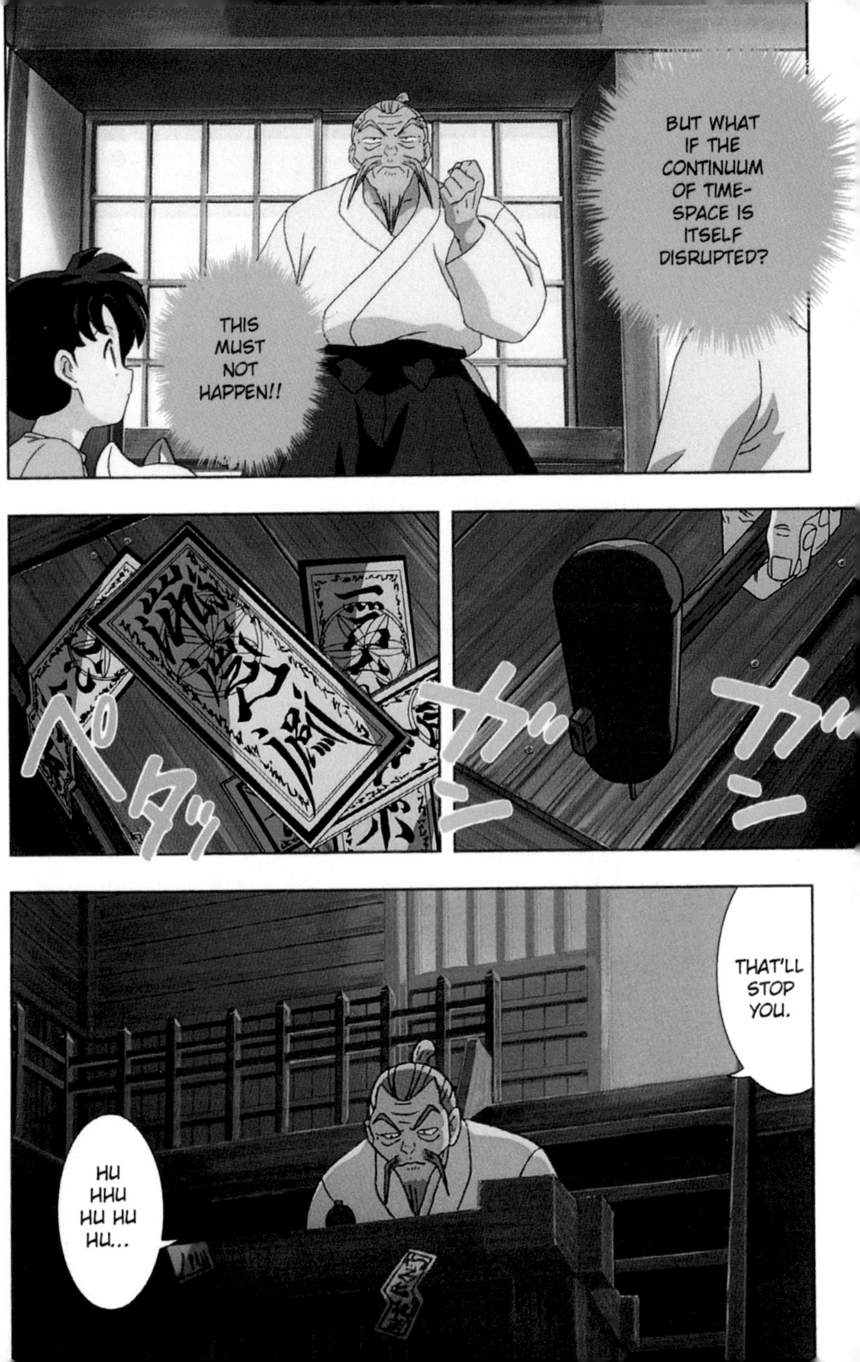
BUT WHAT IF THE CONTINUUM OF TIME-SPACE IS ITSELF DISRUPTED?
THIS MUST NOT HAPPEN!!
ガン
ガン
ペタッ
THAT'LL STOP YOU.
HU HHU HU HU HU...

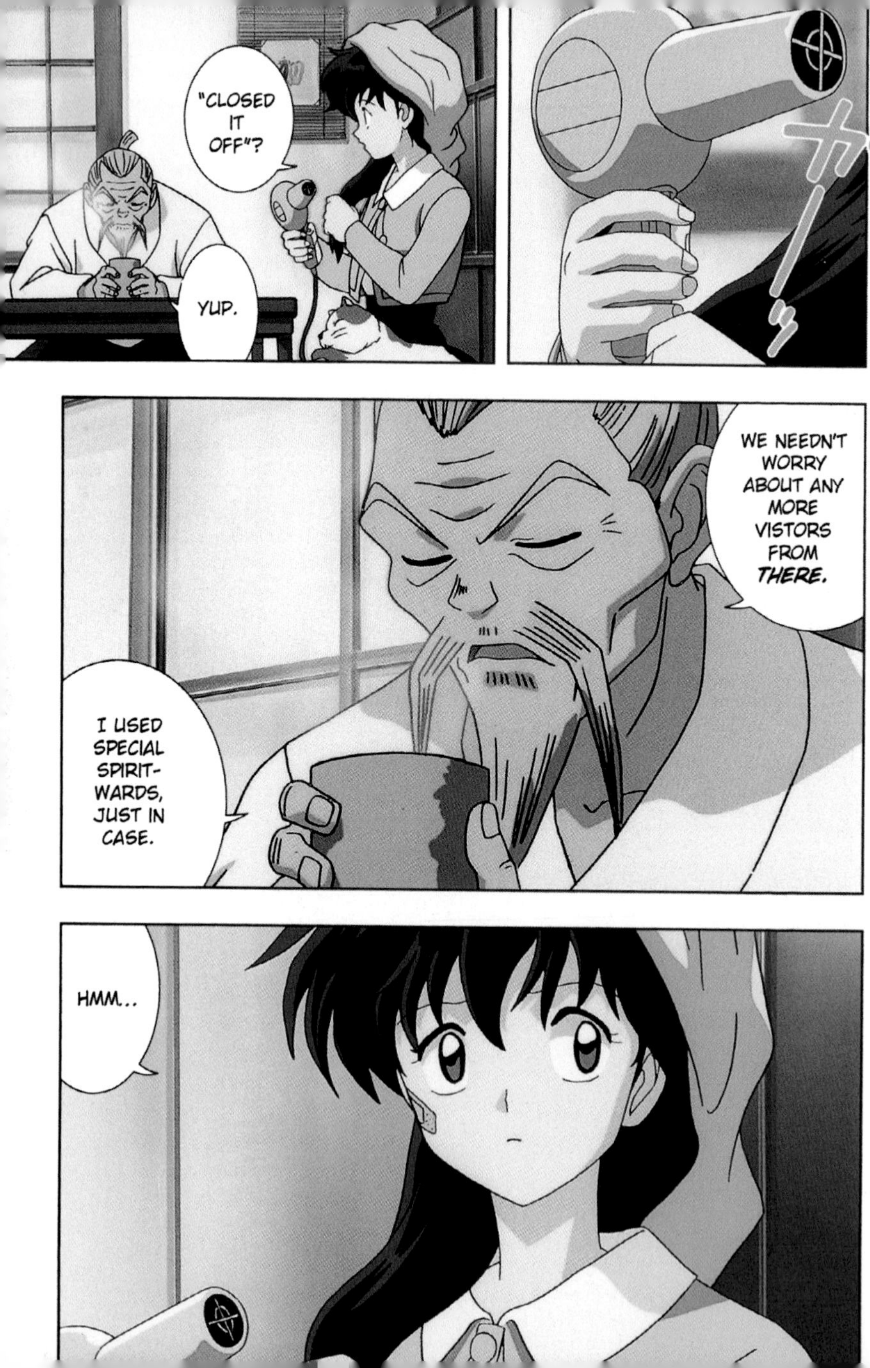
ガーッ
"CLOSED IT OFF"?
YUP.
WE NEEDN'T WORRY ABOUT ANY MORE VISTORS FROM ***THERE.***
I USED SPECIAL SPIRIT-WARDS, JUST IN CASE.
HMM..

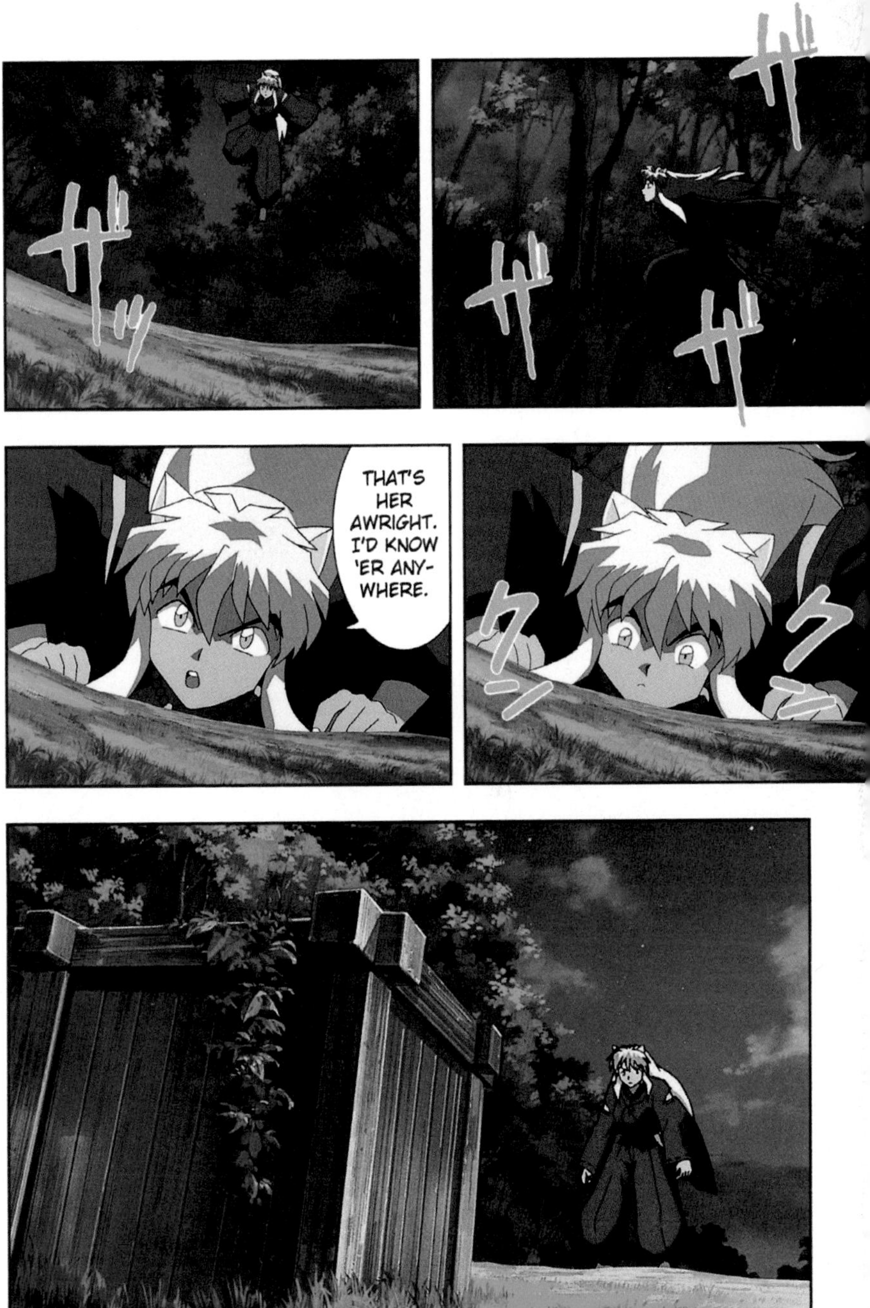
ザ
ザ
ザ
ザッ
クン
クン
THAT'S HER AWRIGHT. I'D KNOW 'ER ANY-WHERE.

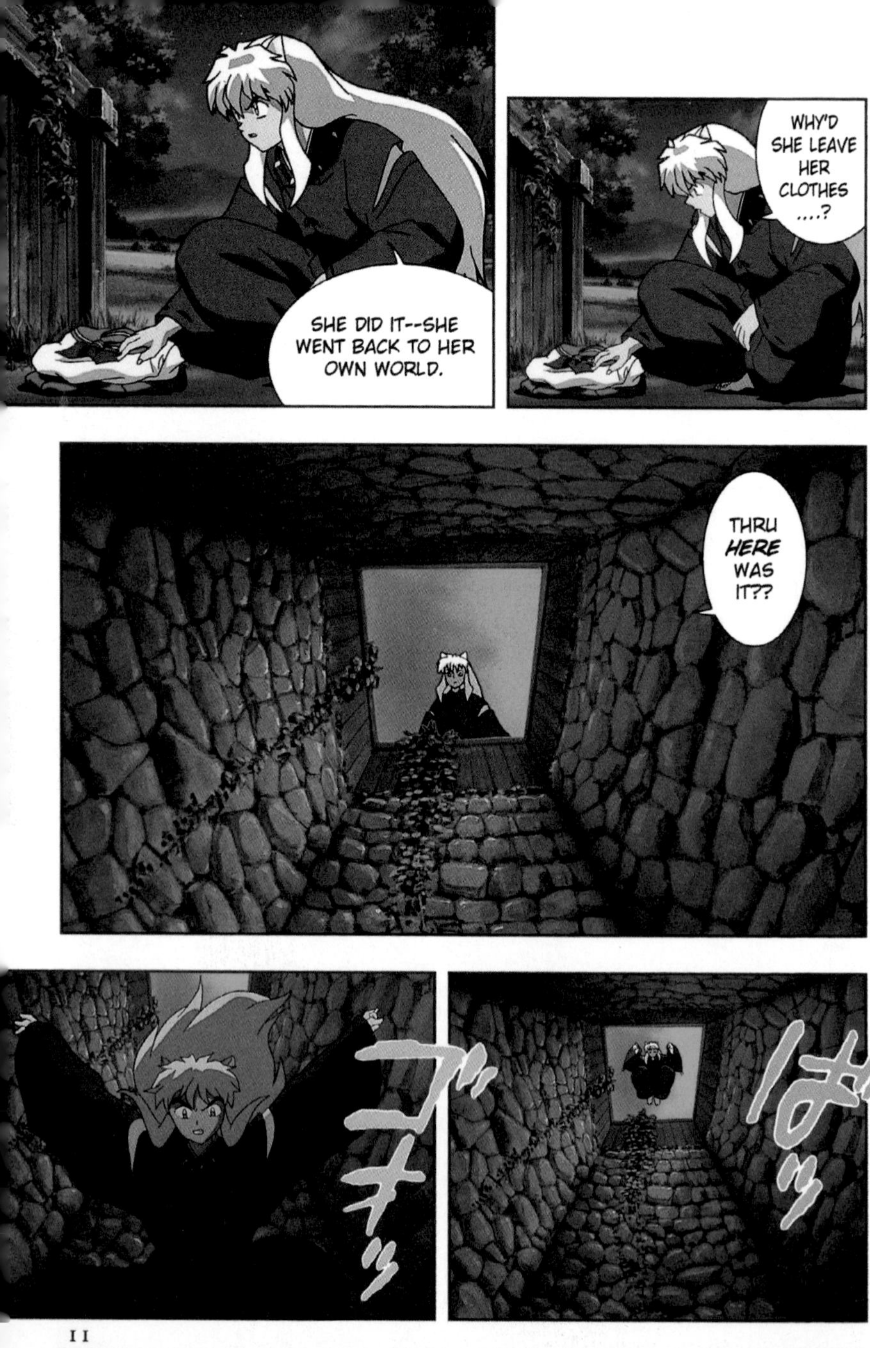
WHY'D SHE LEAVE HER CLOTHES ....?
SHE DID IT--SHE WENT BACK TO HER OWN WORLD.
THRU *HERE* WAS IT??
ばッ
ゴキッ

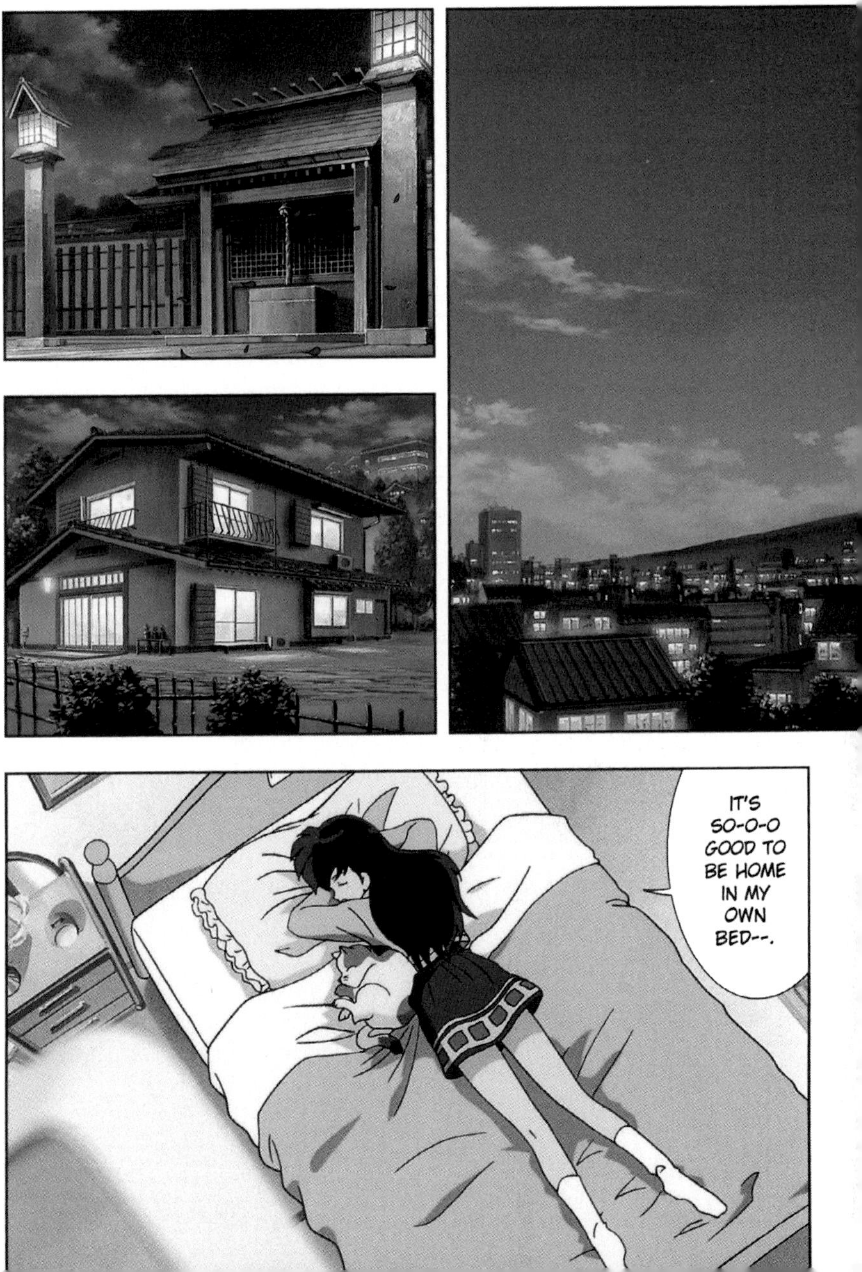
IT'S SO-O-O GOOD TO BE HOME IN MY OWN BED--.

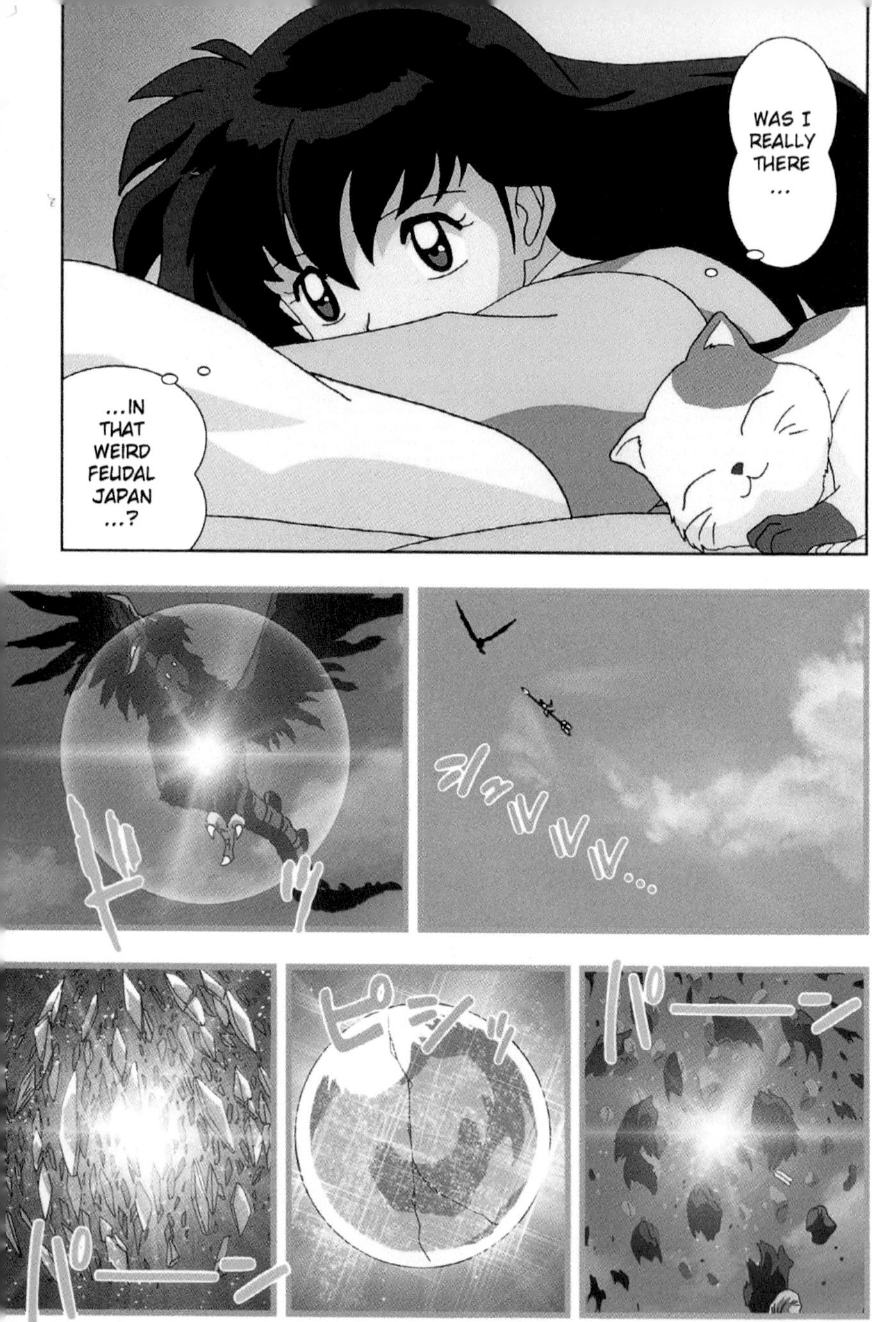
WAS I REALLY THERE ...
...IN THAT WEIRD FEUDAL JAPAN ...?
ドッ
パーーン
ピシッ
パーーン

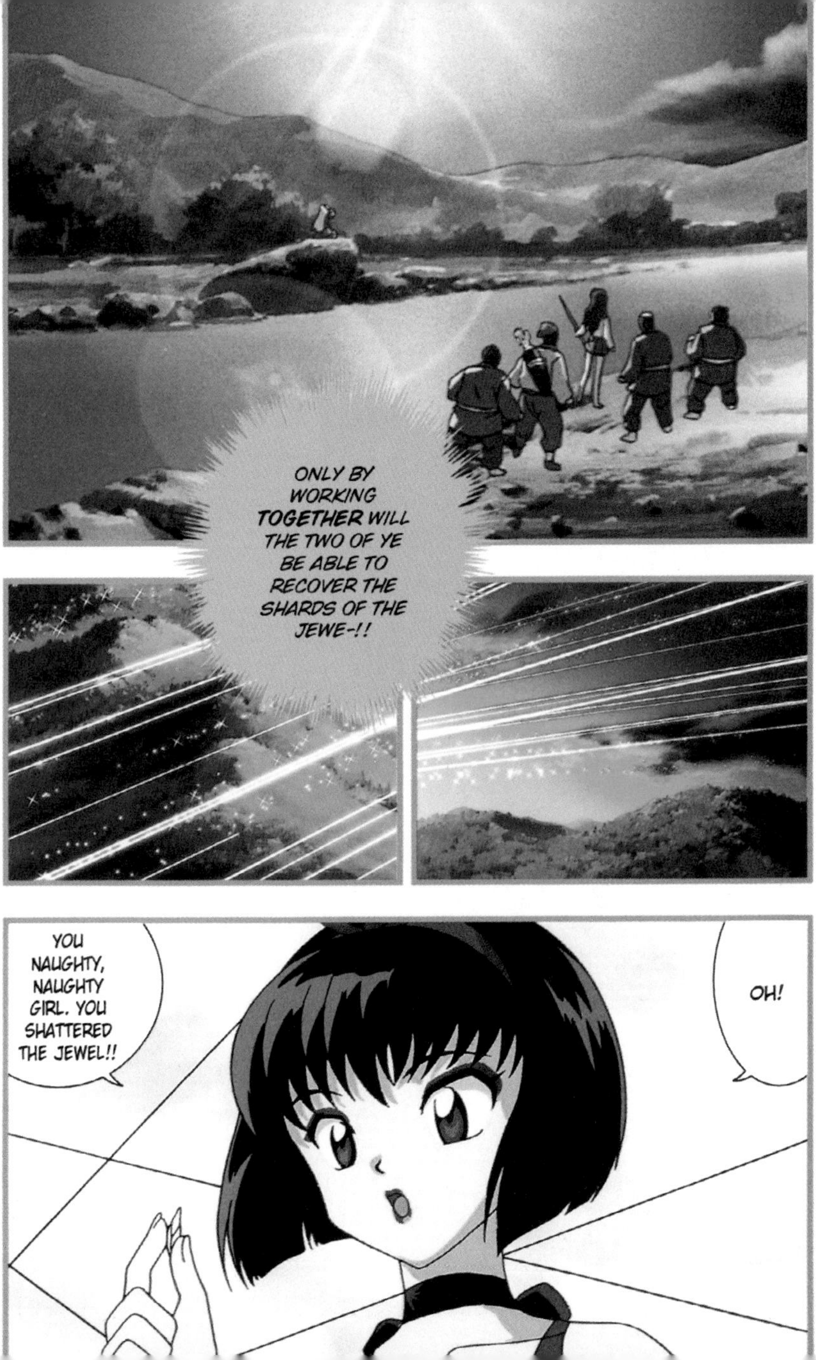
ONLY BY WORKING **TOGETHER** WILL THE TWO OF YE BE ABLE TO RECOVER THE SHARDS OF THE JEWE-!!
OH!
YOU NAUGHTY, NAUGHTY GIRL. YOU SHATTERED THE JEWEL!!

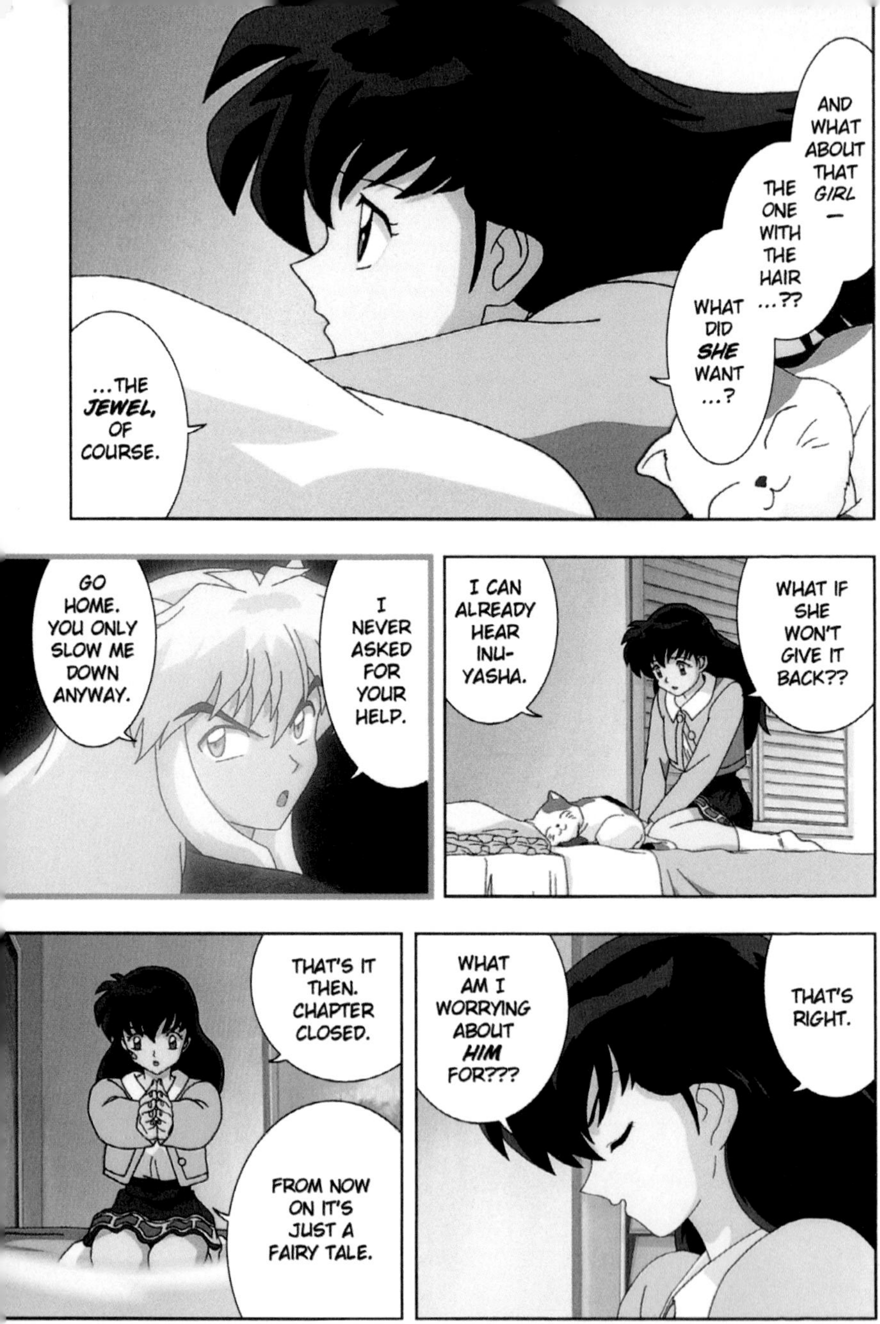
AND WHAT ABOUT THAT *GIRL* —
THE ONE WITH THE HAIR ...??
WHAT DID *SHE* WANT ...?
...THE *JEWEL,* OF COURSE.
WHAT IF SHE WON'T GIVE IT BACK??
I CAN ALREADY HEAR INU-YASHA.
I NEVER ASKED FOR YOUR HELP.
GO HOME. YOU ONLY SLOW ME DOWN ANYWAY.
THAT'S RIGHT.
WHAT AM I WORRYING ABOUT *HIM* FOR???
THAT'S IT THEN. CHAPTER CLOSED.
FROM NOW ON IT'S JUST A FAIRY TALE.

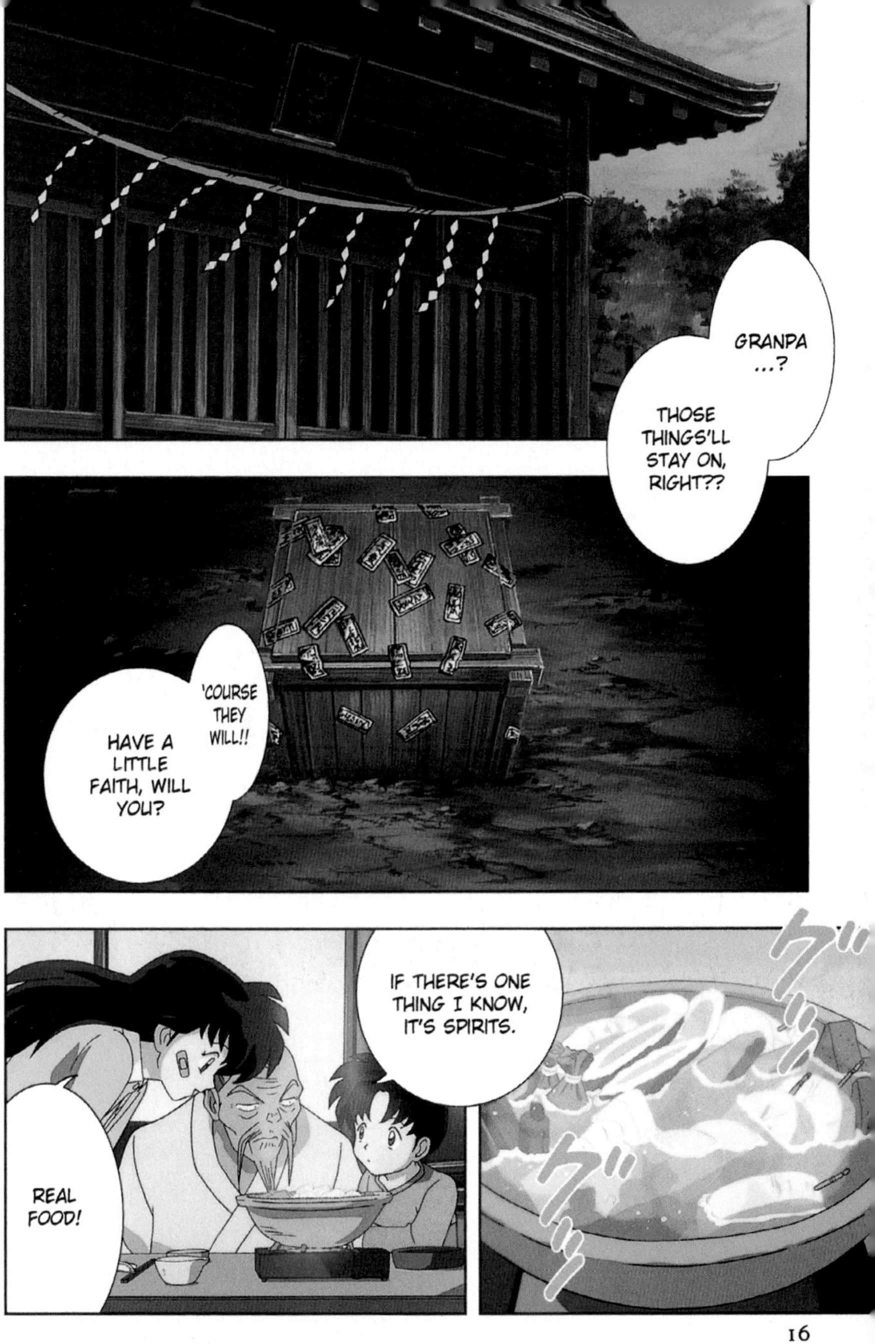
GRANPA ...?
THOSE THINGS'LL STAY ON, RIGHT??
'COURSE THEY WILL!!
HAVE A LITTLE FAITH, WILL YOU?
IF THERE'S ONE THING I KNOW, IT'S SPIRITS.
REAL FOOD!

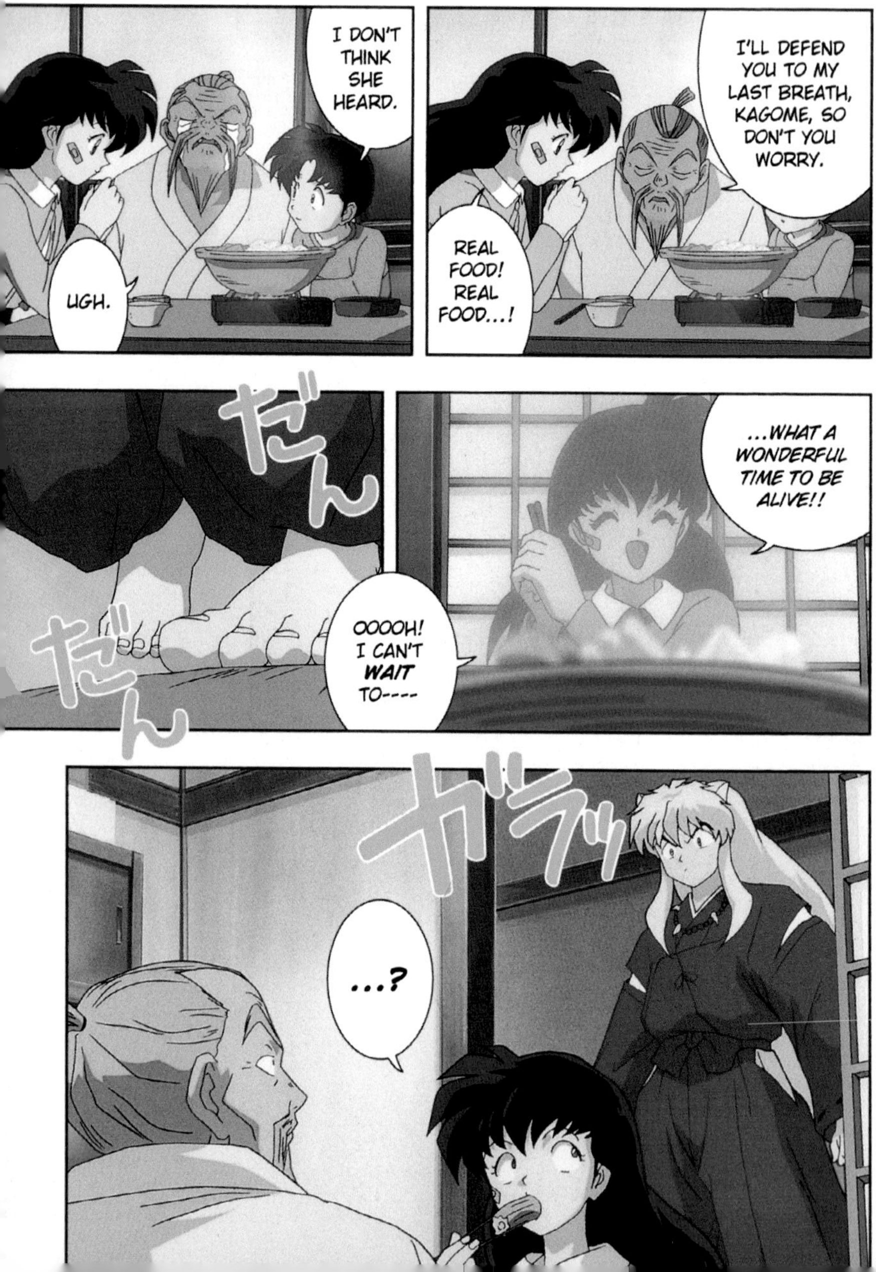
I'LL DEFEND YOU TO MY LAST BREATH, KAGOME, SO DON'T YOU WORRY.
REAL FOOD! REAL FOOD...!
I DON'T THINK SHE HEARD.
UGH.
...WHAT A WONDERFUL TIME TO BE ALIVE!!
OOOOH! I CAN'T WAIT TO----
だん
だん
ガラッ
...?

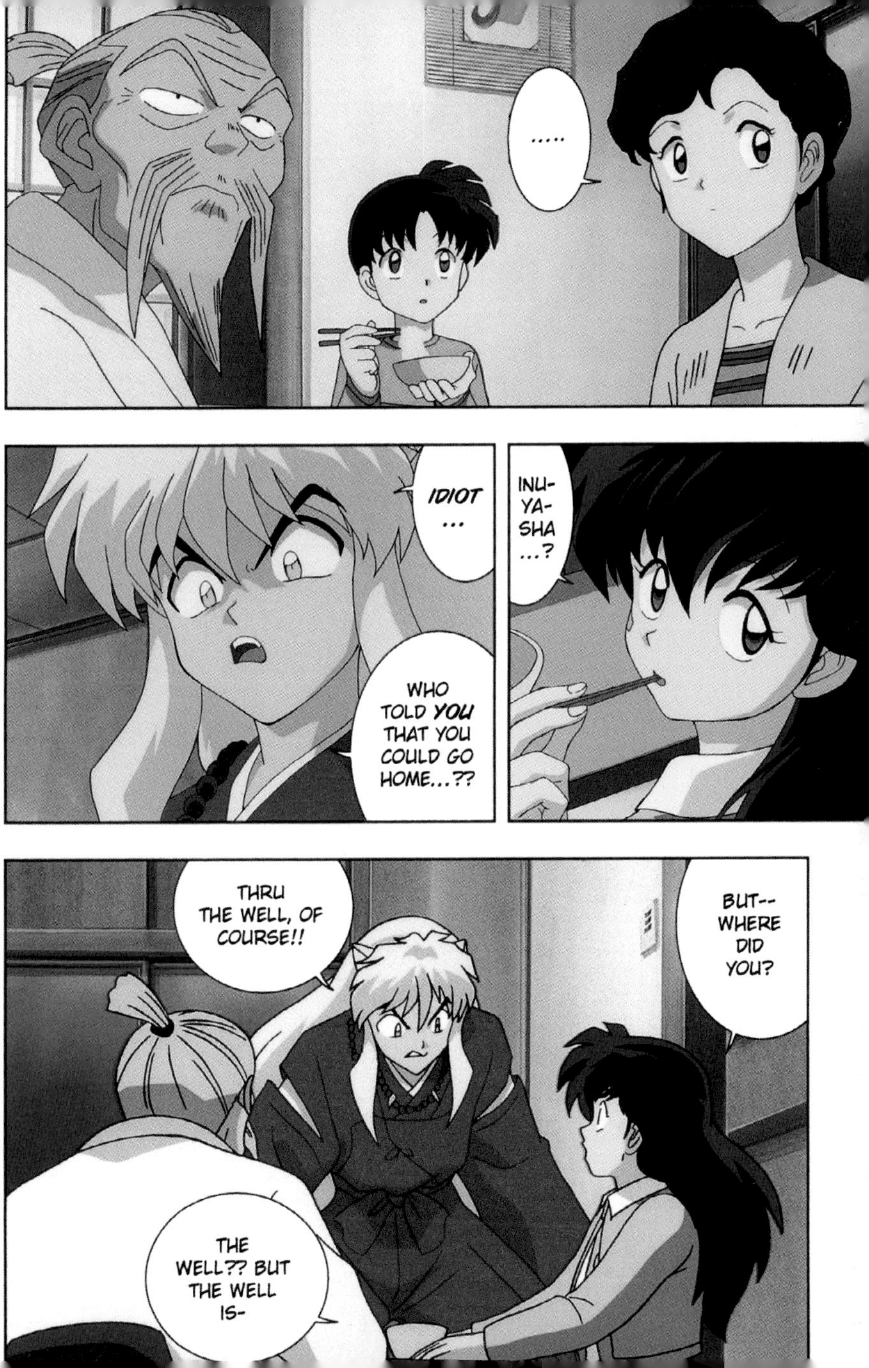
.....
INU-YA-SHA...?
IDIOT...
WHO TOLD YOU THAT YOU COULD GO HOME...??
BUT--WHERE DID YOU?
THRU THE WELL, OF COURSE!!
THE WELL?? BUT THE WELL IS-

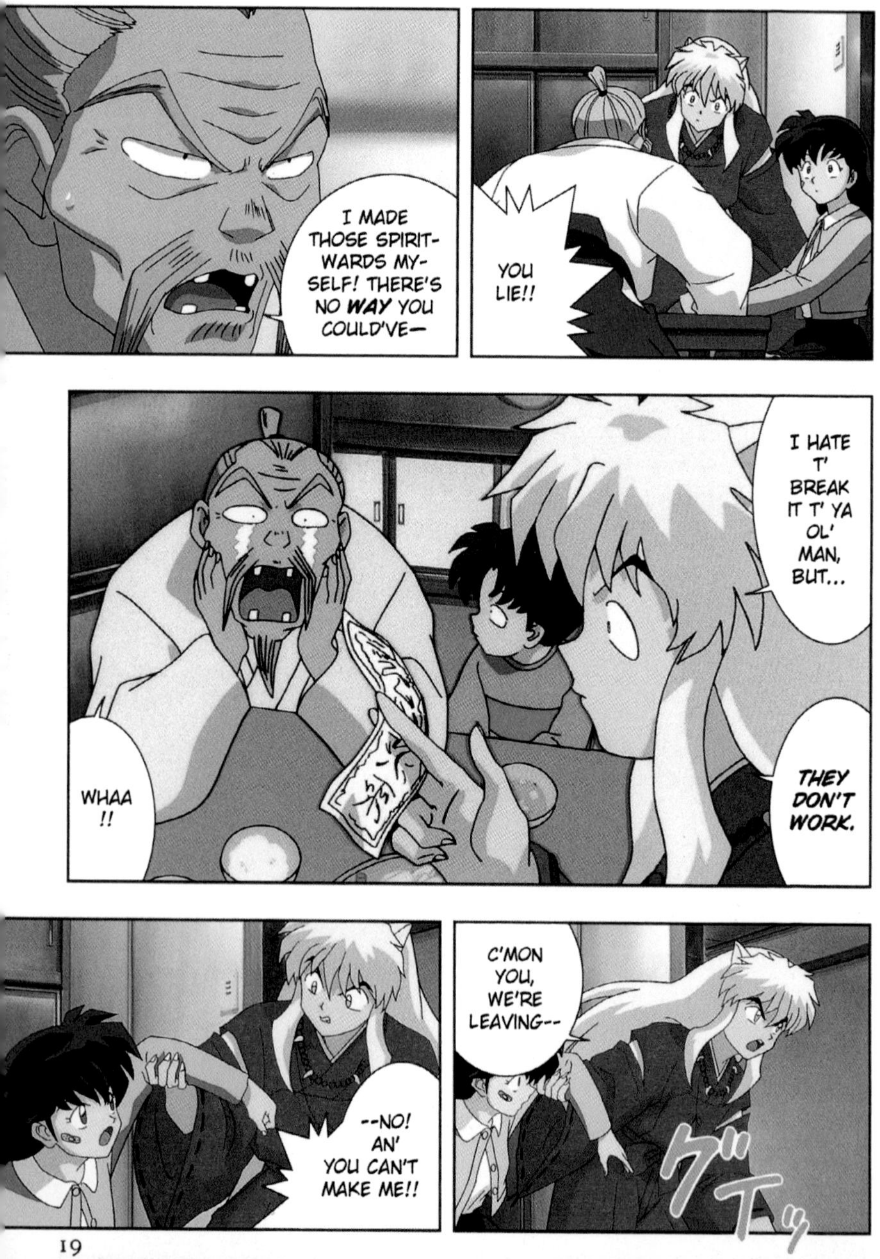
YOU LIE!!
I MADE THOSE SPIRIT-WARDS MY-SELF! THERE'S NO ***WAY*** YOU COULD'VE—
I HATE T' BREAK IT T' YA OL' MAN, BUT...
THEY DON'T WORK.
WHAA !!
C'MON YOU, WE'RE LEAVING--
グッ
--NO! AN' YOU CAN'T MAKE ME!!

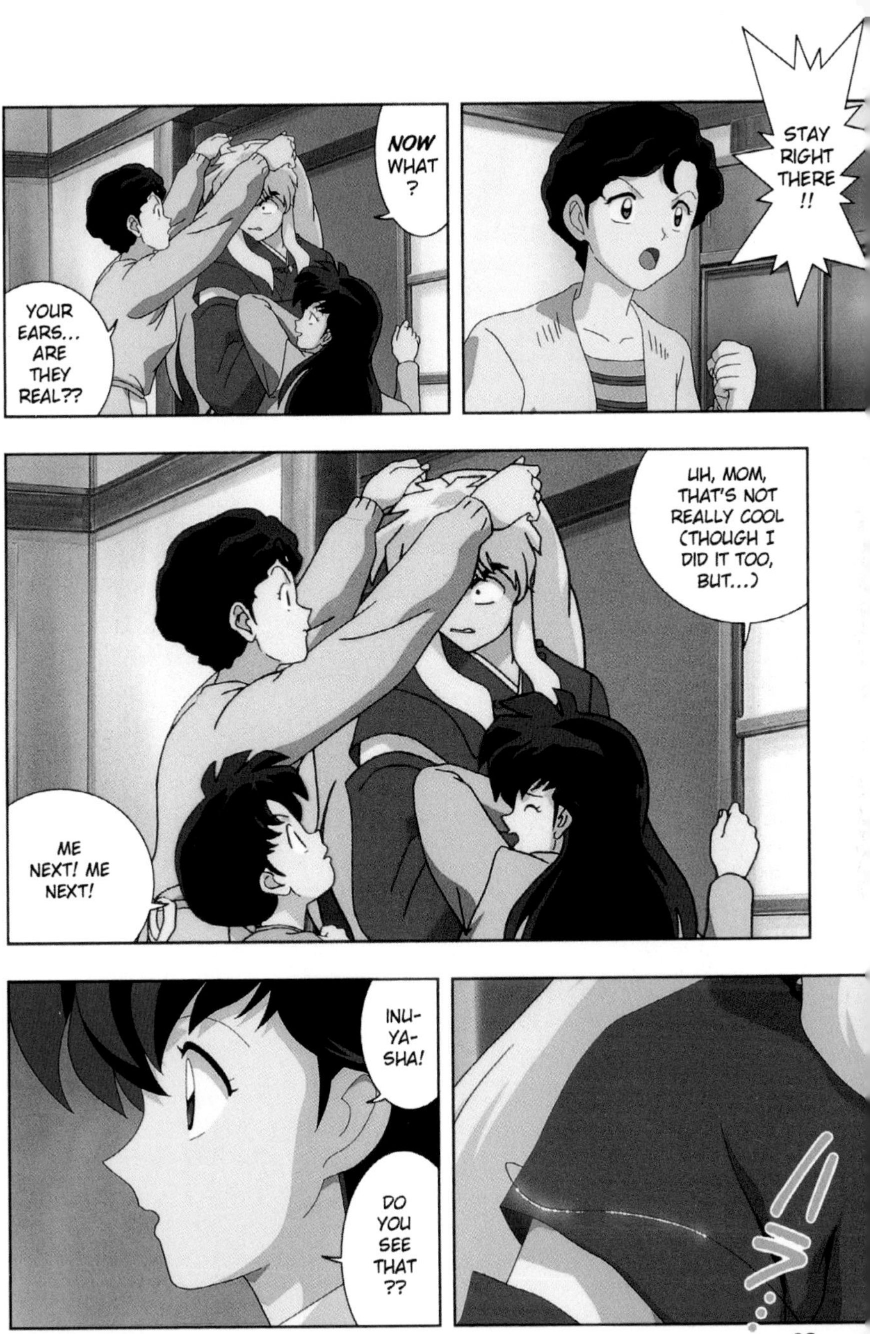
STAY RIGHT THERE!!
NOW WHAT?
YOUR EARS... ARE THEY REAL??
UH, MOM, THAT'S NOT REALLY COOL (THOUGH I DID IT TOO, BUT...)
ME NEXT! ME NEXT!
INU-YASHA!
DO YOU SEE THAT??

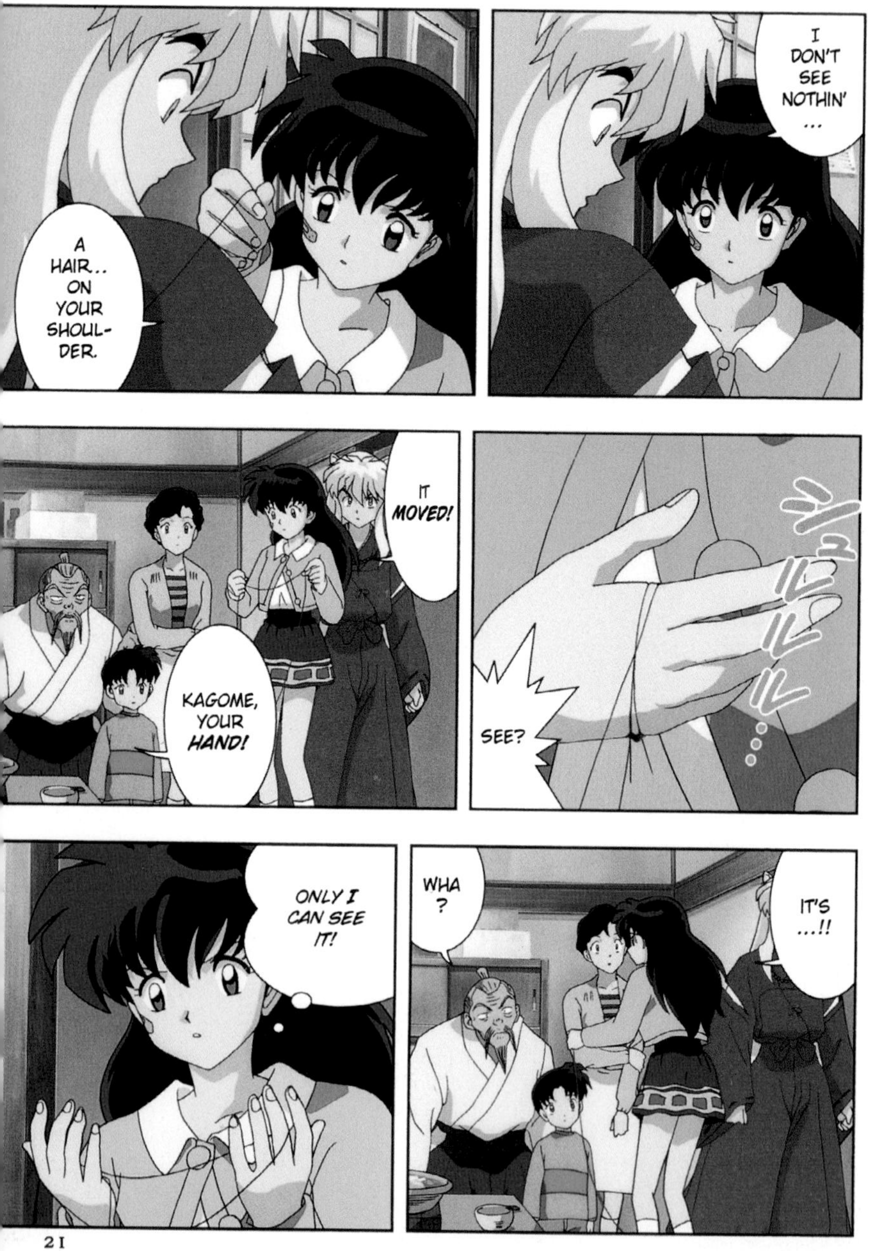

I DON'T SEE NOTHIN' ...
A HAIR... ON YOUR SHOULDER.
SEE?
IT MOVED!
KAGOME, YOUR HAND!
IT'S ...!!
WHA ?
ONLY I CAN SEE IT!

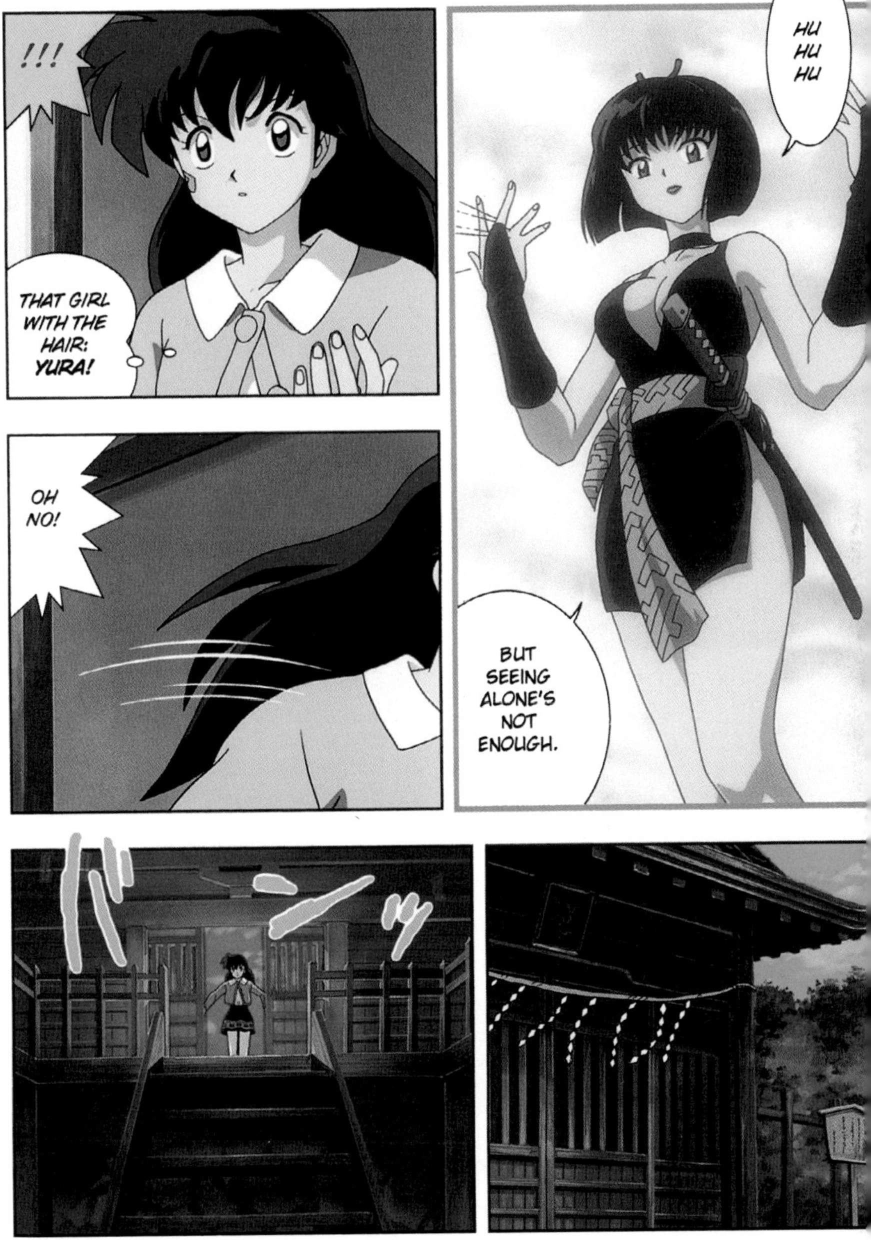
HU
HU
HU
BUT SEEING ALONE'S NOT ENOUGH.
!!!
THAT GIRL WITH THE HAIR: YURA!
OH NO!
バーンッ

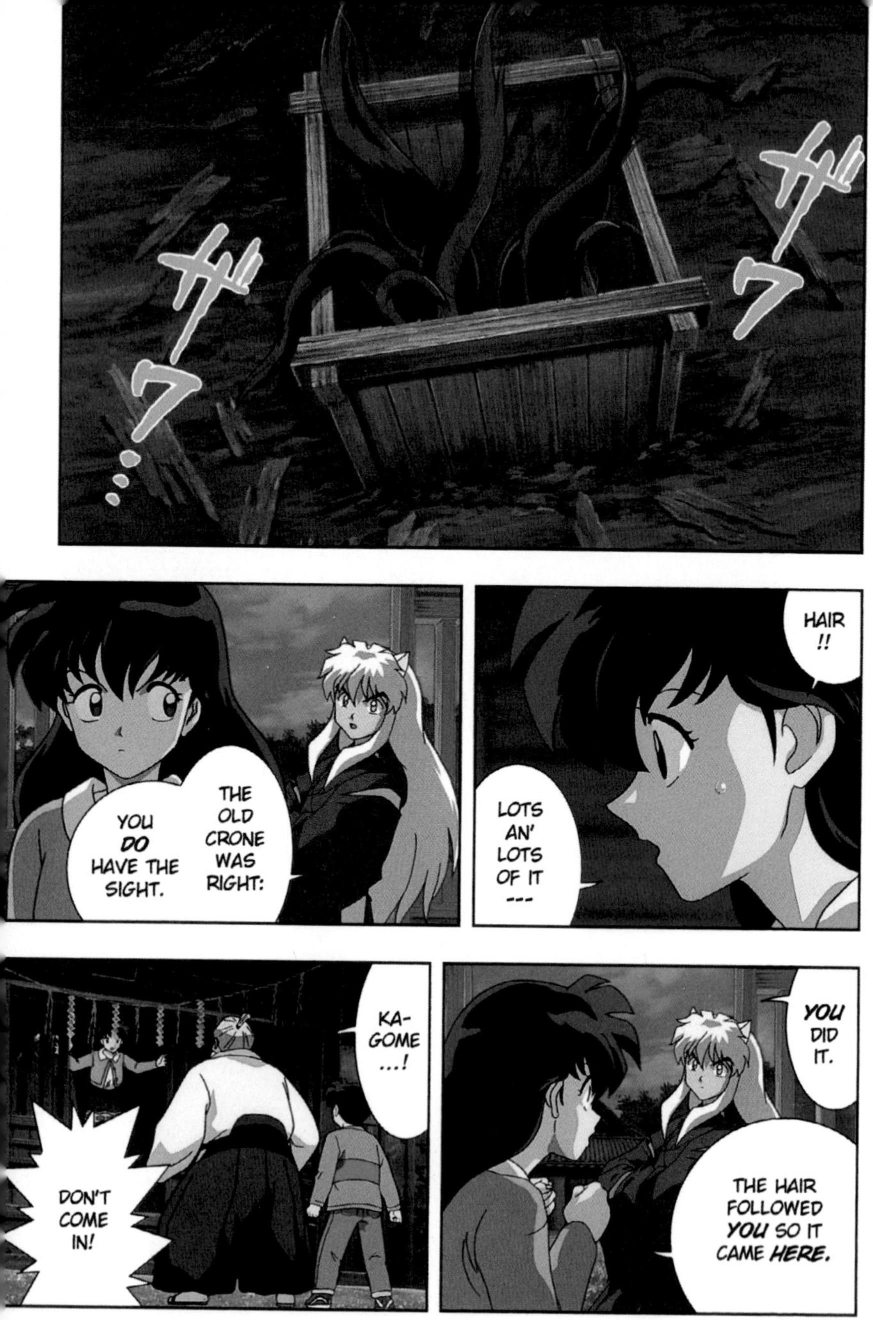
ザワ
ザワ…
HAIR !!
LOTS AN' LOTS OF IT ---
THE OLD CRONE WAS RIGHT:
YOU *DO* HAVE THE SIGHT.
YOU DID IT.
THE HAIR FOLLOWED *YOU* SO IT CAME *HERE.*
KA-GOME ...!
DON'T COME IN!

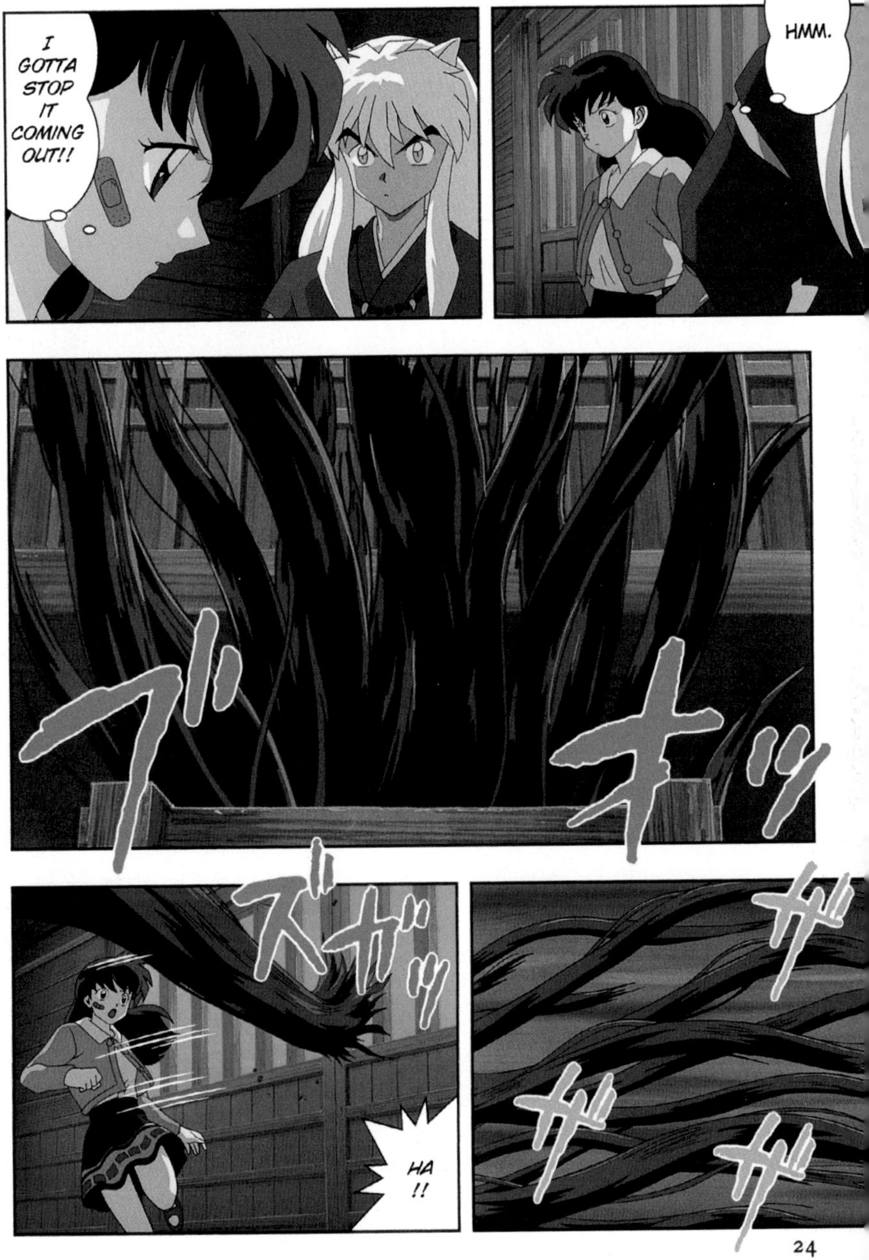
HMM.
I GOTTA STOP IT COMING OUT!!
ブオッ
ザ
ザ
ザ
ズガッ
HA!!

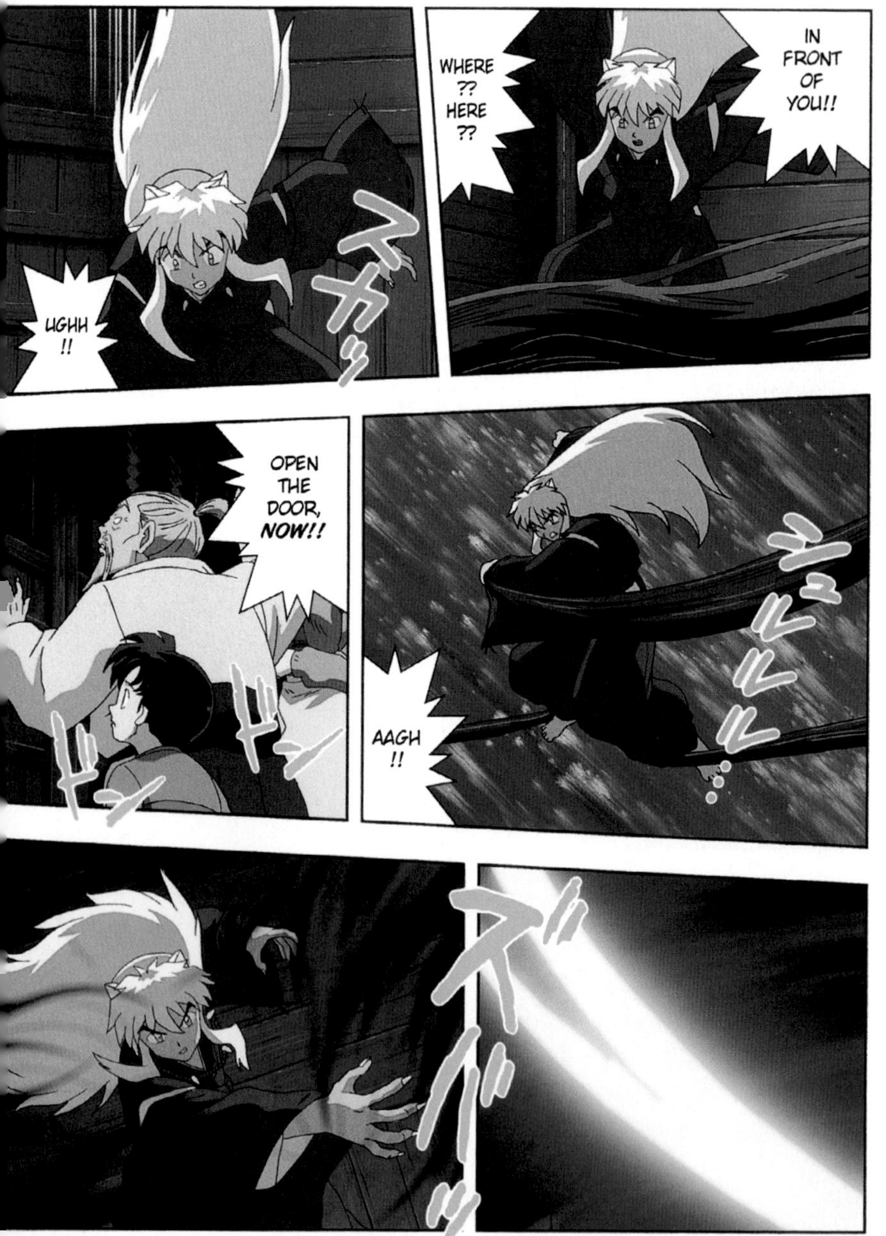
IN FRONT OF YOU!!
WHERE ?? HERE ??
UGHH !!
スカッ
シュルルル
AAGH !!
OPEN THE DOOR, NOW!!
ドン
ドン

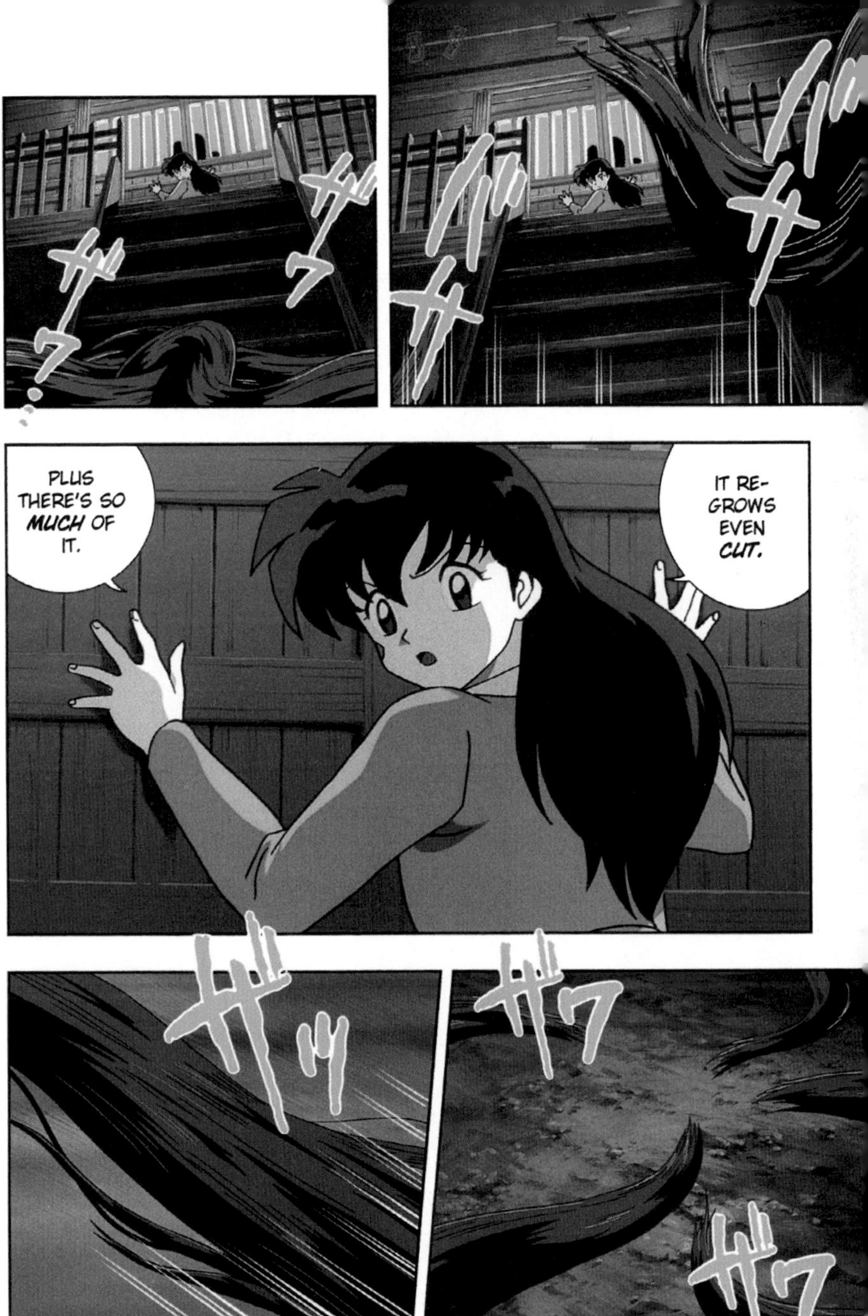
IT RE-GROWS EVEN CUT.
PLUS THERE'S SO MUCH OF IT.

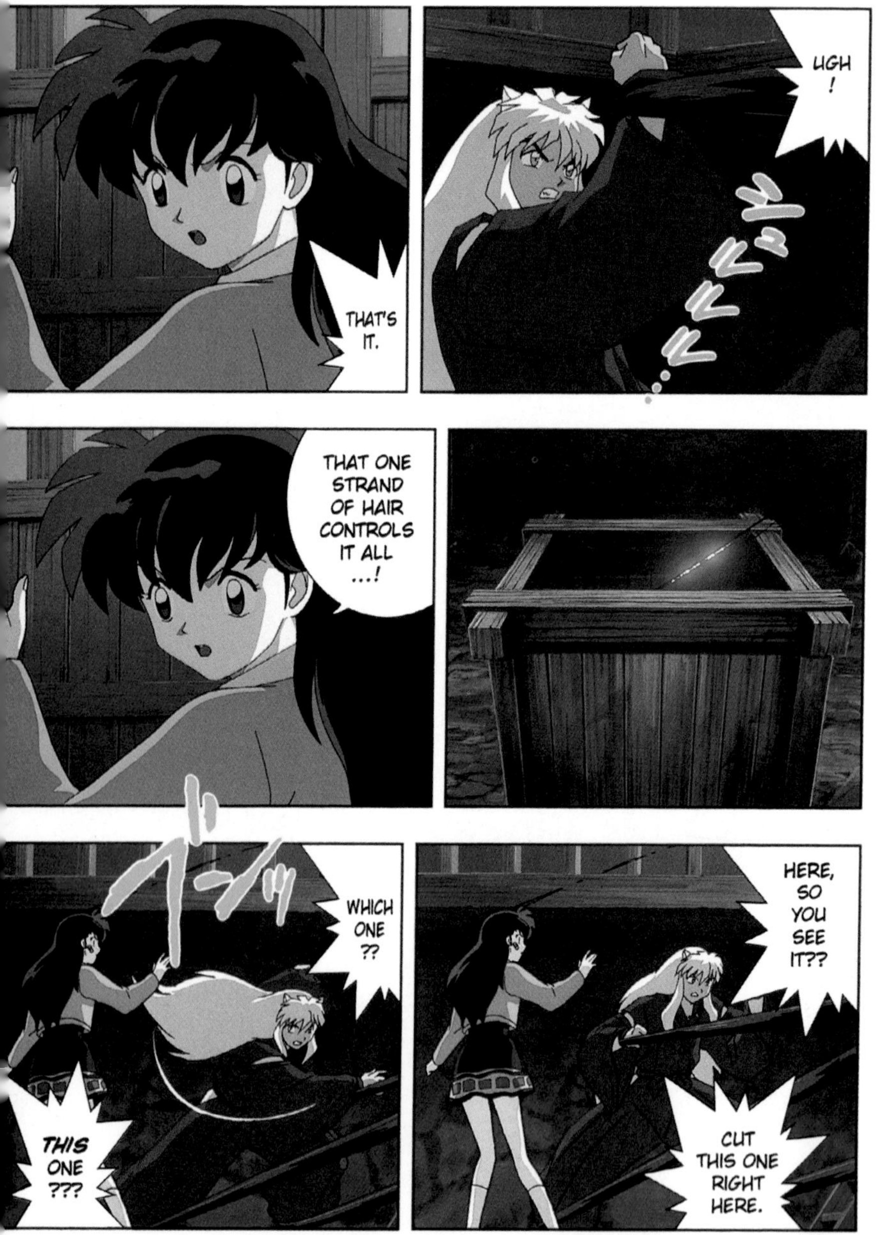
UGH !
THAT'S IT.
THAT ONE STRAND OF HAIR CONTROLS IT ALL ...!
HERE, SO YOU SEE IT??
CUT THIS ONE RIGHT HERE.
WHICH ONE ??
THIS ONE ???

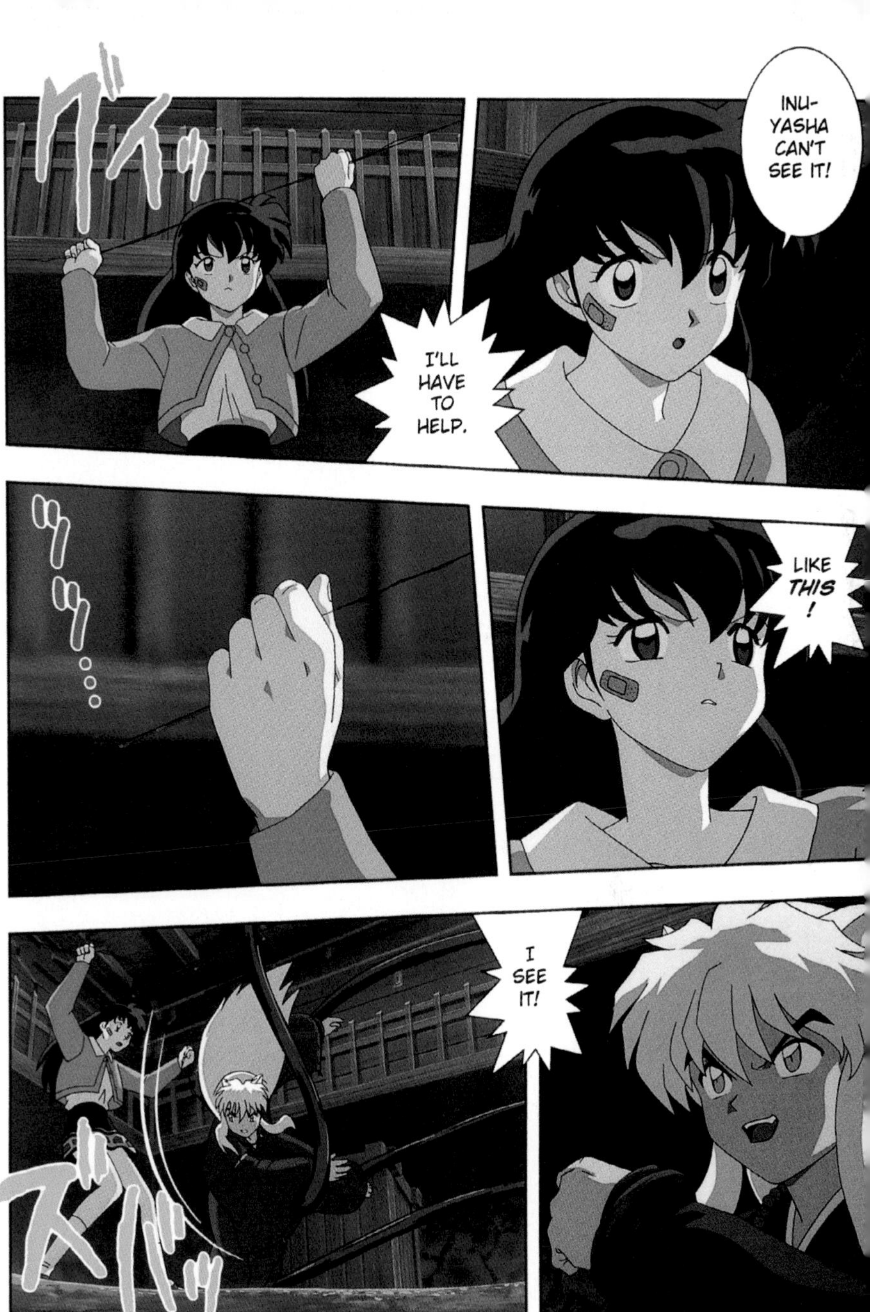
INU-YASHA CAN'T SEE IT!
I'LL HAVE TO HELP.
LIKE THIS!
I SEE IT!

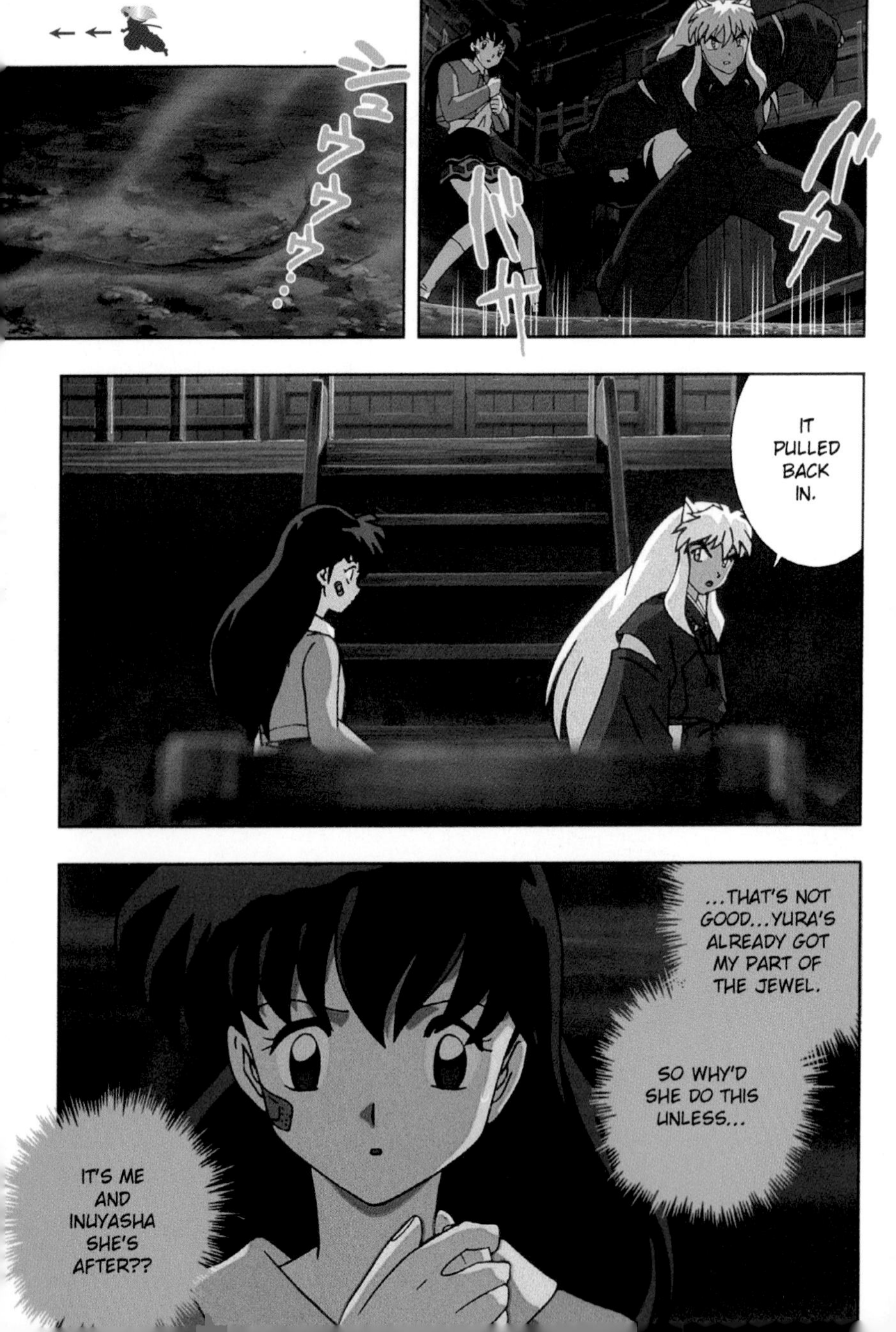
バサ
バサ
シュウウウ…
IT PULLED BACK IN.
...THAT'S NOT GOOD...YURA'S ALREADY GOT MY PART OF THE JEWEL.
SO WHY'D SHE DO THIS UNLESS...
IT'S ME AND INUYASHA SHE'S AFTER??

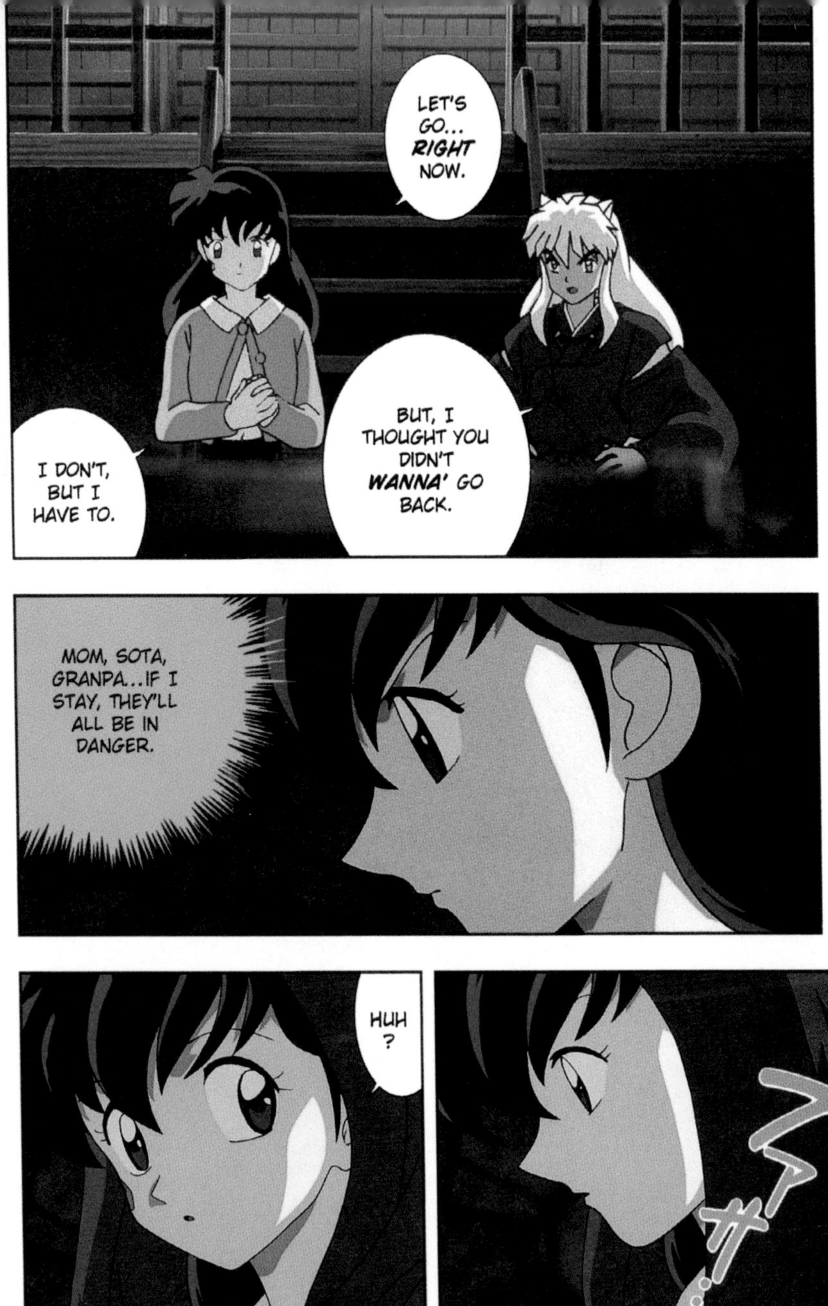
LET'S GO... RIGHT NOW.
BUT, I THOUGHT YOU DIDN'T WANNA' GO BACK.
I DON'T, BUT I HAVE TO.
MOM, SOTA, GRANPA...IF I STAY, THEY'LL ALL BE IN DANGER.
HUH ?

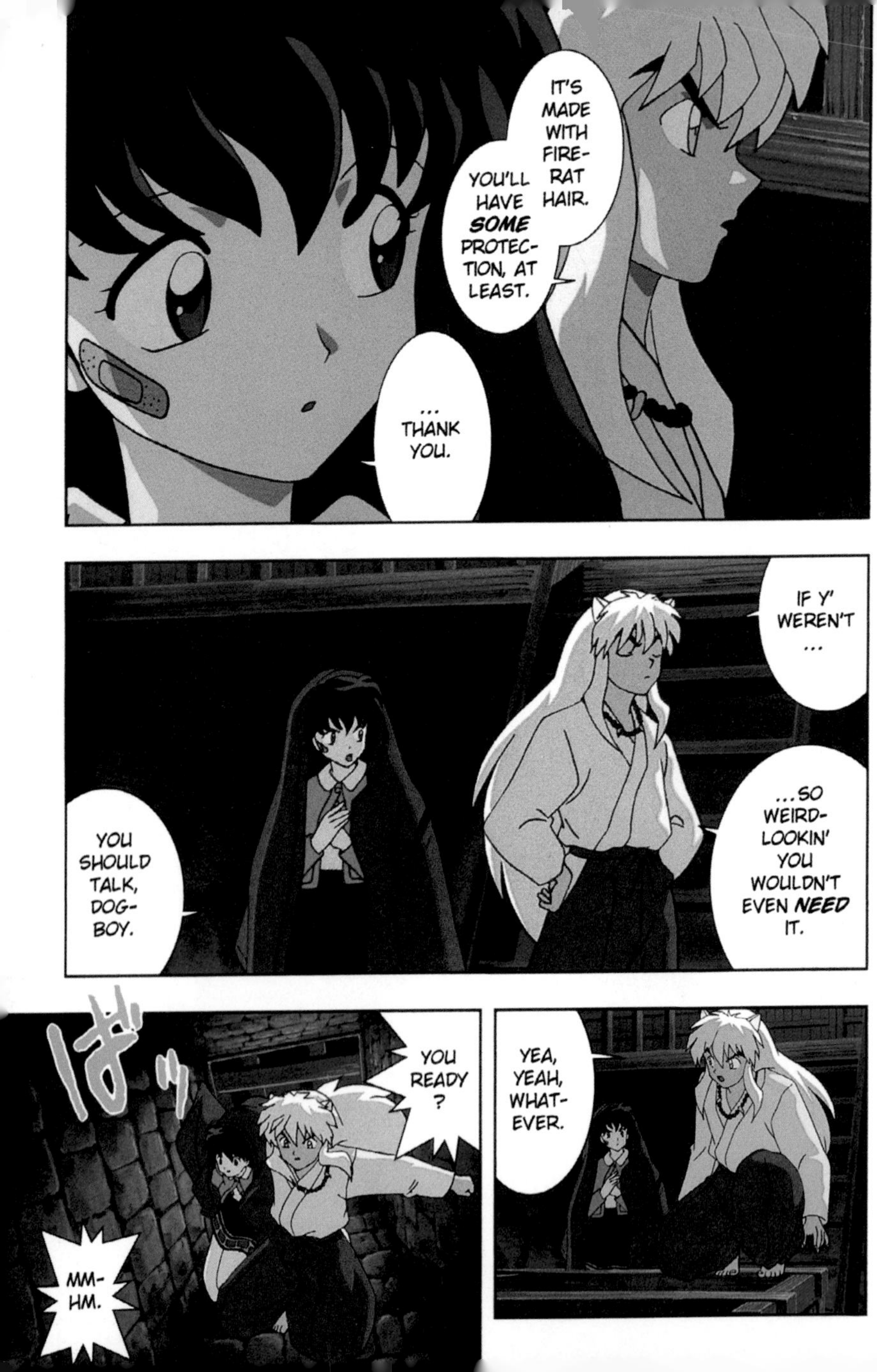

IT'S MADE WITH FIRE-RAT HAIR.
YOU'LL HAVE **SOME** PROTECTION, AT LEAST.
...THANK YOU.
IF Y' WEREN'T ...
...SO WEIRD-LOOKIN' YOU WOULDN'T EVEN **NEED** IT.
YOU SHOULD TALK, DOG-BOY.
YEA, YEAH, WHATEVER.
YOU READY?
ばッ
MM-HM.

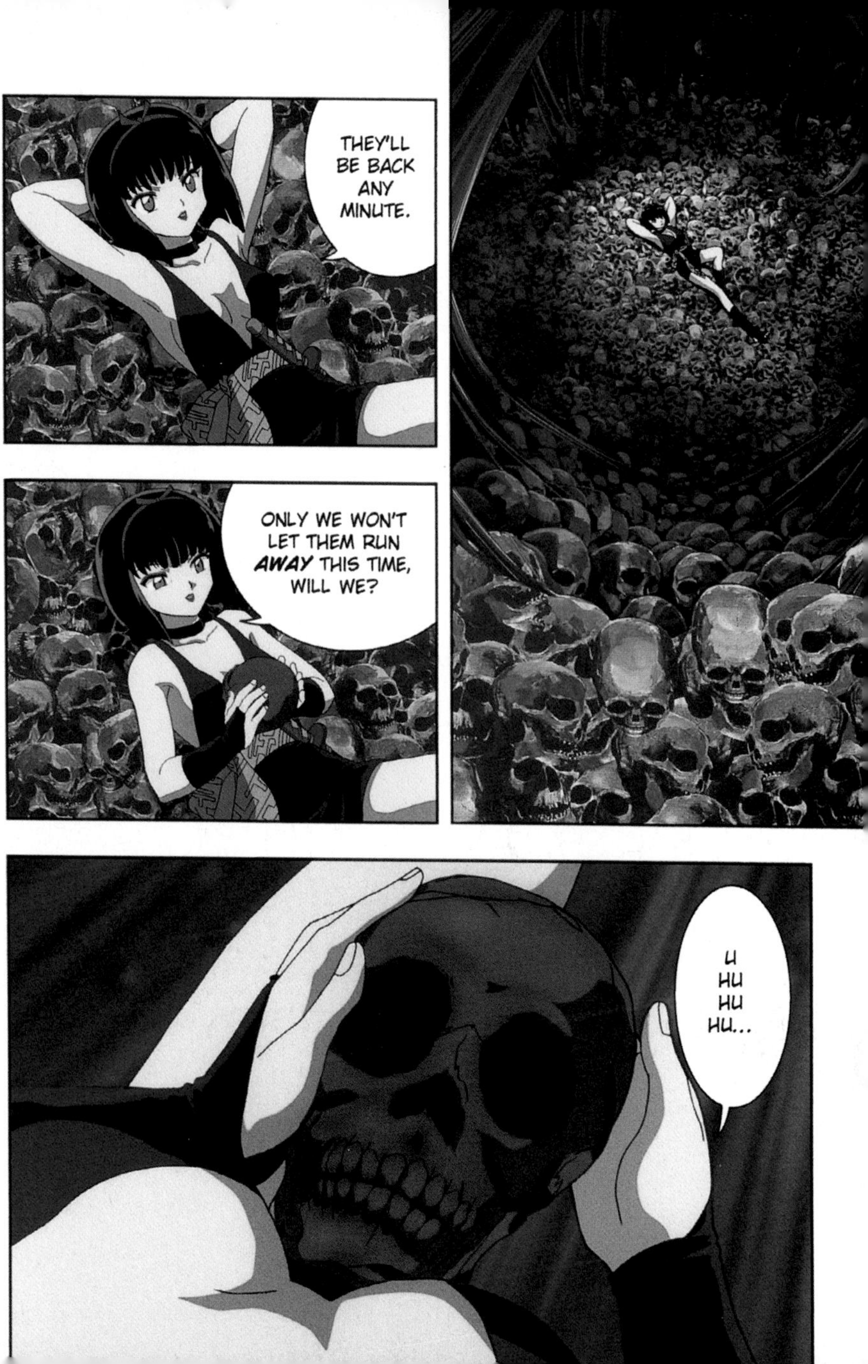
THEY'LL BE BACK ANY MINUTE.
ONLY WE WON'T LET THEM RUN *AWAY* THIS TIME, WILL WE?
U HU HU HU...

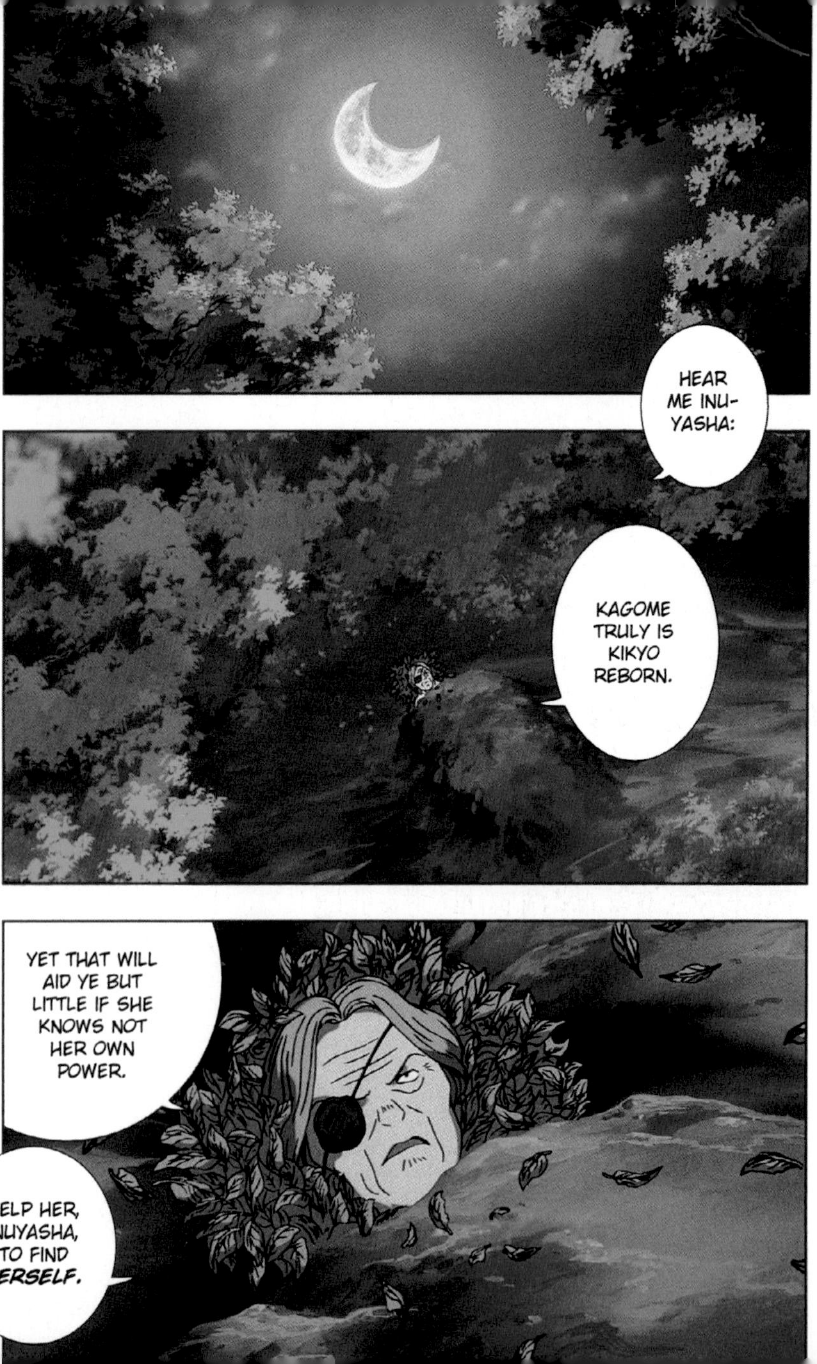
HEAR ME INU-YASHA:
KAGOME TRULY IS KIKYO REBORN.
YET THAT WILL AID YE BUT LITTLE IF SHE KNOWS NOT HER OWN POWER.
HELP HER, INUYASHA, TO FIND *HERSELF.*

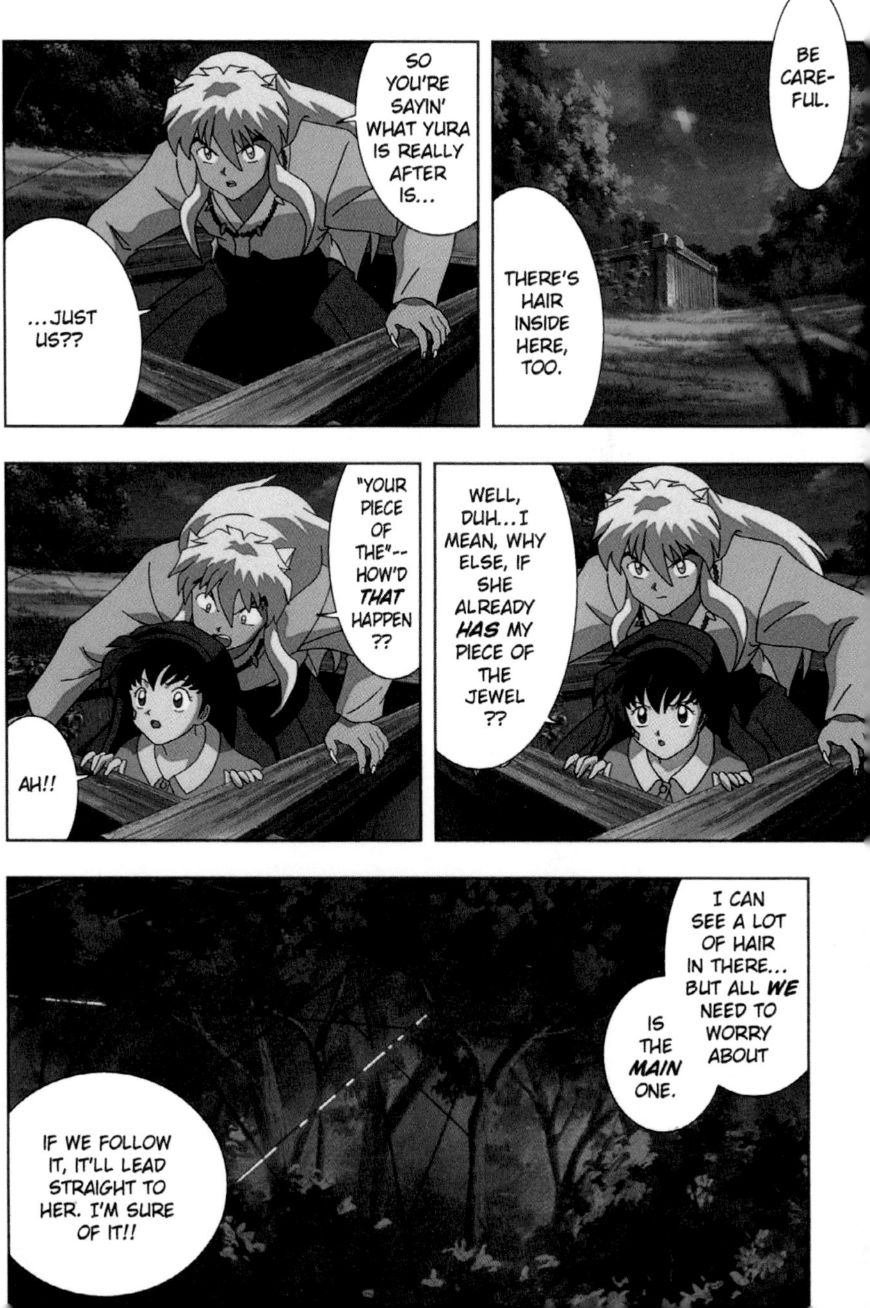
BE CAREFUL.
THERE'S HAIR INSIDE HERE, TOO.
SO YOU'RE SAYIN' WHAT YURA IS REALLY AFTER IS...
...JUST US??
WELL, DUH...I MEAN, WHY ELSE, IF SHE ALREADY *HAS* MY PIECE OF THE JEWEL??
"YOUR PIECE OF THE"--HOW'D *THAT* HAPPEN??
AH!!
I CAN SEE A LOT OF HAIR IN THERE... BUT ALL *WE* NEED TO WORRY ABOUT
IS THE *MAIN* ONE.
IF WE FOLLOW IT, IT'LL LEAD STRAIGHT TO HER. I'M SURE OF IT!!

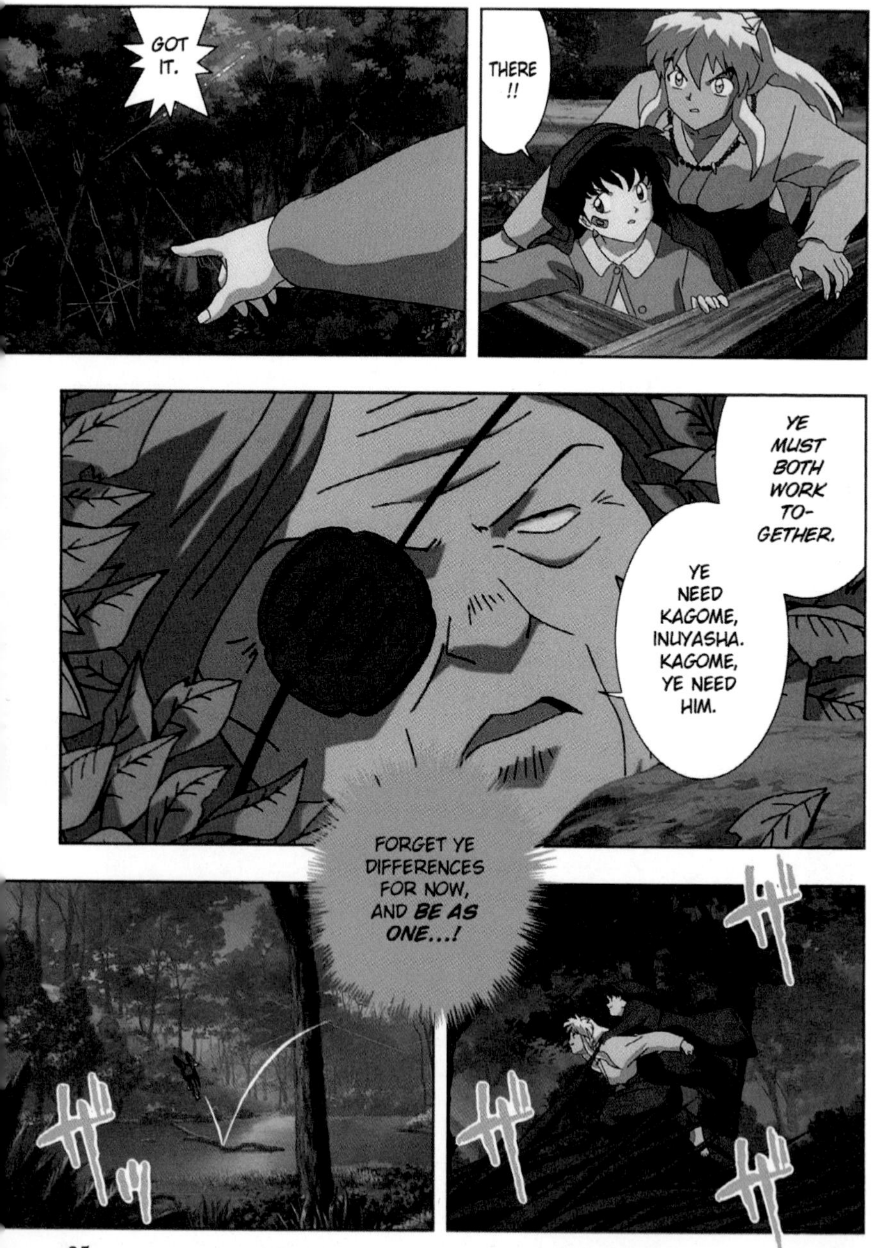
THERE !!
GOT IT.
YE MUST BOTH WORK TO-GETHER.
YE NEED KAGOME, INUYASHA. KAGOME, YE NEED HIM.
FORGET YE DIFFERENCES FOR NOW, AND BE AS ONE...!

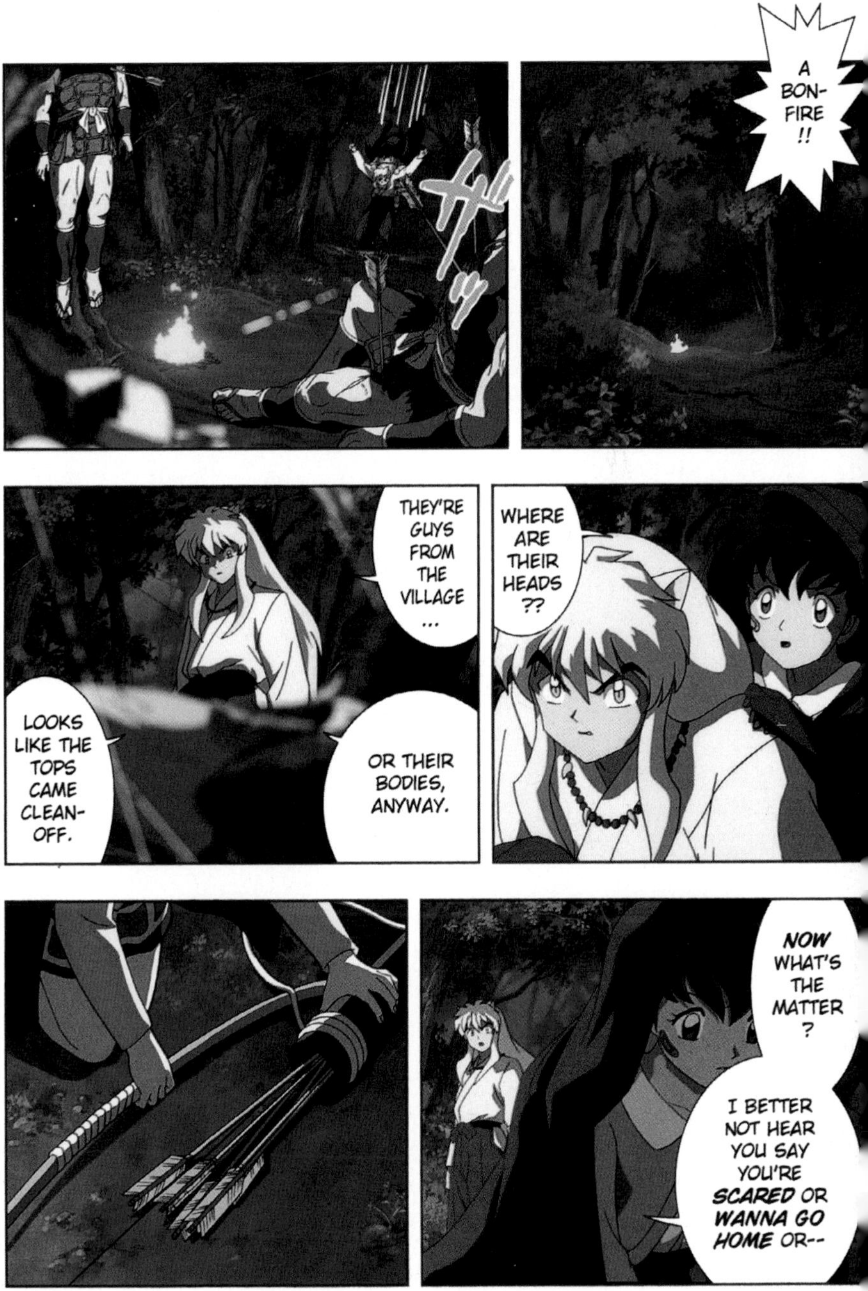
A BON-FIRE!!
WHERE ARE THEIR HEADS??
THEY'RE GUYS FROM THE VILLAGE...
OR THEIR BODIES, ANYWAY.
LOOKS LIKE THE TOPS CAME CLEAN-OFF.
NOW WHAT'S THE MATTER?
I BETTER NOT HEAR YOU SAY YOU'RE SCARED OR WANNA GO HOME OR--

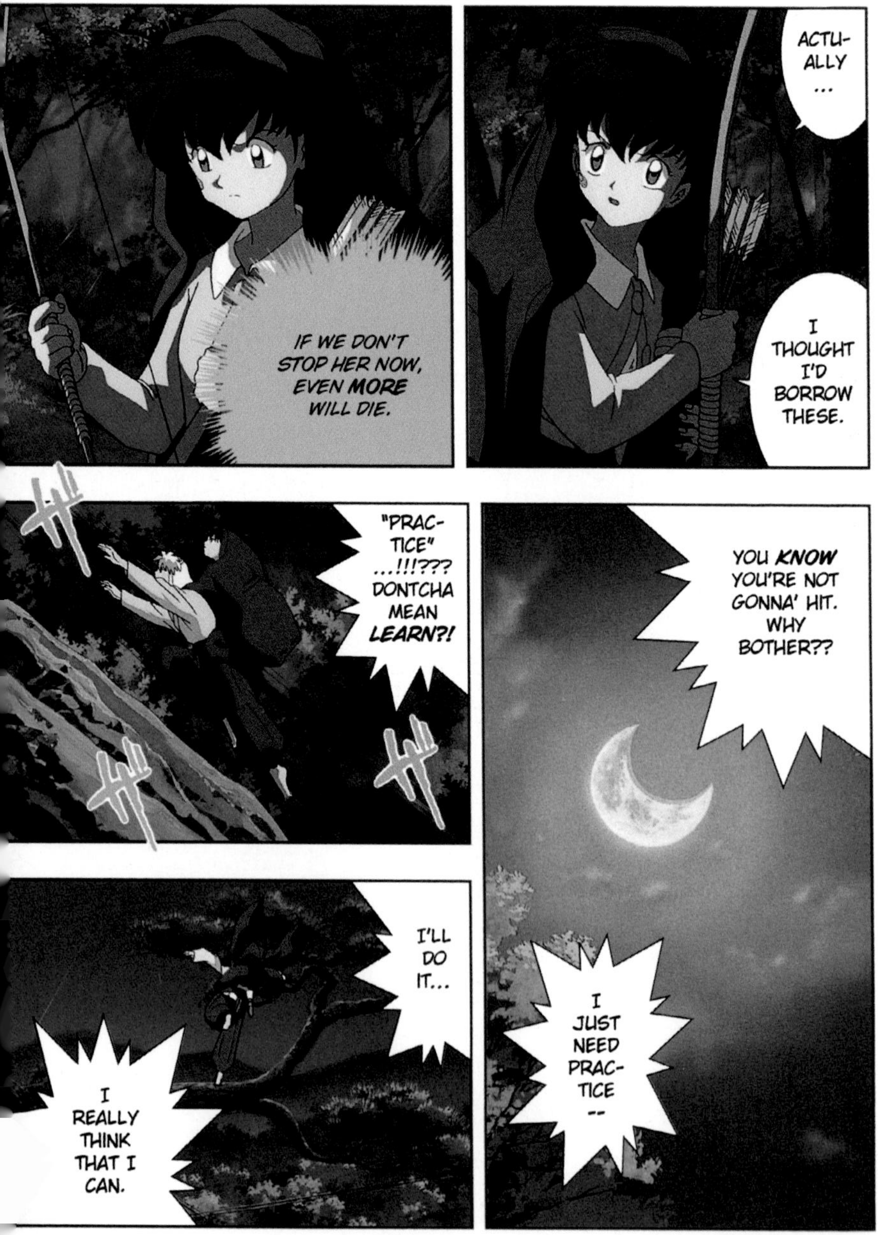
ACTU-ALLY ...
I THOUGHT I'D BORROW THESE.
IF WE DON'T STOP HER NOW, EVEN MORE WILL DIE.
YOU KNOW YOU'RE NOT GONNA' HIT. WHY BOTHER??
I JUST NEED PRAC-TICE --
"PRAC-TICE" ...!!!??? DONTCHA MEAN LEARN?!
I'LL DO IT...
I REALLY THINK THAT I CAN.

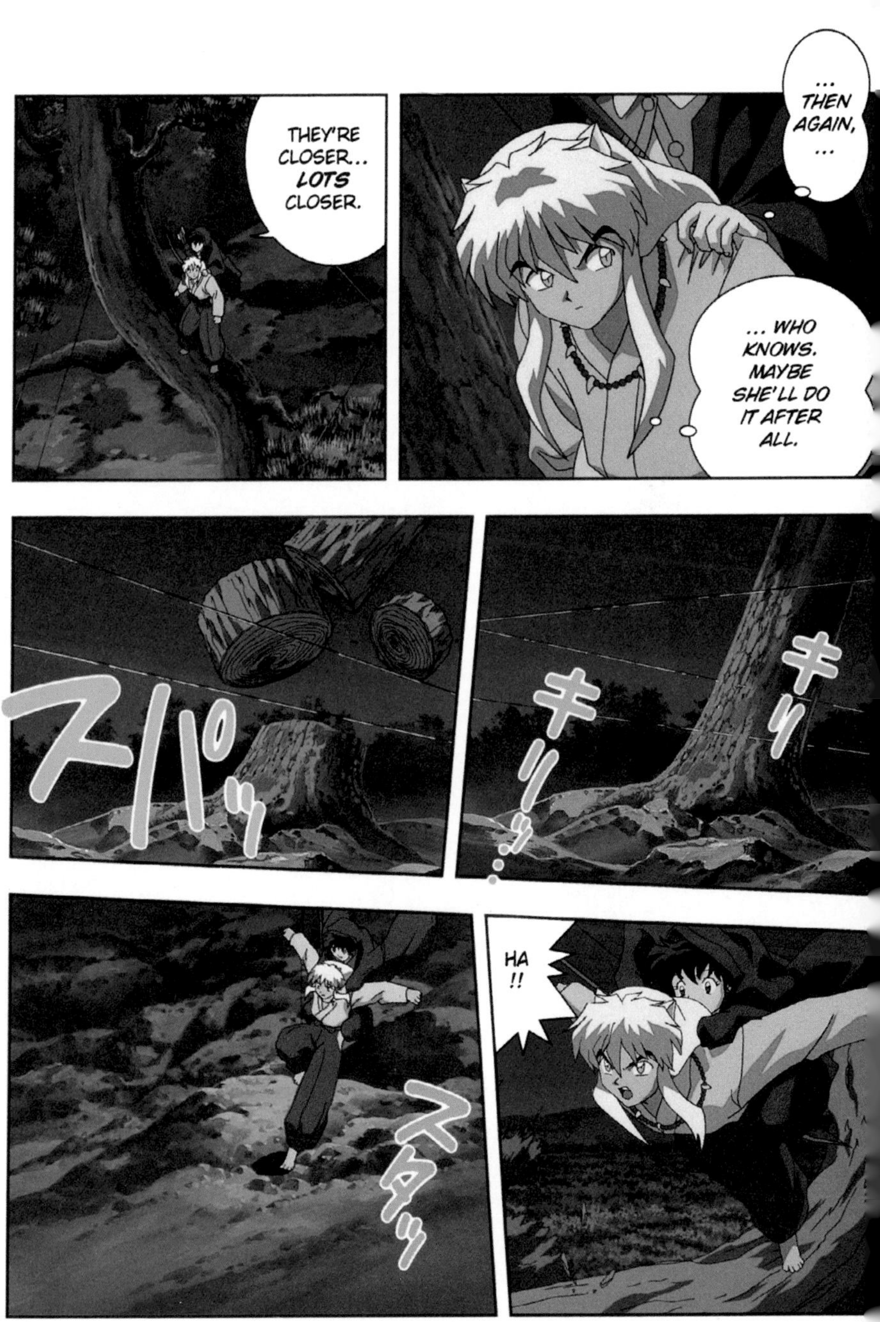
... THEN AGAIN, ...
... WHO KNOWS. MAYBE SHE'LL DO IT AFTER ALL.
THEY'RE CLOSER... LOTS CLOSER.
キリ
キリリッ...
スパッ
HA !!
スタッ

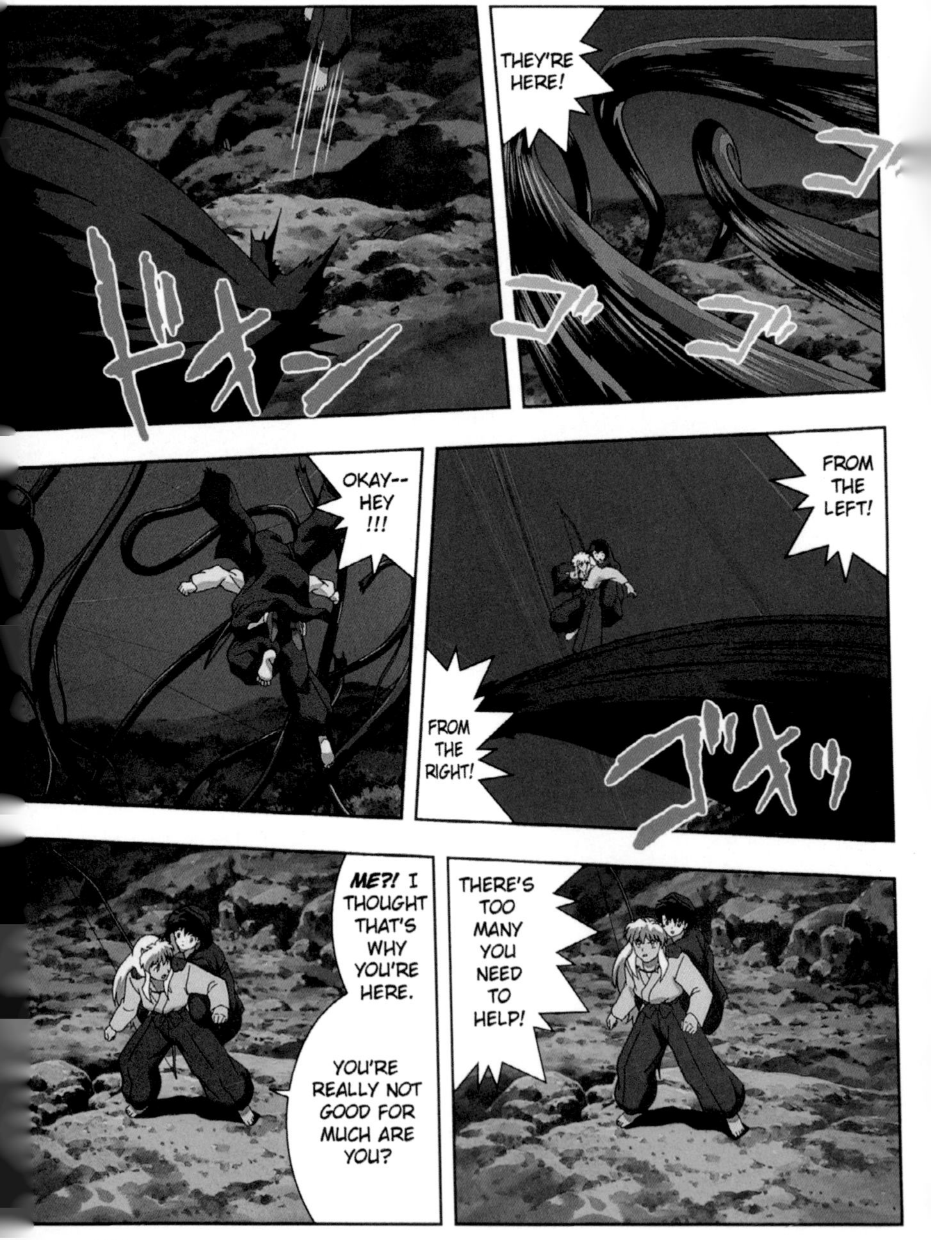
THEY'RE HERE!
ゴゴゴ
ドォーン
FROM THE LEFT!
FROM THE RIGHT!
ゴォッ
OKAY-- HEY !!!
THERE'S TOO MANY YOU NEED TO HELP!
ME?! I THOUGHT THAT'S WHY YOU'RE HERE.
YOU'RE REALLY NOT GOOD FOR MUCH ARE YOU?

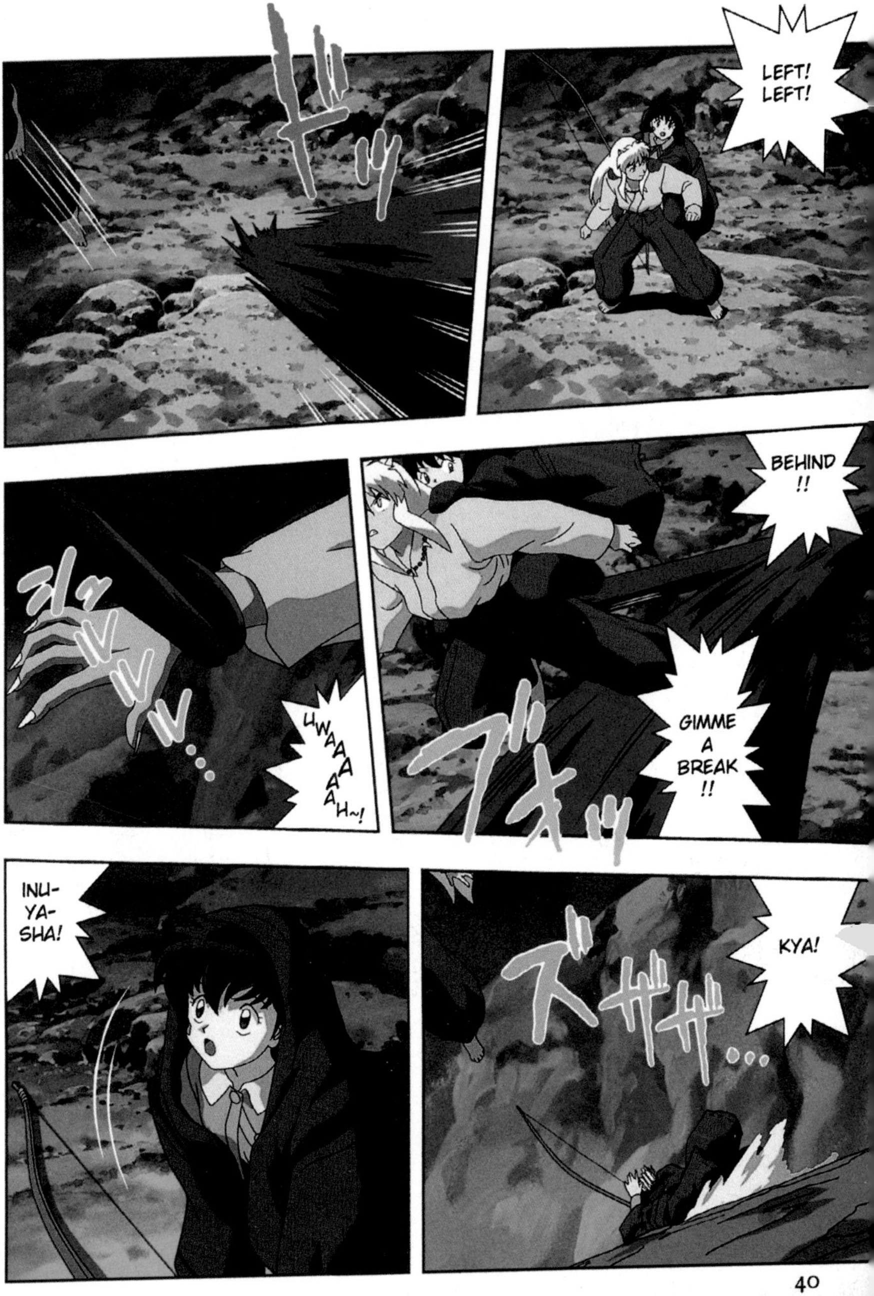
LEFT! LEFT!
BEHIND!!
GIMME A BREAK!!
UWAAAAAAH~!
KYA!
INU-YA-SHA!

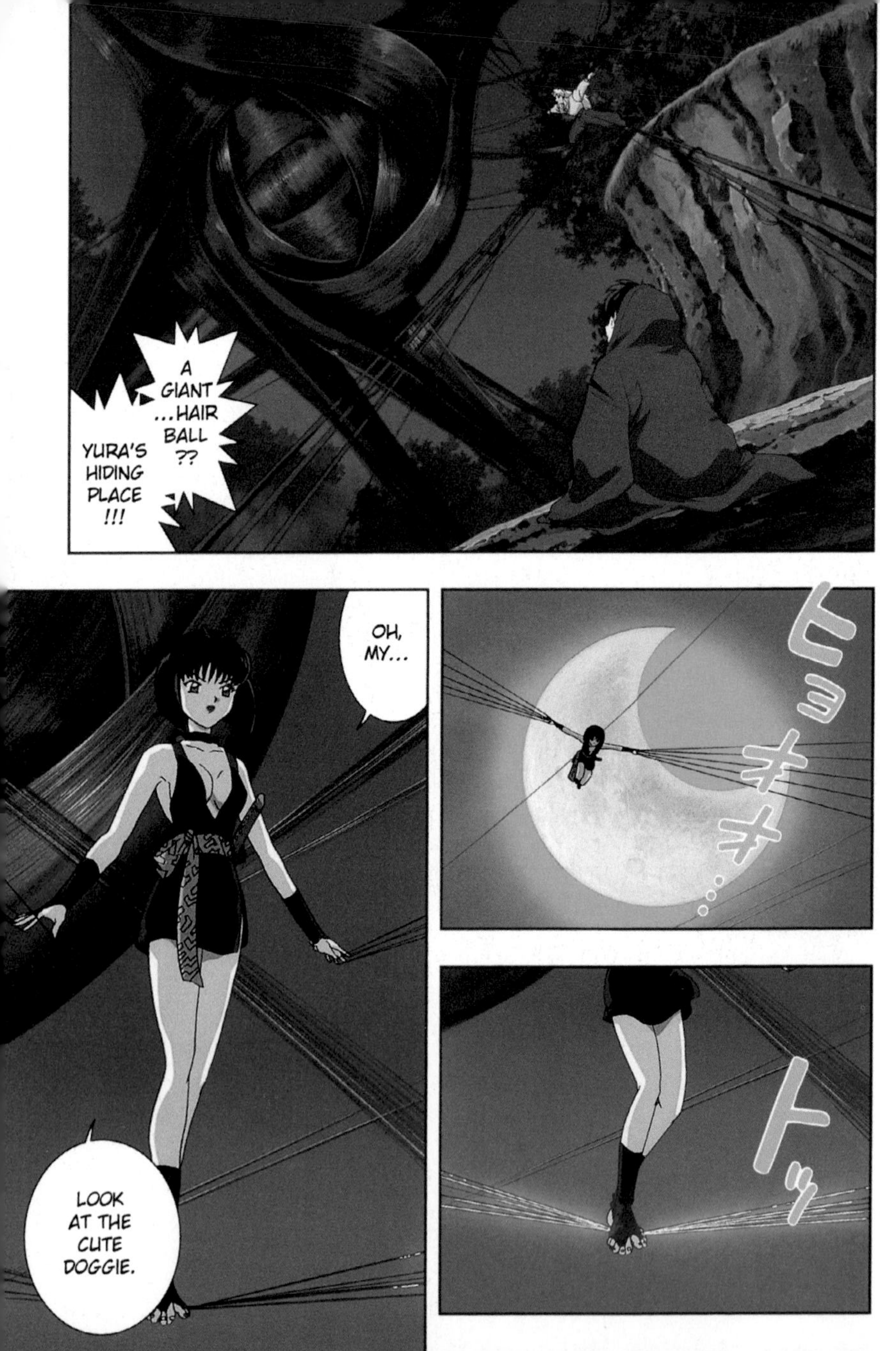
A GIANT ...HAIR BALL ??
YURA'S HIDING PLACE !!!
ヒョオオ…
トッ
OH, MY...
LOOK AT THE CUTE DOGGIE.

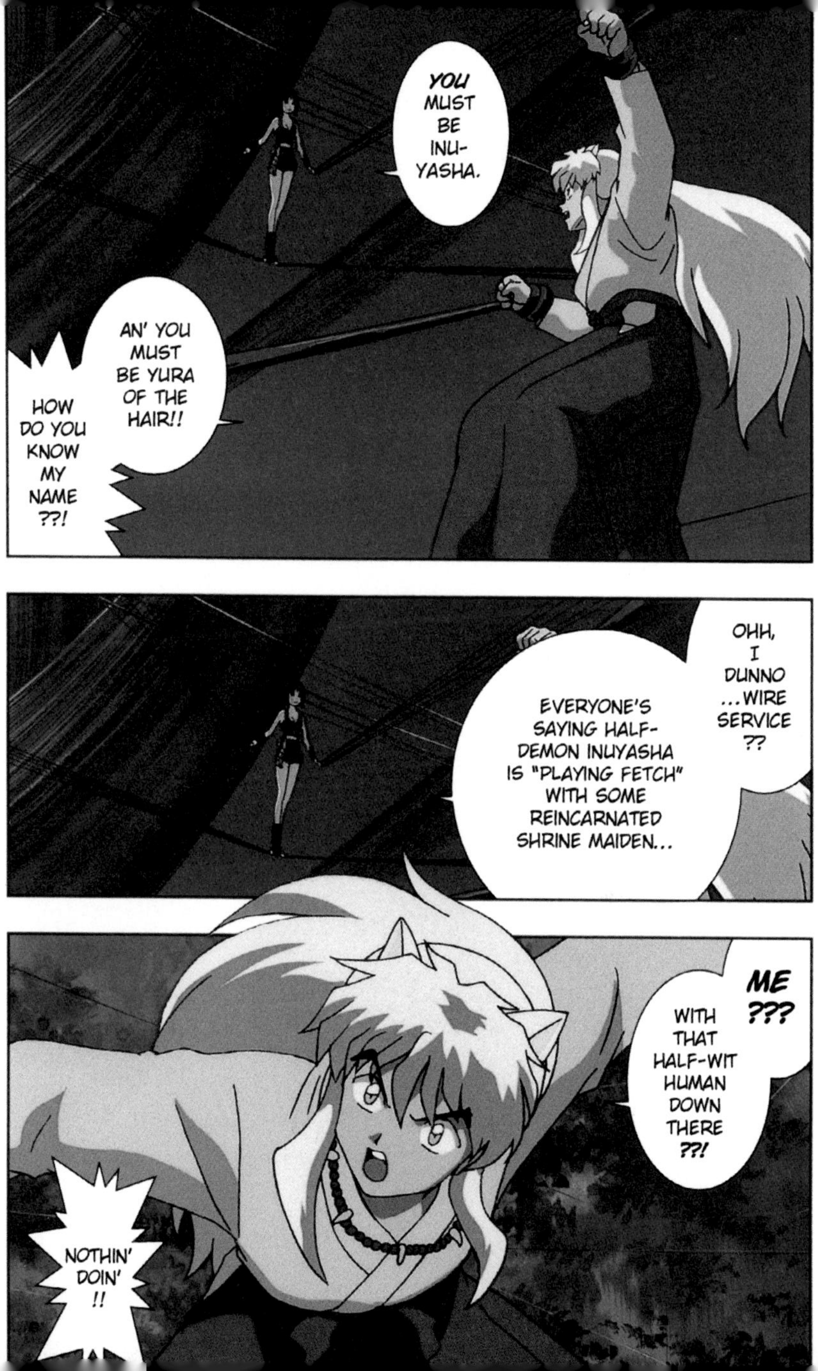
YOU MUST BE INU-YASHA.
AN' YOU MUST BE YURA OF THE HAIR!!
HOW DO YOU KNOW MY NAME ??!
OHH, I DUNNO ...WIRE SERVICE ??
EVERYONE'S SAYING HALF-DEMON INUYASHA IS "PLAYING FETCH" WITH SOME REINCARNATED SHRINE MAIDEN...
ME ???
WITH THAT HALF-WIT HUMAN DOWN THERE ??!
NOTHIN' DOIN' !!

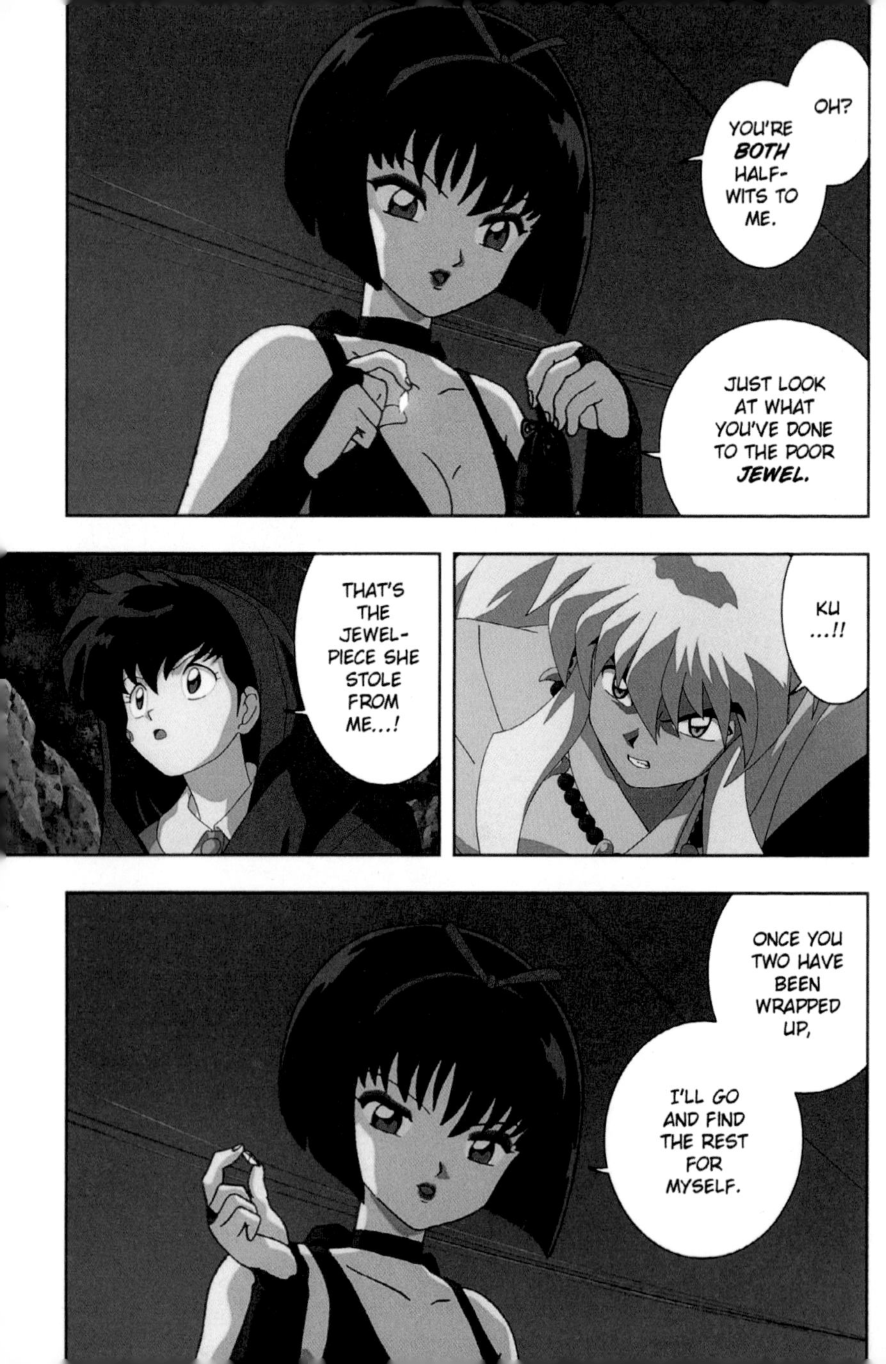
OH? YOU'RE **BOTH** HALF-WITS TO ME.
JUST LOOK AT WHAT YOU'VE DONE TO THE POOR **JEWEL.**
KU ...!!
THAT'S THE JEWEL-PIECE SHE STOLE FROM ME...!
ONCE YOU TWO HAVE BEEN WRAPPED UP,
I'LL GO AND FIND THE REST FOR MYSELF.

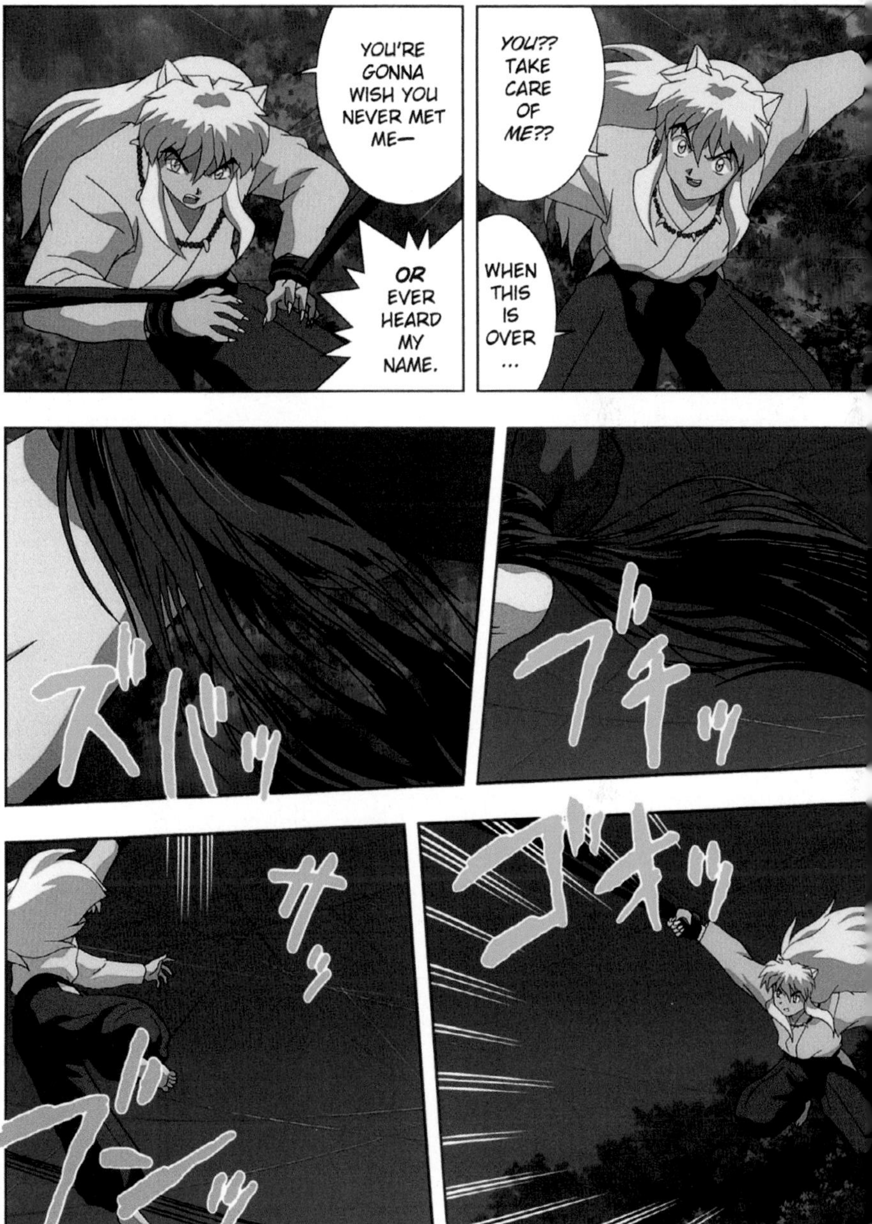
YOU?? TAKE CARE OF ME??
WHEN THIS IS OVER ...
YOU'RE GONNA WISH YOU NEVER MET ME—
OR EVER HEARD MY NAME.
ブチッ
ズバッ
ゴキッ
サッ
ブーンッ

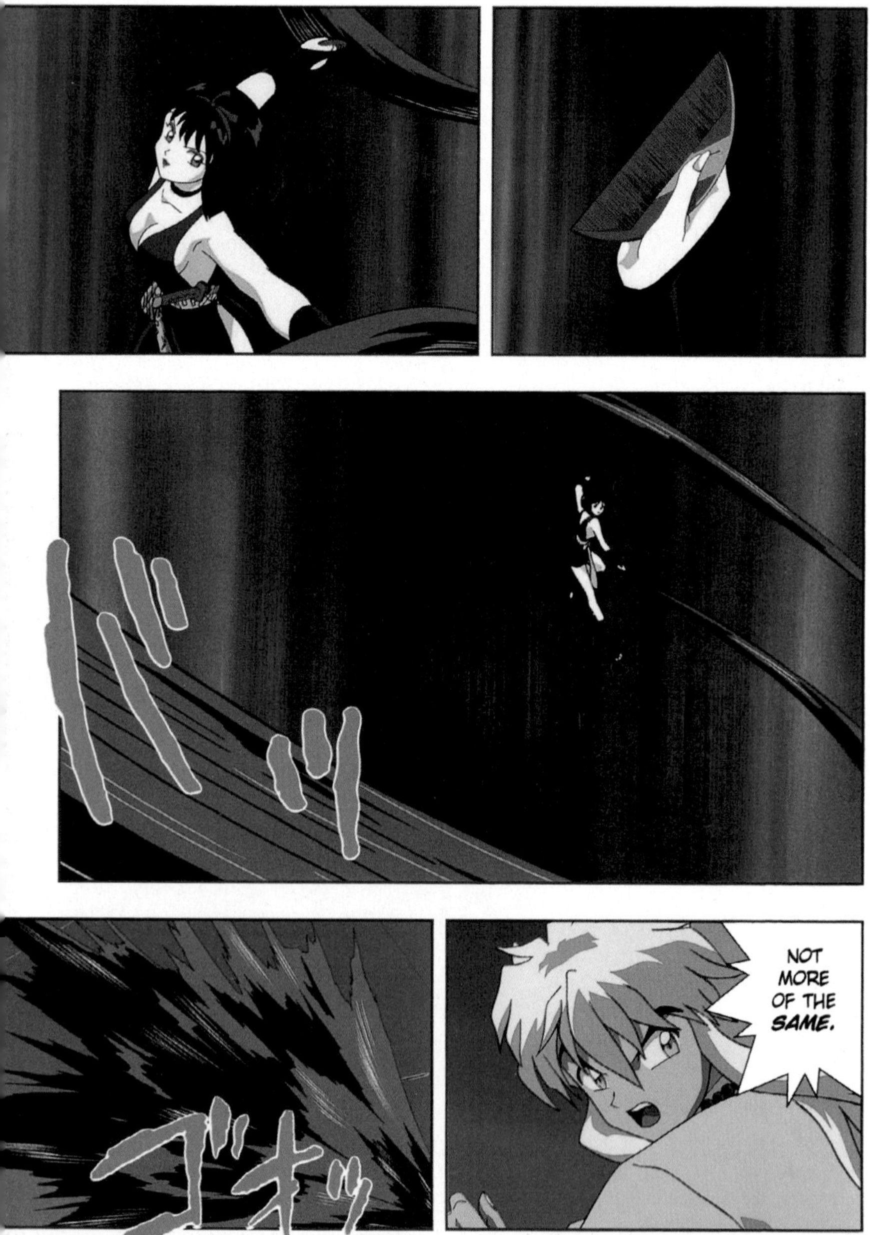
NOT MORE OF THE SAME.
ゴオッ

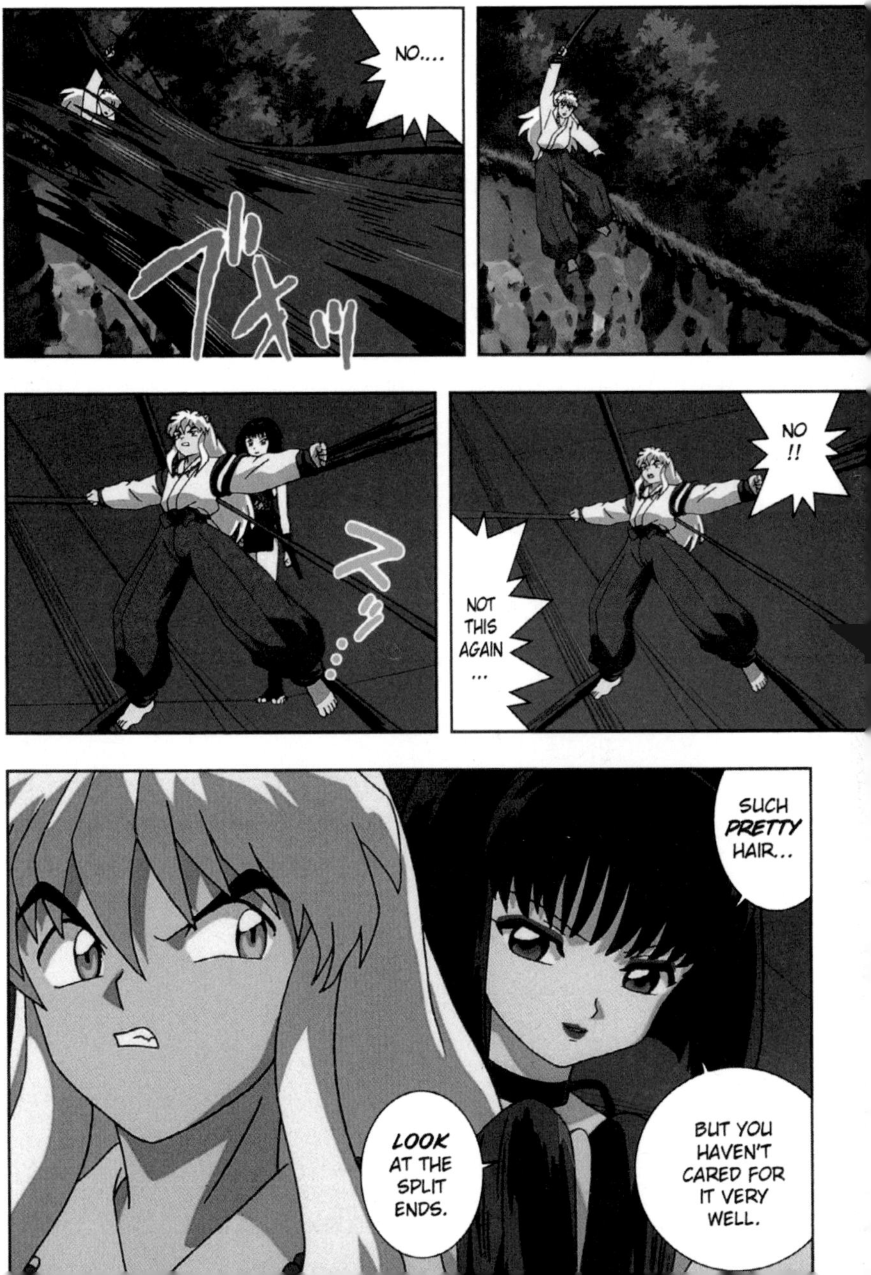
NO....
NO !!
NOT THIS AGAIN ...
スッ
SUCH PRETTY HAIR..
BUT YOU HAVEN'T CARED FOR IT VERY WELL.
LOOK AT THE SPLIT ENDS.

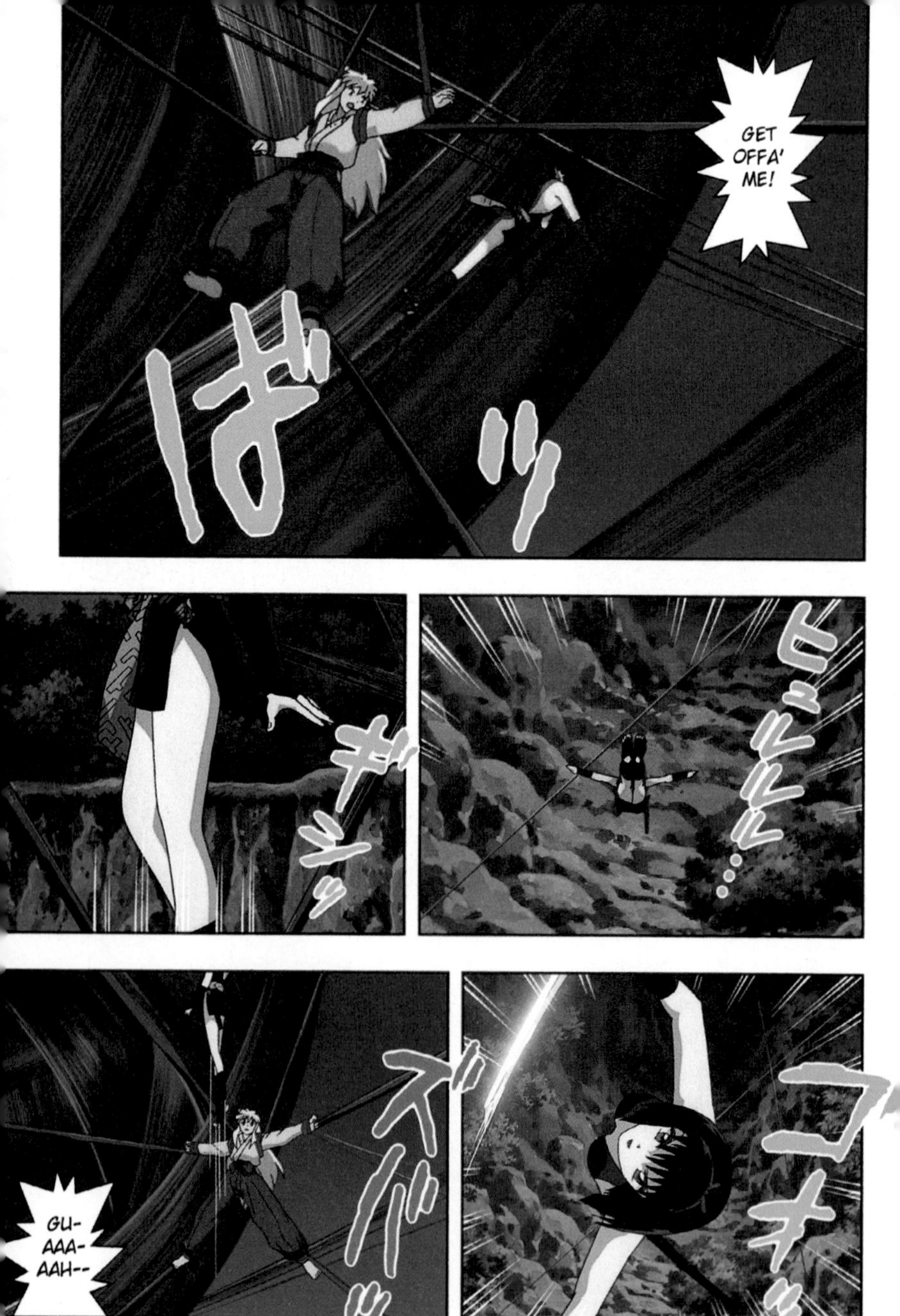
GET OFFA' ME!
GU-AAA-AAH--

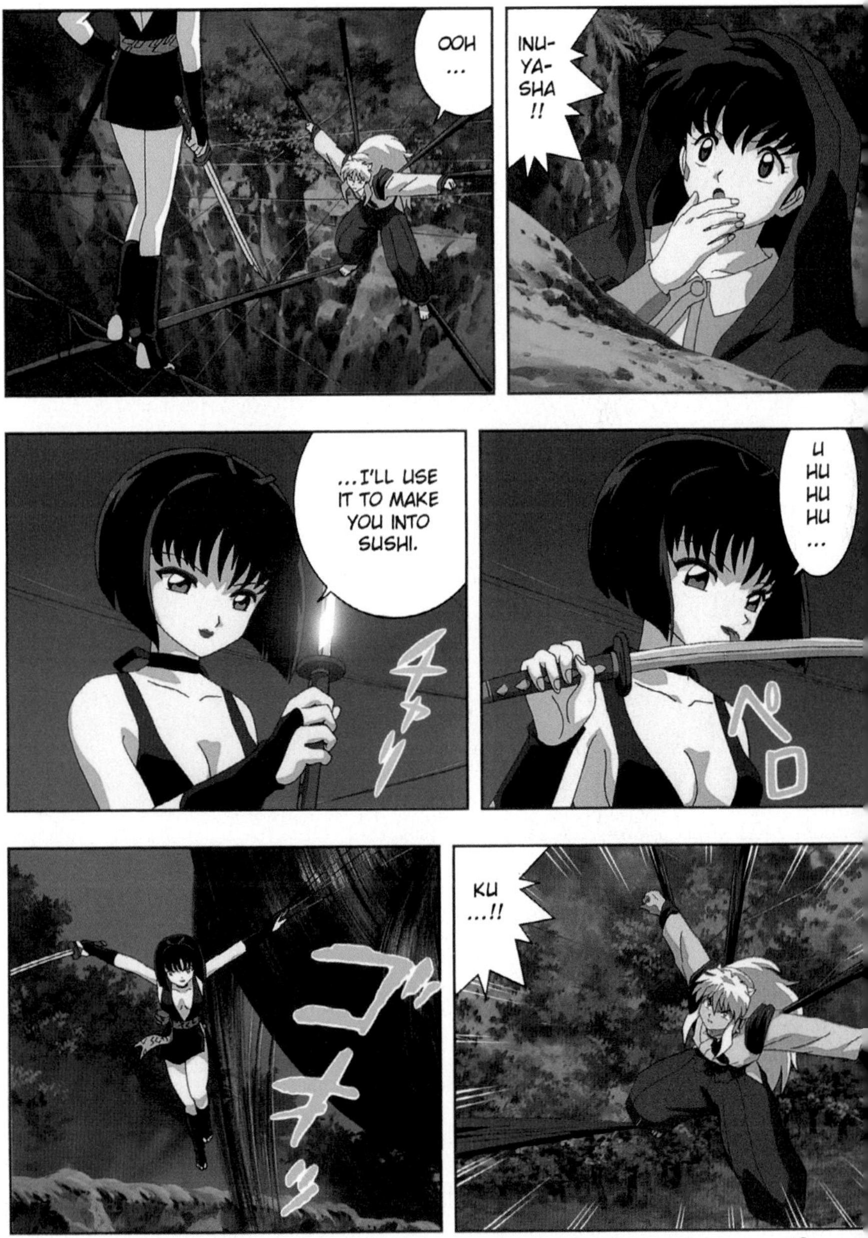
INU-YA-SHA!!
OOH ...
U HU HU HU ...
ペロ
...I'LL USE IT TO MAKE YOU INTO SUSHI.
チャリ
KU ...!!

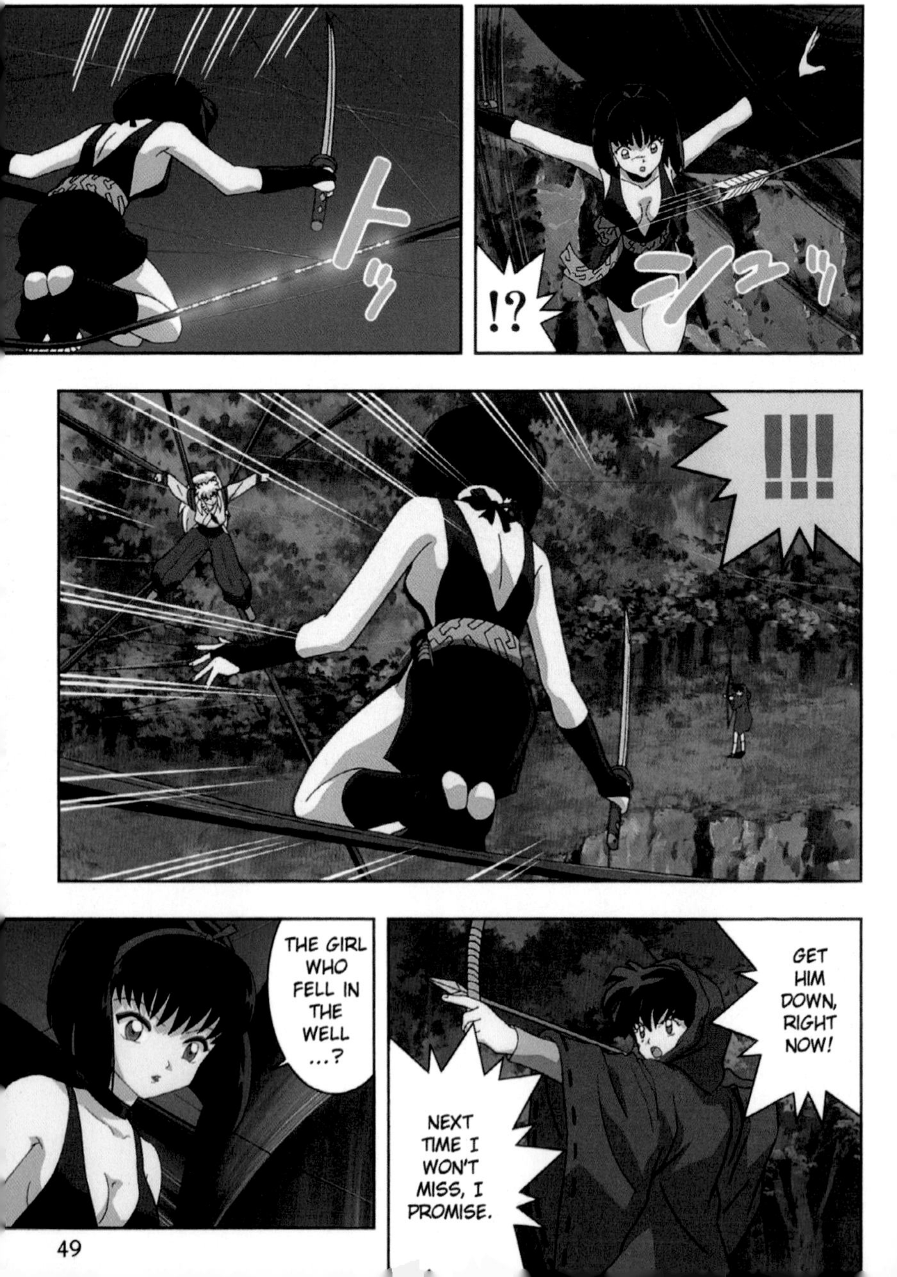
シュッ
!?
トッ
!!!
GET HIM DOWN, RIGHT NOW!
NEXT TIME I WON'T MISS, I PROMISE.
THE GIRL WHO FELL IN THE WELL ...?

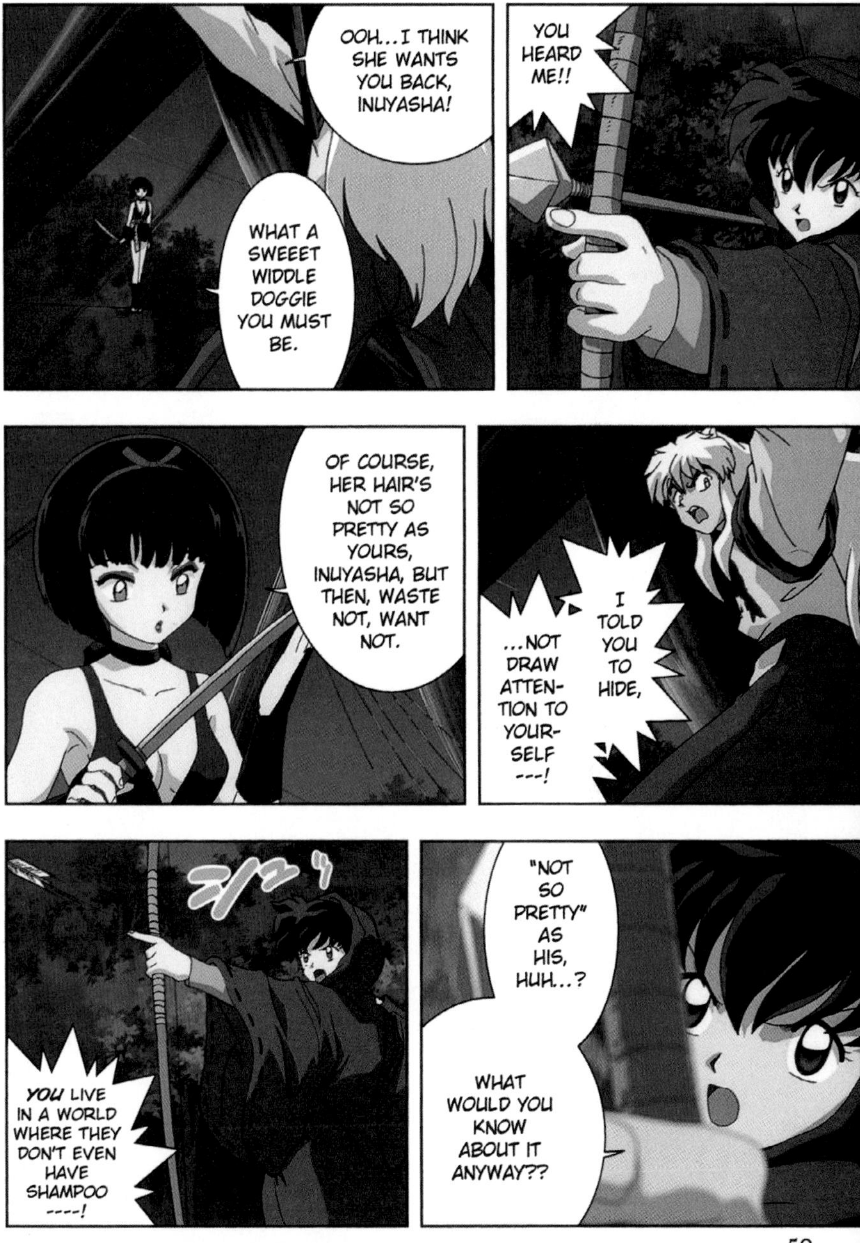
YOU HEARD ME!!
OOH...I THINK SHE WANTS YOU BACK, INUYASHA!
WHAT A SWEEET WIDDLE DOGGIE YOU MUST BE.
I TOLD YOU TO HIDE,
...NOT DRAW ATTENTION TO YOURSELF ---!
OF COURSE, HER HAIR'S NOT SO PRETTY AS YOURS, INUYASHA, BUT THEN, WASTE NOT, WANT NOT.
"NOT SO PRETTY" AS HIS, HUH...?
WHAT WOULD YOU KNOW ABOUT IT ANYWAY??
YOU LIVE IN A WORLD WHERE THEY DON'T EVEN HAVE SHAMPOO ----!

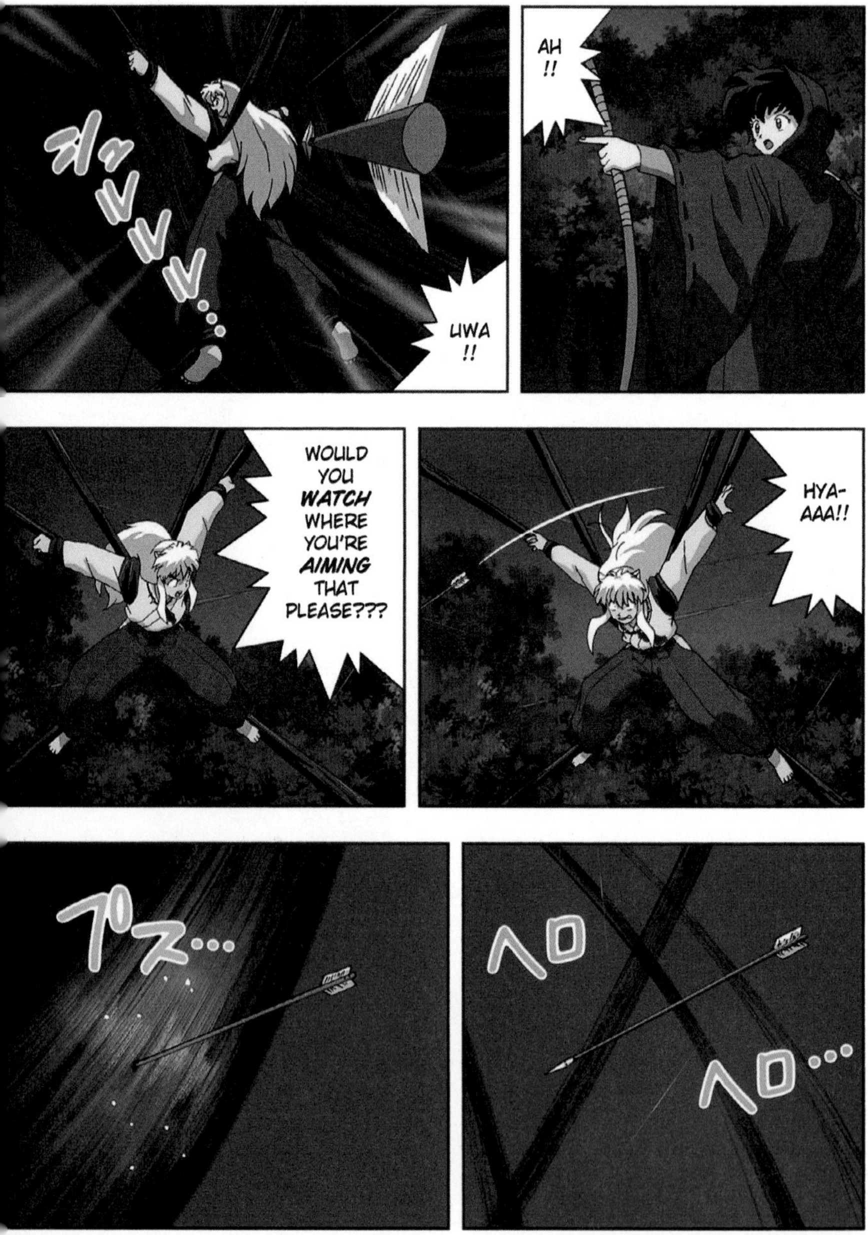

AH !!
UWA !!
HYA-AAA!!
WOULD YOU WATCH WHERE YOU'RE AIMING THAT PLEASE???
ヘロ
ヘロ…
プス…

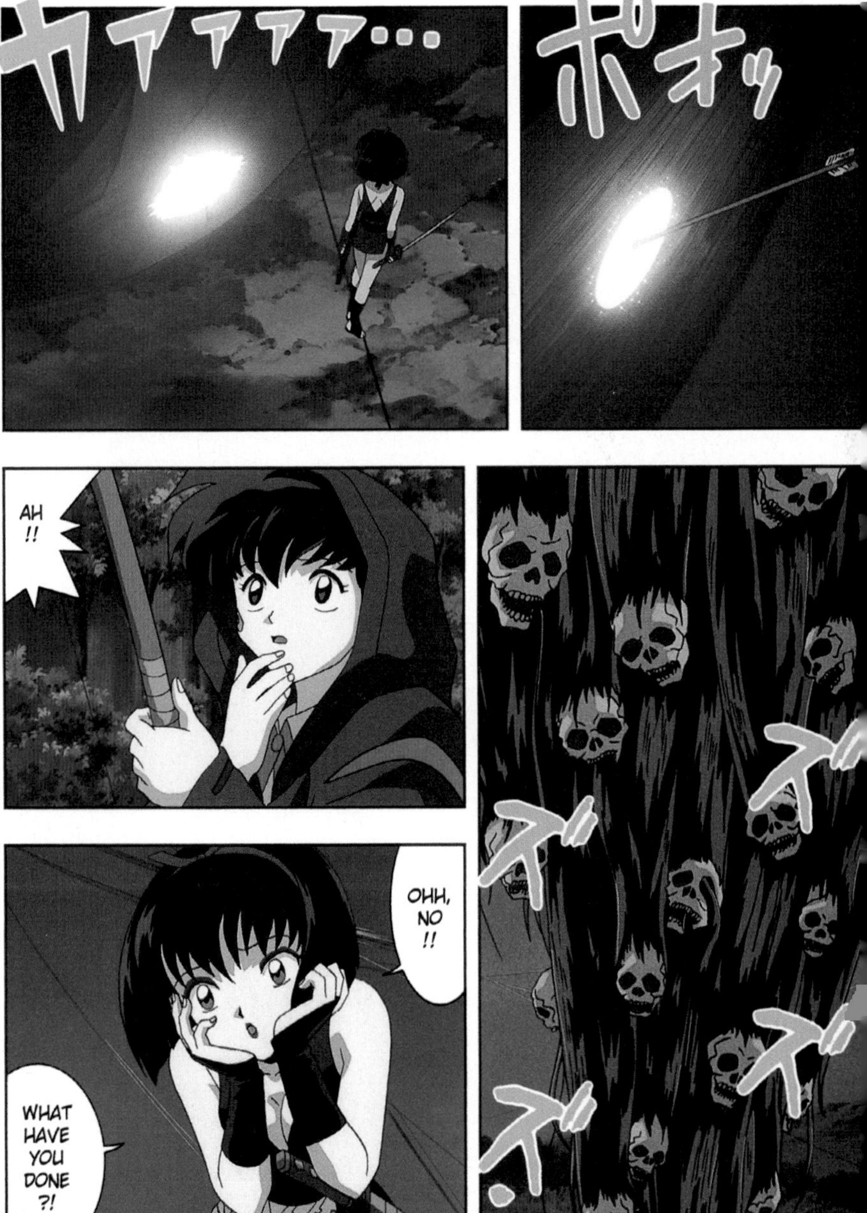
ポォッ
カァァァァ…
ズ
ズ
ズ
ズ
AH !!
OHH, NO !!
WHAT HAVE YOU DONE ?!

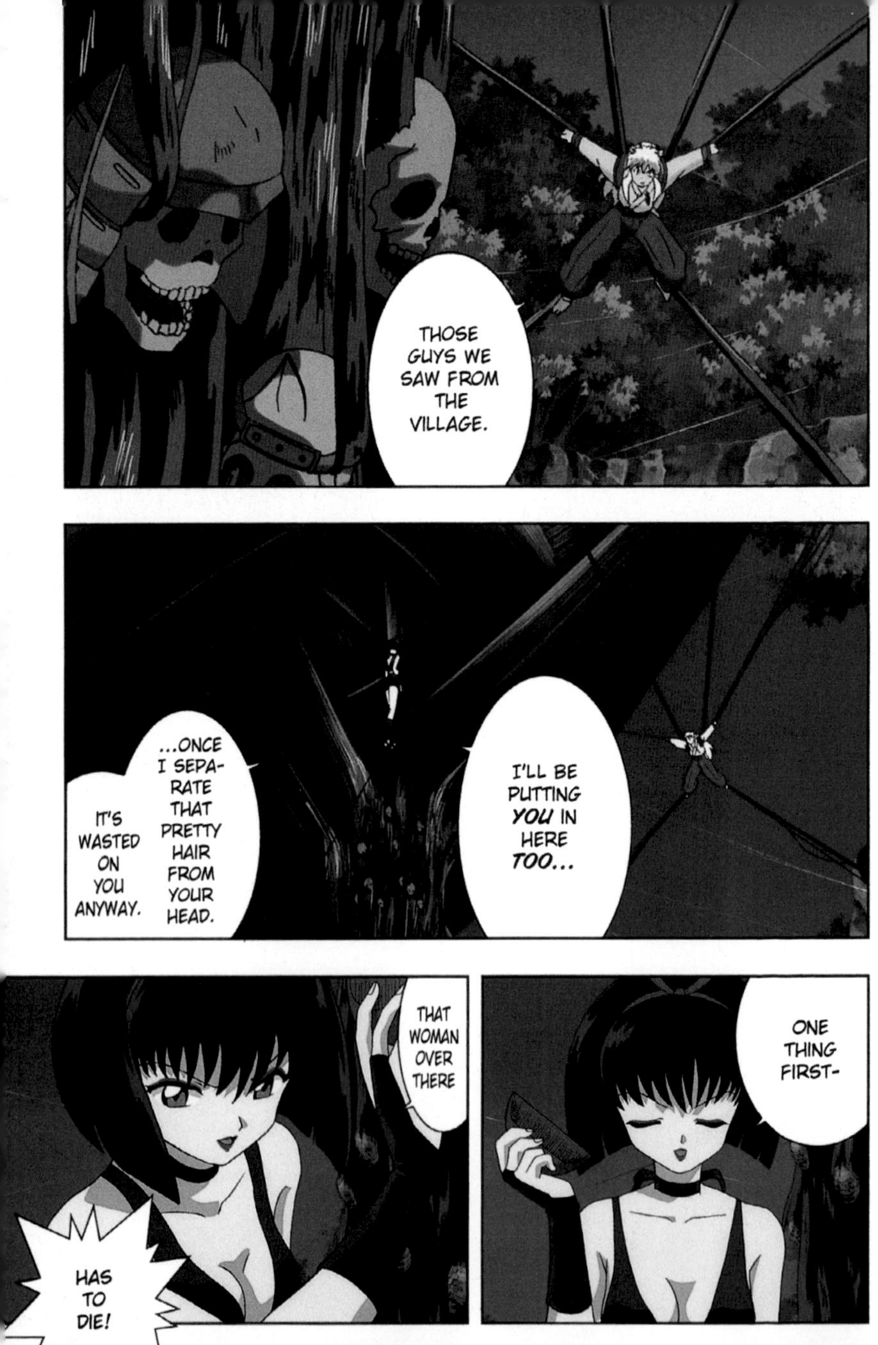
THOSE GUYS WE SAW FROM THE VILLAGE.
I'LL BE PUTTING *YOU* IN HERE *TOO*...
...ONCE I SEPA-RATE THAT PRETTY HAIR FROM YOUR HEAD.
IT'S WASTED ON YOU ANYWAY.
ONE THING FIRST-
THAT WOMAN OVER THERE
HAS TO DIE!

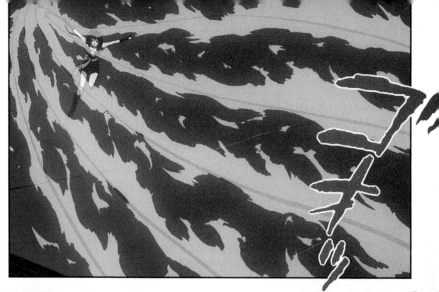

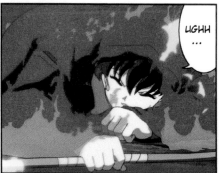

UGHH ...

AHH!

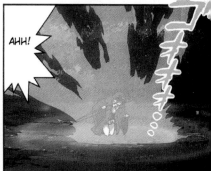

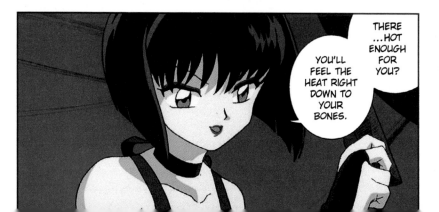

THERE ...HOT ENOUGH FOR YOU?

YOU'LL FEEL THE HEAT RIGHT DOWN TO YOUR BONES.

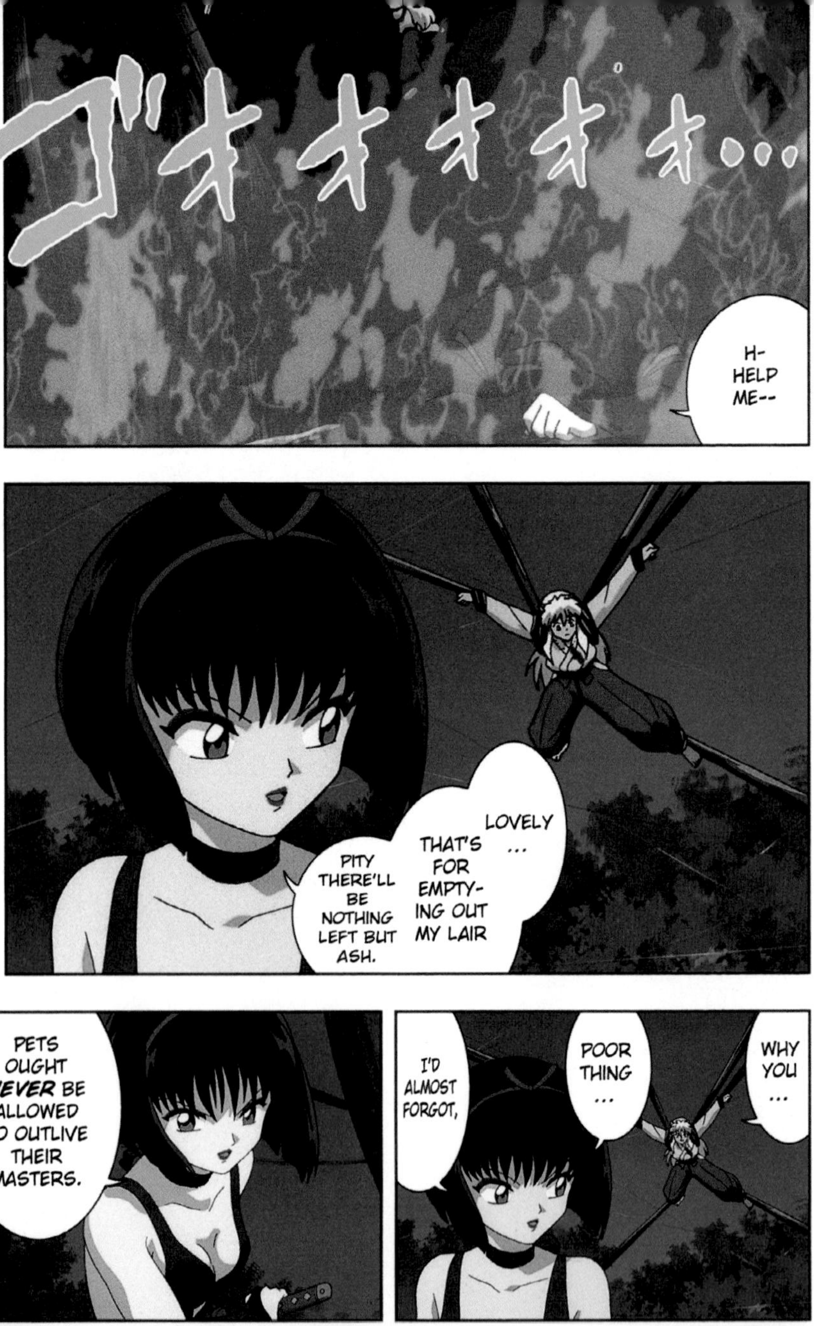
ゴオオオオオ...
H- HELP ME--
LOVELY ...
THAT'S FOR EMPTY-ING OUT MY LAIR
PITY THERE'LL BE NOTHING LEFT BUT ASH.
WHY YOU ...
POOR THING ...
I'D ALMOST FORGOT,
PETS OUGHT **NEVER** BE ALLOWED TO OUTLIVE THEIR MASTERS.

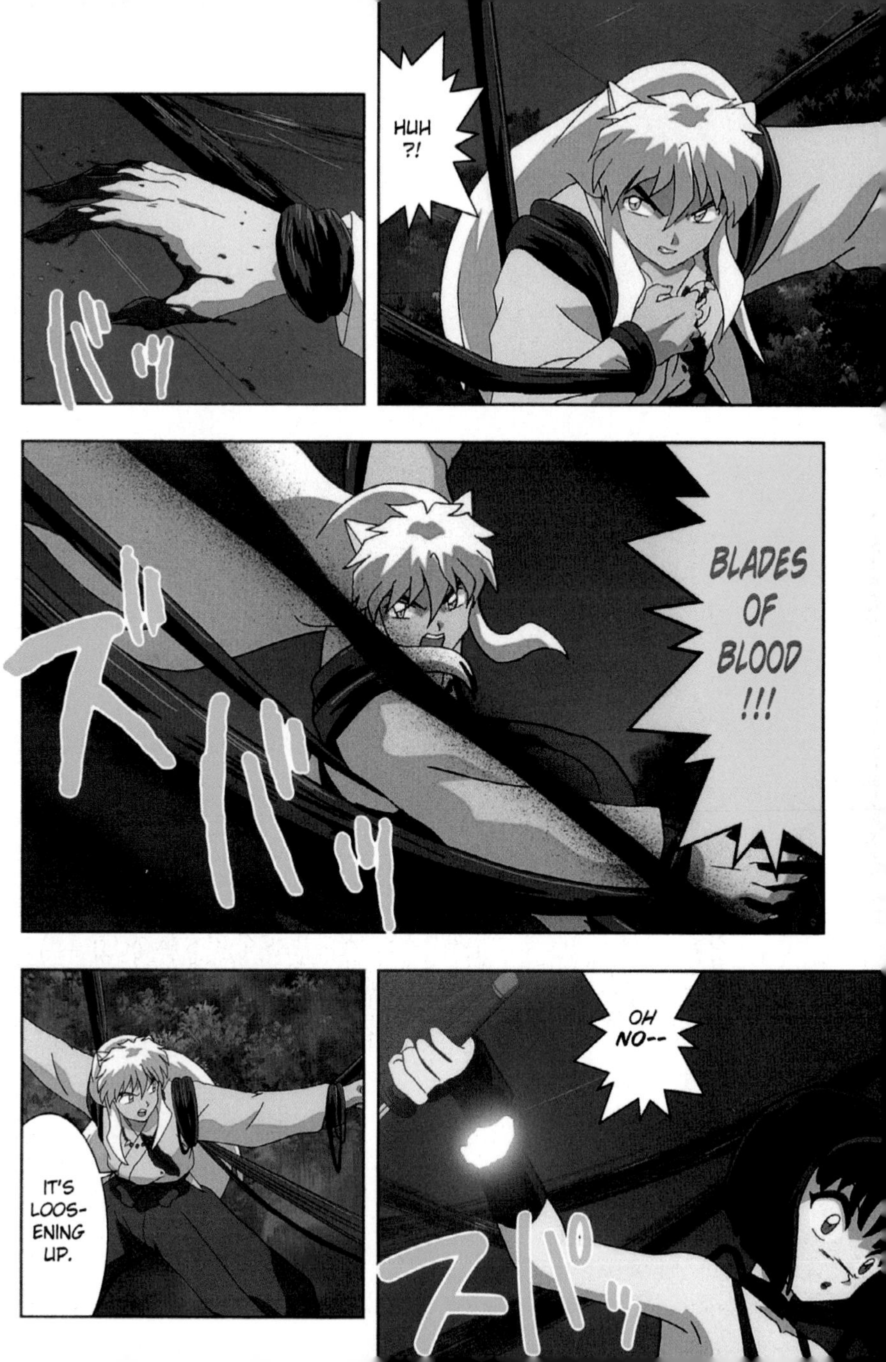
HUH ?!
バッ
BLADES OF BLOOD !!!
ズバッ
OH NO--
スパッ
IT'S LOOS-ENING UP.

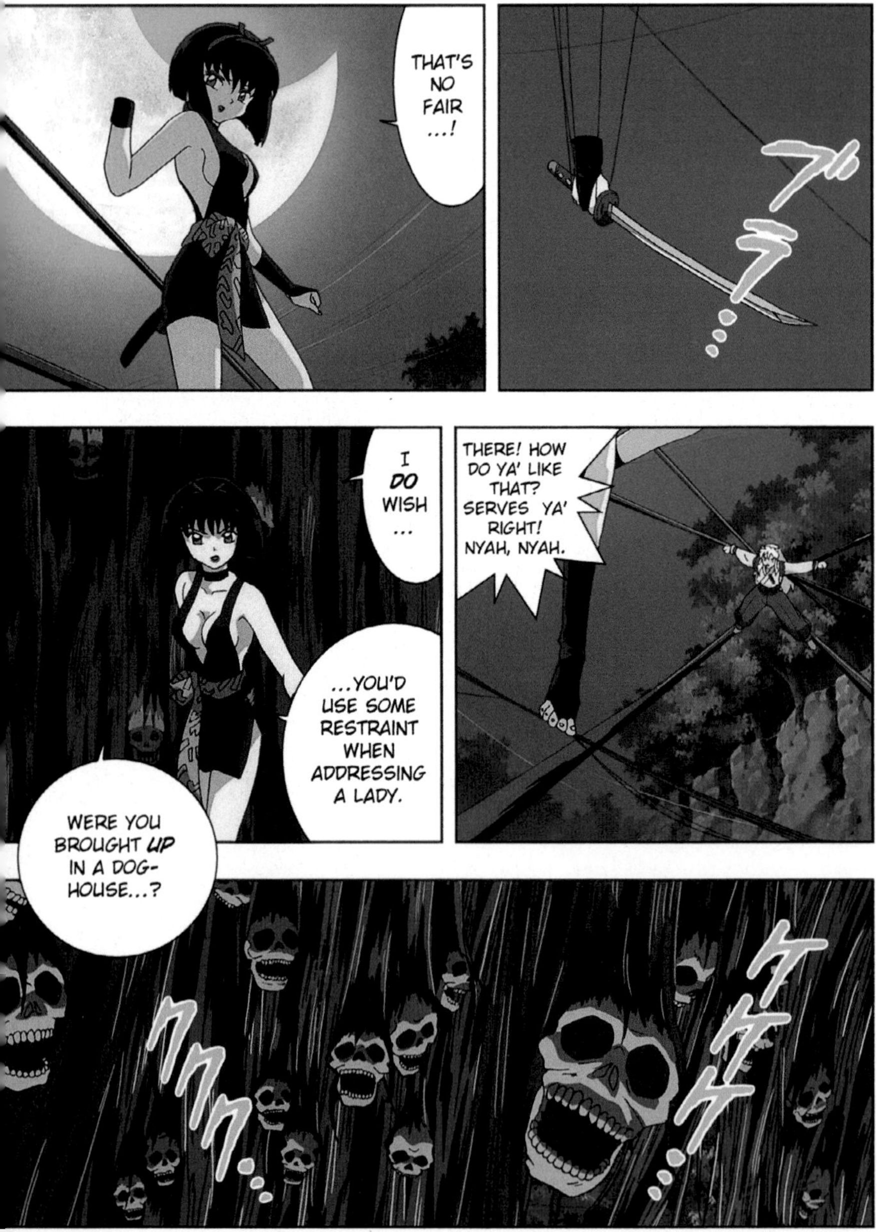
ブラ…
THAT'S NO FAIR...!
THERE! HOW DO YA' LIKE THAT? SERVES YA' RIGHT! NYAH, NYAH.
I *DO* WISH...
...YOU'D USE SOME RESTRAINT WHEN ADDRESSING A LADY.
WERE YOU BROUGHT *UP* IN A DOG-HOUSE...?
ケケケケ…
ククク…

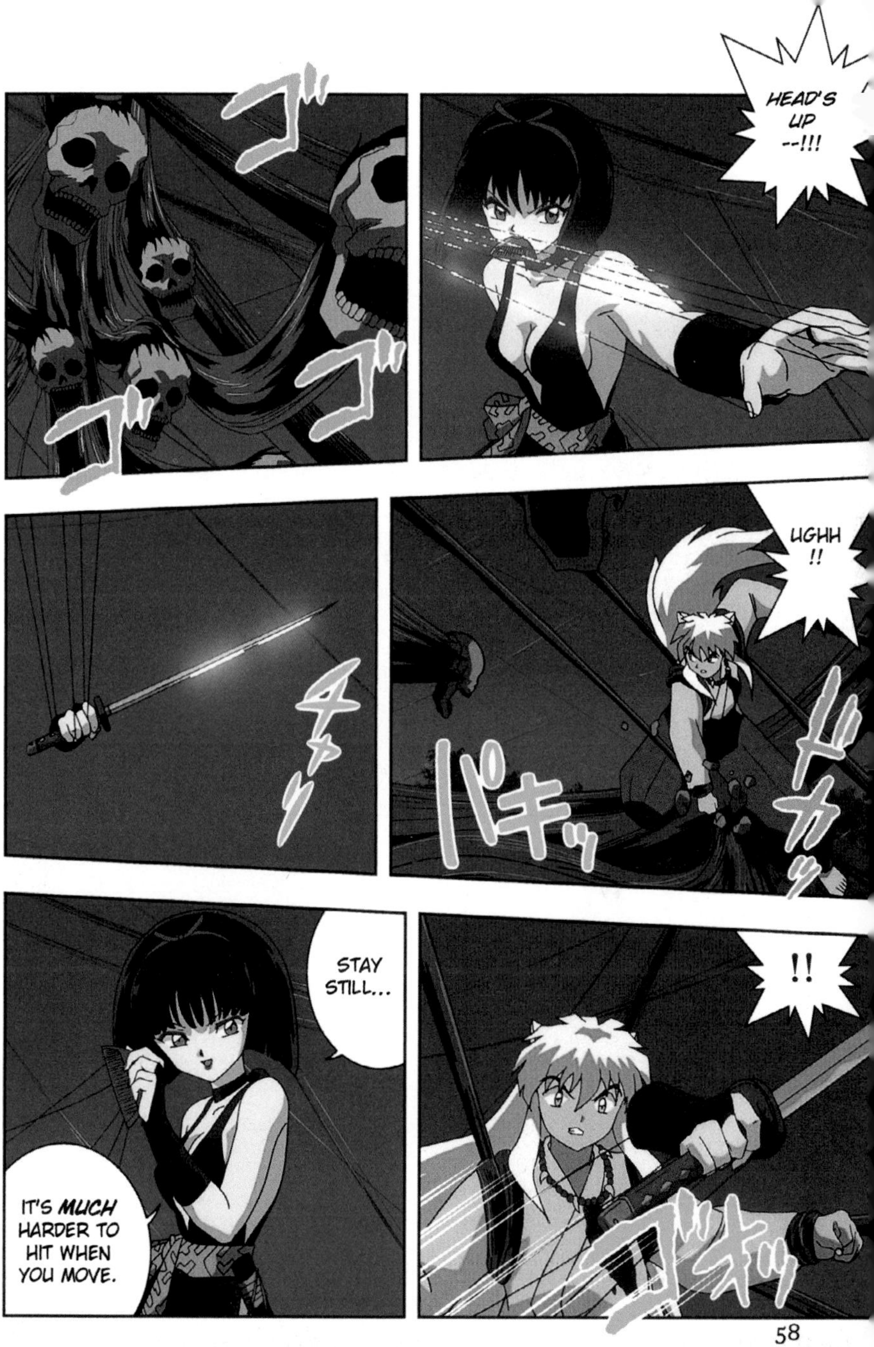
HEAD'S UP --!!!
ゴゴゴ
UGHH !!
ドカッ
パキッ
チャッ
!!
ゴキッ
STAY STILL...
IT'S *MUCH* HARDER TO HIT WHEN YOU MOVE.

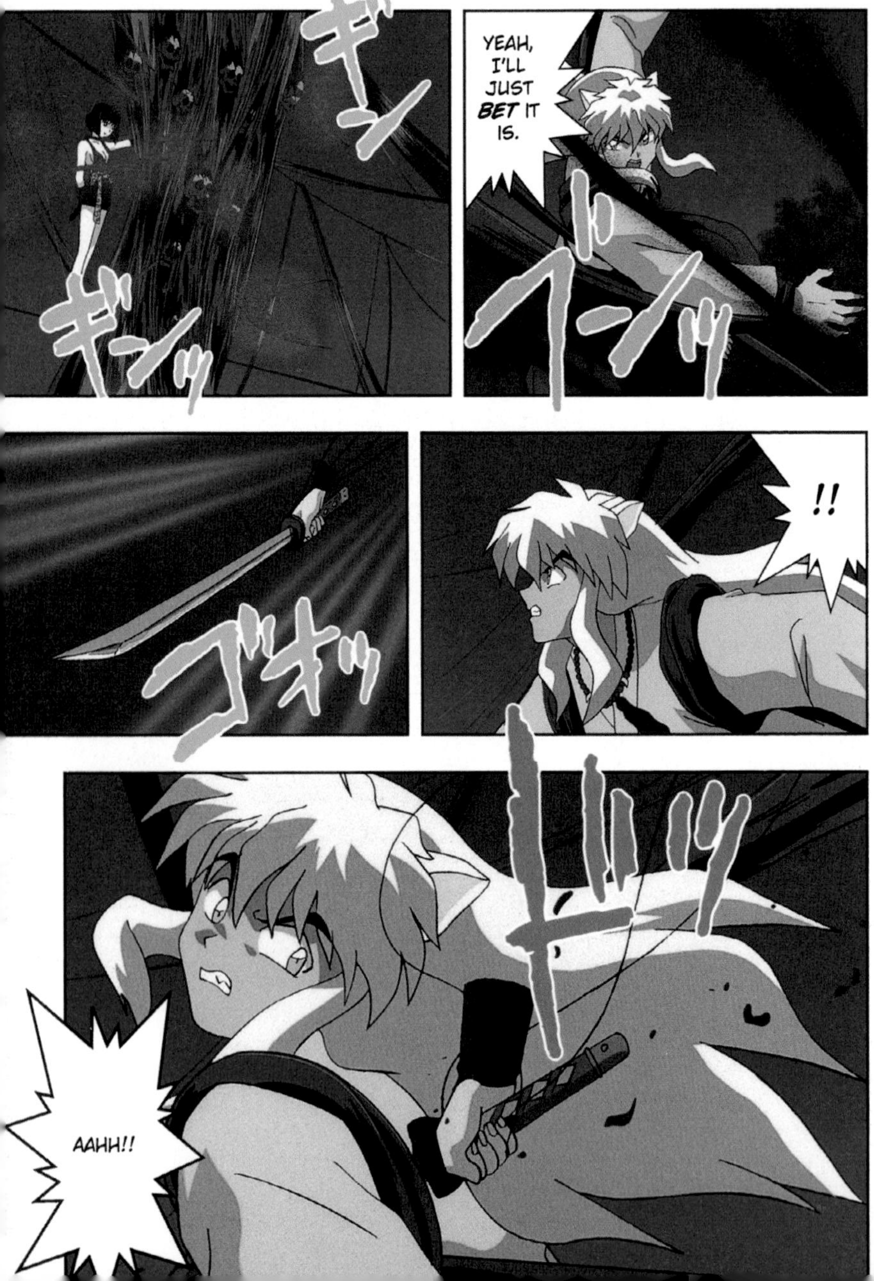
YEAH, I'LL JUST **BET** IT IS.
!!
AAHH!!

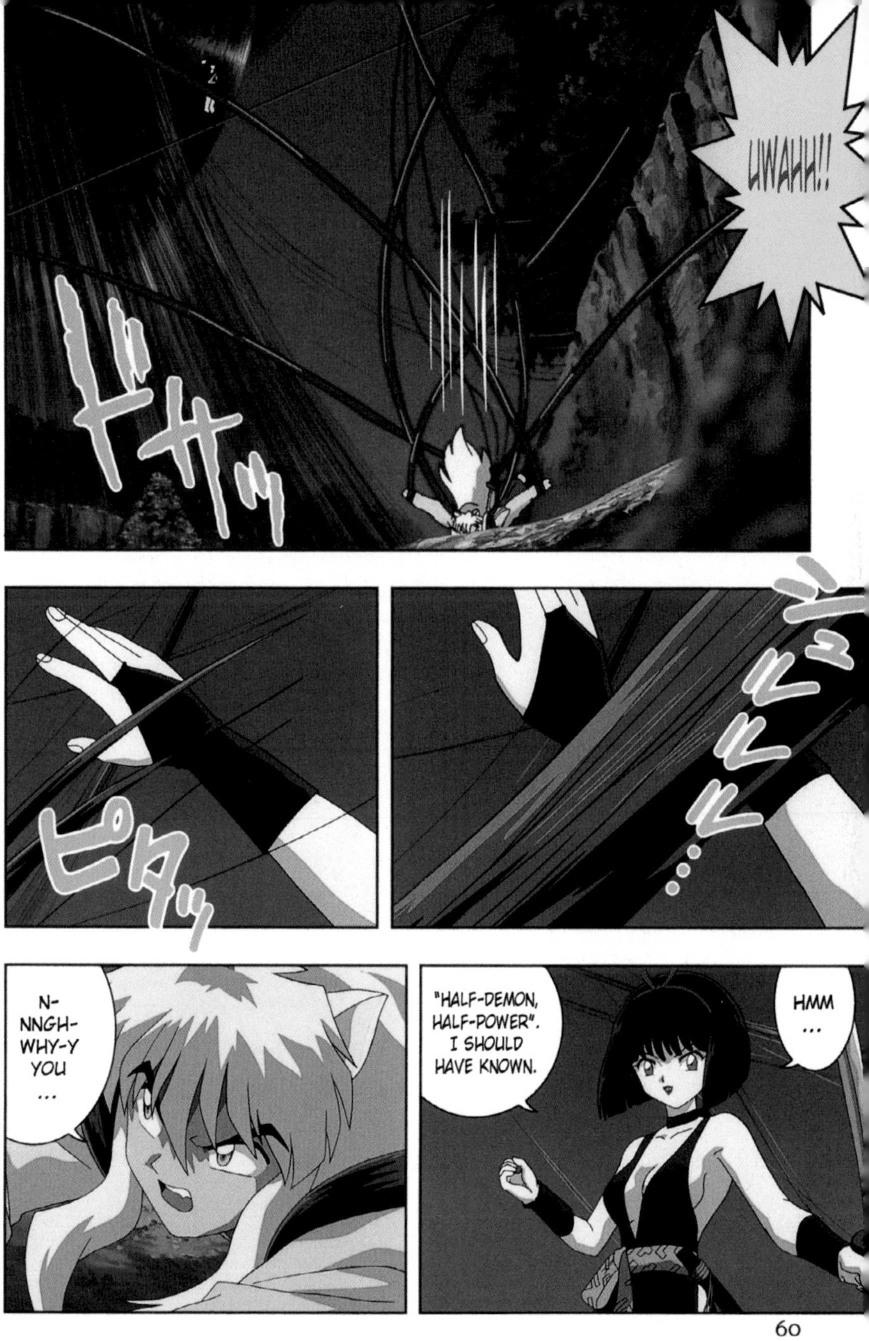
UWAHH!!
ドサッ
HMM ...
"HALF-DEMON, HALF-POWER". I SHOULD HAVE KNOWN.
N- NNGH- WHY-Y YOU ...
ピタッ

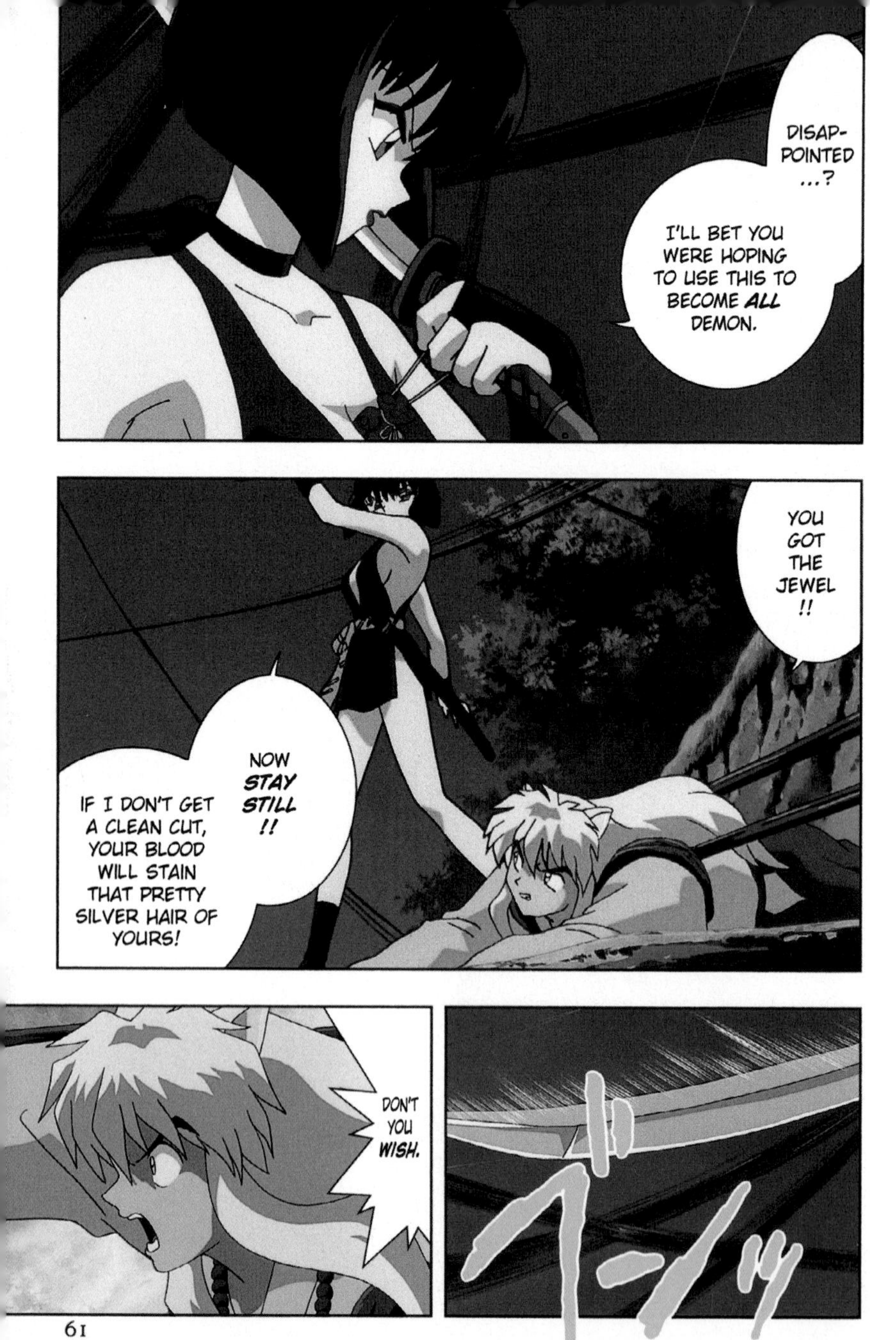
DISAP-POINTED ...?
I'LL BET YOU WERE HOPING TO USE THIS TO BECOME ALL DEMON.
YOU GOT THE JEWEL !!
NOW STAY STILL !!
IF I DON'T GET A CLEAN CUT, YOUR BLOOD WILL STAIN THAT PRETTY SILVER HAIR OF YOURS!
ブンッ
DON'T YOU WISH.

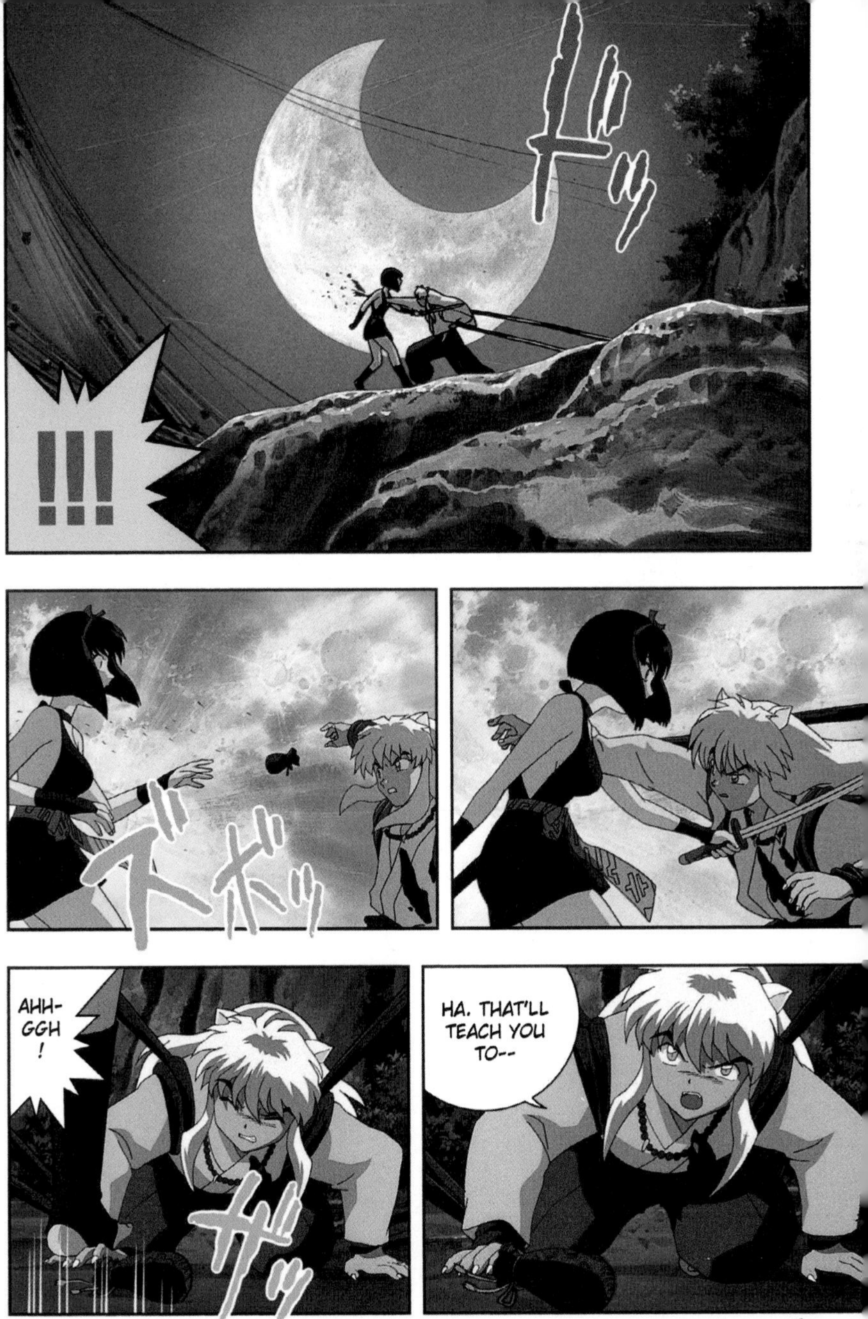
ドッ
!!!
ズボッ
HA. THAT'LL TEACH YOU TO--
AHH-GGH!
ザッ

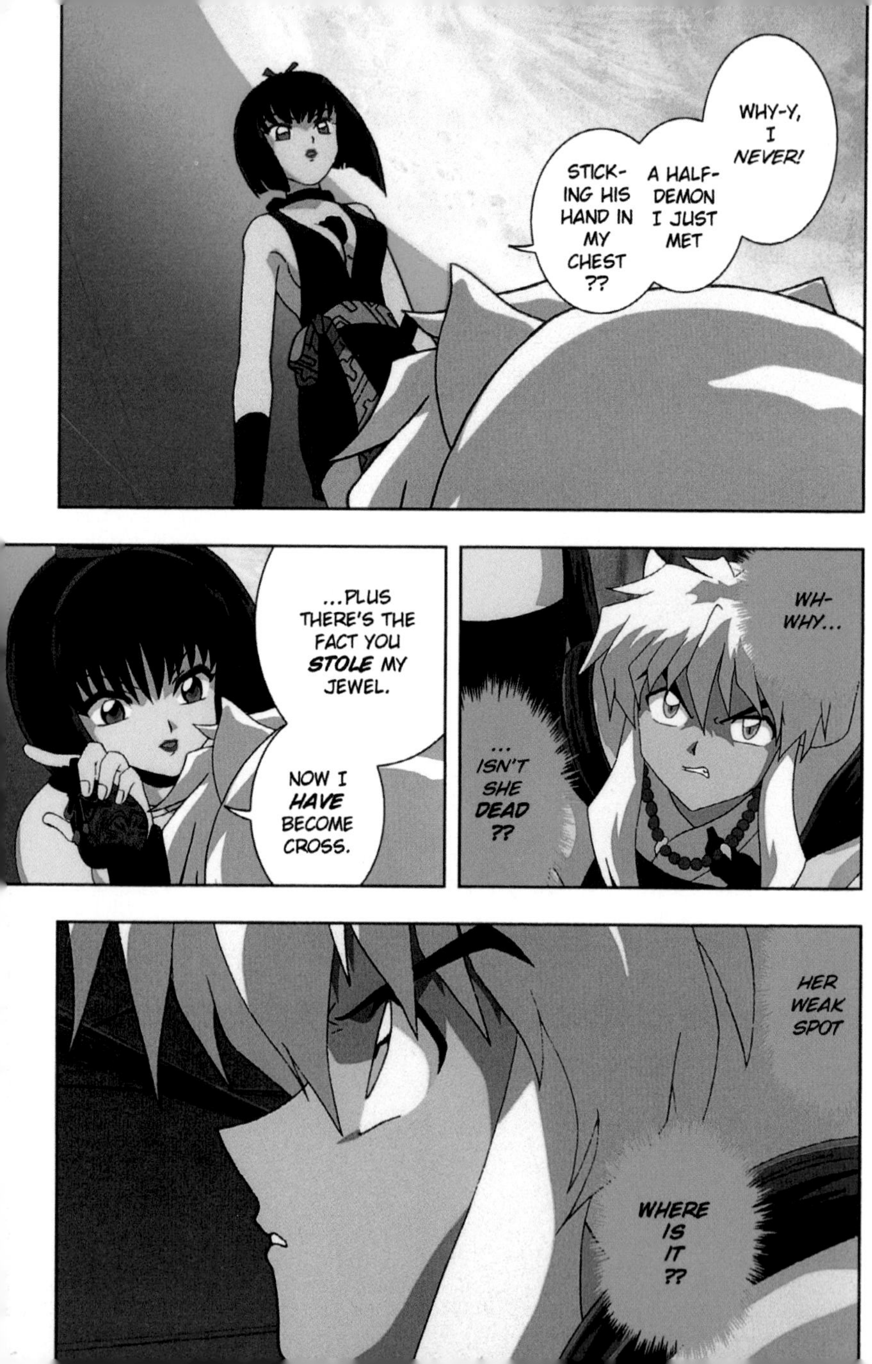

WHY-Y, I NEVER!
A HALF-DEMON I JUST MET
STICKING HIS HAND IN MY CHEST ??
WH- WHY...
...ISN'T SHE DEAD ??
...PLUS THERE'S THE FACT YOU STOLE MY JEWEL.
NOW I HAVE BECOME CROSS.
HER WEAK SPOT
WHERE IS IT ??

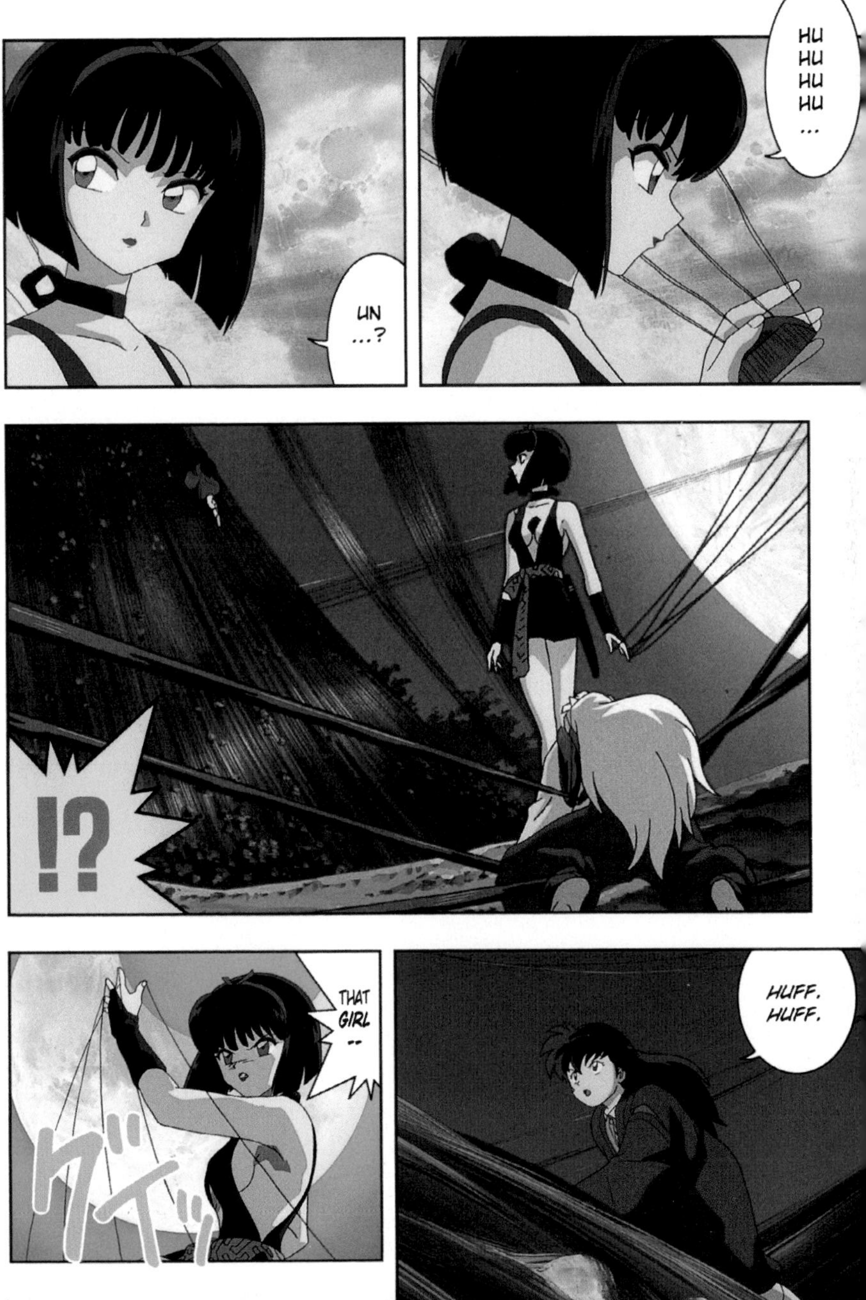
HU HU HU HU ...
UN ...?
!?
HUFF. HUFF.
THAT GIRL --
グイッ

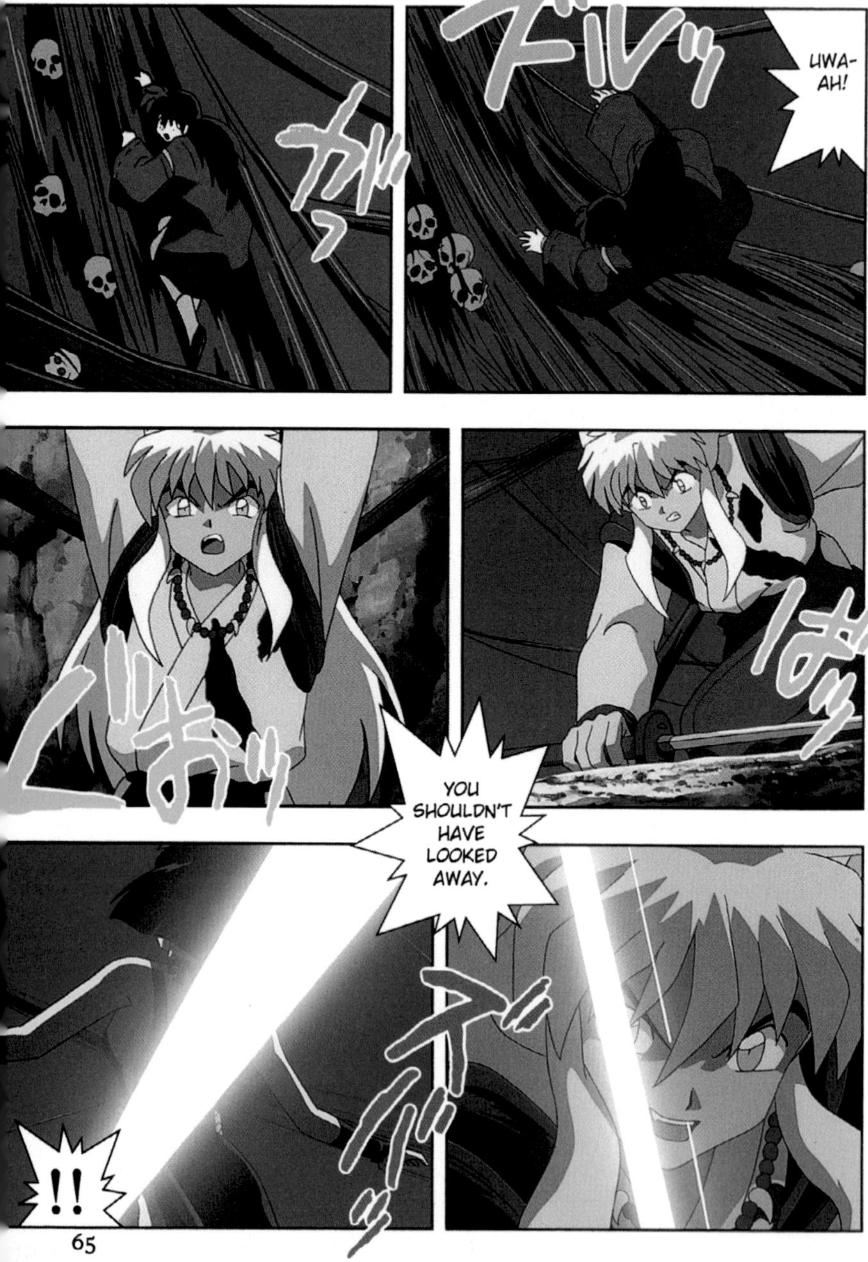
ズルッ
UWA-AH!
ガッ
ばっ
YOU SHOULDN'T HAVE LOOKED AWAY.
!!

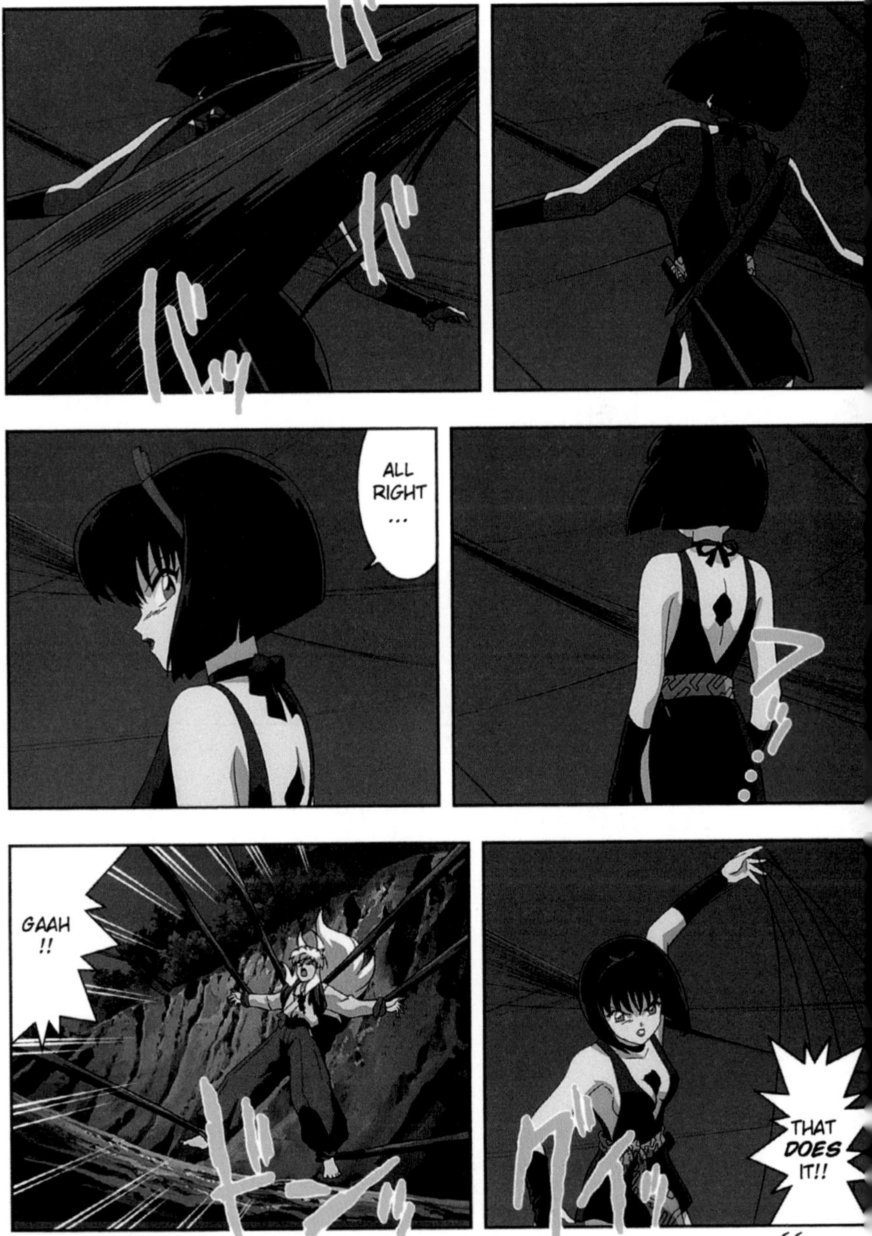
ALL RIGHT ...
THAT **DOES** IT!!
GAAH !!

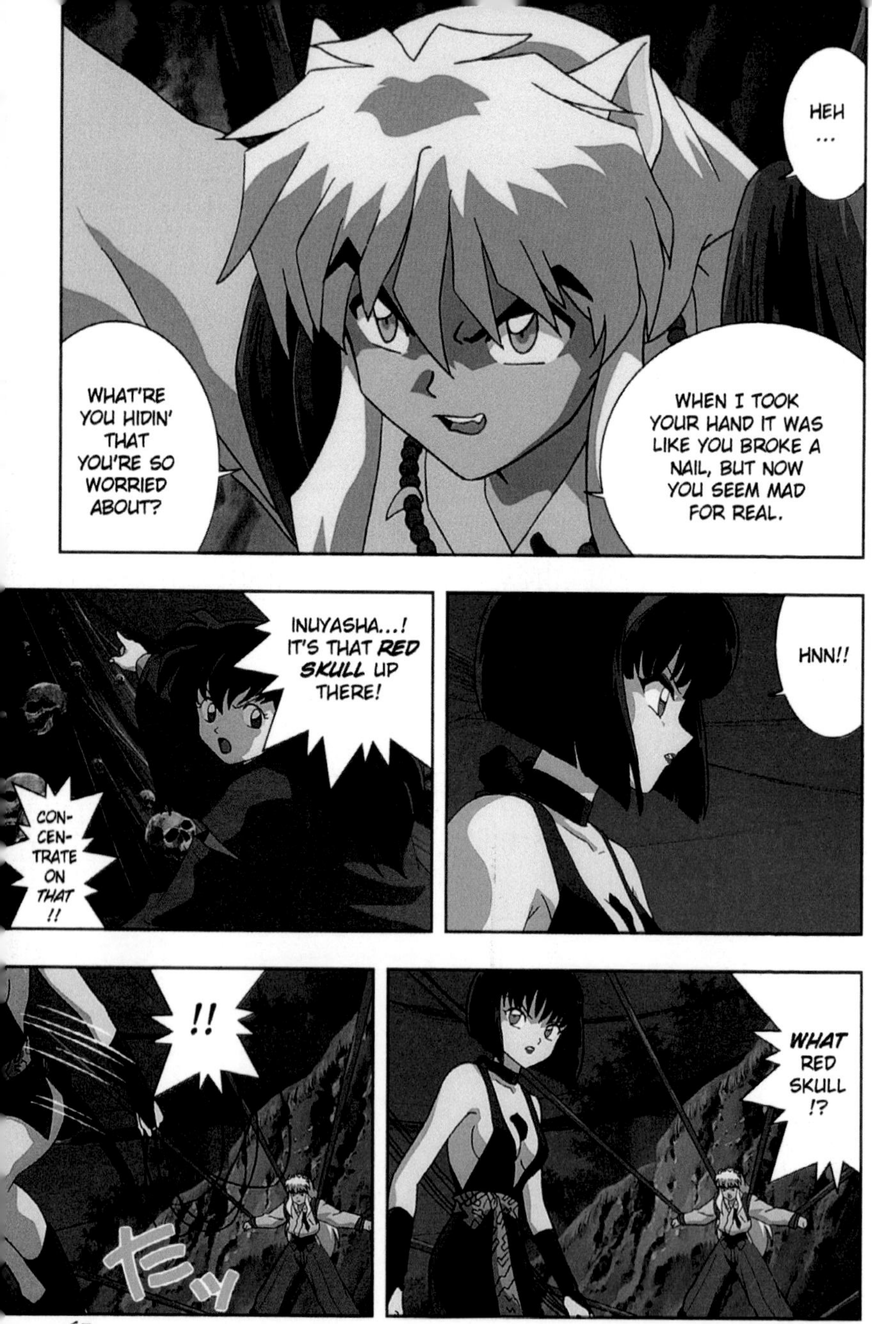
HEH ...
WHEN I TOOK YOUR HAND IT WAS LIKE YOU BROKE A NAIL, BUT NOW YOU SEEM MAD FOR REAL.
WHAT'RE YOU HIDIN' THAT YOU'RE SO WORRIED ABOUT?
HNN!!
INUYASHA...! IT'S THAT *RED SKULL* UP THERE!
CON-CEN-TRATE ON *THAT* !!
WHAT RED SKULL !?
!!

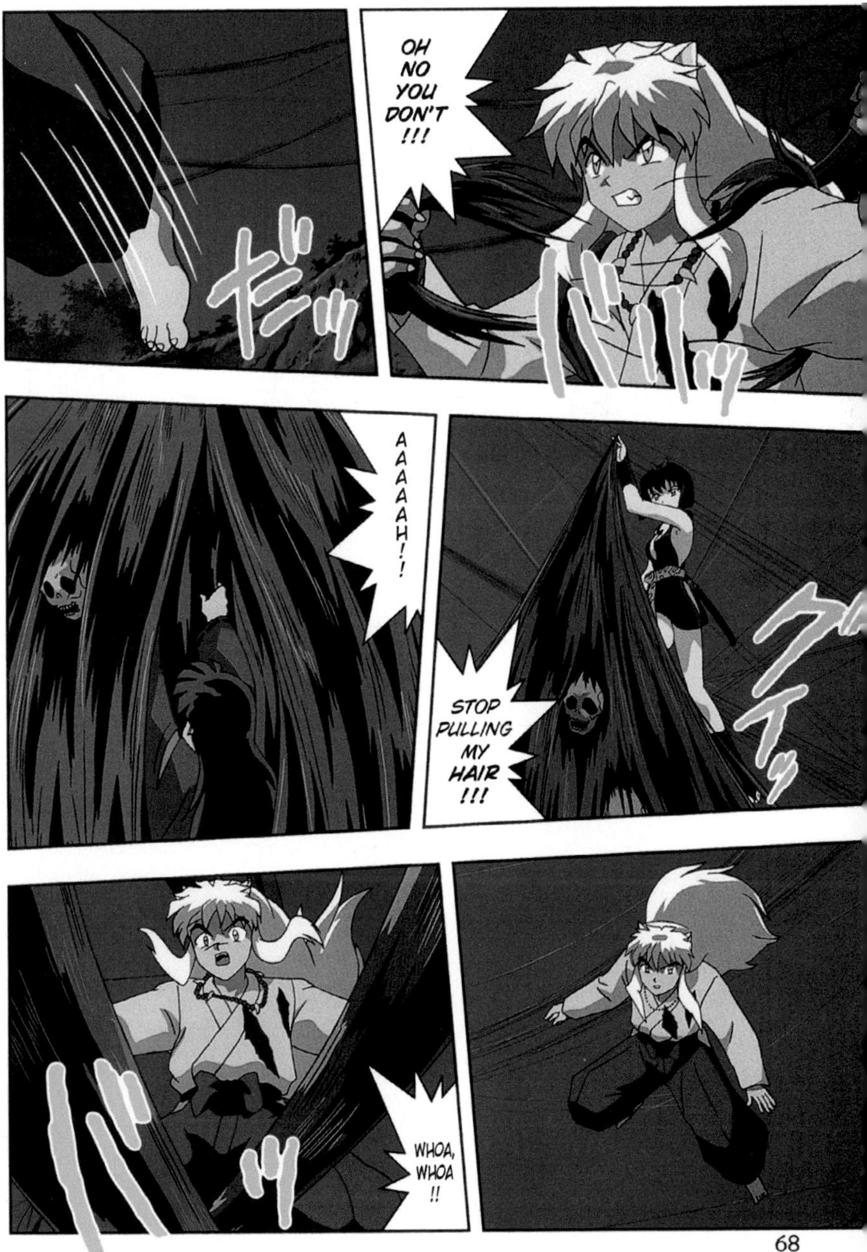
OH NO YOU DON'T!!!
STOP PULLING MY HAIR!!!
AAAAAH!!
WHOA, WHOA!!

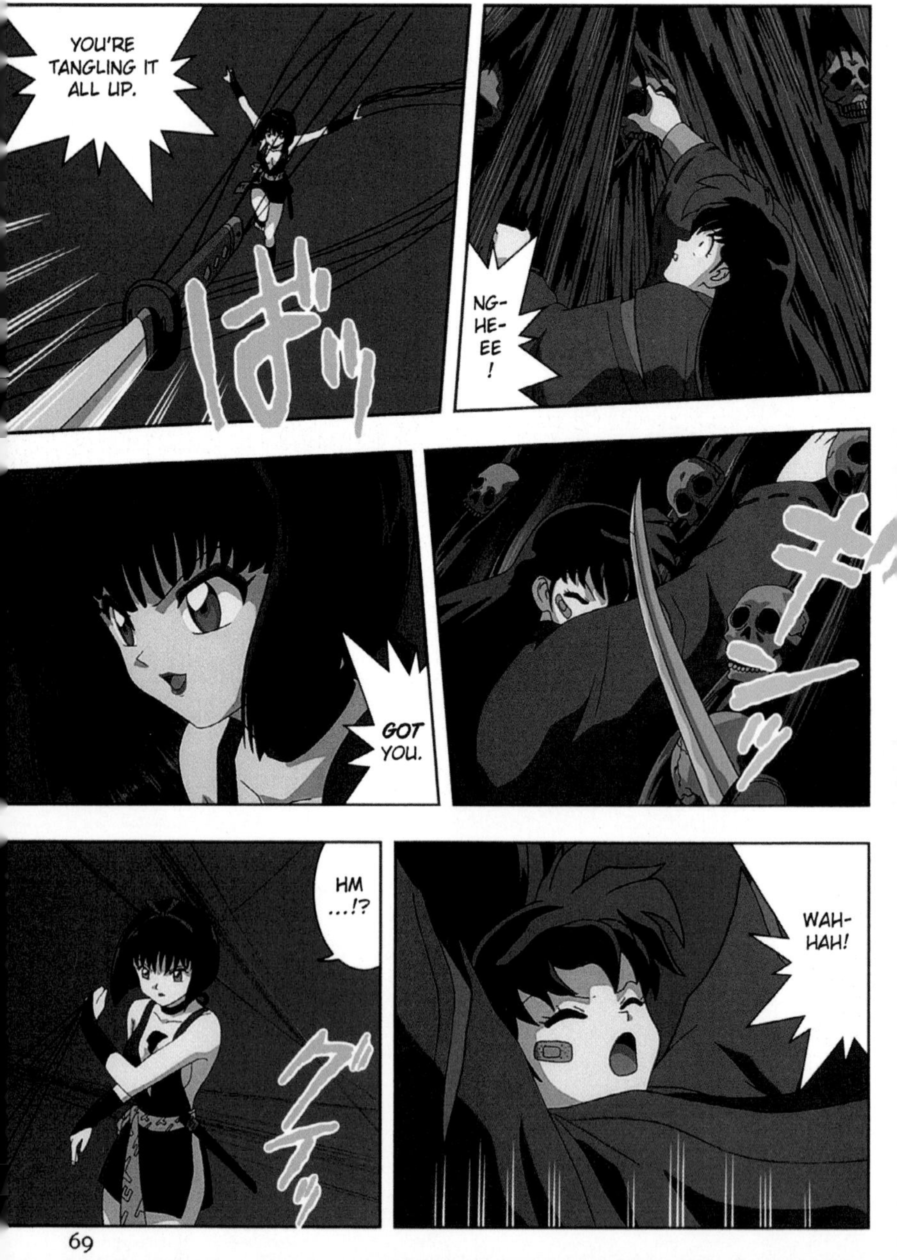
NG-HE-EE!
YOU'RE TANGLING IT ALL UP.
ばッ
キーンッ
GOT YOU.
WAH-HAH!
HM ...!?
グイッ

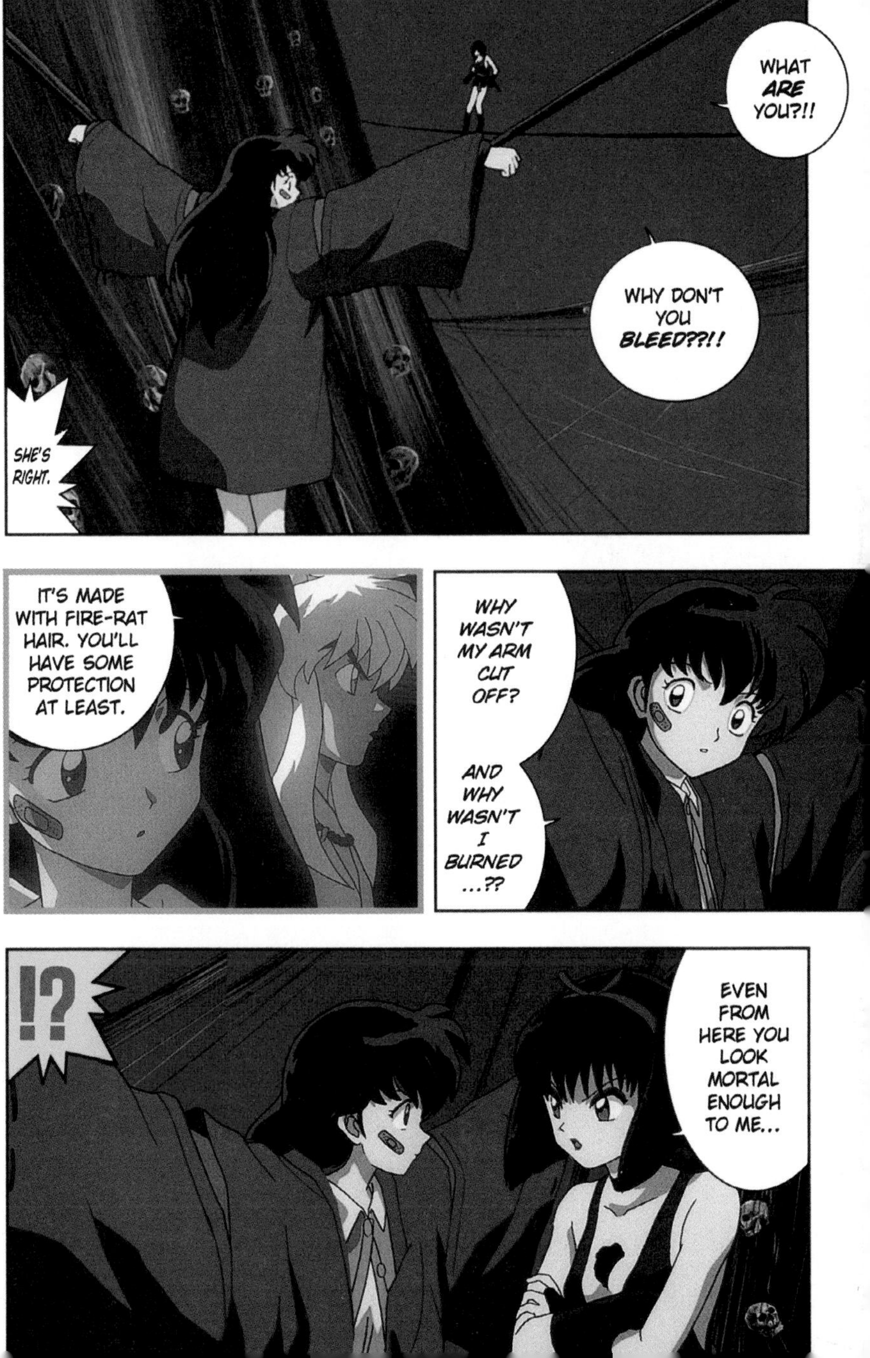
WHAT ARE YOU?!!
WHY DON'T YOU BLEED??!!
SHE'S RIGHT.
WHY WASN'T MY ARM CUT OFF?
AND WHY WASN'T I BURNED ...??
IT'S MADE WITH FIRE-RAT HAIR. YOU'LL HAVE SOME PROTECTION AT LEAST.
EVEN FROM HERE YOU LOOK MORTAL ENOUGH TO ME...
!?

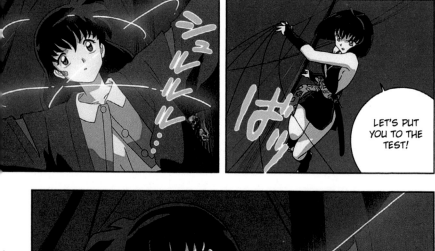

LET'S PUT YOU TO THE TEST!

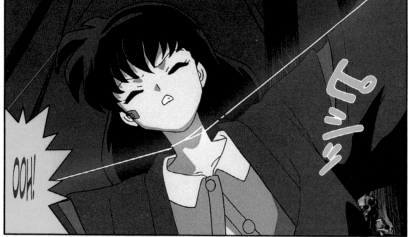

OOH!

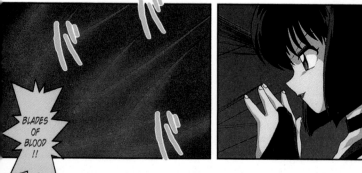

BLADES OF BLOOD !!

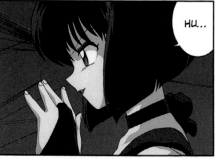

HU...

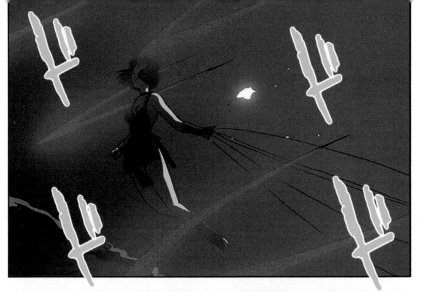

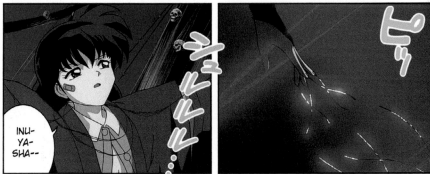

INU-
YA-
SHA--

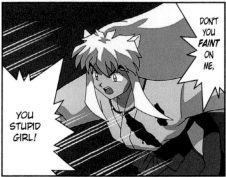

DON'T
YOU
FAINT
ON
ME,

YOU
STUPID
GIRL!

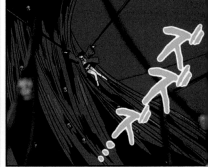

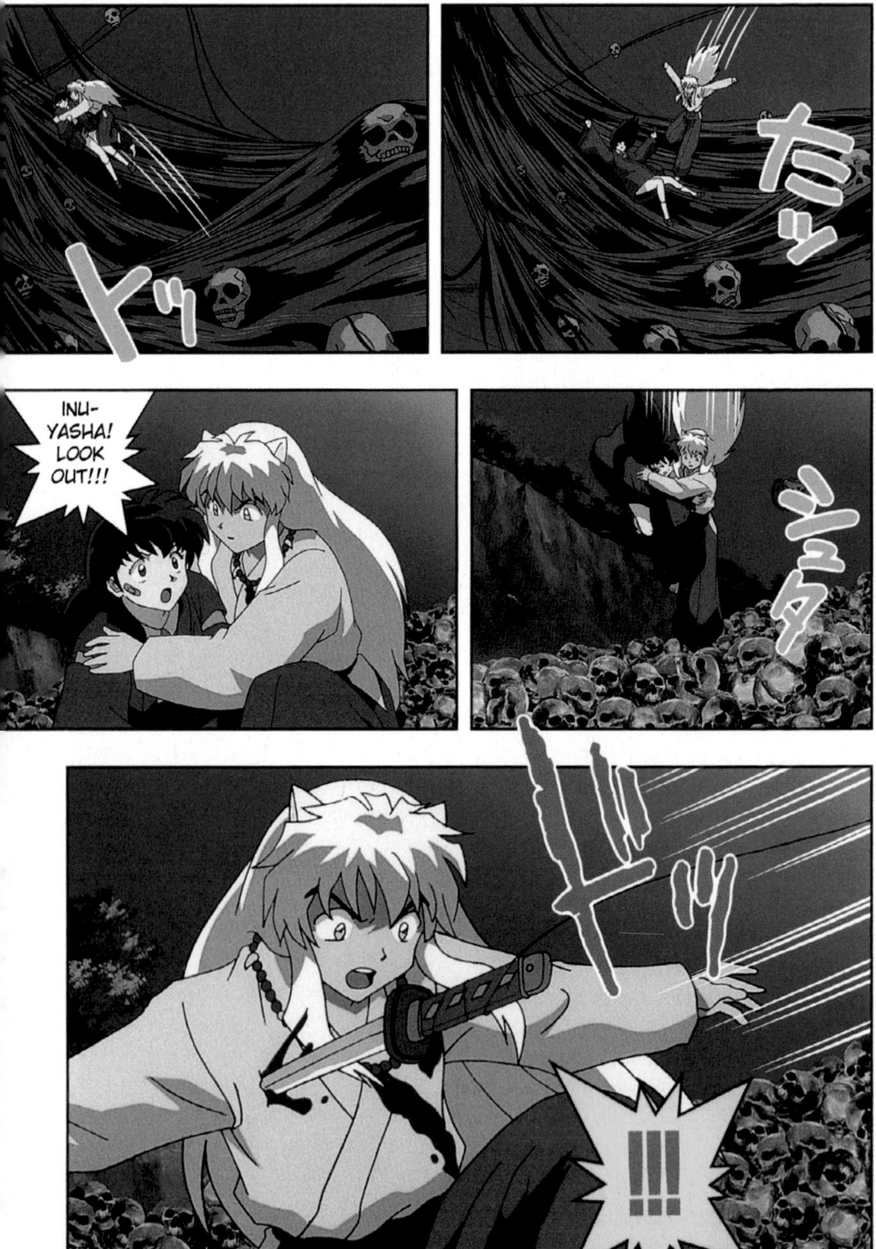

ダッ
ドッ
シュタ
INU-YASHA! LOOK OUT!!!
ドッ
!!!

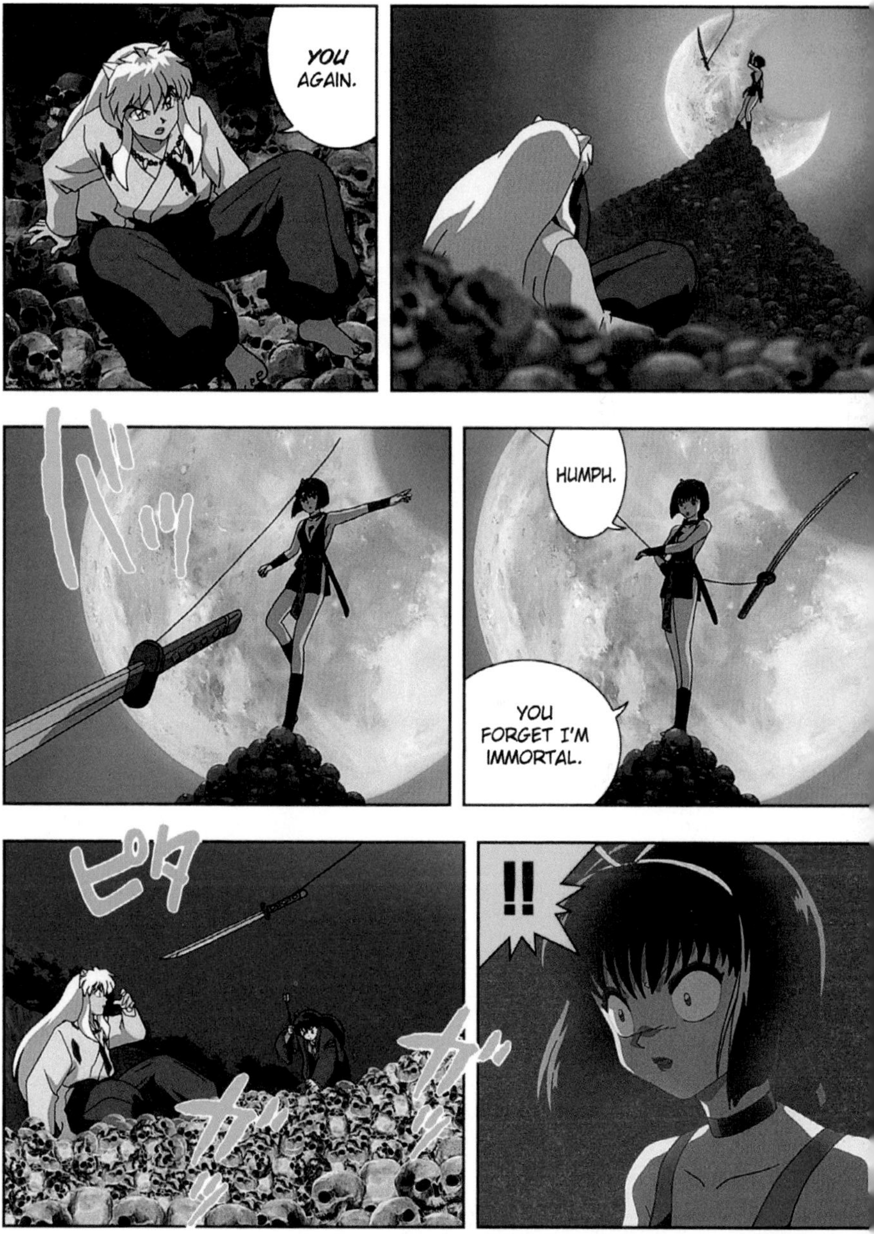
YOU AGAIN.
HUMPH.
YOU FORGET I'M IMMORTAL.
バッ
!!
ガッ
ガッ
ピタ

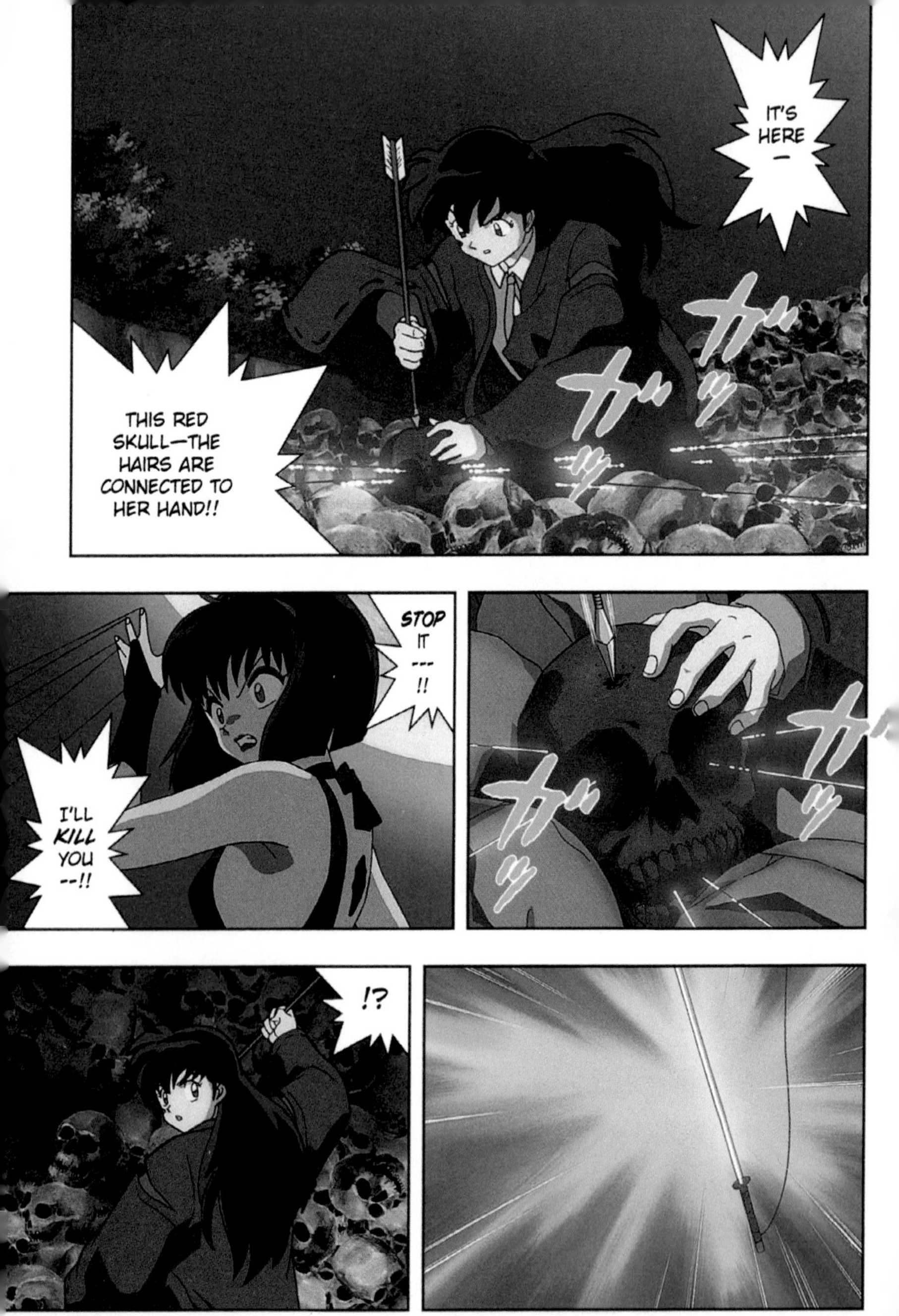
IT'S HERE —
THIS RED SKULL—THE HAIRS ARE CONNECTED TO HER HAND!!
ガッ ガッ
ガッ ガッ
STOP IT ---!!
I'LL KILL YOU --!!
!?

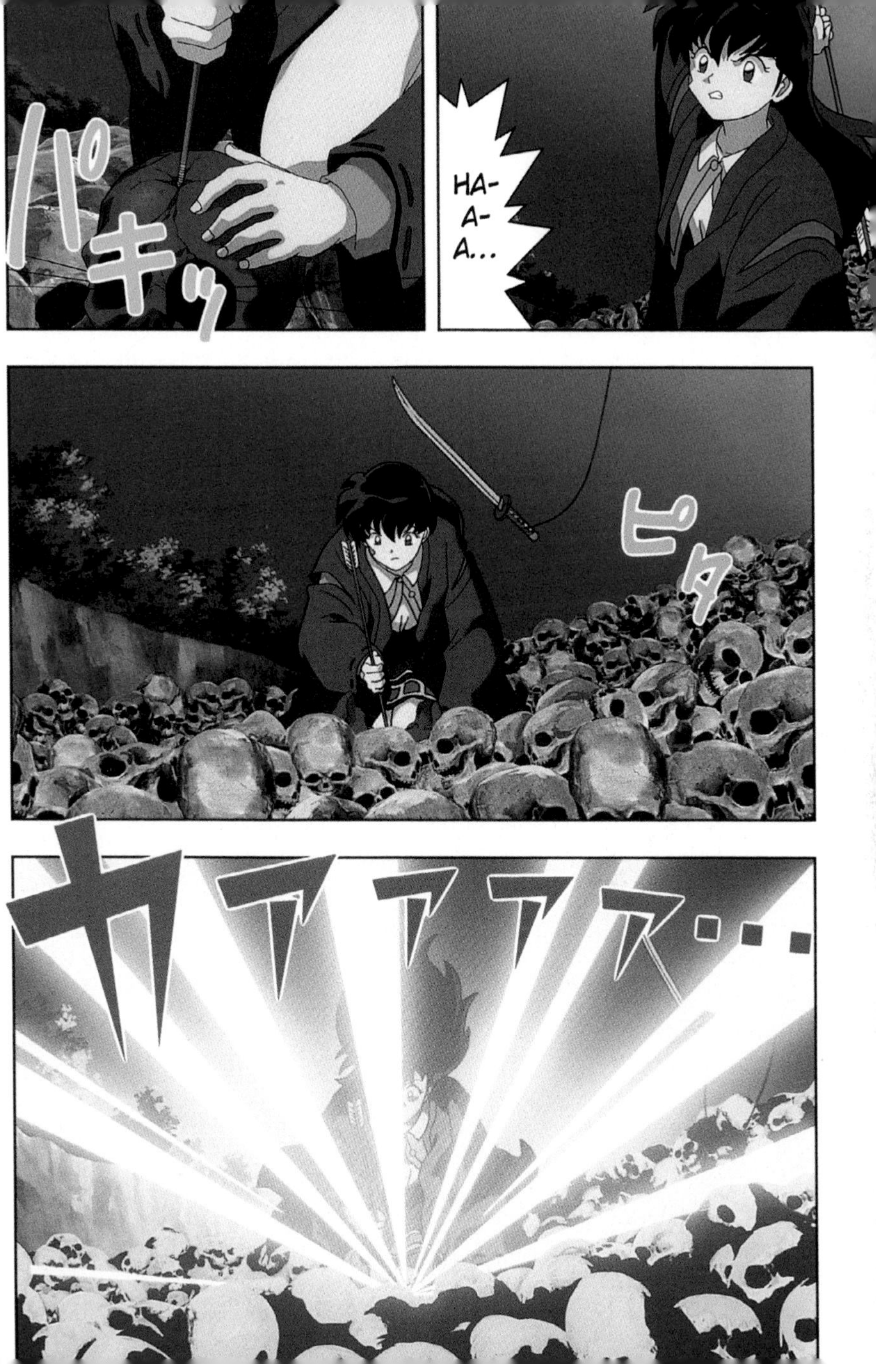
HA-
A-
A...
パキッ
ピタ
カァァァァ…

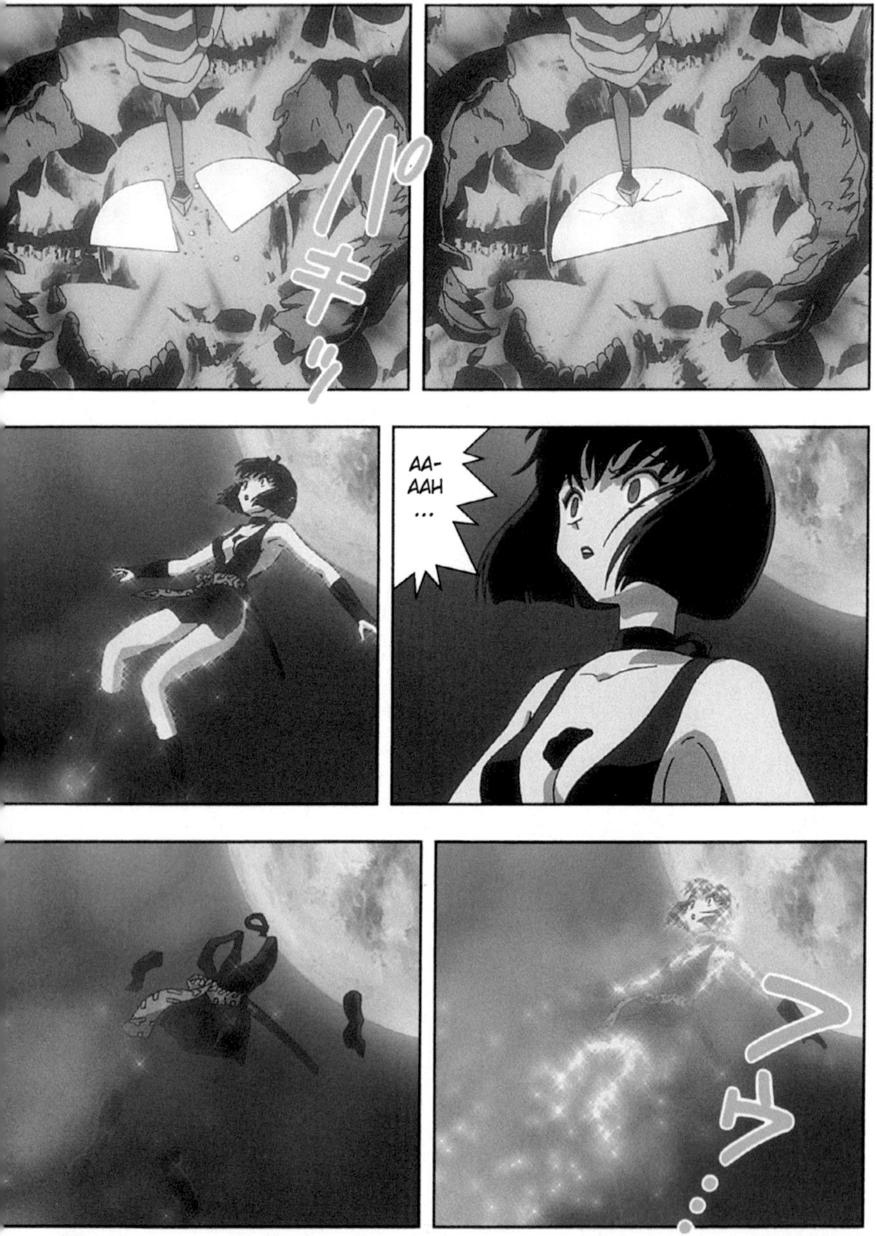
パキッ
AA-AAH ...
ヘァ…

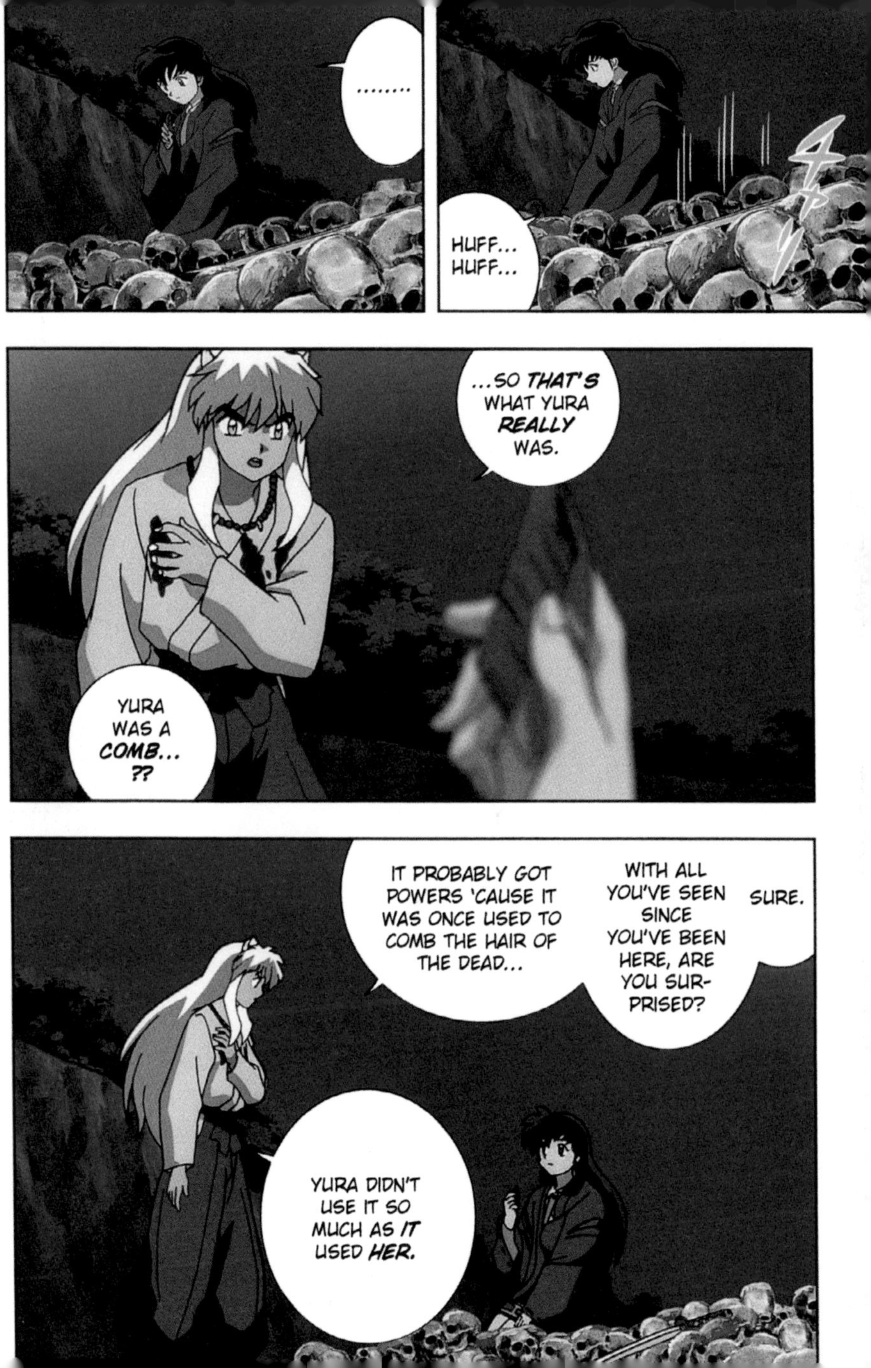
HUFF... HUFF...
....
...SO THAT'S WHAT YURA REALLY WAS.
YURA WAS A COMB...??
SURE.
WITH ALL YOU'VE SEEN SINCE YOU'VE BEEN HERE, ARE YOU SURPRISED?
IT PROBABLY GOT POWERS 'CAUSE IT WAS ONCE USED TO COMB THE HAIR OF THE DEAD...
YURA DIDN'T USE IT SO MUCH AS IT USED HER.

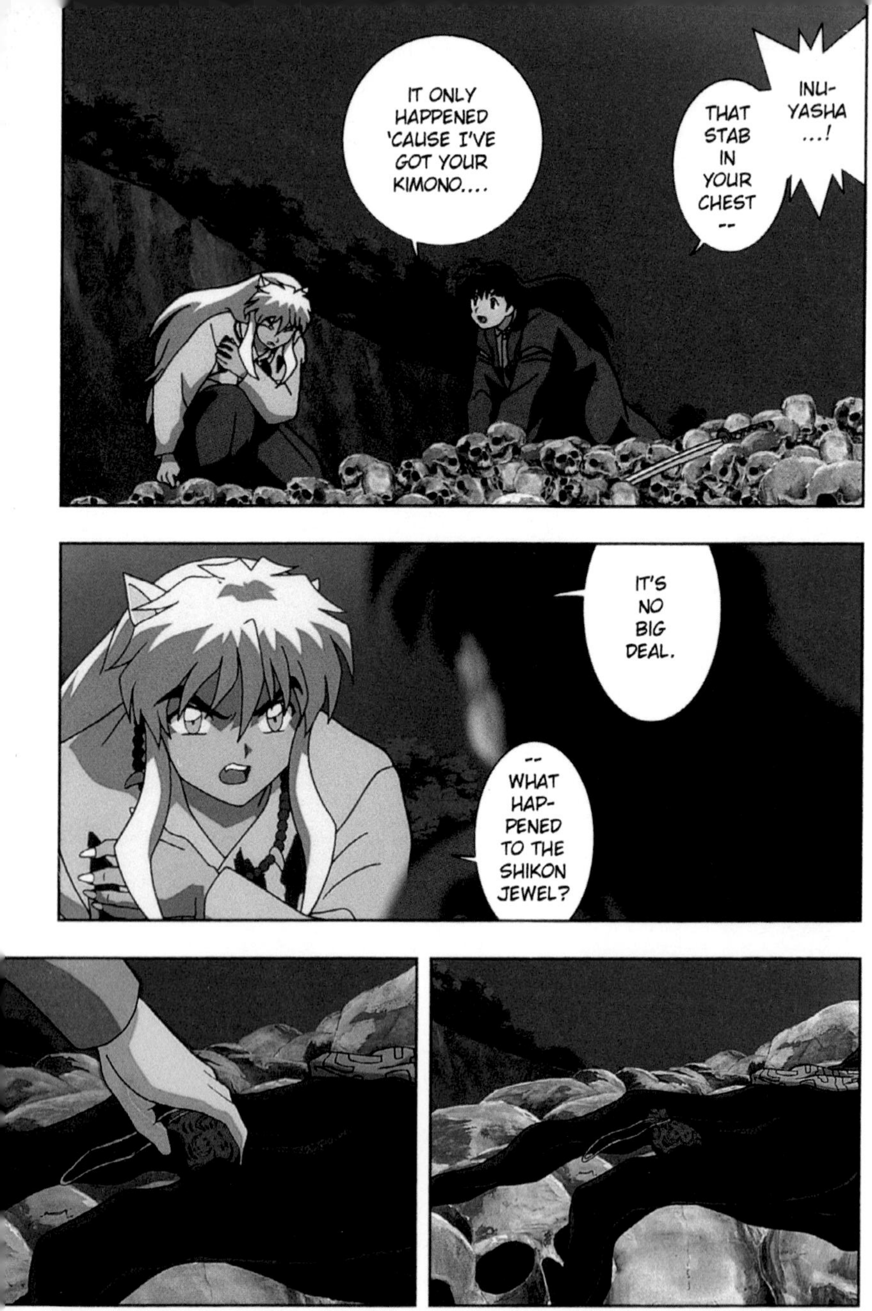
INU-YASHA ...!
THAT STAB IN YOUR CHEST --
IT ONLY HAPPENED 'CAUSE I'VE GOT YOUR KIMONO....
IT'S NO BIG DEAL.
-- WHAT HAPPENED TO THE SHIKON JEWEL?

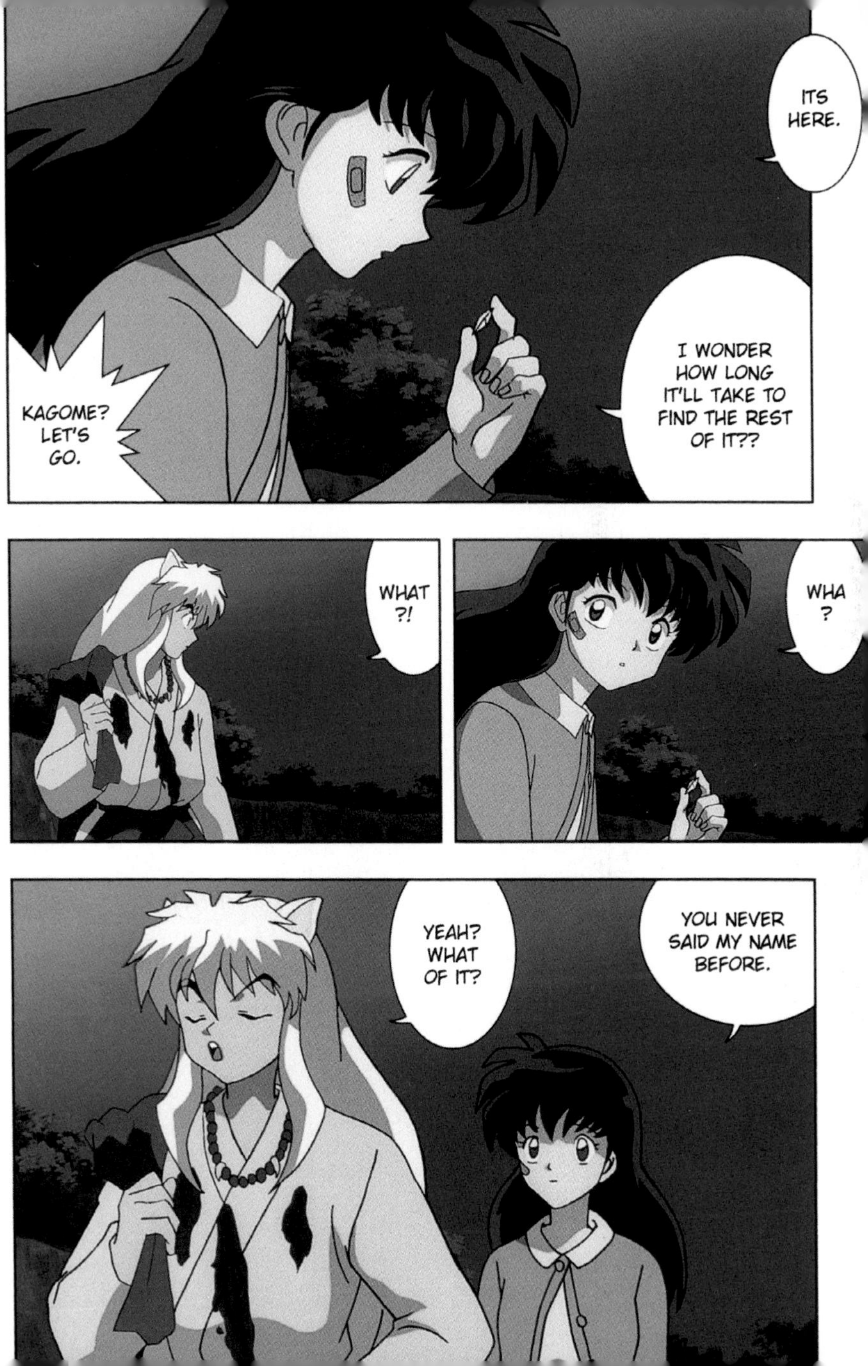
ITS HERE.
I WONDER HOW LONG IT'LL TAKE TO FIND THE REST OF IT??
KAGOME? LET'S GO.
WHA ?
WHAT ?!
YOU NEVER SAID MY NAME BEFORE.
YEAH? WHAT OF IT?

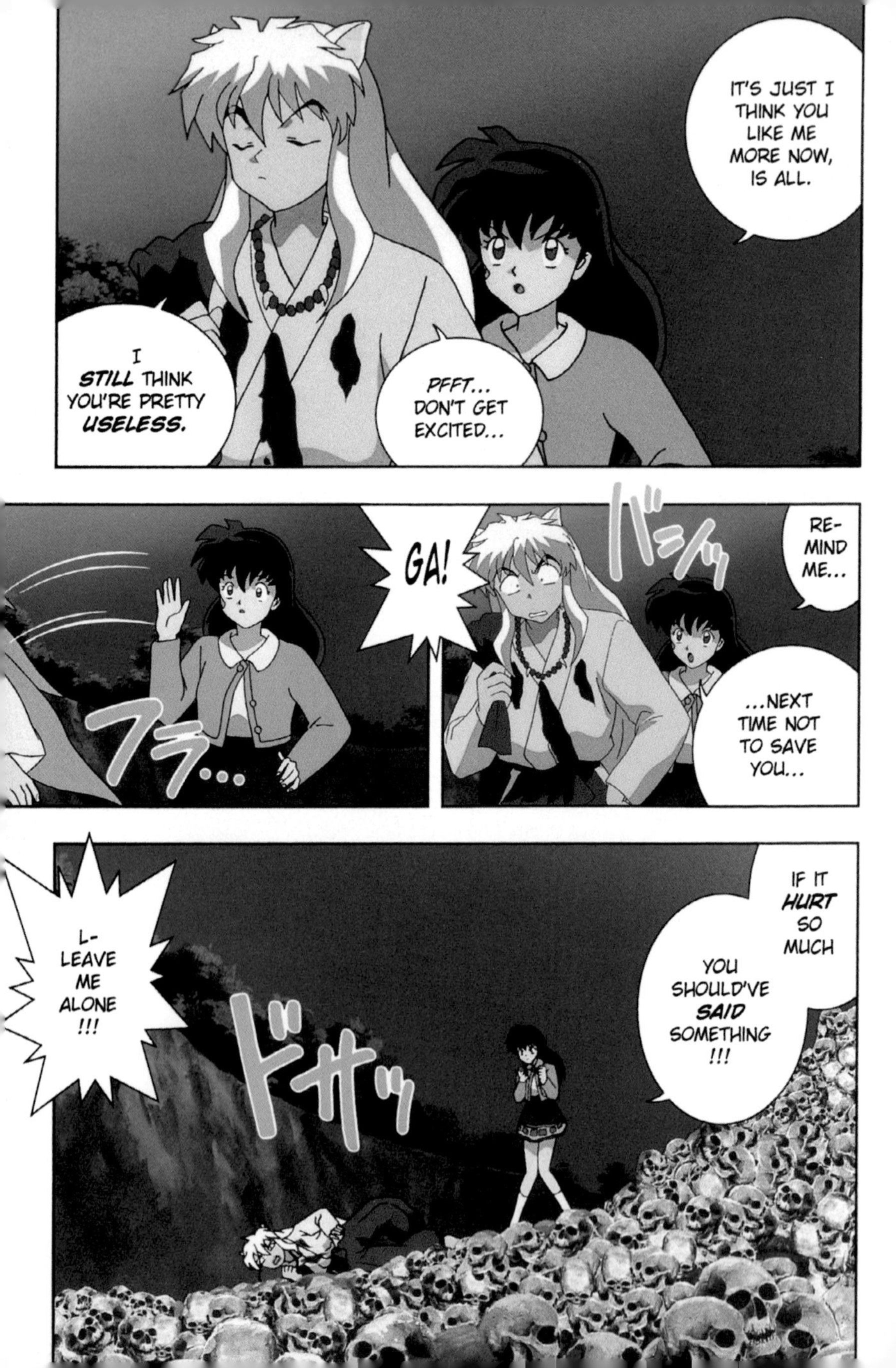
IT'S JUST I THINK YOU LIKE ME MORE NOW, IS ALL.
PFFT... DON'T GET EXCITED...
I STILL THINK YOU'RE PRETTY USELESS.
バシッ
RE-MIND ME...
...NEXT TIME NOT TO SAVE YOU...
GA!
フラ...
IF IT HURT SO MUCH
YOU SHOULD'VE SAID SOMETHING !!!
ドサッ
L- LEAVE ME ALONE !!!

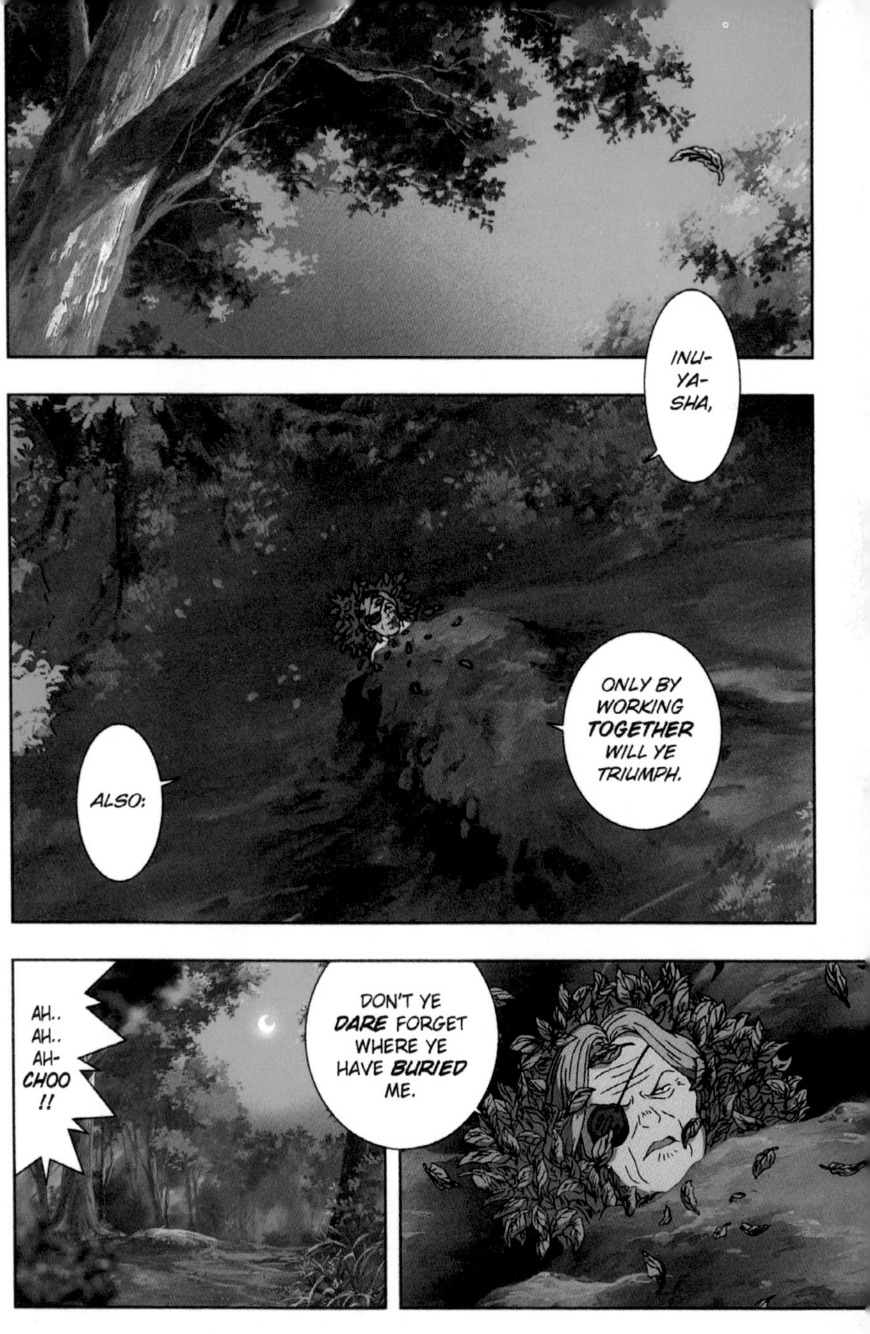
INU-YASHA,
ONLY BY WORKING **TOGETHER** WILL YE TRIUMPH.
ALSO:
DON'T YE **DARE** FORGET WHERE YE HAVE **BURIED** ME.
AH.. AH.. AH-**CHOO** !!

5
ARISTOCRATIC ASSASSIN, SESSHOMARU

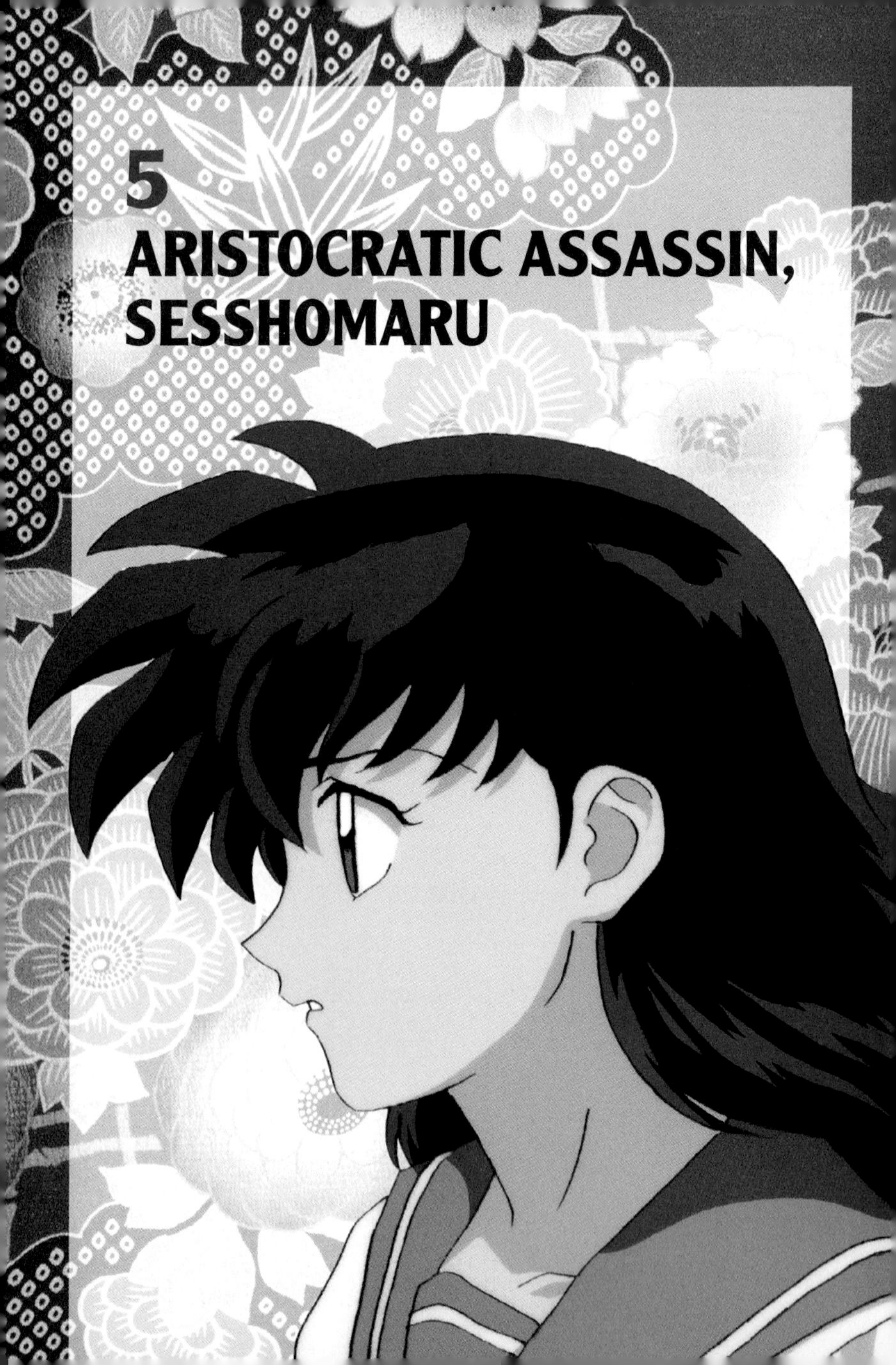

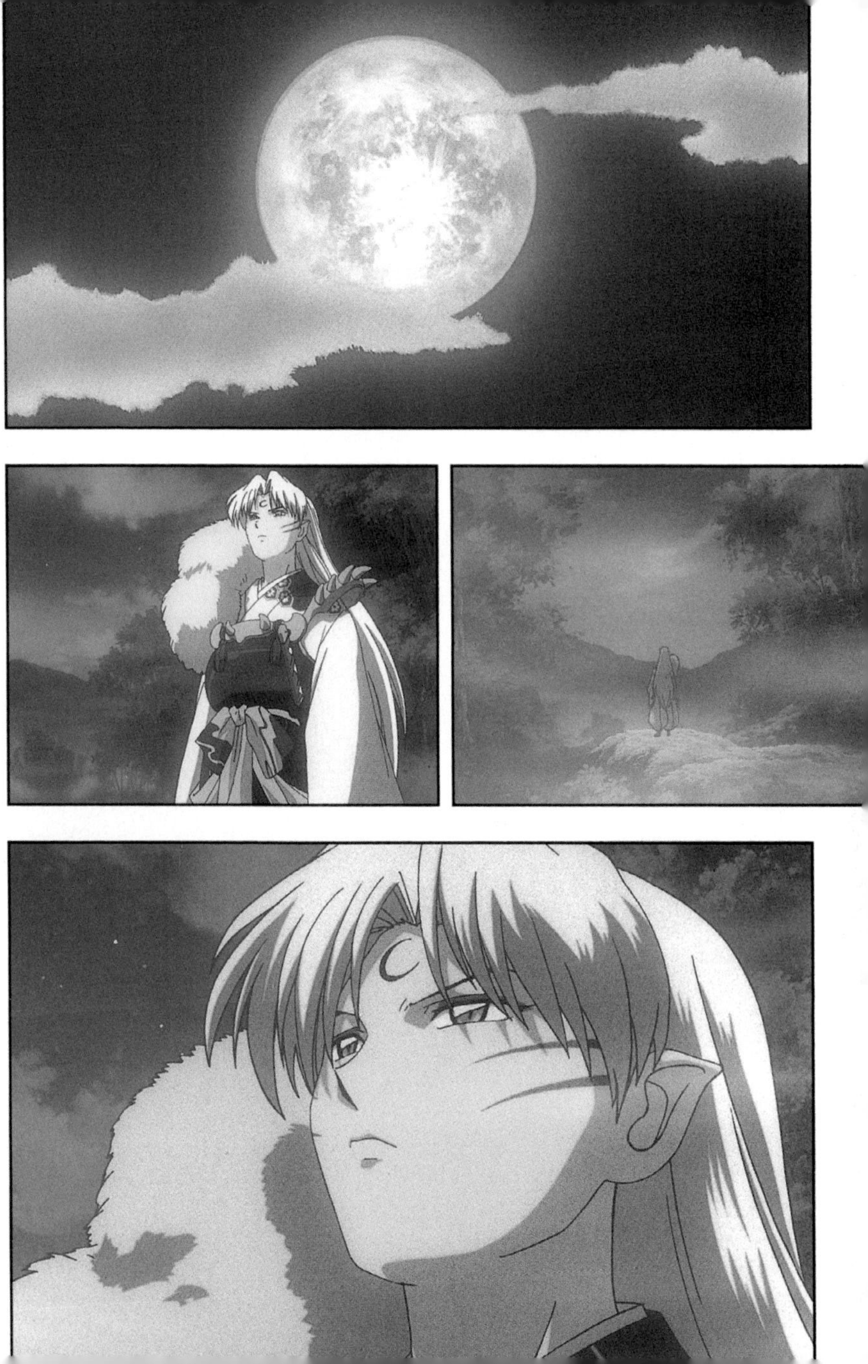

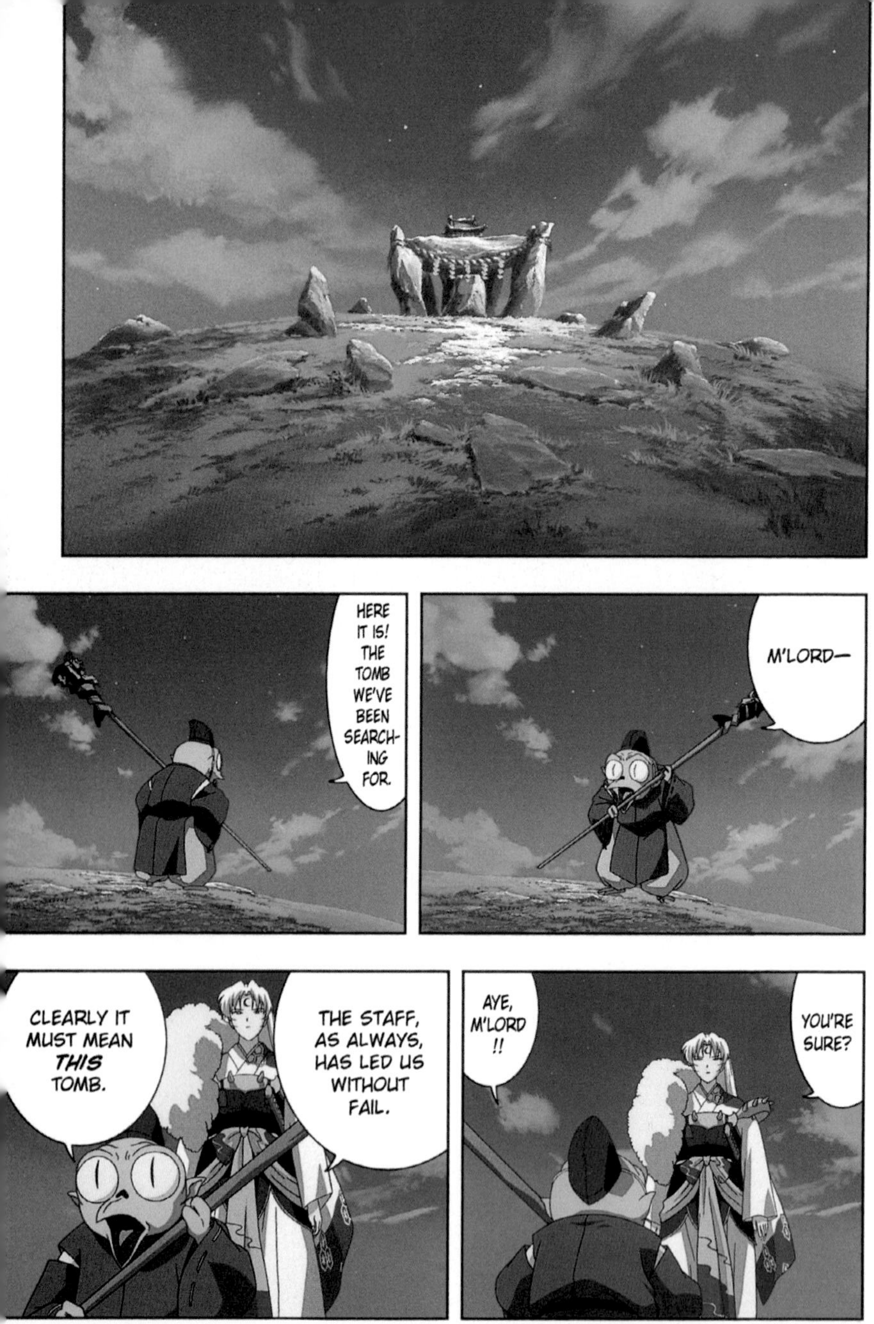
M'LORD—
HERE IT IS! THE TOMB WE'VE BEEN SEARCHING FOR.
YOU'RE SURE?
AYE, M'LORD !!
THE STAFF, AS ALWAYS, HAS LED US WITHOUT FAIL.
CLEARLY IT MUST MEAN *THIS* TOMB.

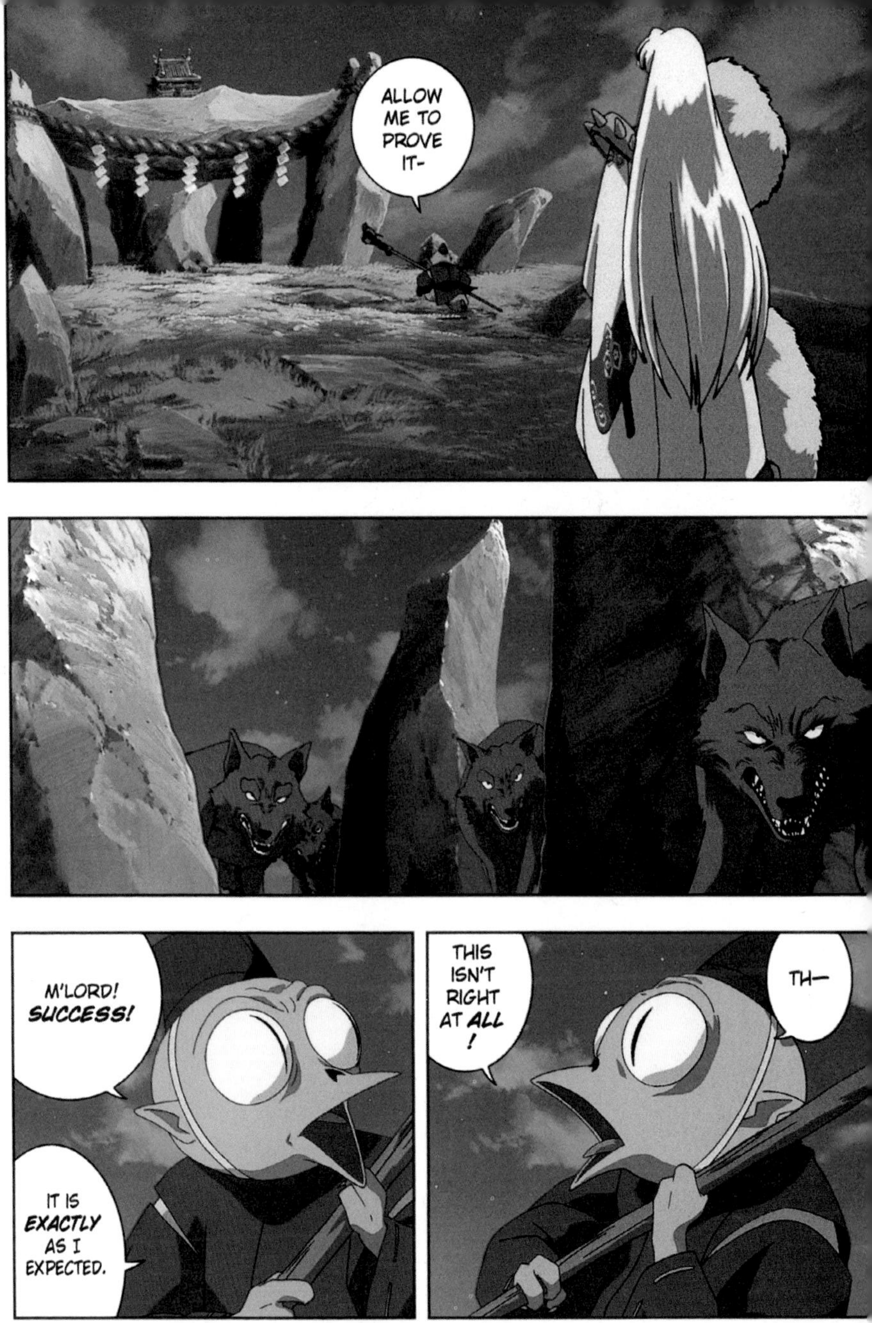
ALLOW ME TO PROVE IT-
TH—
THIS ISN'T RIGHT AT **ALL**!
M'LORD! **SUCCESS!**
IT IS **EXACTLY** AS I EXPECTED.

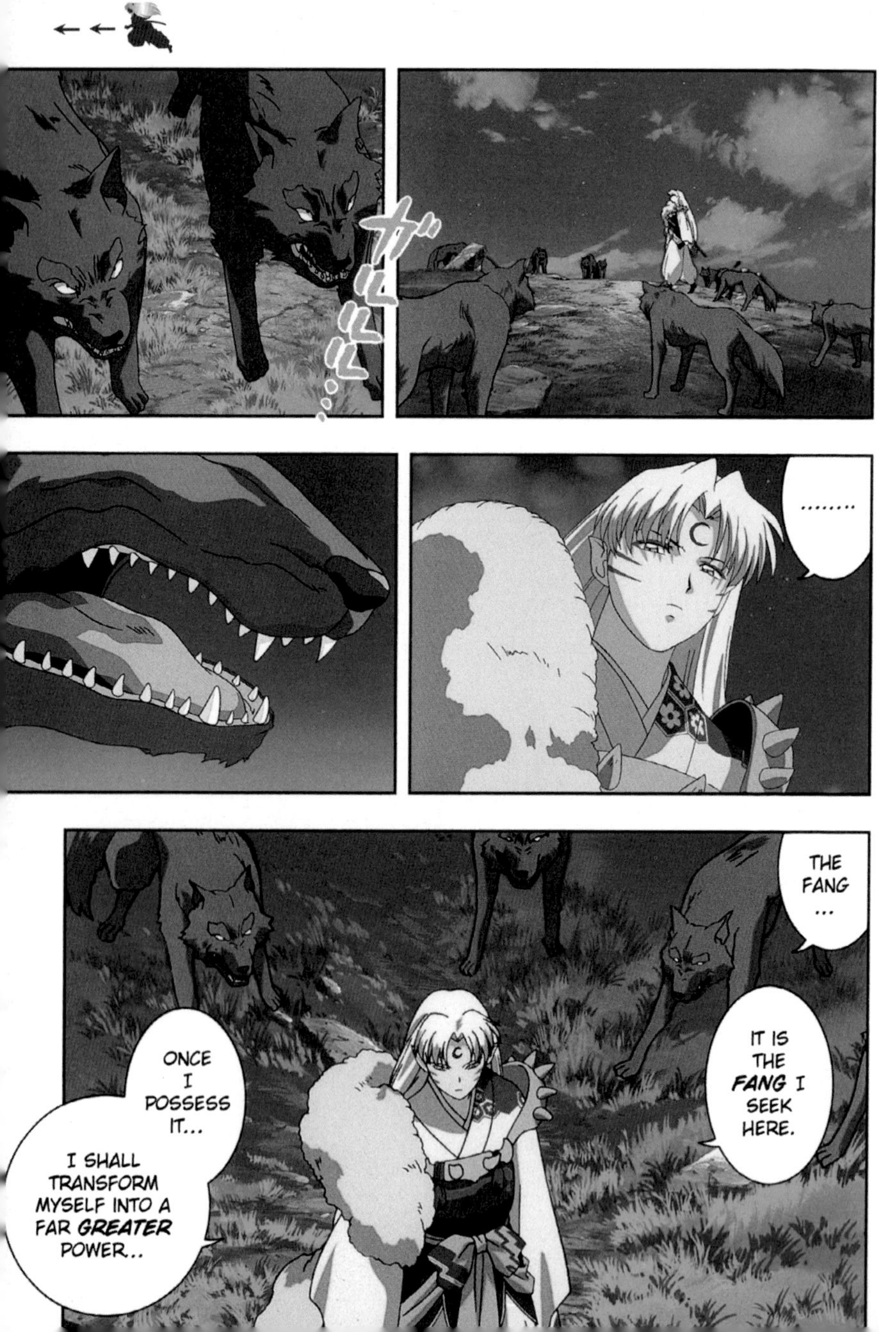
ガルルル…
....
THE FANG ...
IT IS THE FANG I SEEK HERE.
ONCE I POSSESS IT...
I SHALL TRANSFORM MYSELF INTO A FAR GREATER POWER..

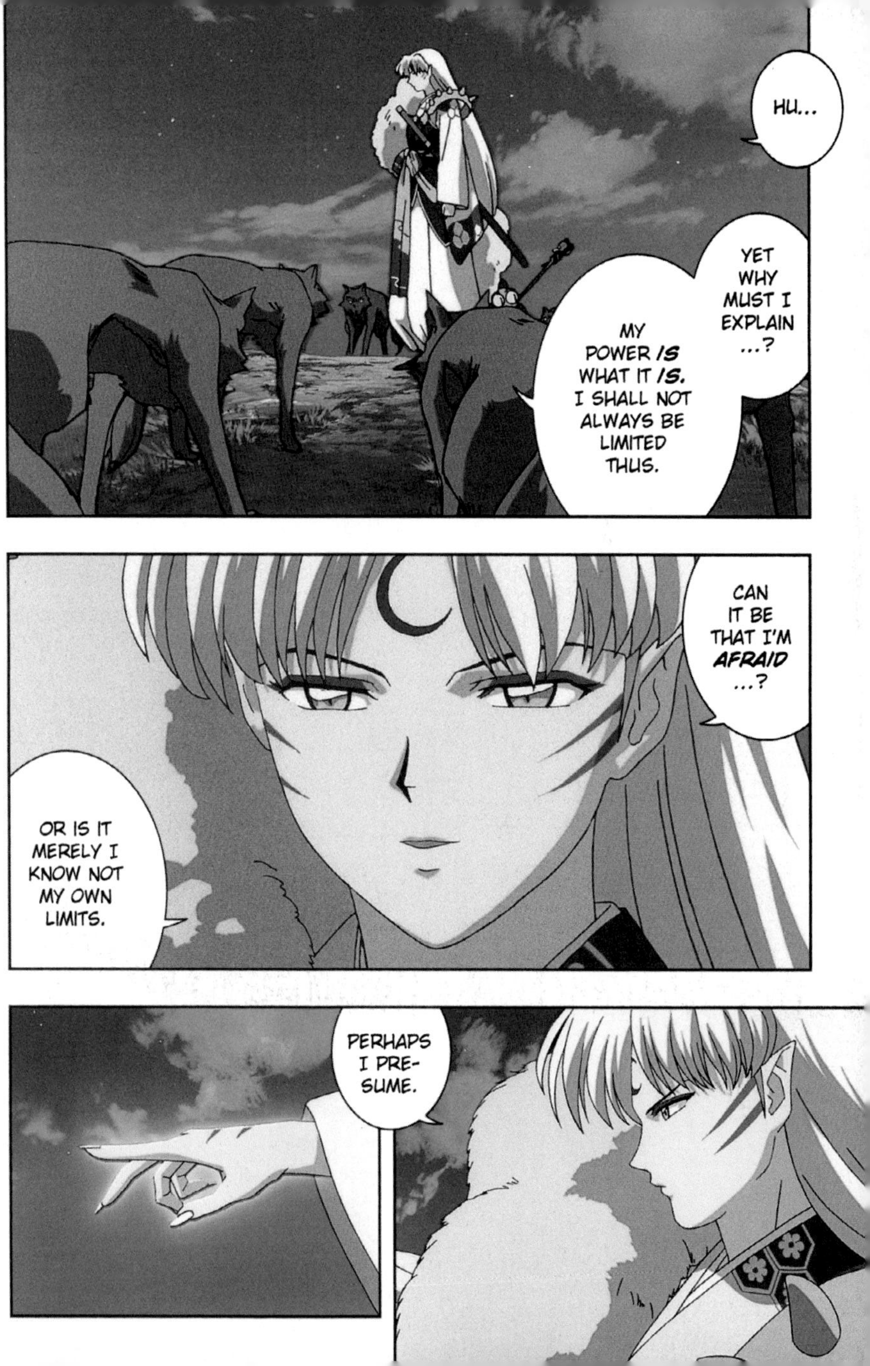
HU...
YET WHY MUST I EXPLAIN ...?
MY POWER *IS* WHAT IT *IS.* I SHALL NOT ALWAYS BE LIMITED THUS.
CAN IT BE THAT I'M *AFRAID* ...?
OR IS IT MERELY I KNOW NOT MY OWN LIMITS.
PERHAPS I PRE- SUME.

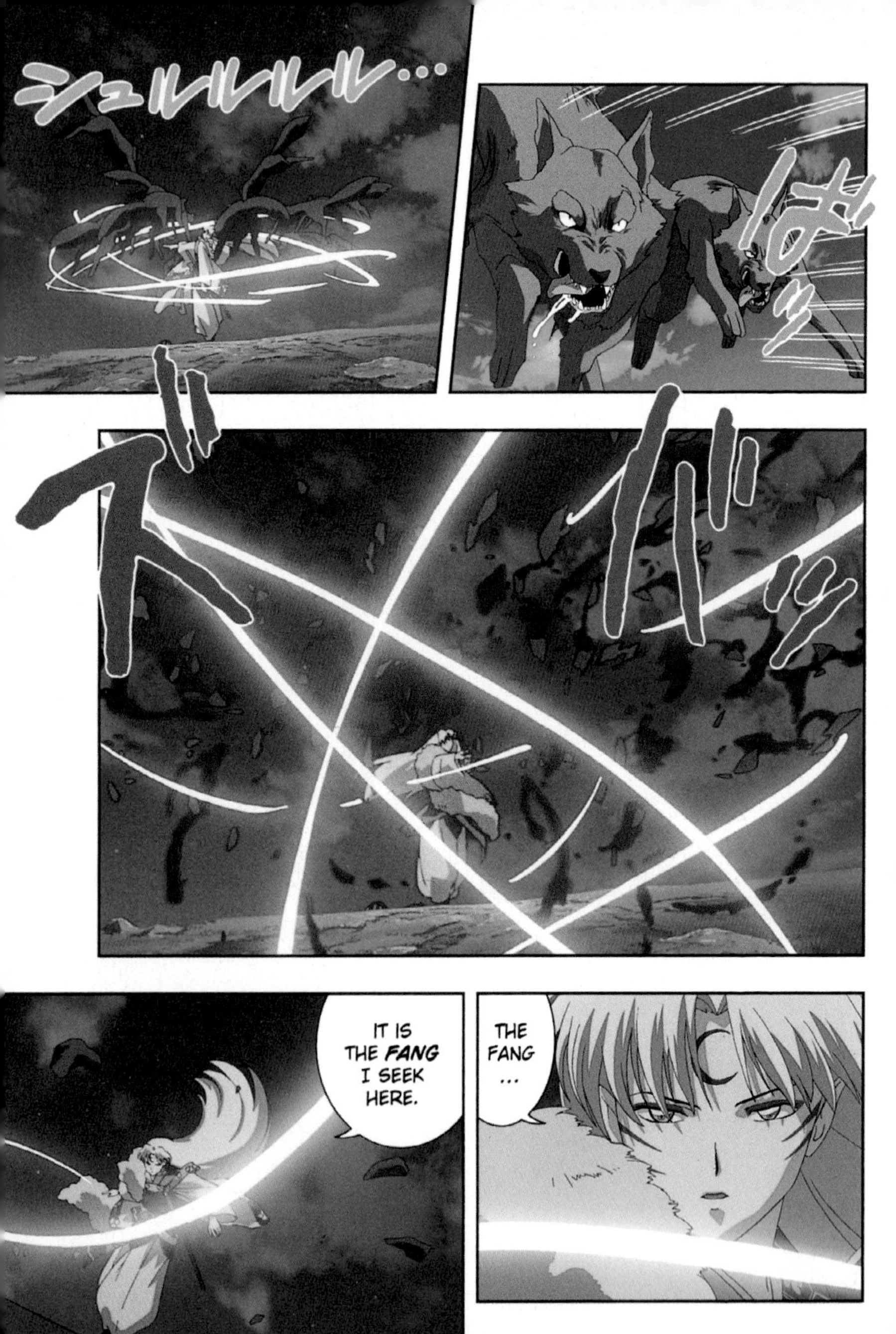
ばッ
シュルルルルル…
ズバッ
THE FANG …
IT IS THE *FANG* I SEEK HERE.

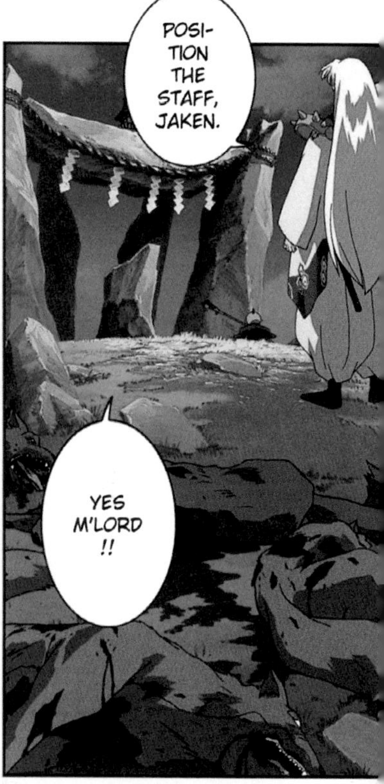
POSI-
TION
THE
STAFF,
JAKEN.
YES
M'LORD
!!

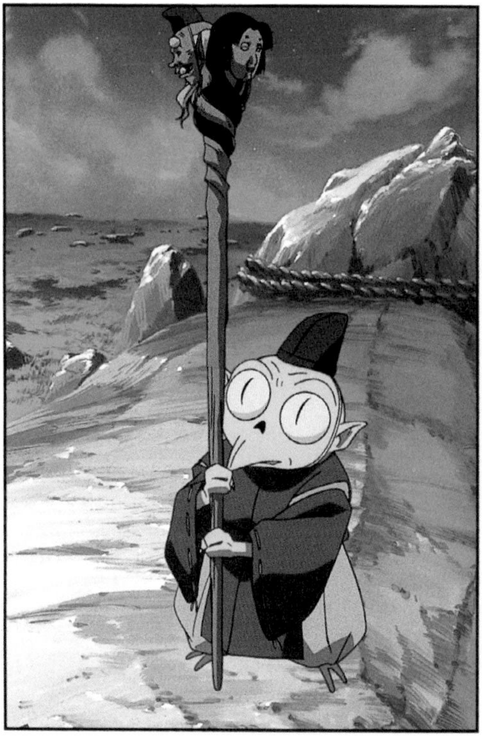

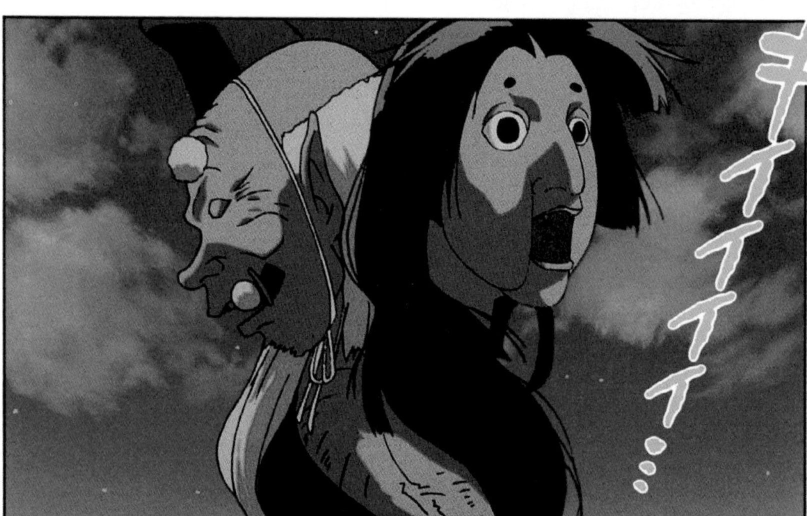
キイイイイ…

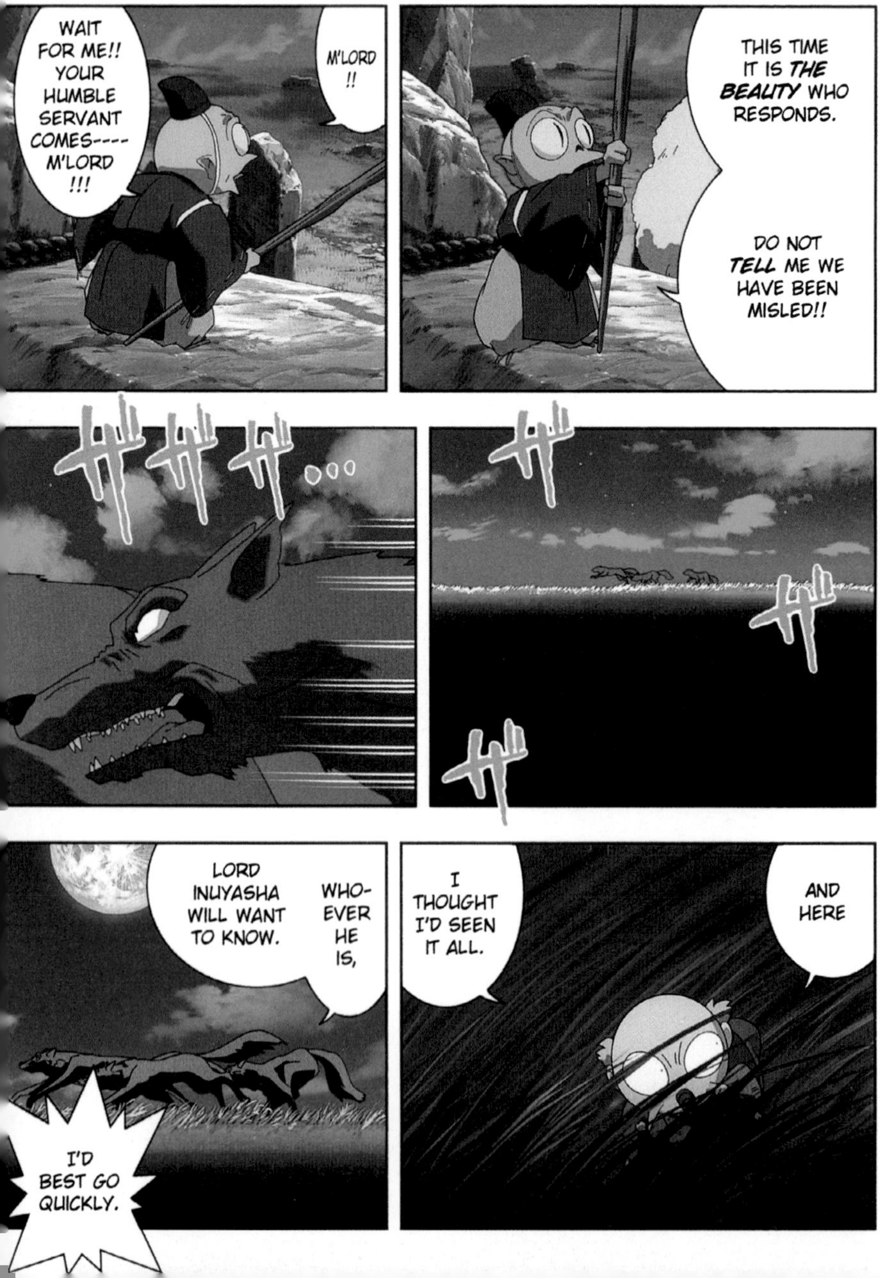
THIS TIME IT IS THE BEAUTY WHO RESPONDS.
DO NOT TELL ME WE HAVE BEEN MISLED!!
M'LORD!!
WAIT FOR ME!! YOUR HUMBLE SERVANT COMES---- M'LORD!!!
AND HERE
I THOUGHT I'D SEEN IT ALL.
WHO-EVER HE IS,
LORD INUYASHA WILL WANT TO KNOW.
I'D BEST GO QUICKLY.

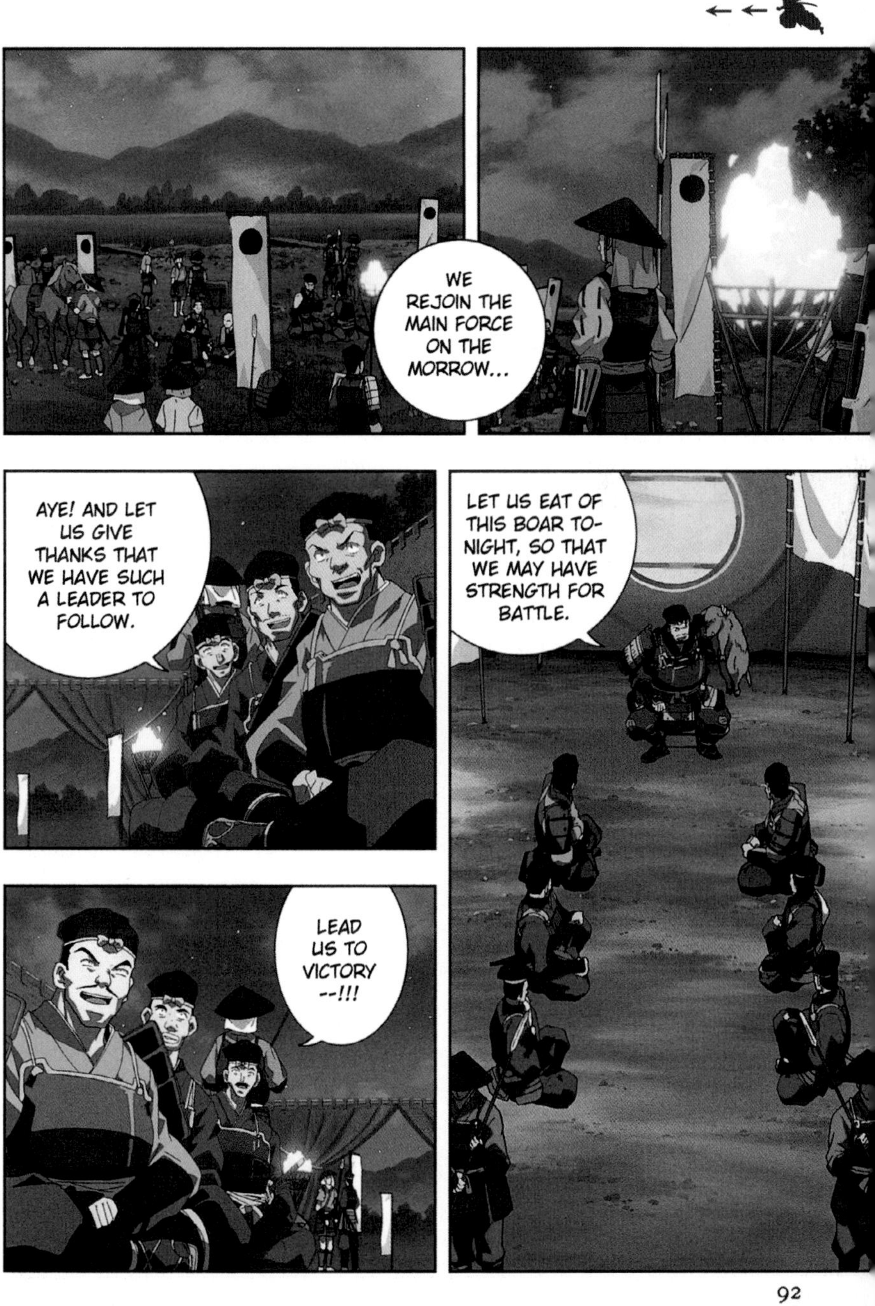
WE REJOIN THE MAIN FORCE ON THE MORROW...
LET US EAT OF THIS BOAR TO-NIGHT, SO THAT WE MAY HAVE STRENGTH FOR BATTLE.
AYE! AND LET US GIVE THANKS THAT WE HAVE SUCH A LEADER TO FOLLOW.
LEAD US TO VICTORY --!!!

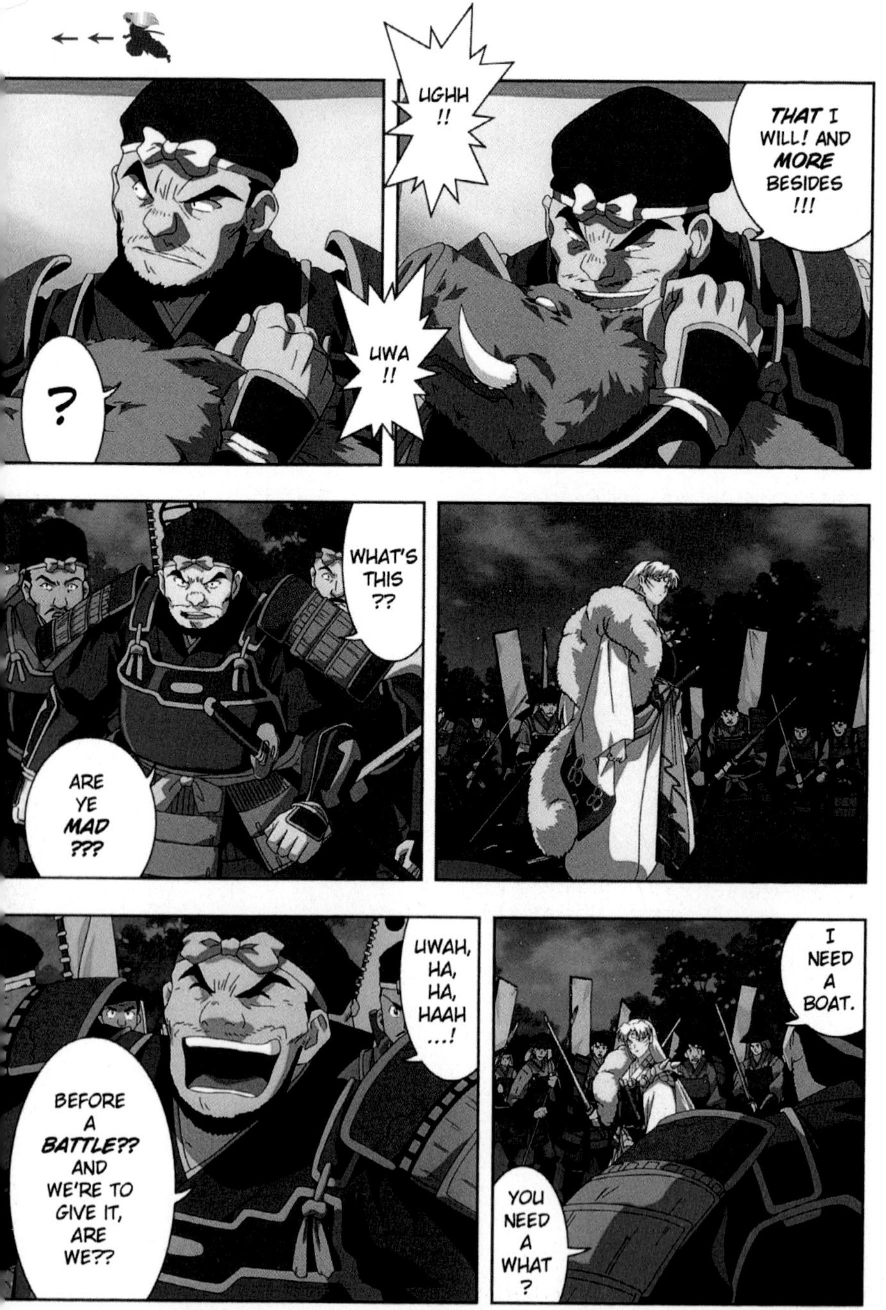
THAT I WILL! AND MORE BESIDES!!!
UGHH!!
UWA!!
?
WHAT'S THIS??
ARE YE MAD???
I NEED A BOAT.
YOU NEED A WHAT?
UWAH, HA, HA, HAAH...!
BEFORE A BATTLE?? AND WE'RE TO GIVE IT, ARE WE??

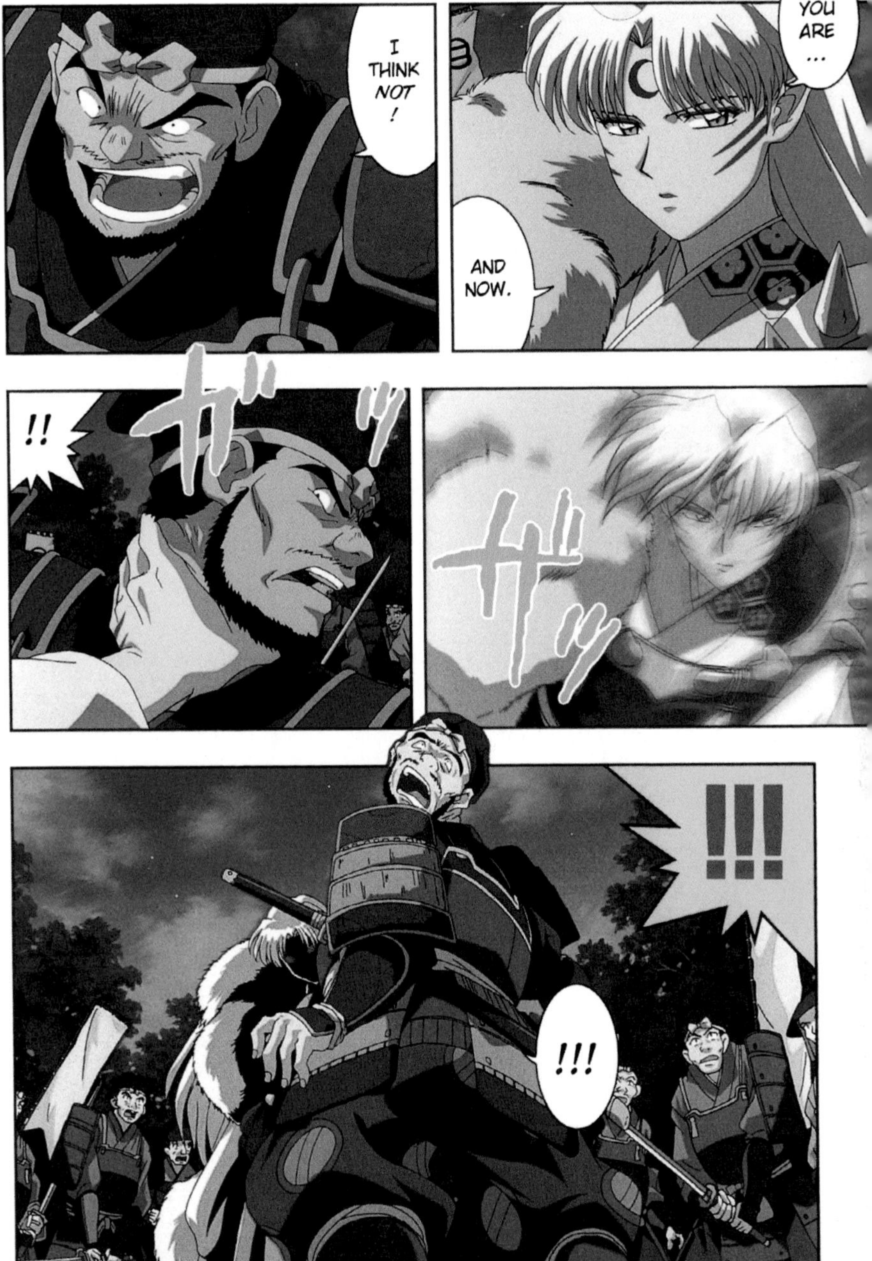

YES, YOU ARE ...
AND NOW.
I THINK NOT!
ザッ
!!
ガッ
!!!
!!!

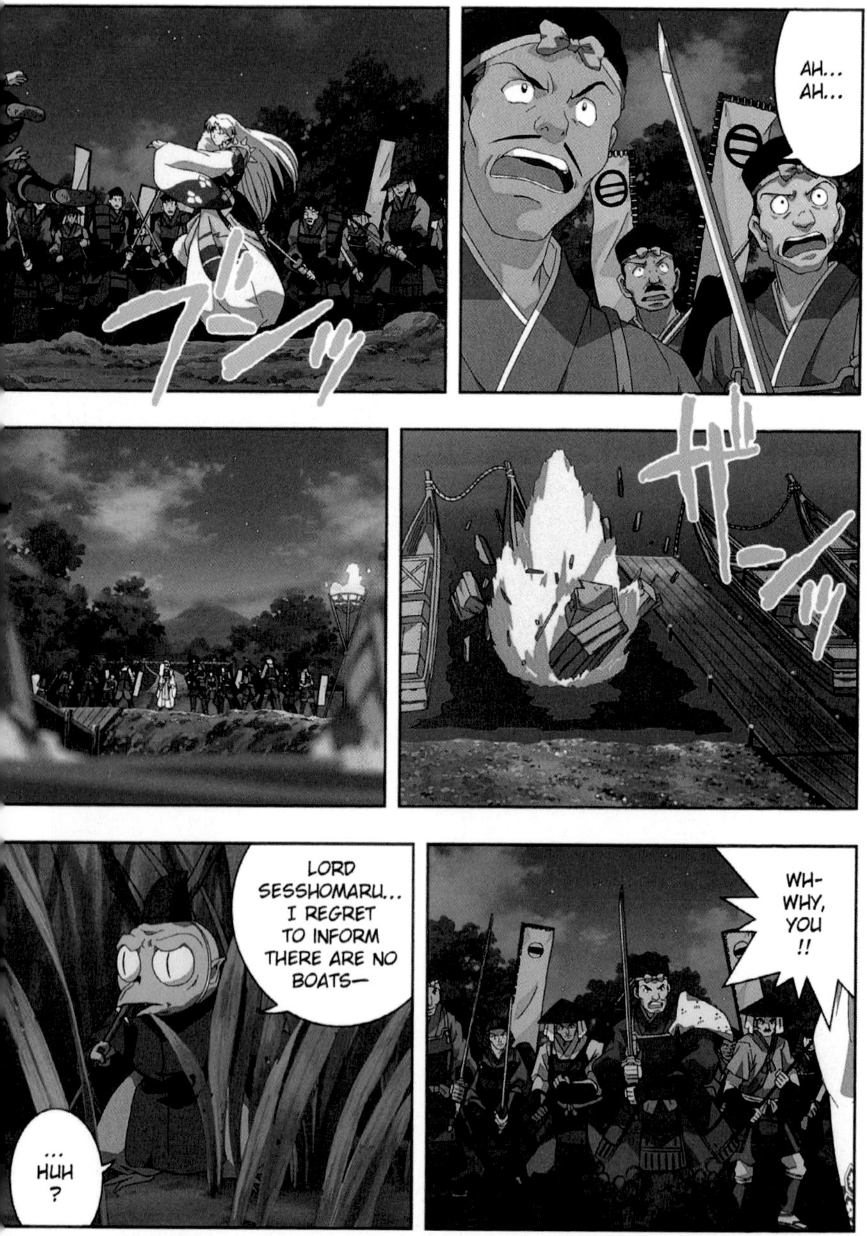
AH... AH...
ブンッ
ザーンッ
WH- WHY, YOU !!
LORD SESSHOMARU... I REGRET TO INFORM THERE ARE NO BOATS—
... HUH ?

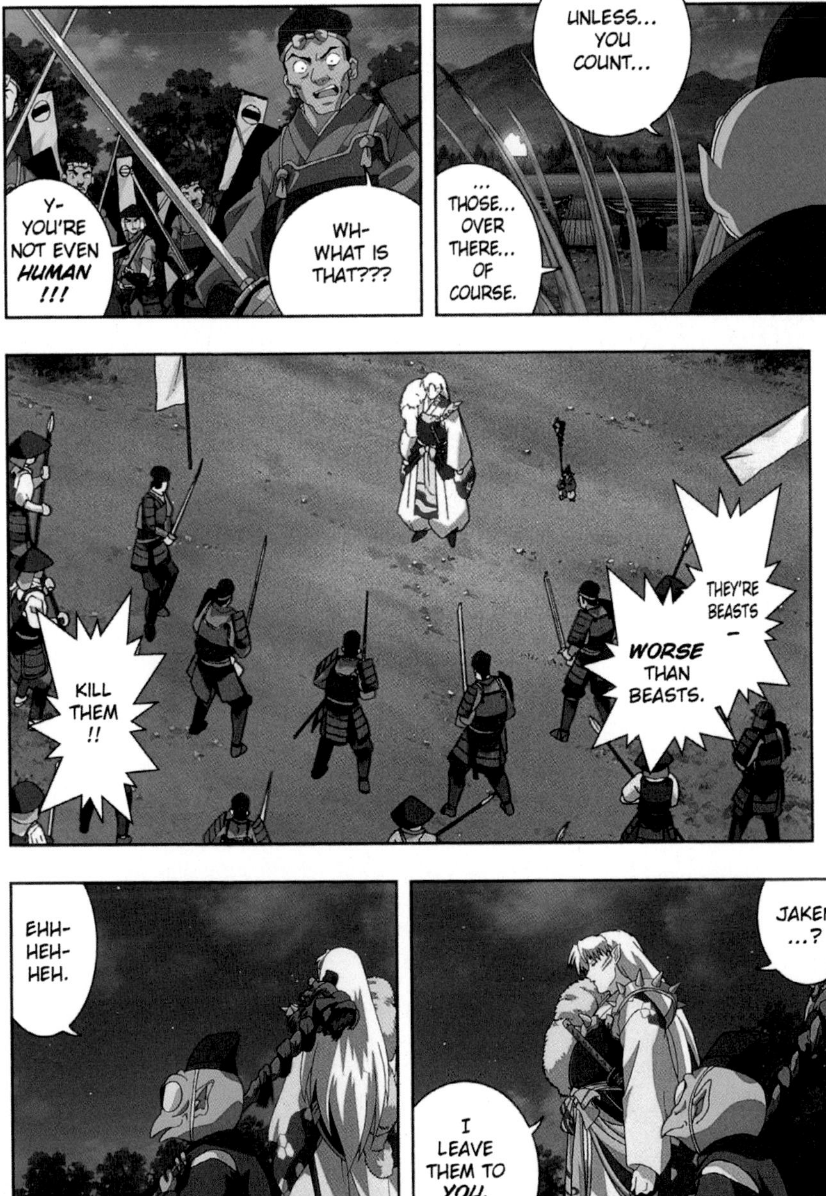
UNLESS... YOU COUNT...
...THOSE... OVER THERE... OF COURSE.
WH- WHAT IS THAT???
Y- YOU'RE NOT EVEN **HUMAN** !!!
THEY'RE BEASTS — **WORSE** THAN BEASTS.
KILL THEM !!
JAKEN ...?
I LEAVE THEM TO **YOU.**
EHH- HEH- HEH.

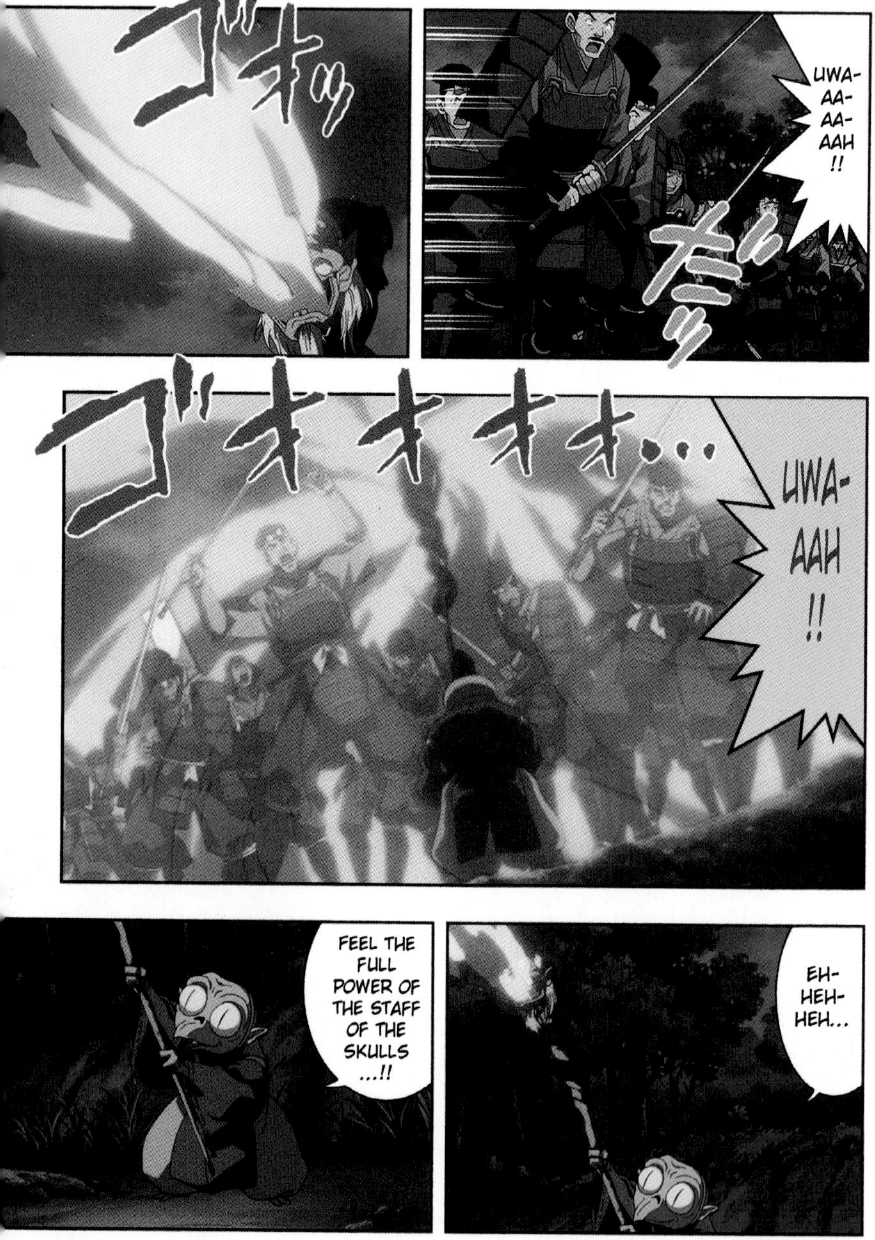
UWA-AA-AA-AAH!!
ダッ
ゴオッ
ゴオオオオ…
UWA-AAH!!
EH-HEH-HEH...
FEEL THE FULL POWER OF THE STAFF OF THE SKULLS ...!!

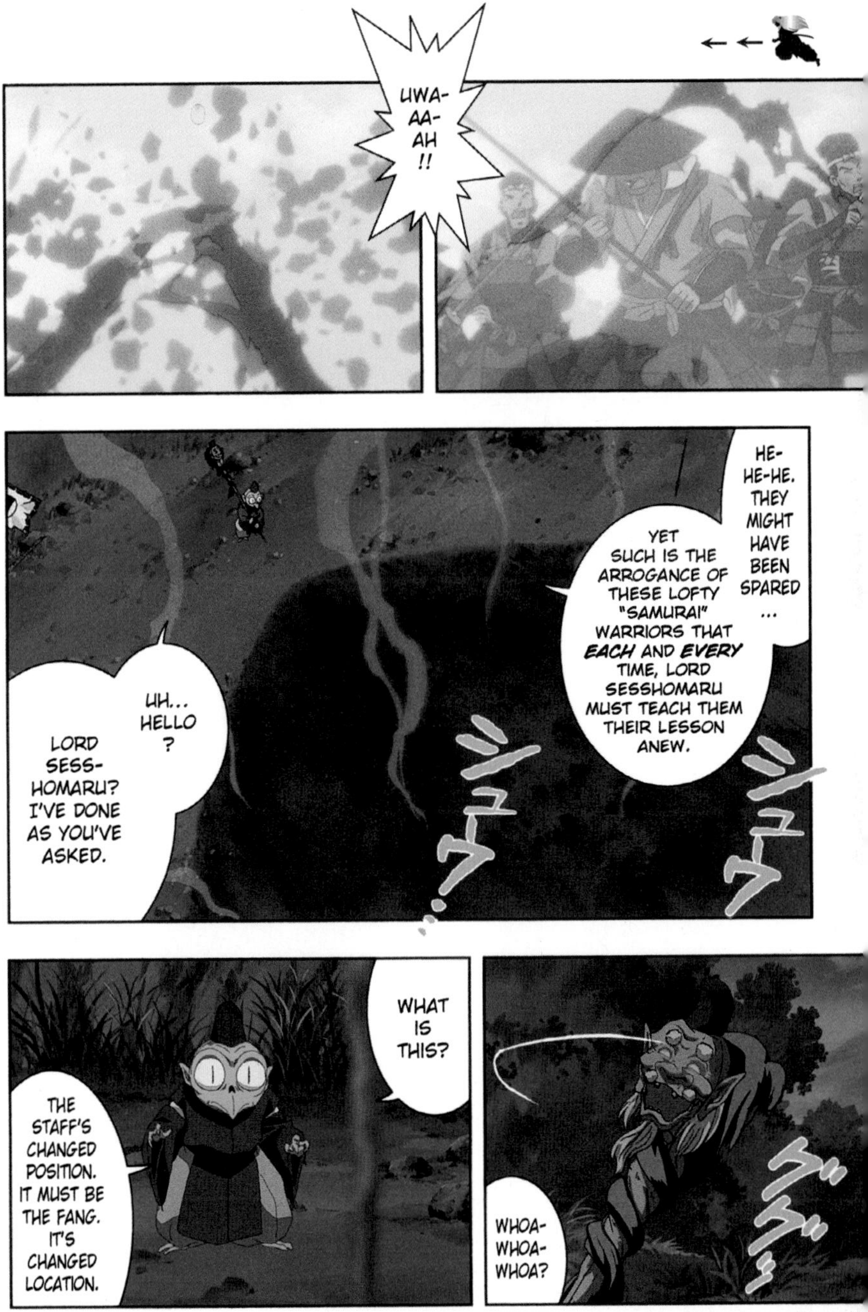
UWA-AA-AH!!
HE-HE-HE. THEY MIGHT HAVE BEEN SPARED...
YET SUCH IS THE ARROGANCE OF THESE LOFTY "SAMURAI" WARRIORS THAT ***EACH*** AND ***EVERY*** TIME, LORD SESSHOMARU MUST TEACH THEM THEIR LESSON ANEW.
UH... HELLO?
LORD SESS-HOMARU? I'VE DONE AS YOU'VE ASKED.
WHOA-WHOA-WHOA?
WHAT IS THIS?
THE STAFF'S CHANGED POSITION. IT MUST BE THE FANG. IT'S CHANGED LOCATION.

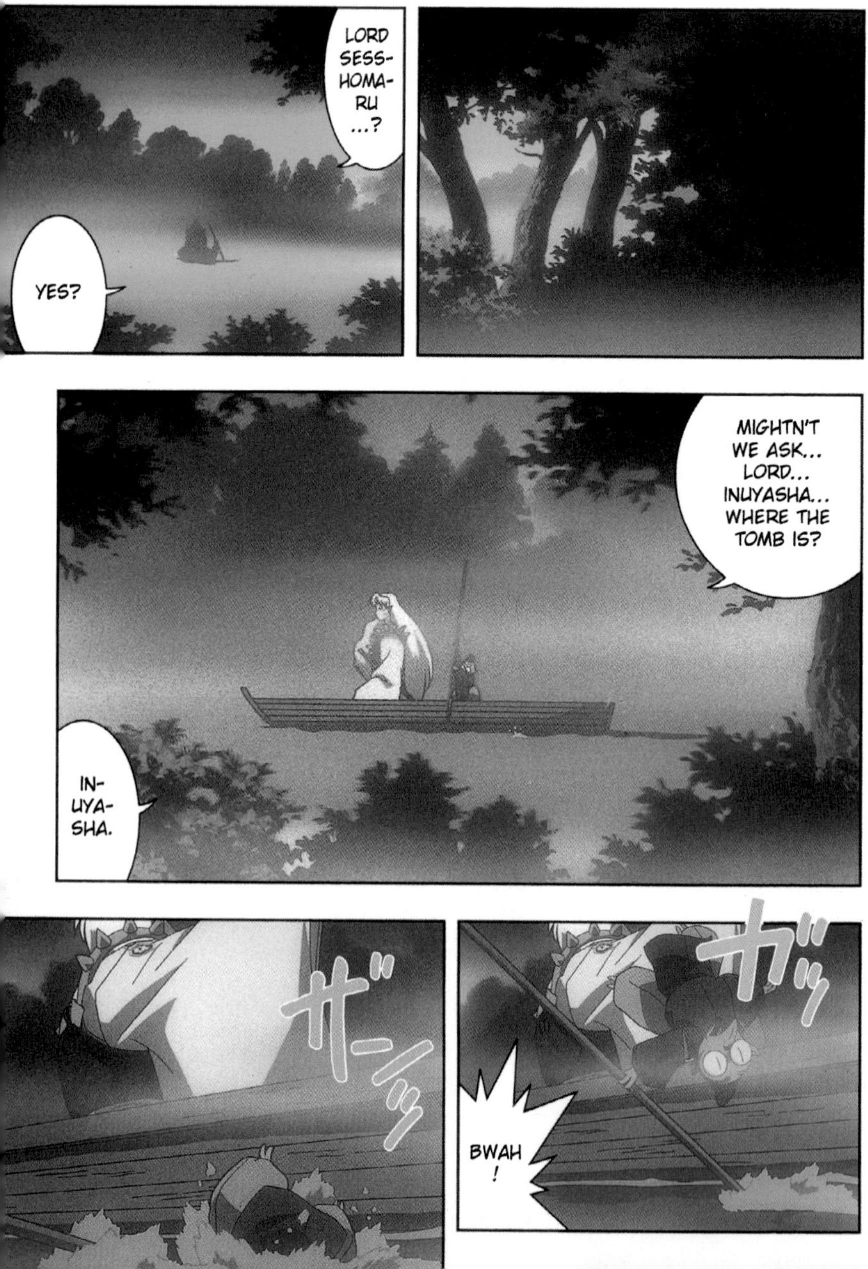
LORD SESS-HOMA-RU ...?
YES?
MIGHTN'T WE ASK... LORD... INUYASHA... WHERE THE TOMB IS?
IN-UYA-SHA.
ガッ
BWAH!
ザーンッ

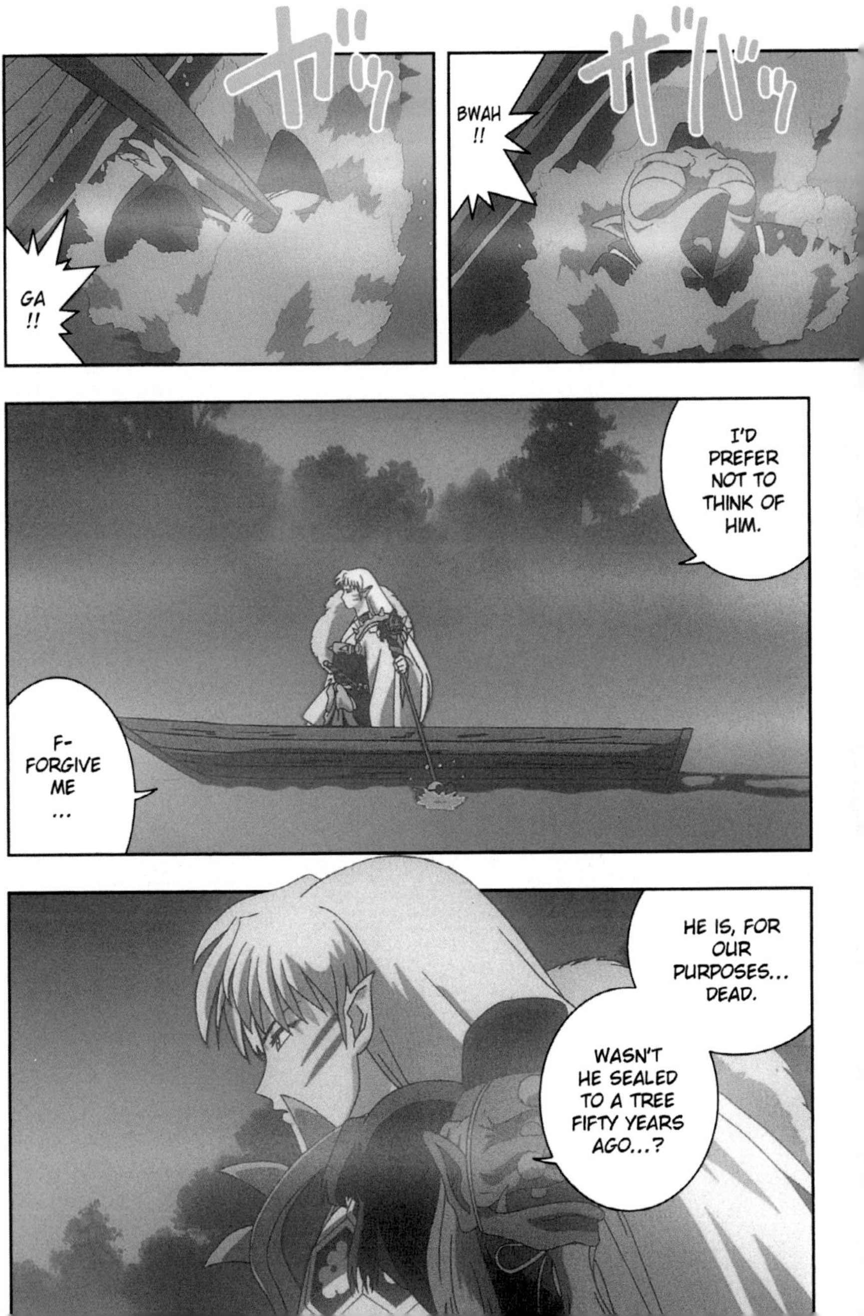
ザバッ
BWAH !!
ガッ
GA !!
I'D PREFER NOT TO THINK OF HIM.
F-FORGIVE ME ...
HE IS, FOR OUR PURPOSES... DEAD.
WASN'T HE SEALED TO A TREE FIFTY YEARS AGO...?

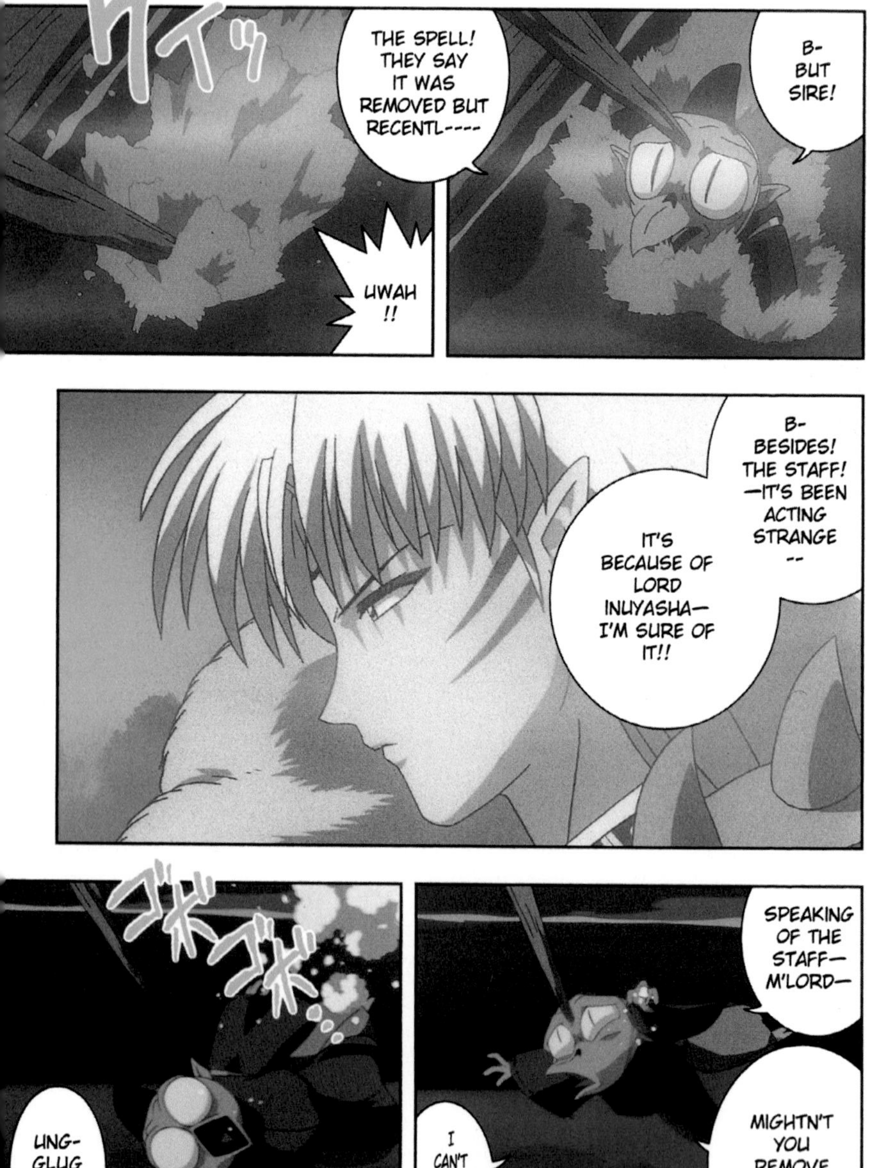
B- BUT SIRE!
グイッ
THE SPELL! THEY SAY IT WAS REMOVED BUT RECENTL----
UWAH !!
B- BESIDES! THE STAFF! —IT'S BEEN ACTING STRANGE --
IT'S BECAUSE OF LORD INUYASHA— I'M SURE OF IT!!
SPEAKING OF THE STAFF— M'LORD—
MIGHTN'T YOU REMOVE IT??
I CAN'T BREATHE ---
ゴボゴボ...
UNG-GLUG ...

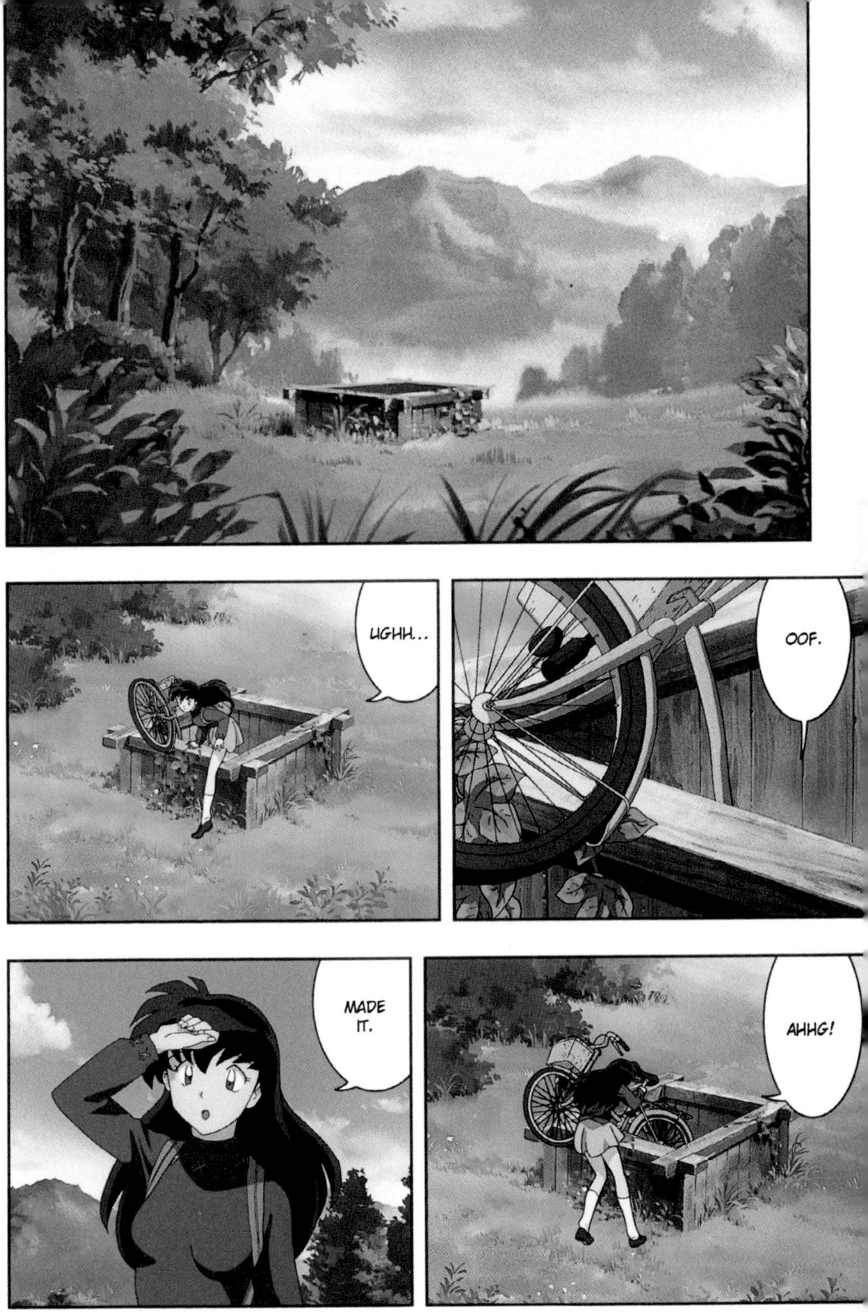
OOF.
UGHH...
AHHG!
MADE IT.

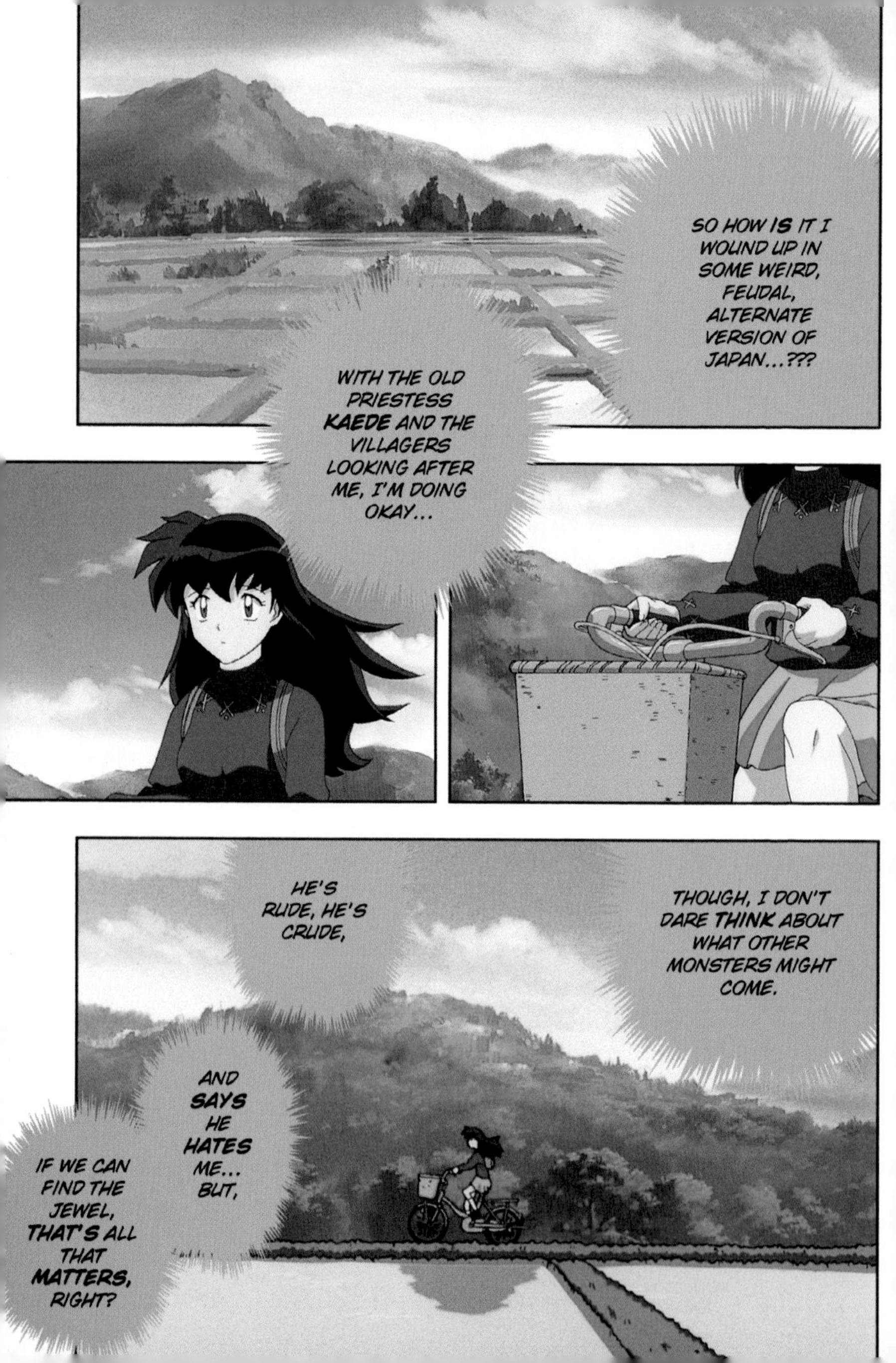
SO HOW IS IT I WOUND UP IN SOME WEIRD, FEUDAL, ALTERNATE VERSION OF JAPAN...???
WITH THE OLD PRIESTESS KAEDE AND THE VILLAGERS LOOKING AFTER ME, I'M DOING OKAY...
THOUGH, I DON'T DARE THINK ABOUT WHAT OTHER MONSTERS MIGHT COME.
HE'S RUDE, HE'S CRUDE,
AND SAYS HE HATES ME... BUT,
IF WE CAN FIND THE JEWEL, THAT'S ALL THAT MATTERS, RIGHT?

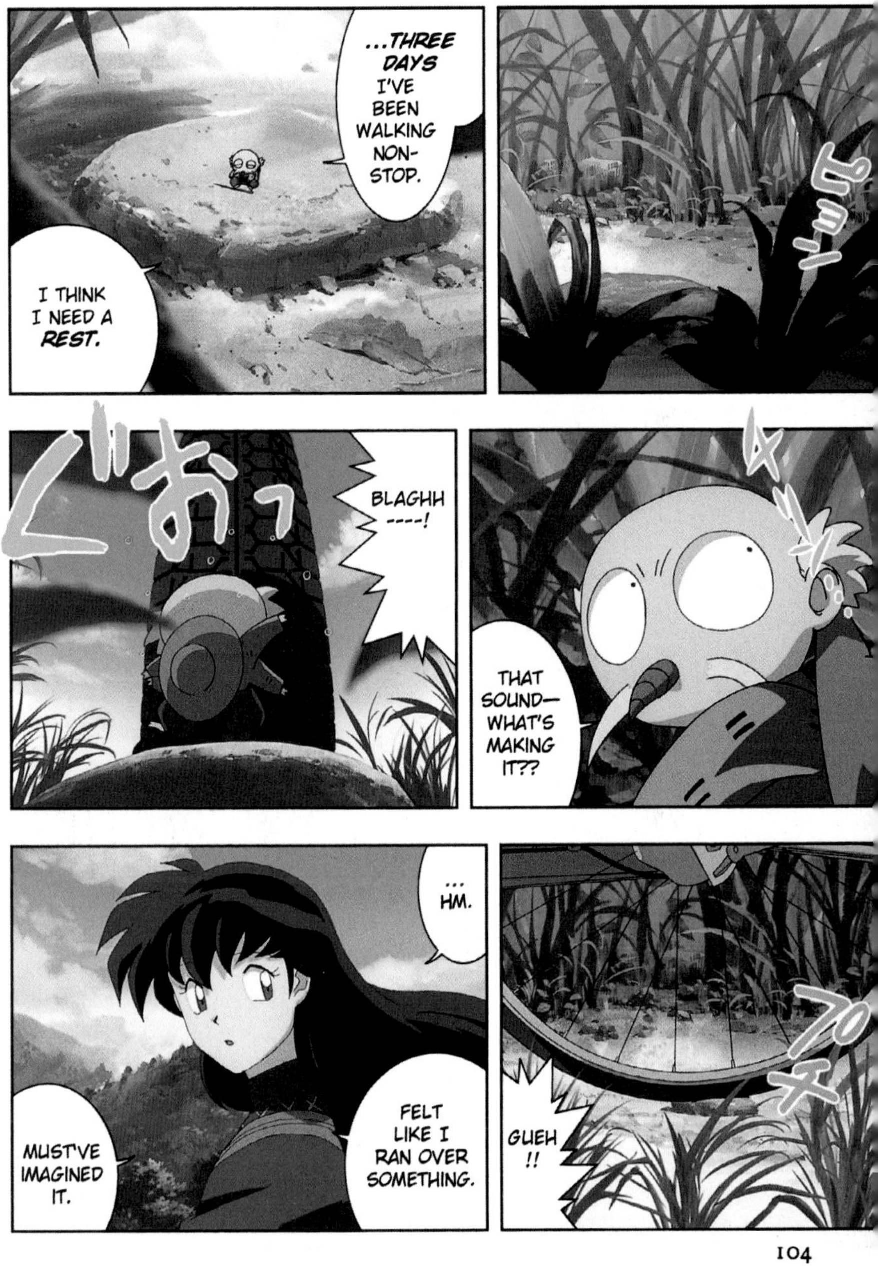
ピョン
...THREE DAYS I'VE BEEN WALKING NON-STOP.
I THINK I NEED A REST.
THAT SOUND— WHAT'S MAKING IT??
ぐおっ
BLAGHH ----!
プチ
GUEH !!
... HM.
FELT LIKE I RAN OVER SOMETHING.
MUST'VE IMAGINED IT.

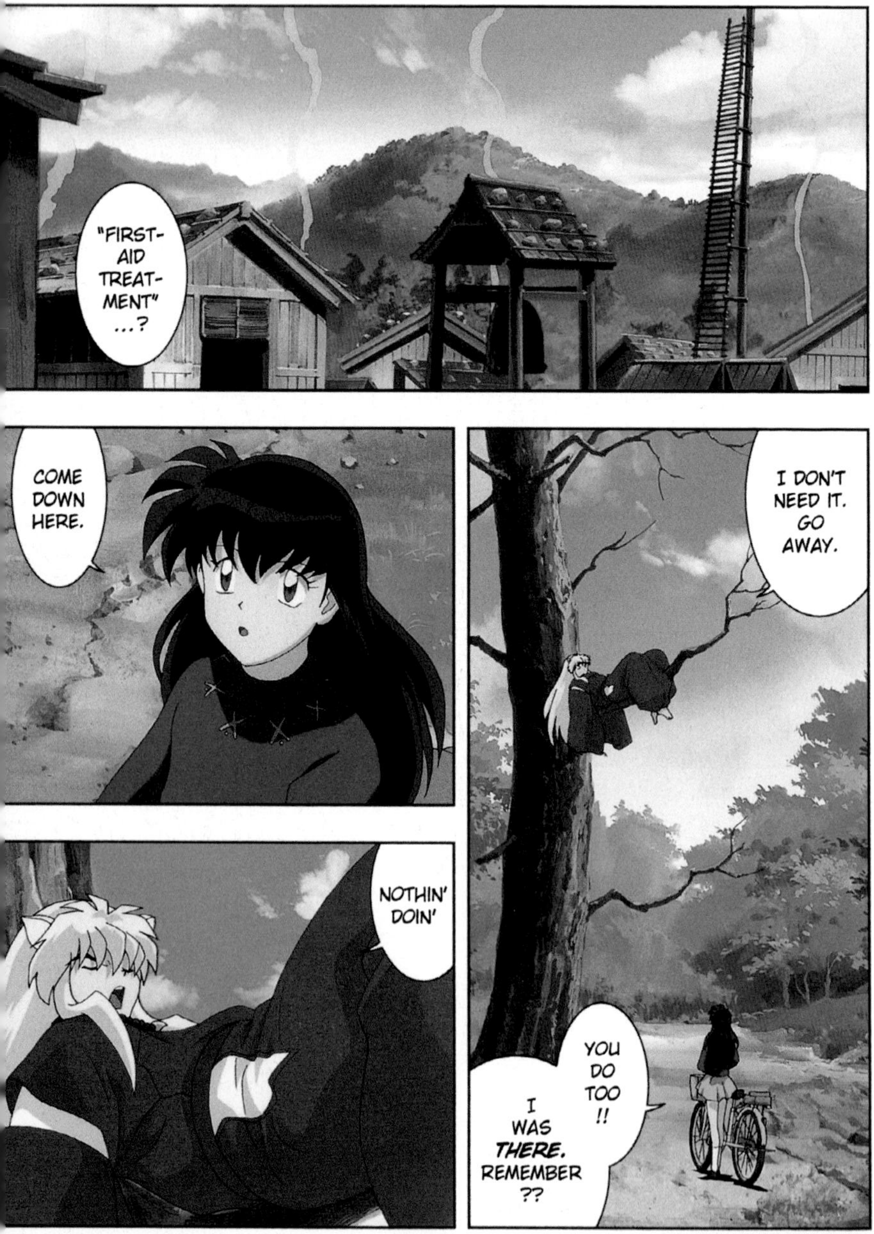
"FIRST-AID TREATMENT"...?
I DON'T NEED IT. GO AWAY.
YOU DO TOO!!
I WAS *THERE.* REMEMBER??
COME DOWN HERE.
NOTHIN' DOIN'

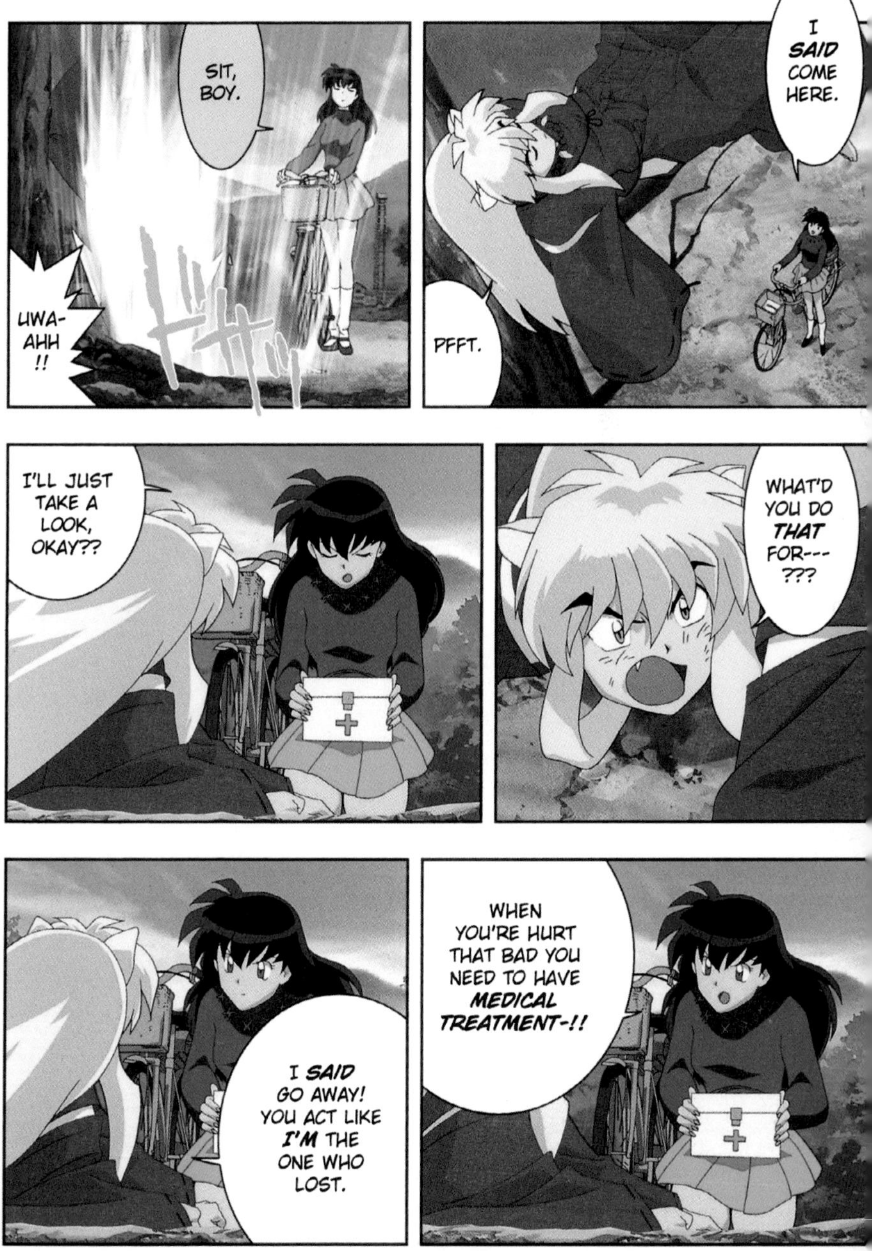
I SAID COME HERE.
PFFT.
SIT, BOY.
UWA-AHH !!
WHAT'D YOU DO THAT FOR--- ???
I'LL JUST TAKE A LOOK, OKAY??
WHEN YOU'RE HURT THAT BAD YOU NEED TO HAVE MEDICAL TREATMENT-!!
I SAID GO AWAY! YOU ACT LIKE I'M THE ONE WHO LOST.

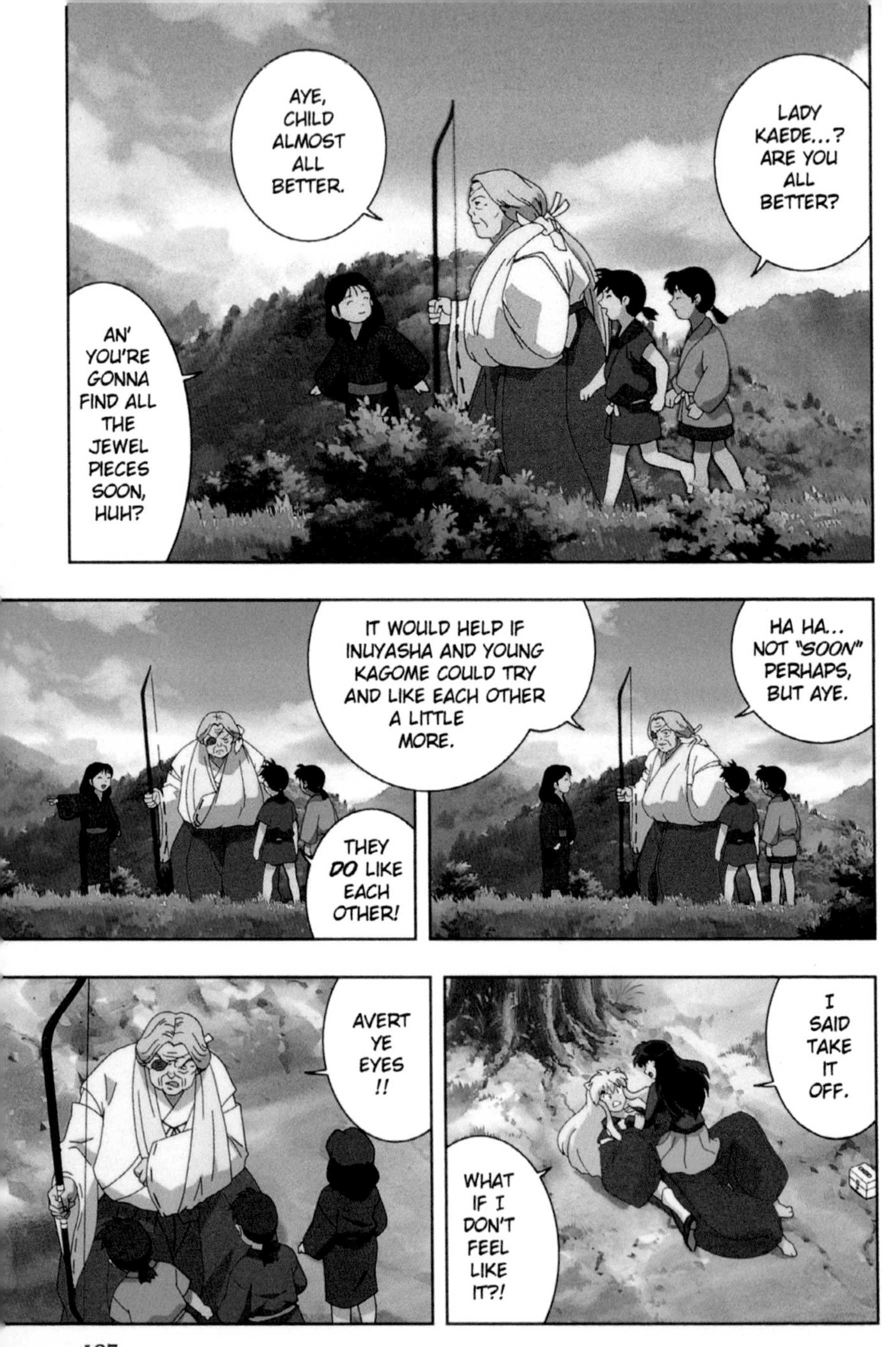
LADY KAEDE...? ARE YOU ALL BETTER?
AYE, CHILD ALMOST ALL BETTER.
AN' YOU'RE GONNA FIND ALL THE JEWEL PIECES SOON, HUH?
HA HA... NOT "*SOON*" PERHAPS, BUT AYE.
IT WOULD HELP IF INUYASHA AND YOUNG KAGOME COULD TRY AND LIKE EACH OTHER A LITTLE MORE.
THEY ***DO*** LIKE EACH OTHER!
I SAID TAKE IT OFF.
WHAT IF I DON'T FEEL LIKE IT?!
AVERT YE EYES!!

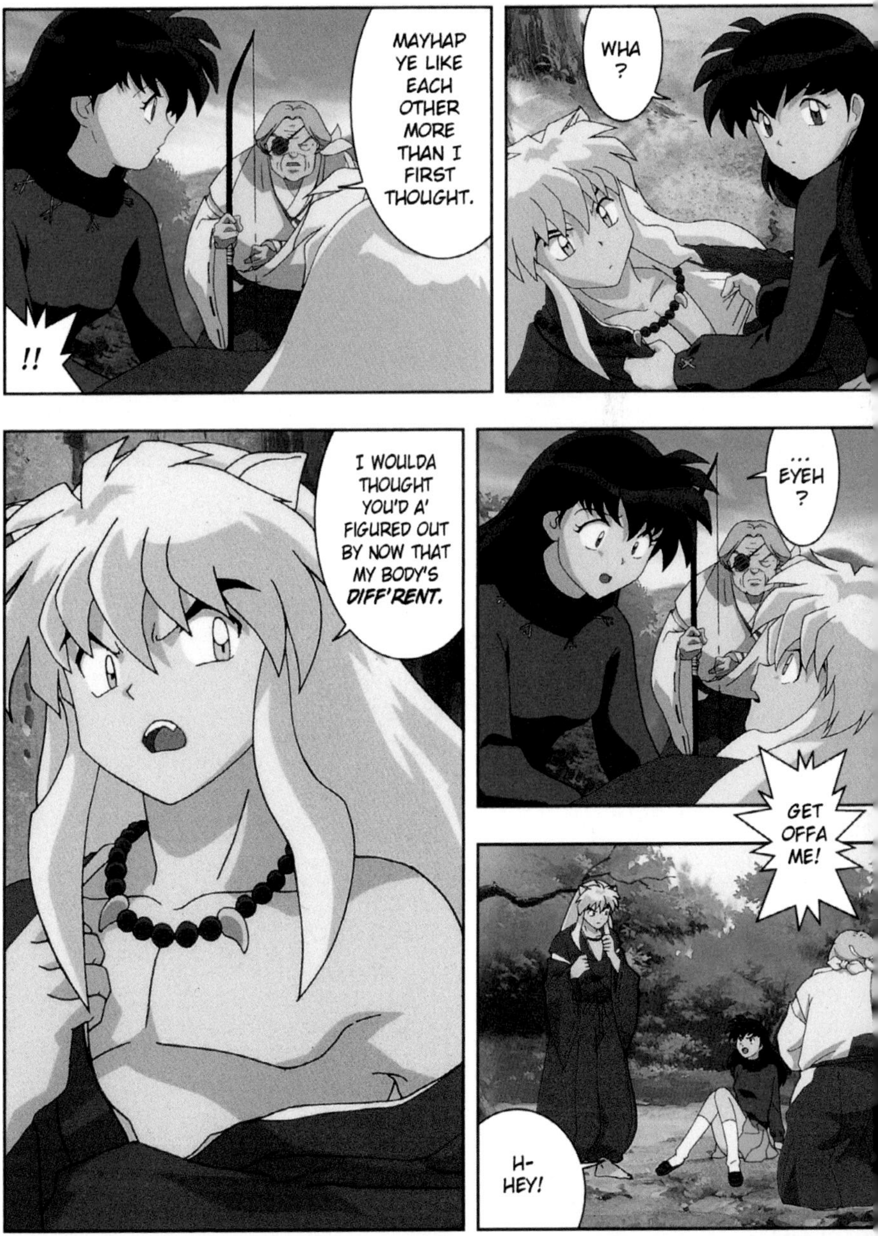
WHA ?
MAYHAP YE LIKE EACH OTHER MORE THAN I FIRST THOUGHT.
!!
... EYEH ?
GET OFFA ME!
H- HEY!
I WOULDA THOUGHT YOU'D A' FIGURED OUT BY NOW THAT MY BODY'S DIFF'RENT.

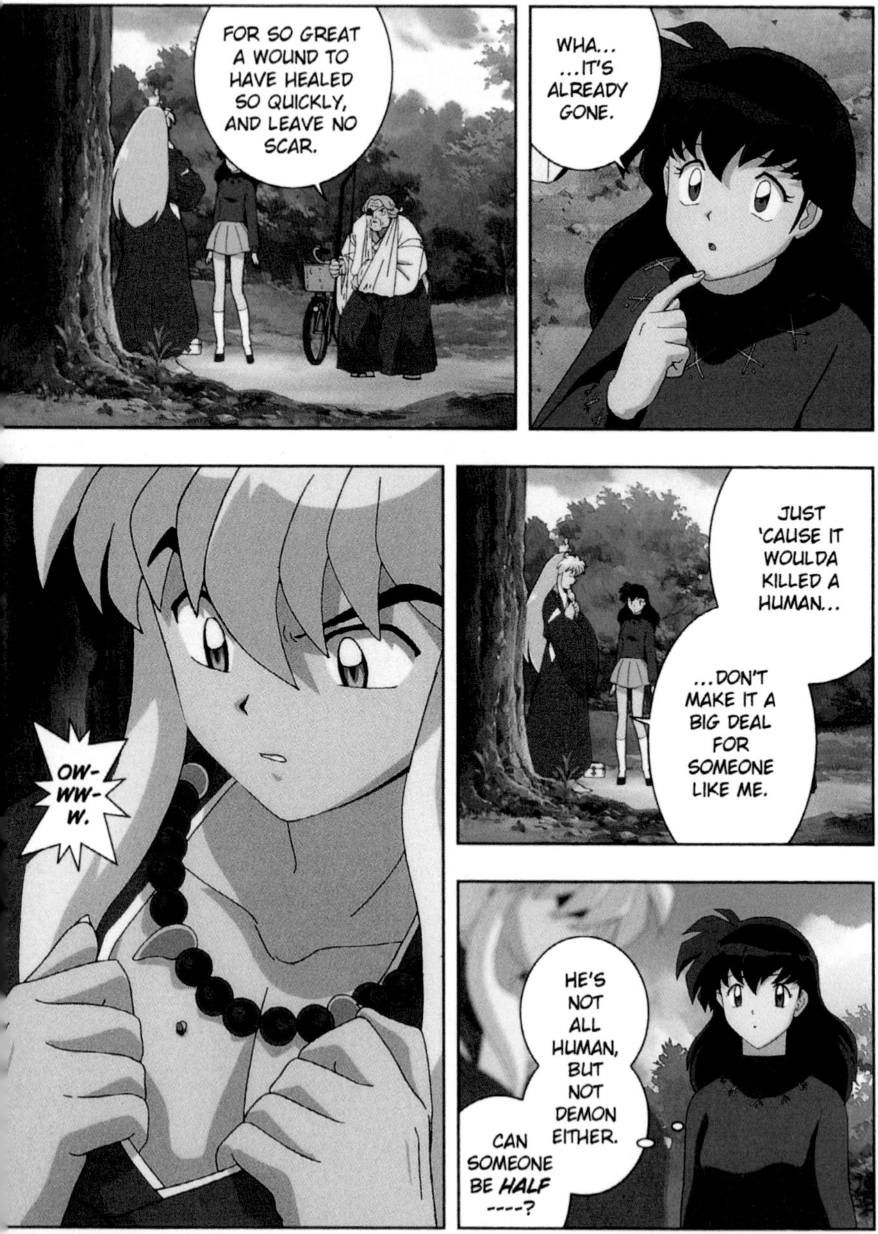
WHA...
...IT'S ALREADY GONE.
FOR SO GREAT A WOUND TO HAVE HEALED SO QUICKLY, AND LEAVE NO SCAR.
JUST 'CAUSE IT WOULDA KILLED A HUMAN...
...DON'T MAKE IT A BIG DEAL FOR SOMEONE LIKE ME.
HE'S NOT ALL HUMAN, BUT NOT DEMON EITHER.
CAN SOMEONE BE *HALF* ----?
OW-WWW-W.

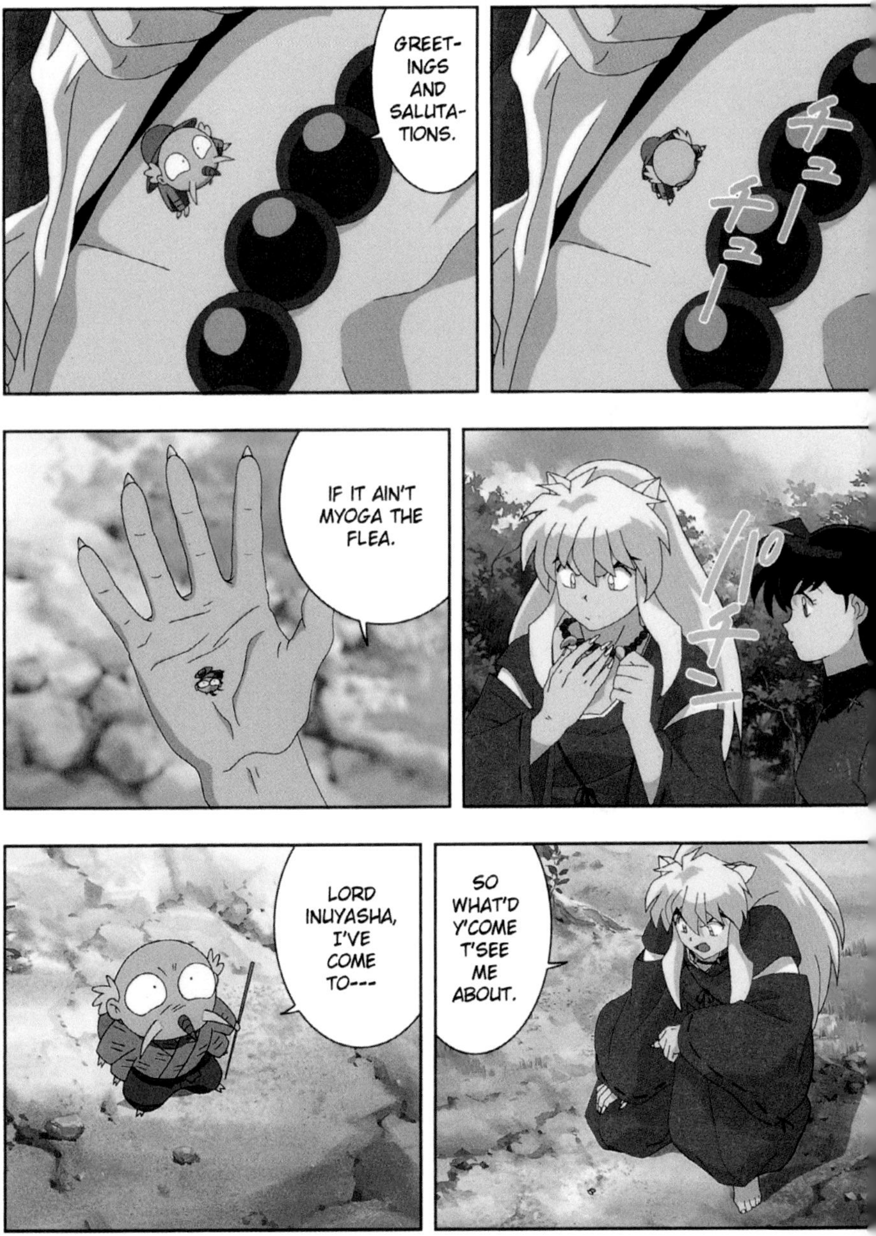

チューチュー
GREET-INGS AND SALUTA-TIONS.
パチン
IF IT AIN'T MYOGA THE FLEA.
SO WHAT'D Y'COME T'SEE ME ABOUT.
LORD INUYASHA, I'VE COME TO---

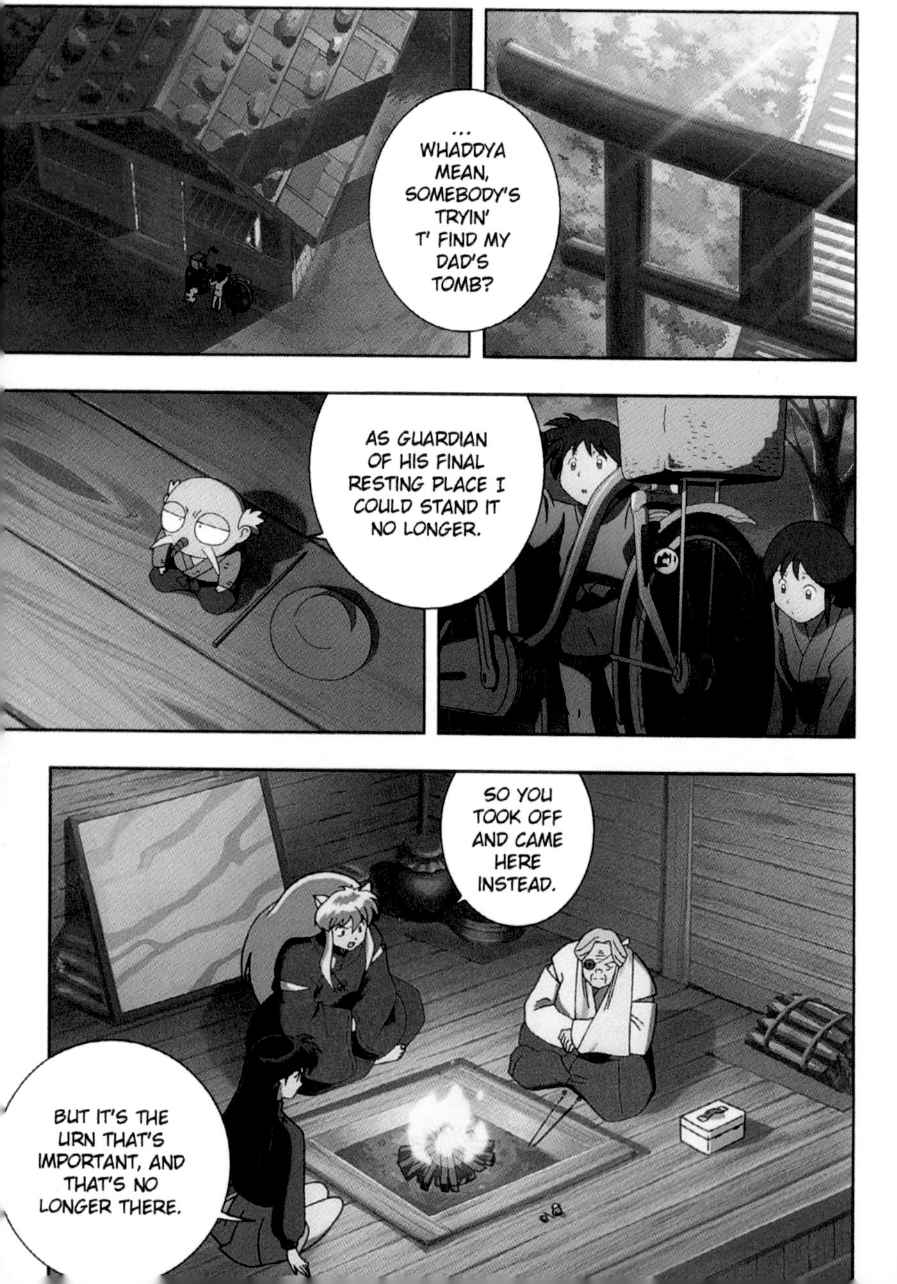
... WHADDYA MEAN, SOMEBODY'S TRYIN' T' FIND MY DAD'S TOMB?
AS GUARDIAN OF HIS FINAL RESTING PLACE I COULD STAND IT NO LONGER.
SO YOU TOOK OFF AND CAME HERE INSTEAD.
BUT IT'S THE URN THAT'S IMPORTANT, AND THAT'S NO LONGER THERE.

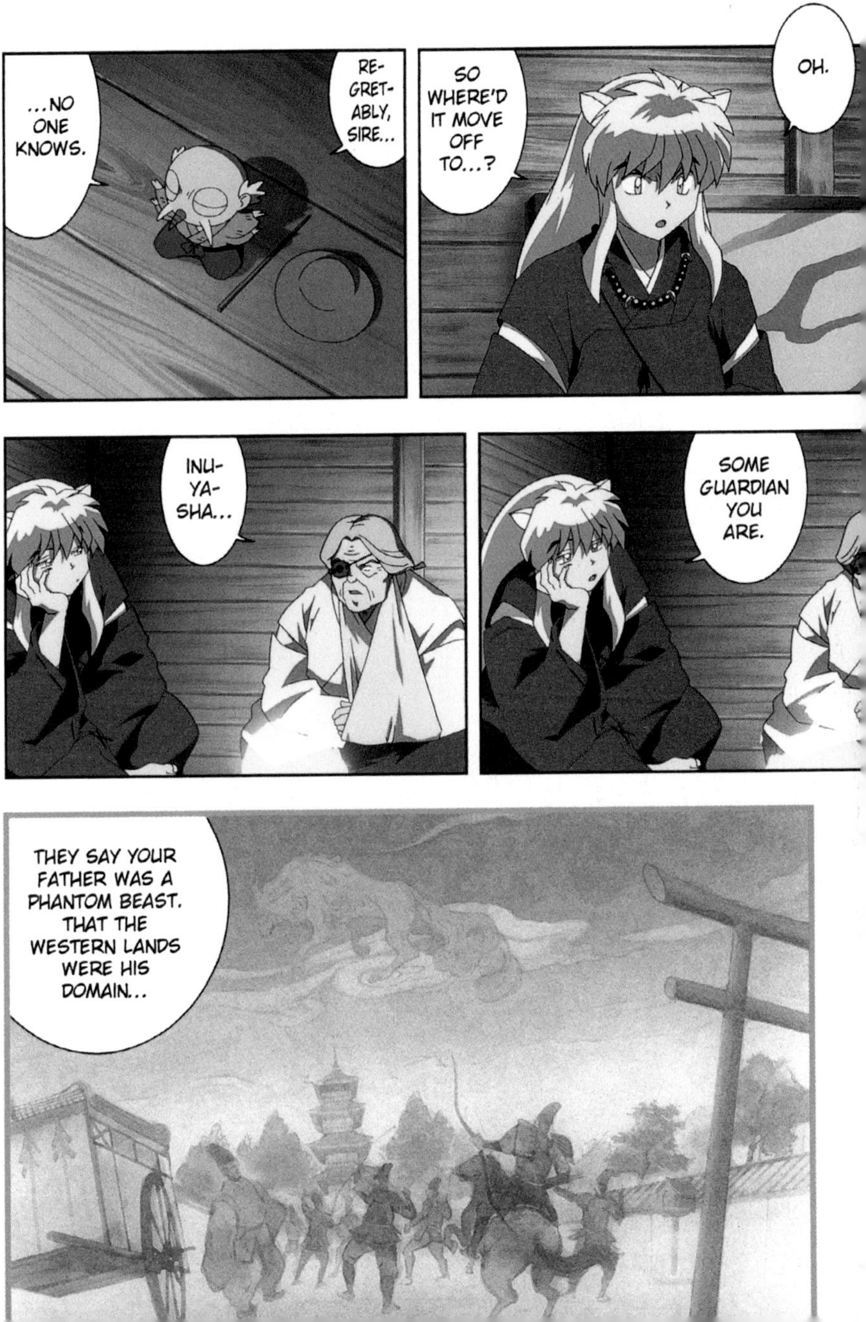
OH.
SO WHERE'D IT MOVE OFF TO...?
RE-GRET-ABLY, SIRE...
...NO ONE KNOWS.
SOME GUARDIAN YOU ARE.
INU-YASHA...
THEY SAY YOUR FATHER WAS A PHANTOM BEAST. THAT THE WESTERN LANDS WERE HIS DOMAIN...

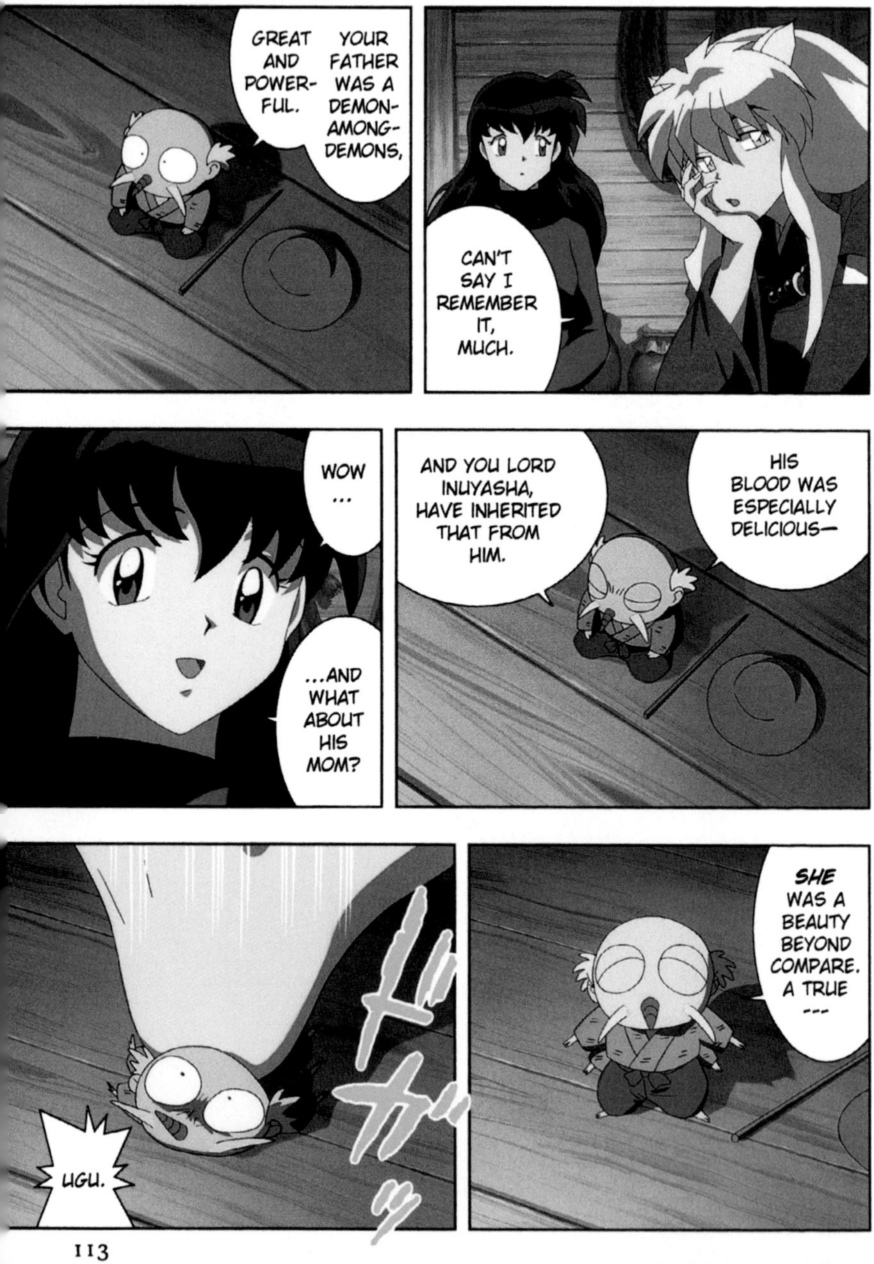
CAN'T SAY I REMEMBER IT, MUCH.
YOUR FATHER WAS A DEMON-AMONG-DEMONS,
GREAT AND POWER-FUL.
HIS BLOOD WAS ESPECIALLY DELICIOUS—
AND YOU LORD INUYASHA, HAVE INHERITED THAT FROM HIM.
WOW ...
...AND WHAT ABOUT HIS MOM?
SHE WAS A BEAUTY BEYOND COMPARE. A TRUE ---
UGU.

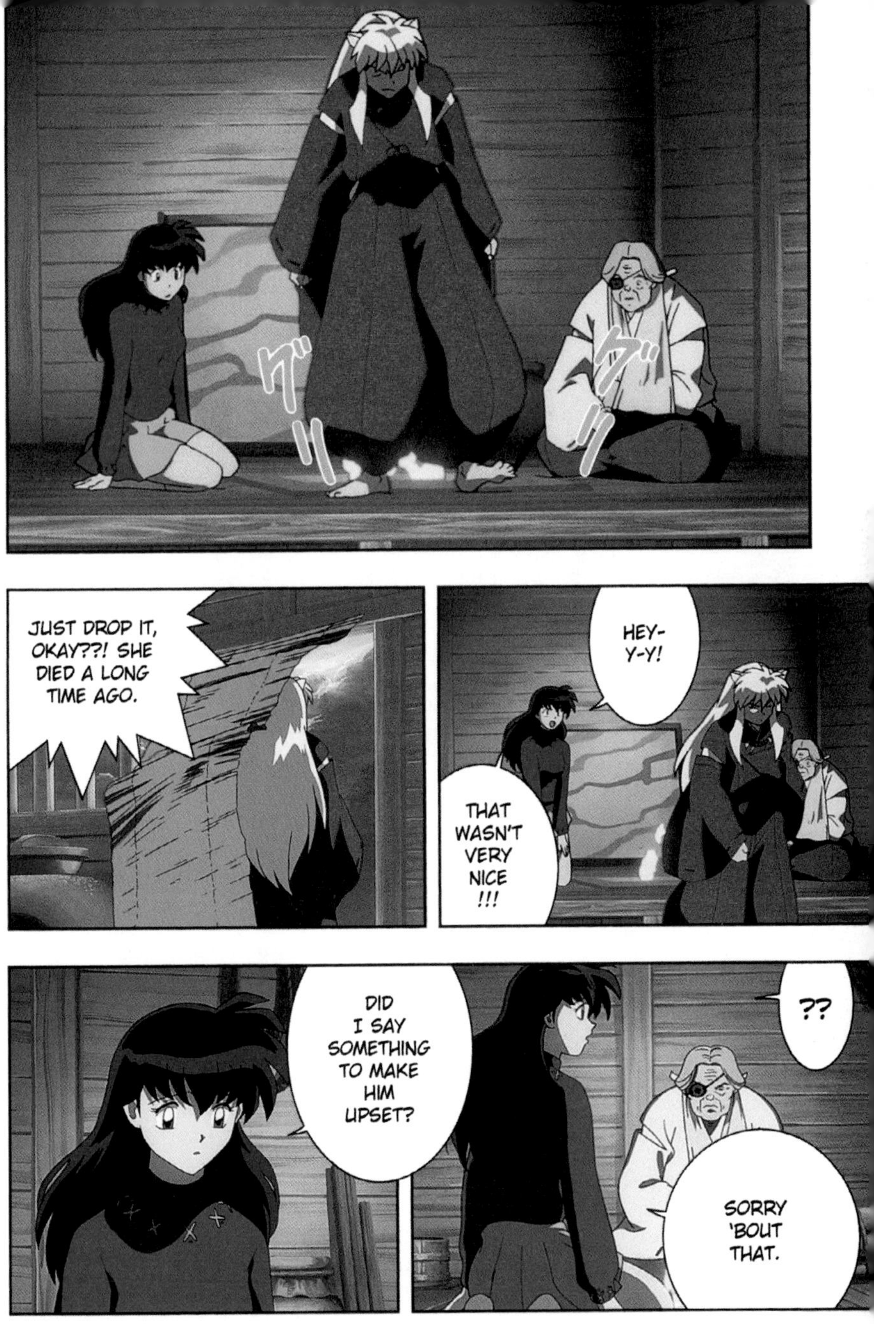
HEY-Y-Y!
THAT WASN'T VERY NICE!!!
JUST DROP IT, OKAY??! SHE DIED A LONG TIME AGO.
??
SORRY 'BOUT THAT.
DID I SAY SOMETHING TO MAKE HIM UPSET?

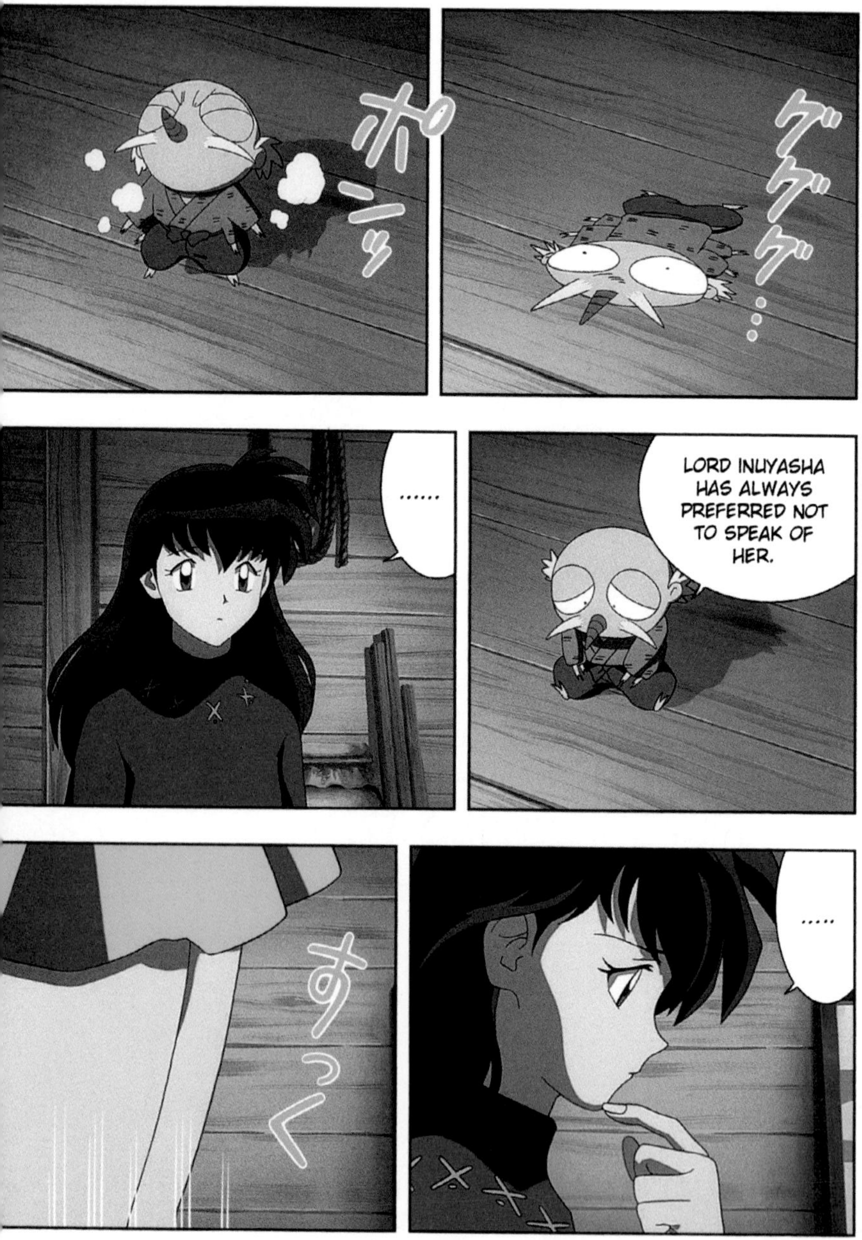
グググ…
ポンッ
LORD INUYASHA HAS ALWAYS PREFERRED NOT TO SPEAK OF HER.
……
……
すっく

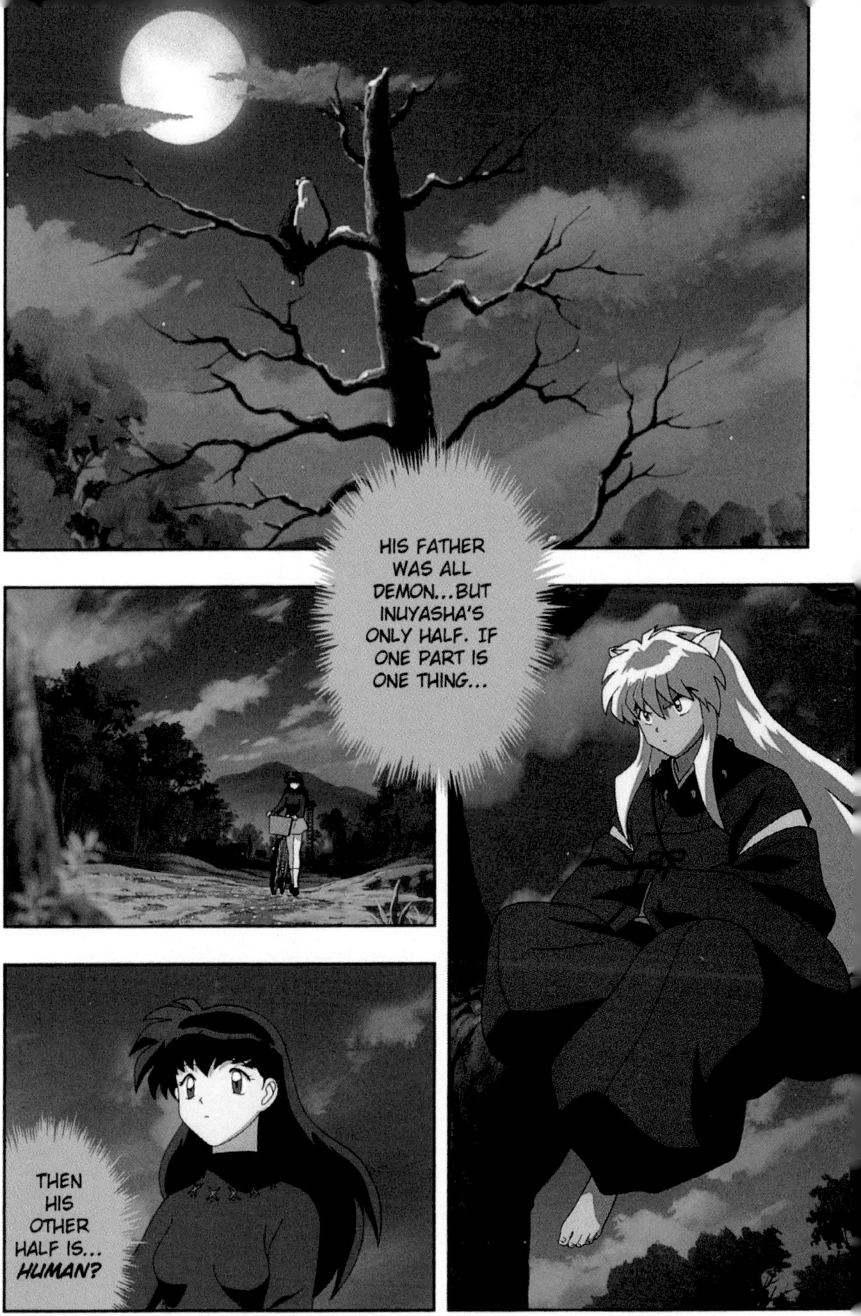
HIS FATHER WAS ALL DEMON...BUT INUYASHA'S ONLY HALF. IF ONE PART IS ONE THING...
THEN HIS OTHER HALF IS... ***HUMAN?***

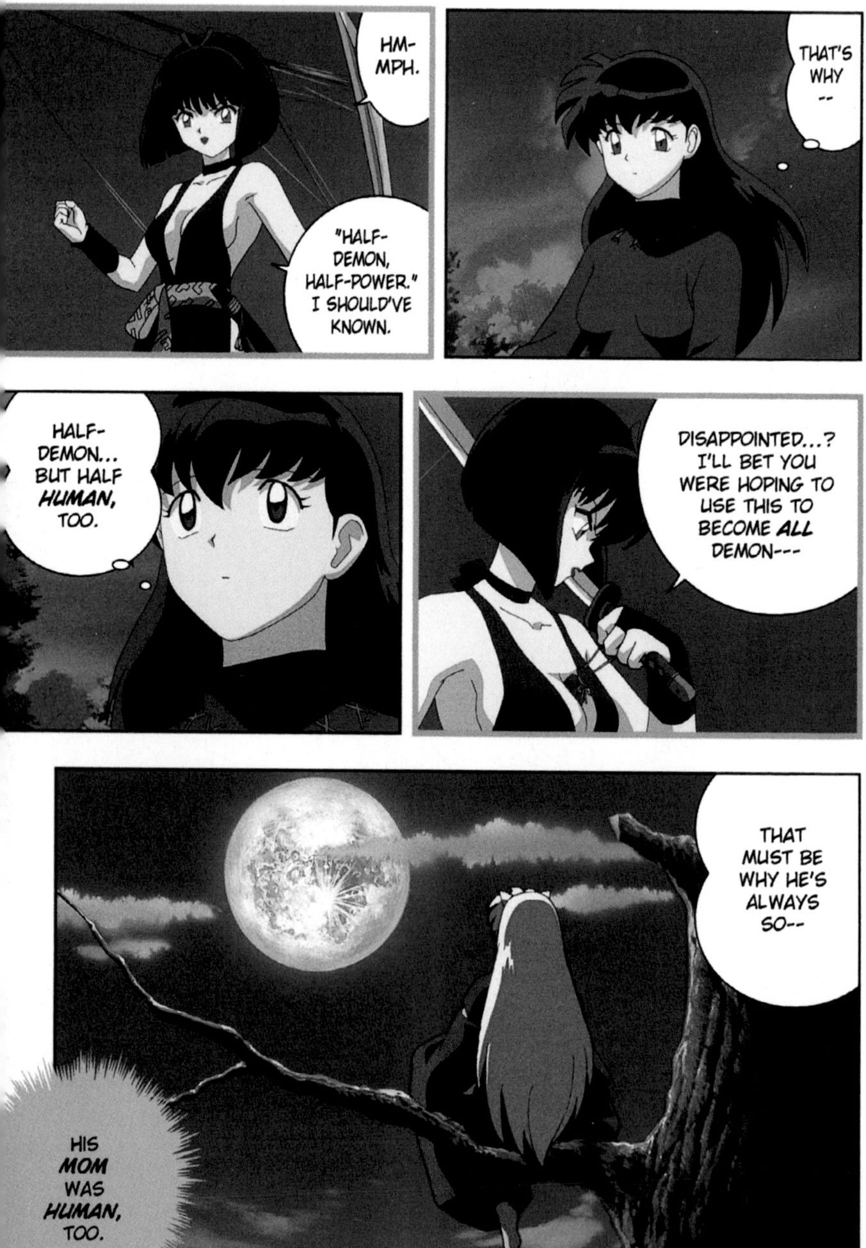
THAT'S WHY --
HM- MPH.
"HALF-DEMON, HALF-POWER." I SHOULD'VE KNOWN.
DISAPPOINTED...? I'LL BET YOU WERE HOPING TO USE THIS TO BECOME *ALL* DEMON---
HALF-DEMON... BUT HALF *HUMAN,* TOO.
THAT MUST BE WHY HE'S ALWAYS SO--
HIS *MOM* WAS *HUMAN,* TOO.

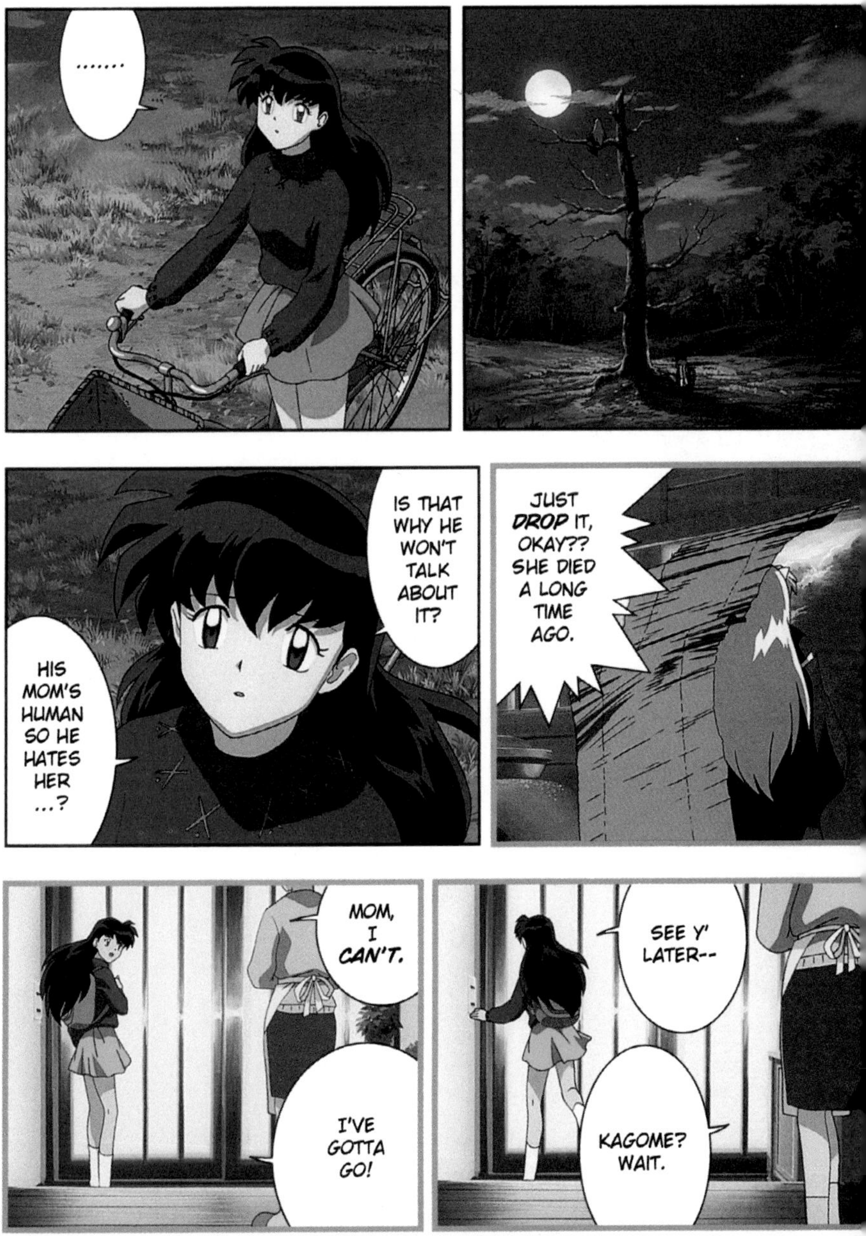
....
JUST DROP IT, OKAY?? SHE DIED A LONG TIME AGO.
IS THAT WHY HE WON'T TALK ABOUT IT?
HIS MOM'S HUMAN SO HE HATES HER ...?
SEE Y' LATER--
KAGOME? WAIT.
MOM, I CAN'T.
I'VE GOTTA GO!

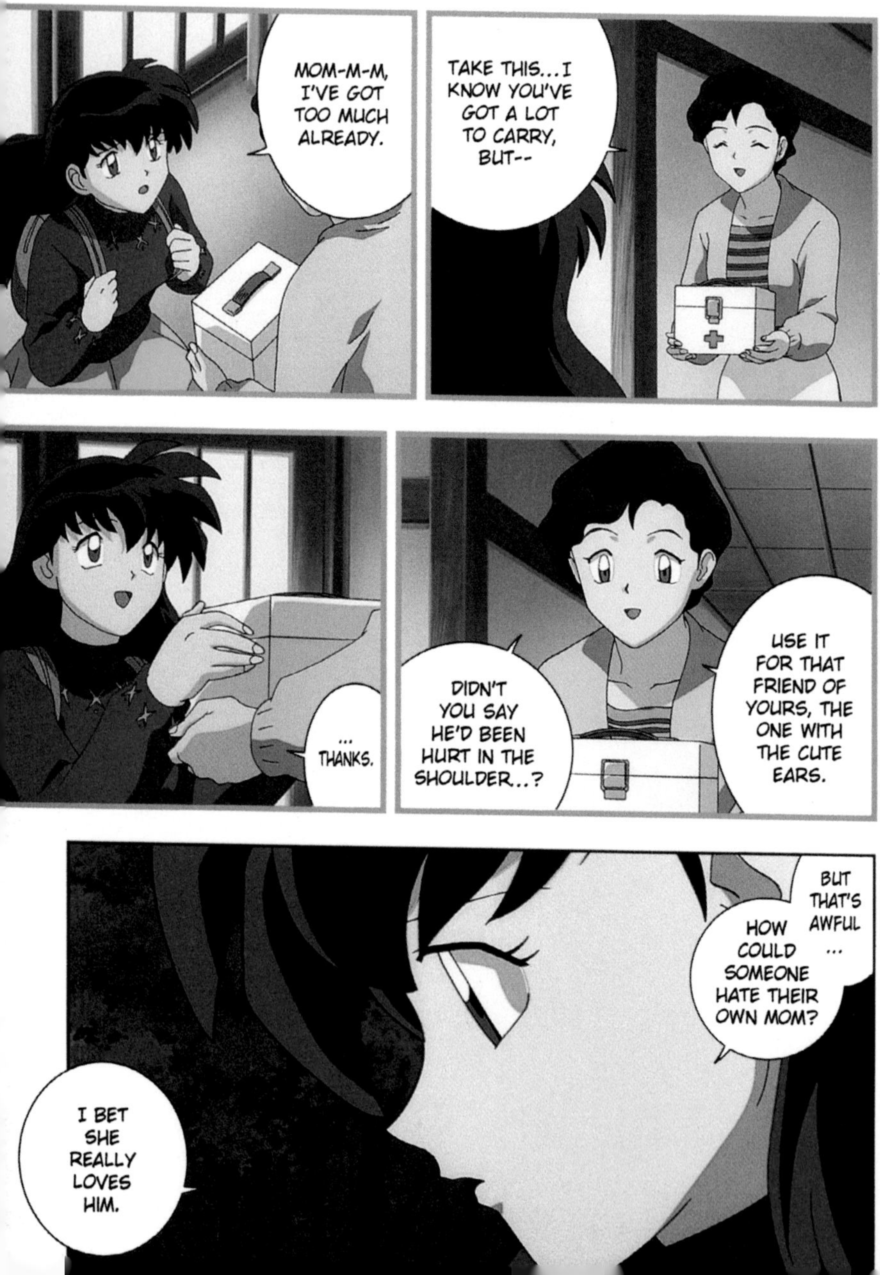
TAKE THIS...I KNOW YOU'VE GOT A LOT TO CARRY, BUT--
MOM-M-M, I'VE GOT TOO MUCH ALREADY.
USE IT FOR THAT FRIEND OF YOURS, THE ONE WITH THE CUTE EARS.
DIDN'T YOU SAY HE'D BEEN HURT IN THE SHOULDER...?
...THANKS.
BUT THAT'S AWFUL...
HOW COULD SOMEONE HATE THEIR OWN MOM?
I BET SHE REALLY LOVES HIM.

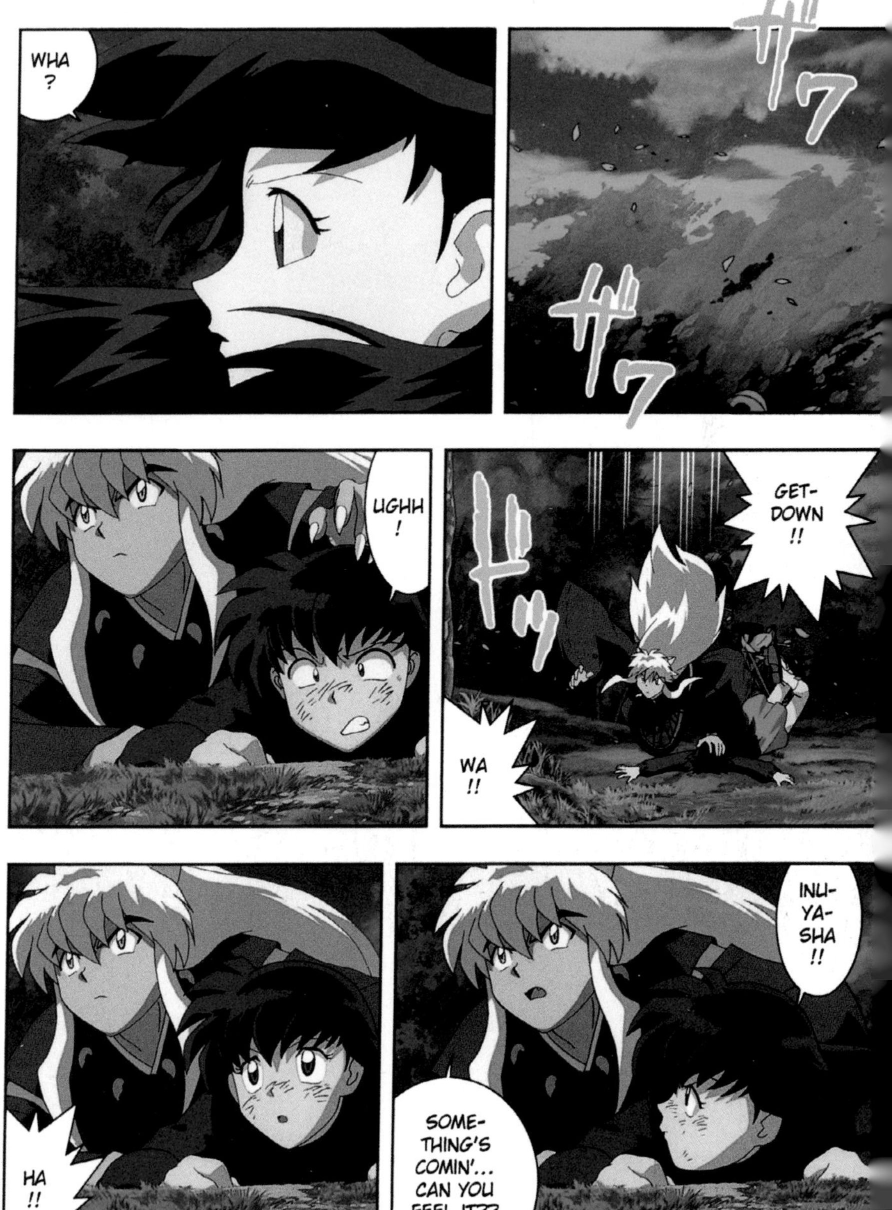
ザワ
ザワ
WHA ?
GET- DOWN !!
ドッ
WA !!
UGHH !
INU- YA- SHA !!
SOME- THING'S COMIN'... CAN YOU FEEL IT??
HA !!

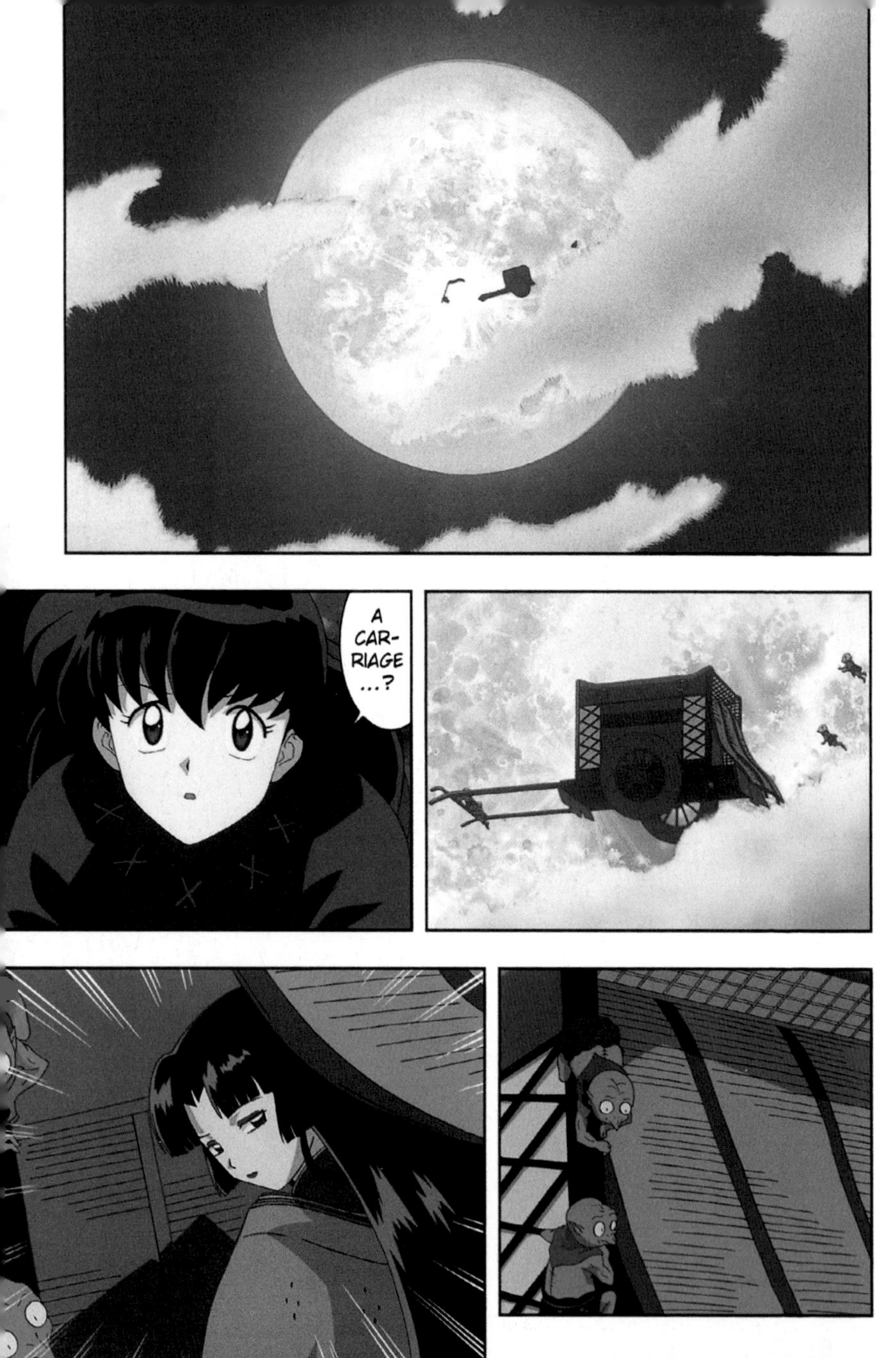
A CAR-RIAGE ...?

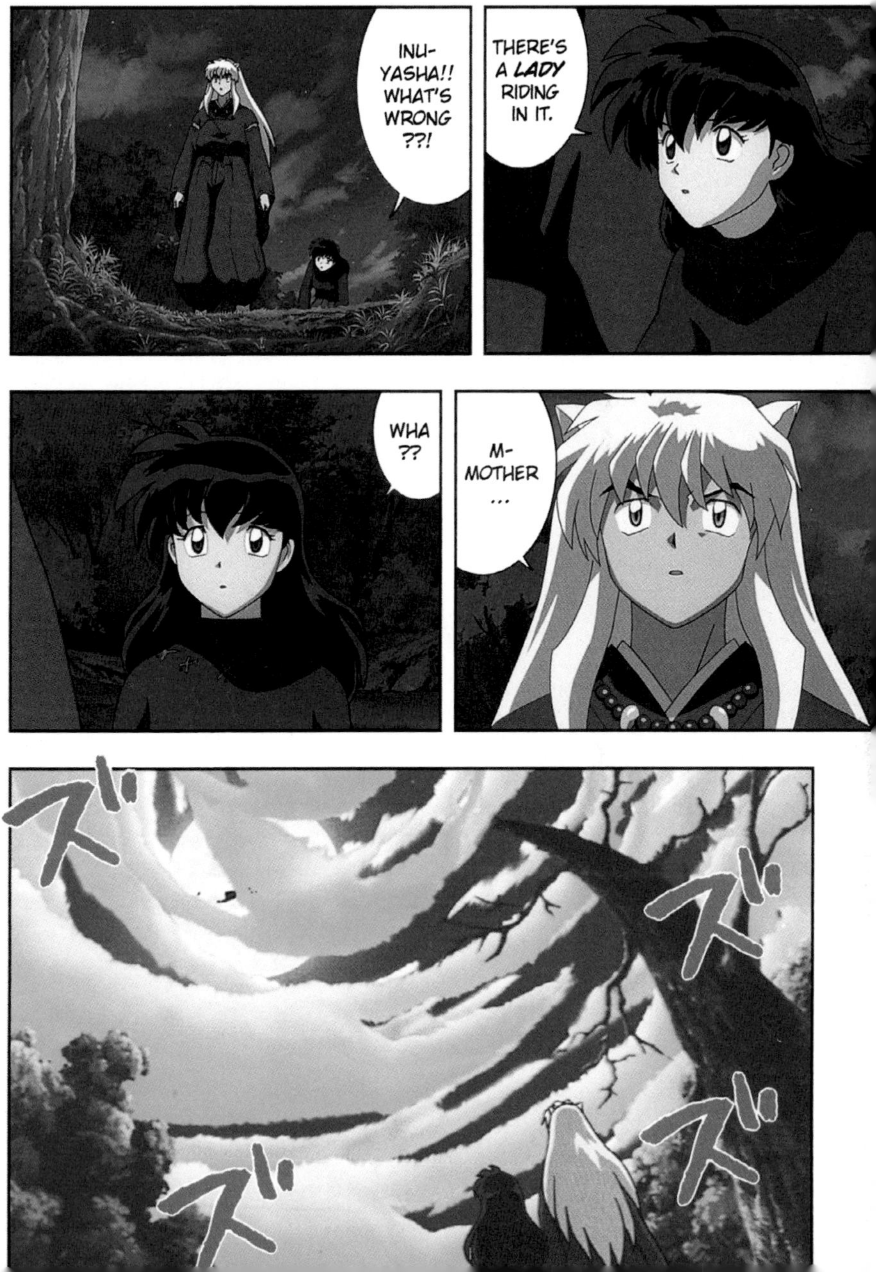
THERE'S A *LADY* RIDING IN IT.
INU-YASHA!! WHAT'S WRONG??!
M-MOTHER...
WHA??
ズ ズ ズ ズ

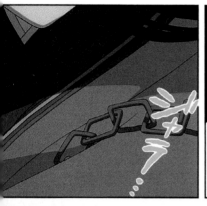

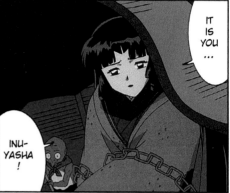

IT
IS
YOU
...

INU-
YASHA
!

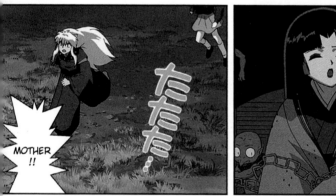

MOTHER
!!

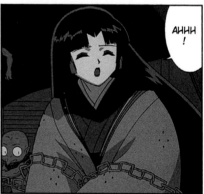

AHHH
!

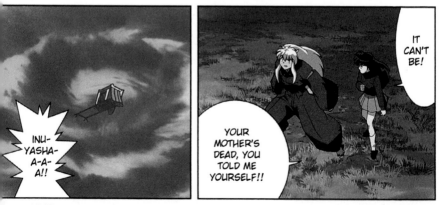

INU-
YASHA-
A-A-
A!!

IT
CAN'T
BE!

YOUR
MOTHER'S
DEAD, YOU
TOLD ME
YOURSELF!!

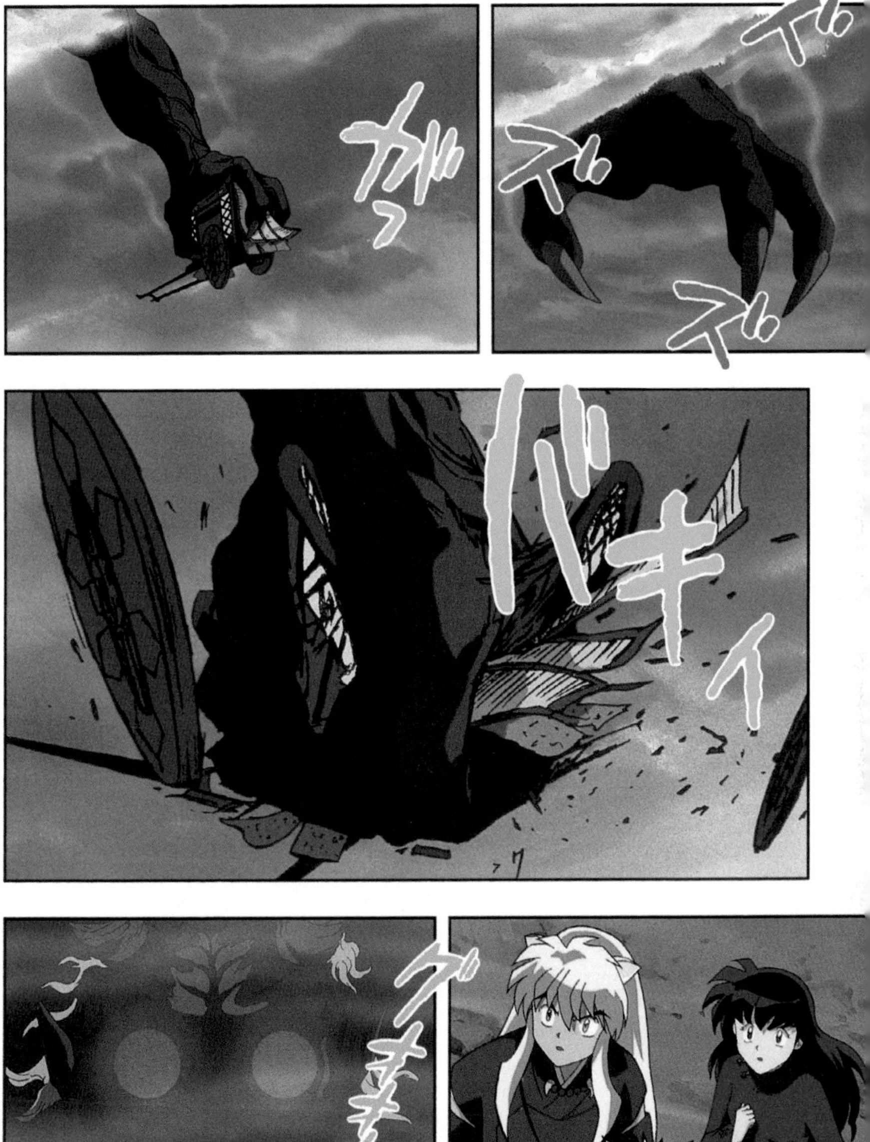
ズ
ズ
ズ
ガッ
バキイ
!
グオオオオオオ

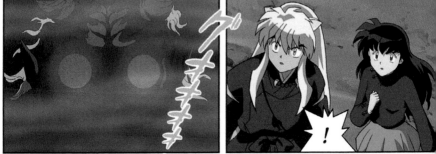

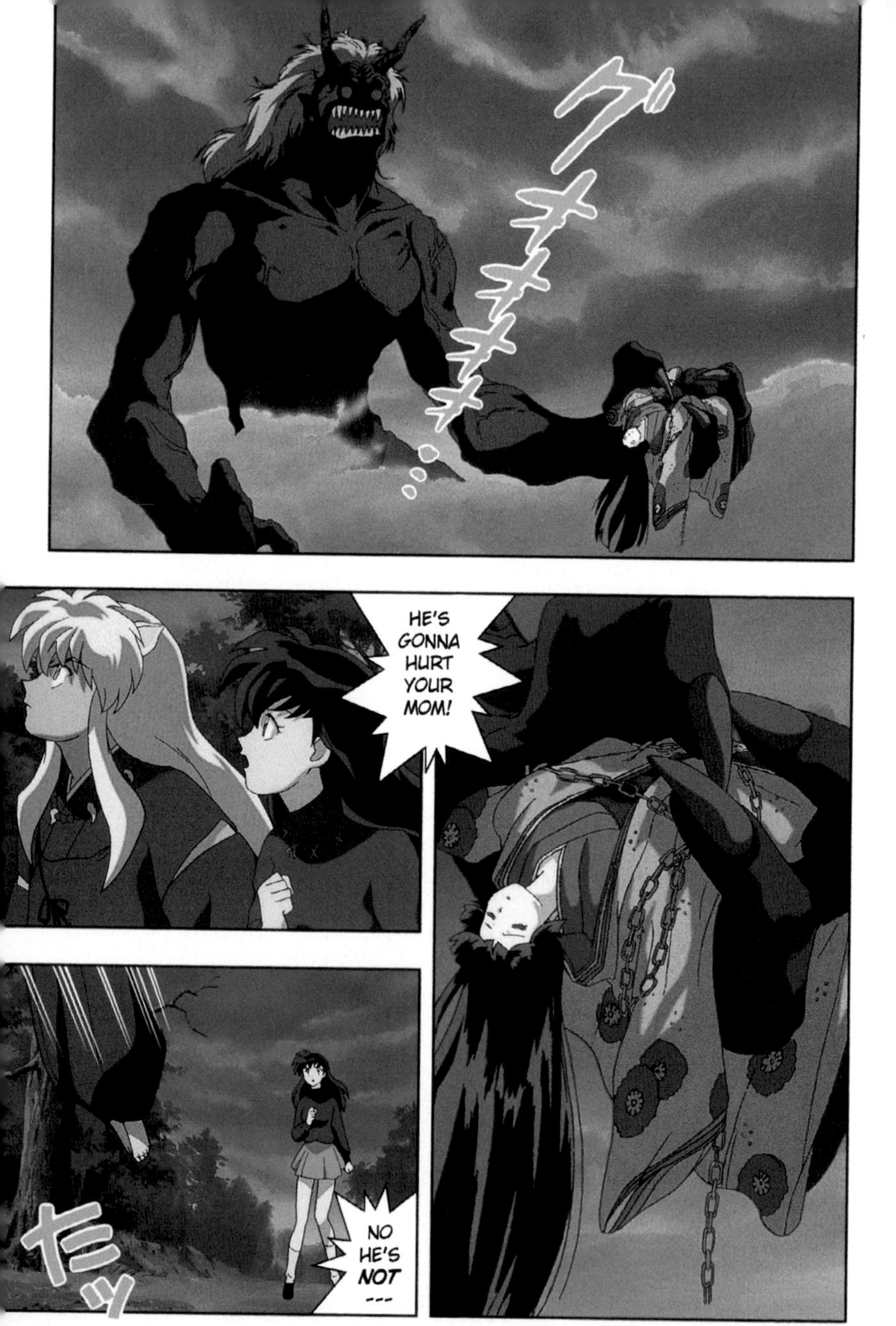

グオオオオオ
HE'S GONNA HURT YOUR MOM!
NO HE'S ***NOT*** ---
タッ

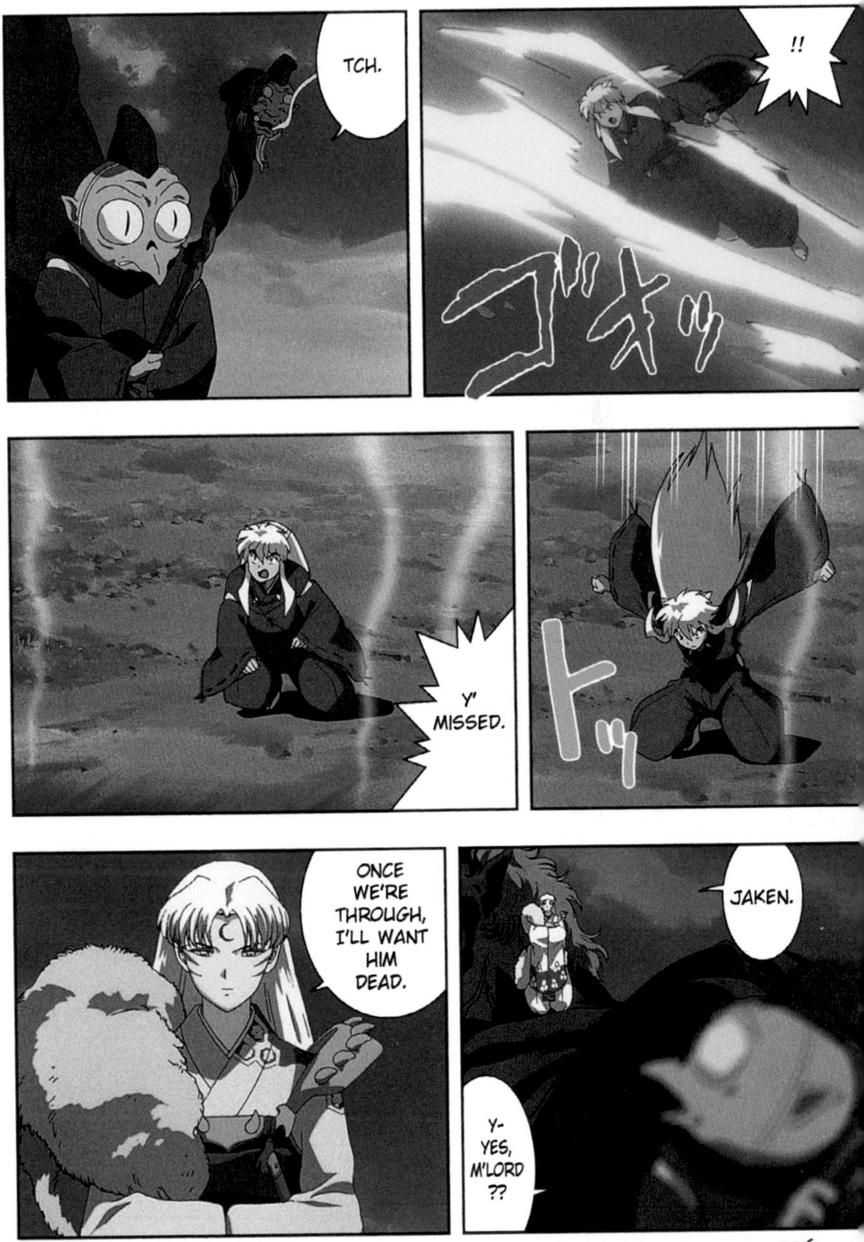
!!
ゴオッ
TCH.
トッ
Y' MISSED.
JAKEN.
Y-YES, M'LORD??
ONCE WE'RE THROUGH, I'LL WANT HIM DEAD.

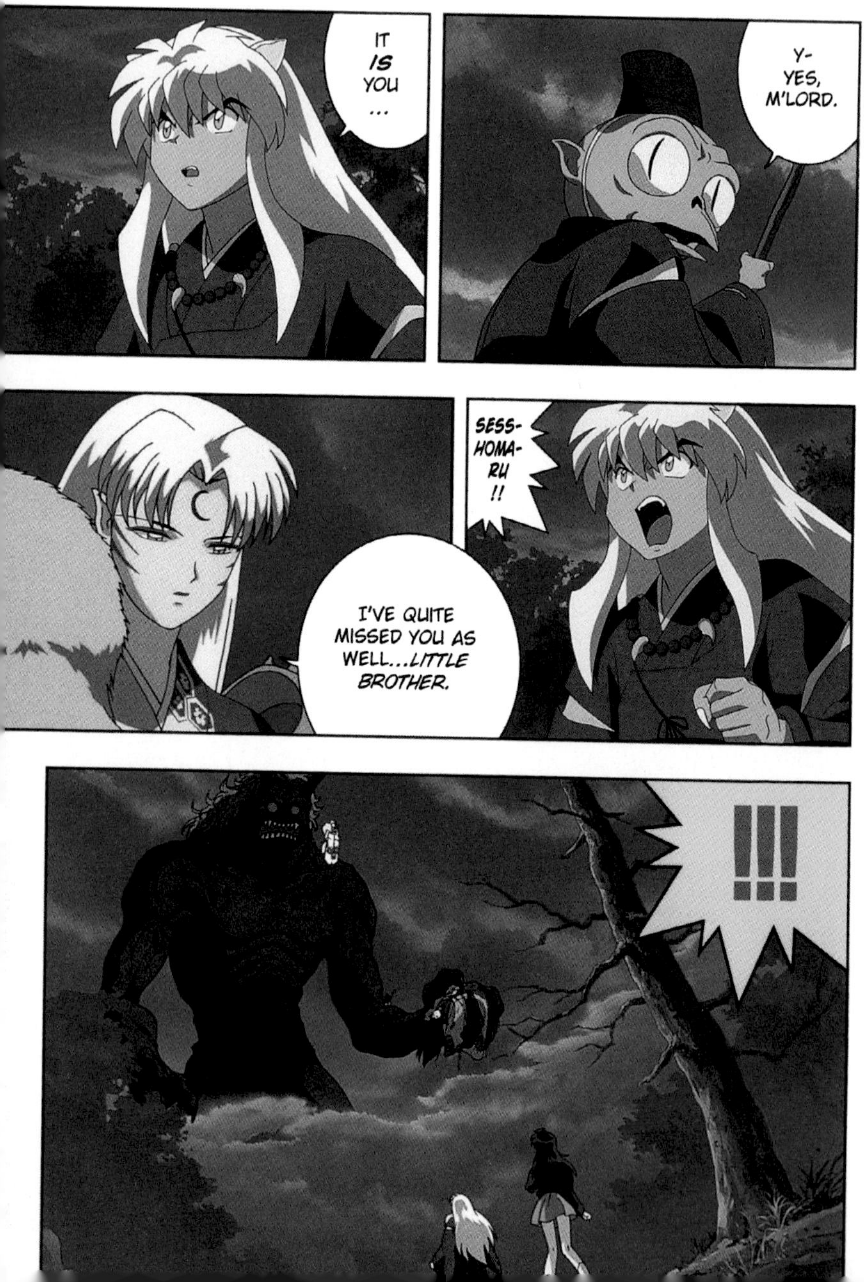

Y-
YES,
M'LORD.
IT
IS
YOU
...
SESS-
HOMA-
RU
!!
I'VE QUITE
MISSED YOU AS
WELL...*LITTLE*
BROTHER.
!!!

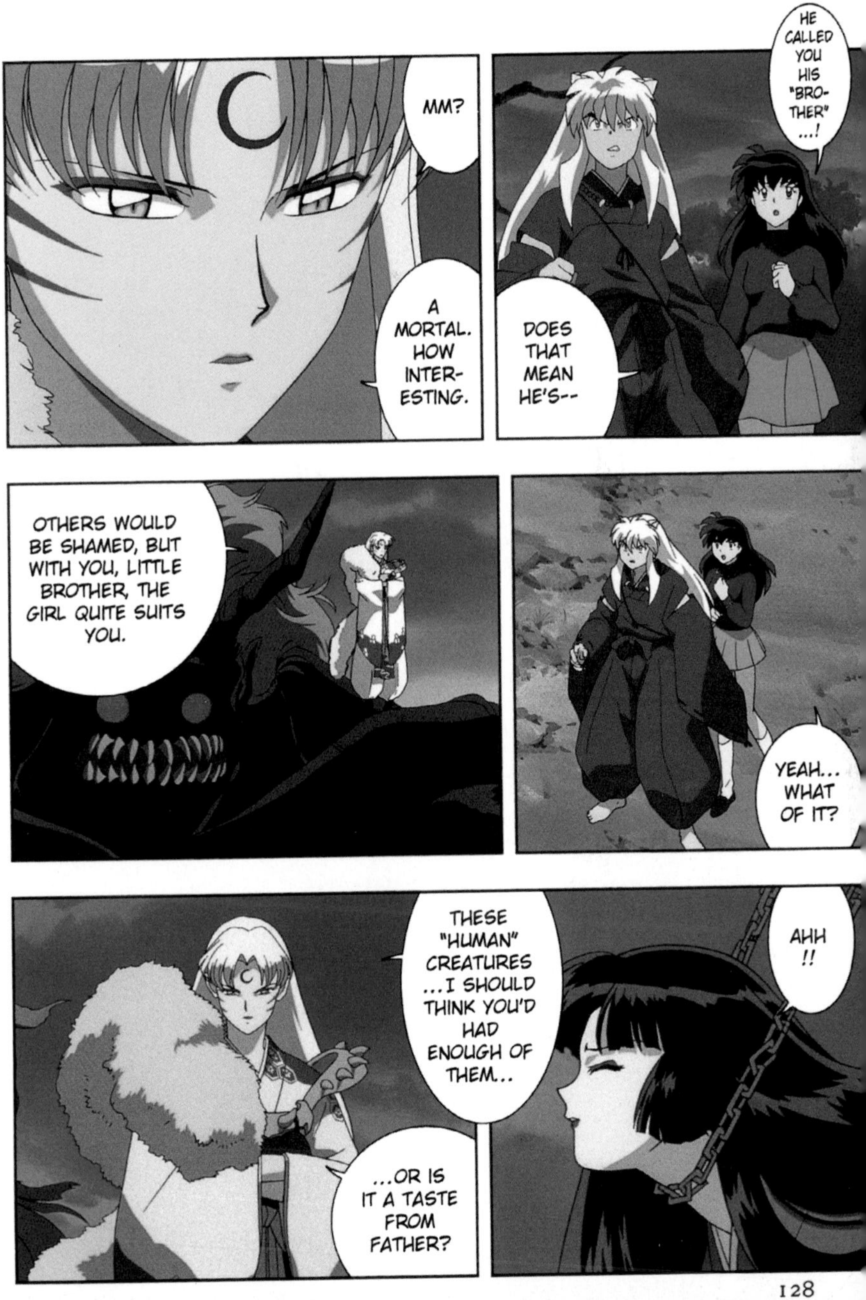
HE CALLED YOU HIS "BROTHER" ...!
DOES THAT MEAN HE'S--
MM?
A MORTAL. HOW INTERESTING.
YEAH... WHAT OF IT?
OTHERS WOULD BE SHAMED, BUT WITH YOU, LITTLE BROTHER, THE GIRL QUITE SUITS YOU.
AHH !!
THESE "HUMAN" CREATURES ...I SHOULD THINK YOU'D HAD ENOUGH OF THEM...
...OR IS IT A TASTE FROM FATHER?

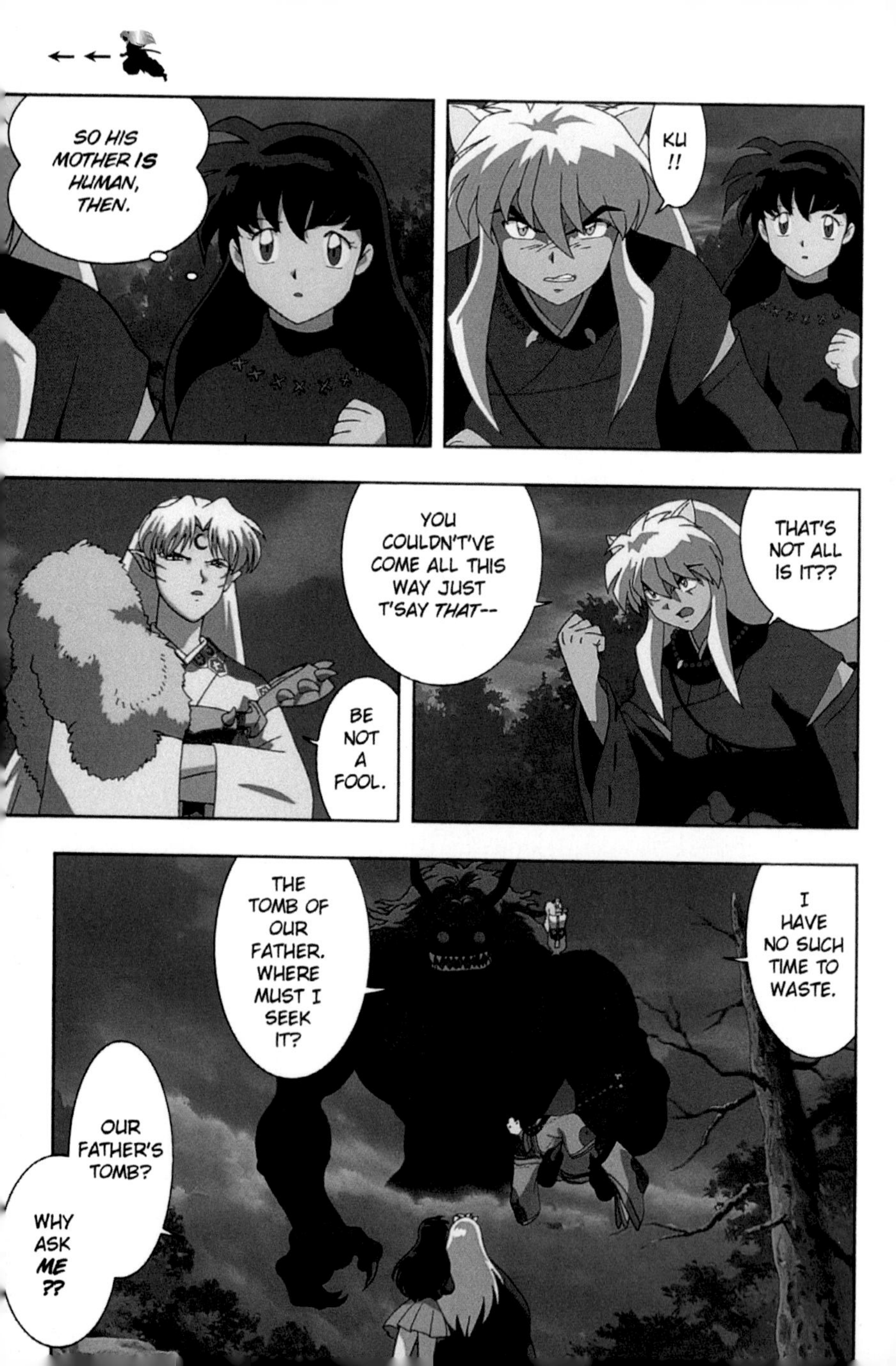
KU !!
SO HIS MOTHER IS HUMAN, THEN.
THAT'S NOT ALL IS IT??
YOU COULDN'T'VE COME ALL THIS WAY JUST T'SAY *THAT*--
BE NOT A FOOL.
I HAVE NO SUCH TIME TO WASTE.
THE TOMB OF OUR FATHER. WHERE MUST I SEEK IT?
OUR FATHER'S TOMB?
WHY ASK **ME** ??

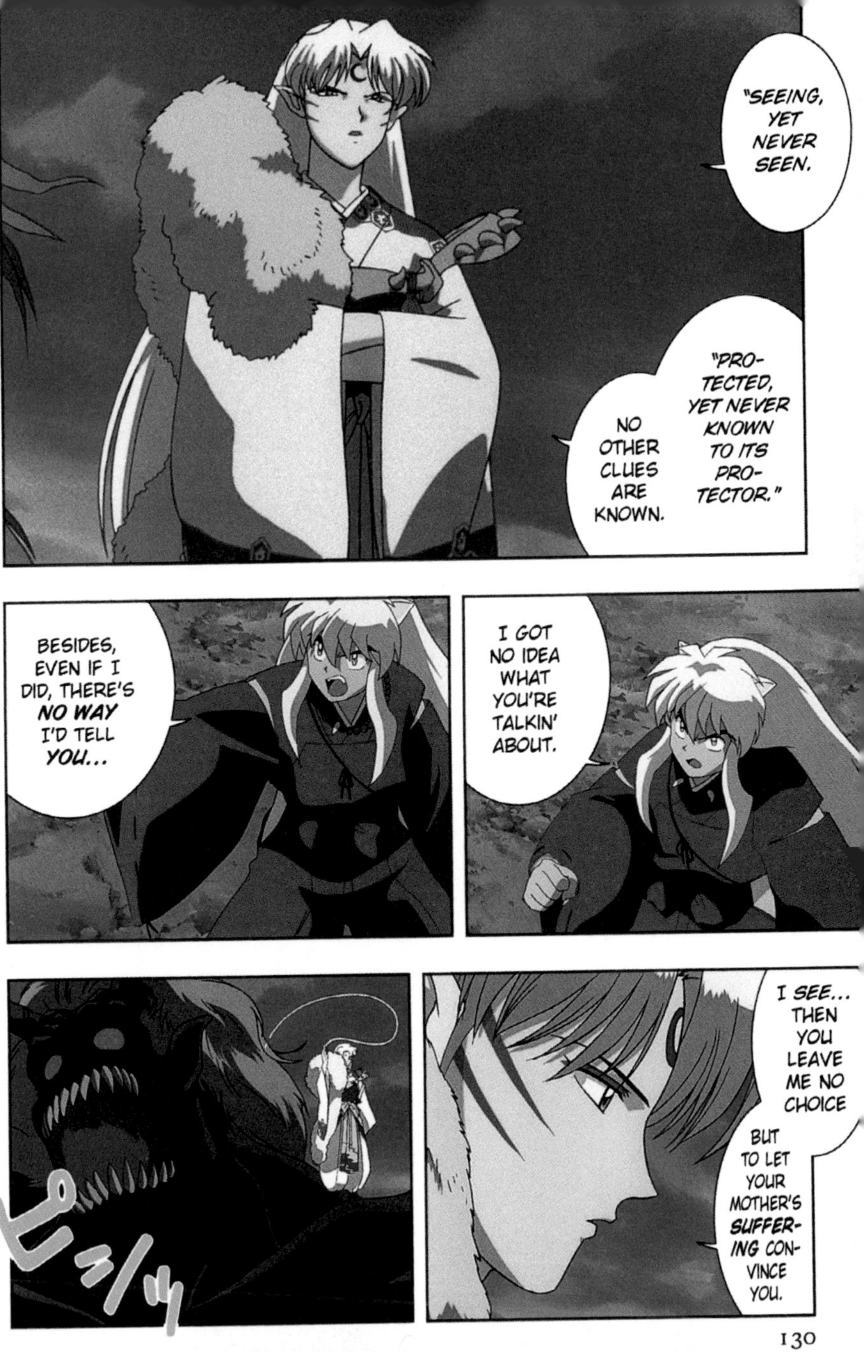
"SEEING, YET NEVER SEEN.
"PROTECTED, YET NEVER KNOWN TO ITS PROTECTOR."
NO OTHER CLUES ARE KNOWN.
I GOT NO IDEA WHAT YOU'RE TALKIN' ABOUT.
BESIDES, EVEN IF I DID, THERE'S **NO WAY** I'D TELL **YOU**...
I SEE... THEN YOU LEAVE ME NO CHOICE
BUT TO LET YOUR MOTHER'S **SUFFERING** CONVINCE YOU.

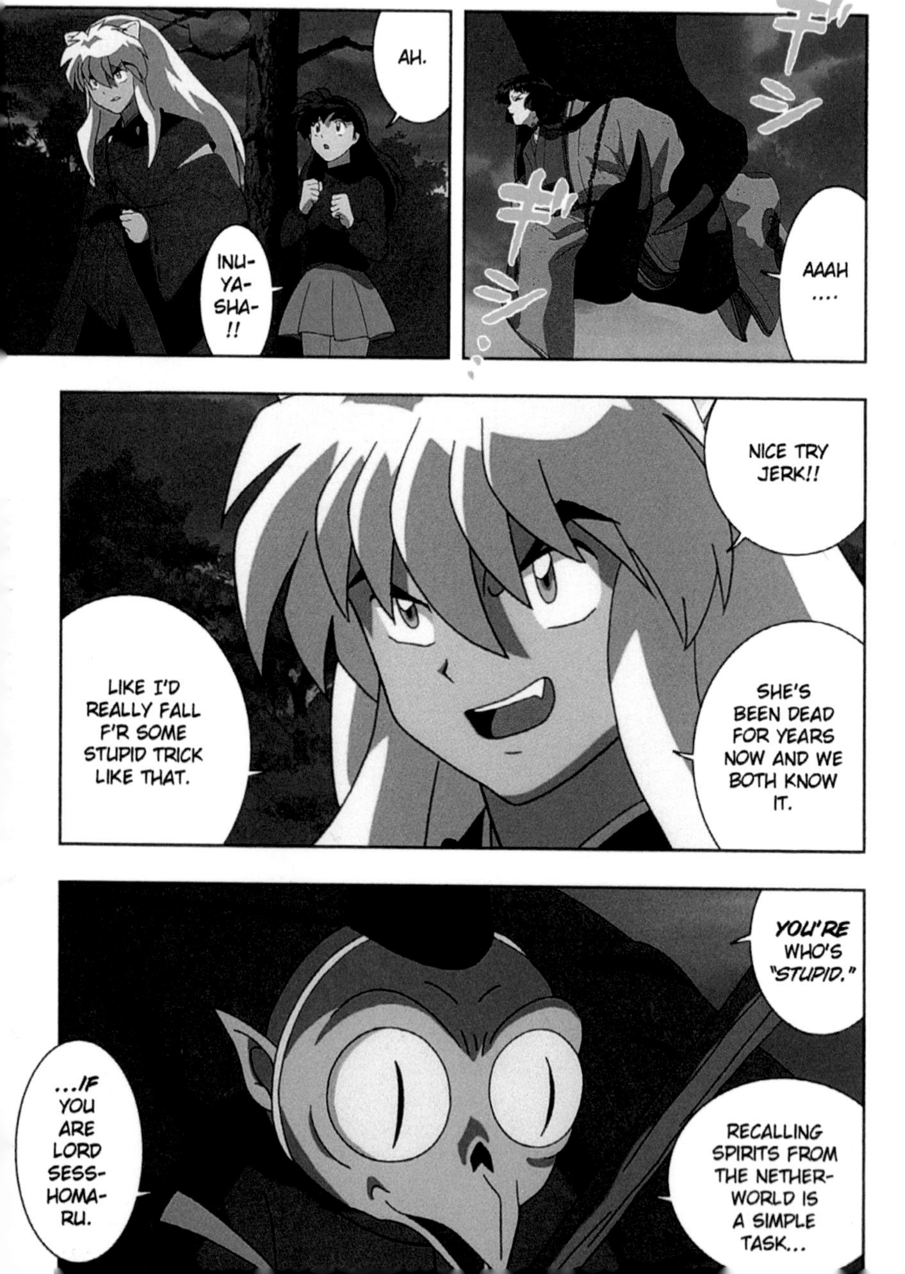

ギシ
ギシ
AAAH ....
AH.
INU-YASHA!!
NICE TRY JERK!!
SHE'S BEEN DEAD FOR YEARS NOW AND WE BOTH KNOW IT.
LIKE I'D REALLY FALL F'R SOME STUPID TRICK LIKE THAT.
YOU'RE WHO'S *"STUPID."*
RECALLING SPIRITS FROM THE NETHER-WORLD IS A SIMPLE TASK...
...IF YOU ARE LORD SESS-HOMA-RU.

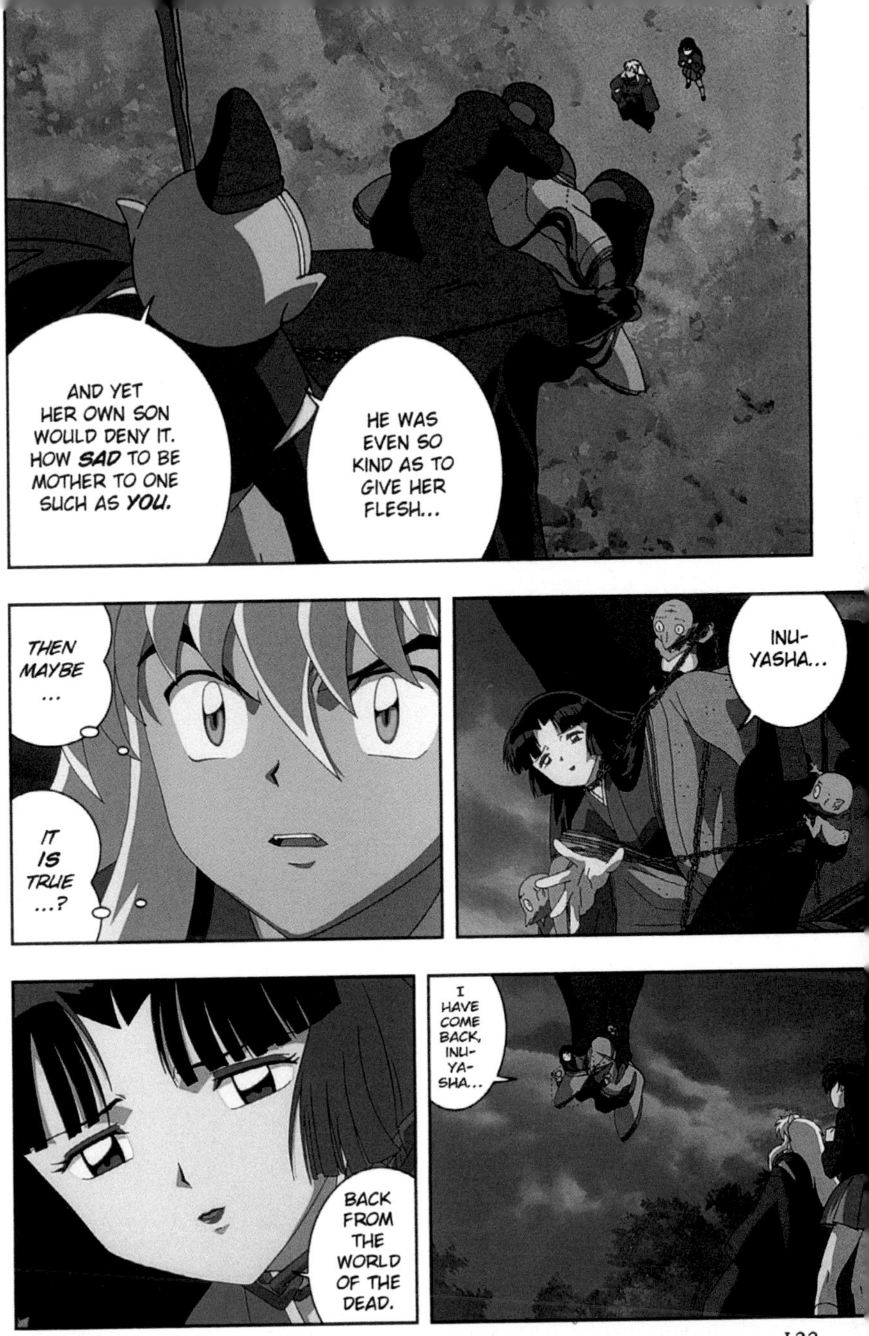
HE WAS EVEN SO KIND AS TO GIVE HER FLESH...
AND YET HER OWN SON WOULD DENY IT. HOW **SAD** TO BE MOTHER TO ONE SUCH AS **YOU.**
INU-YASHA...
THEN MAYBE ...
*IT **IS** TRUE ...?*
I HAVE COME BACK, INU-YA-SHA...
BACK FROM THE WORLD OF THE DEAD.

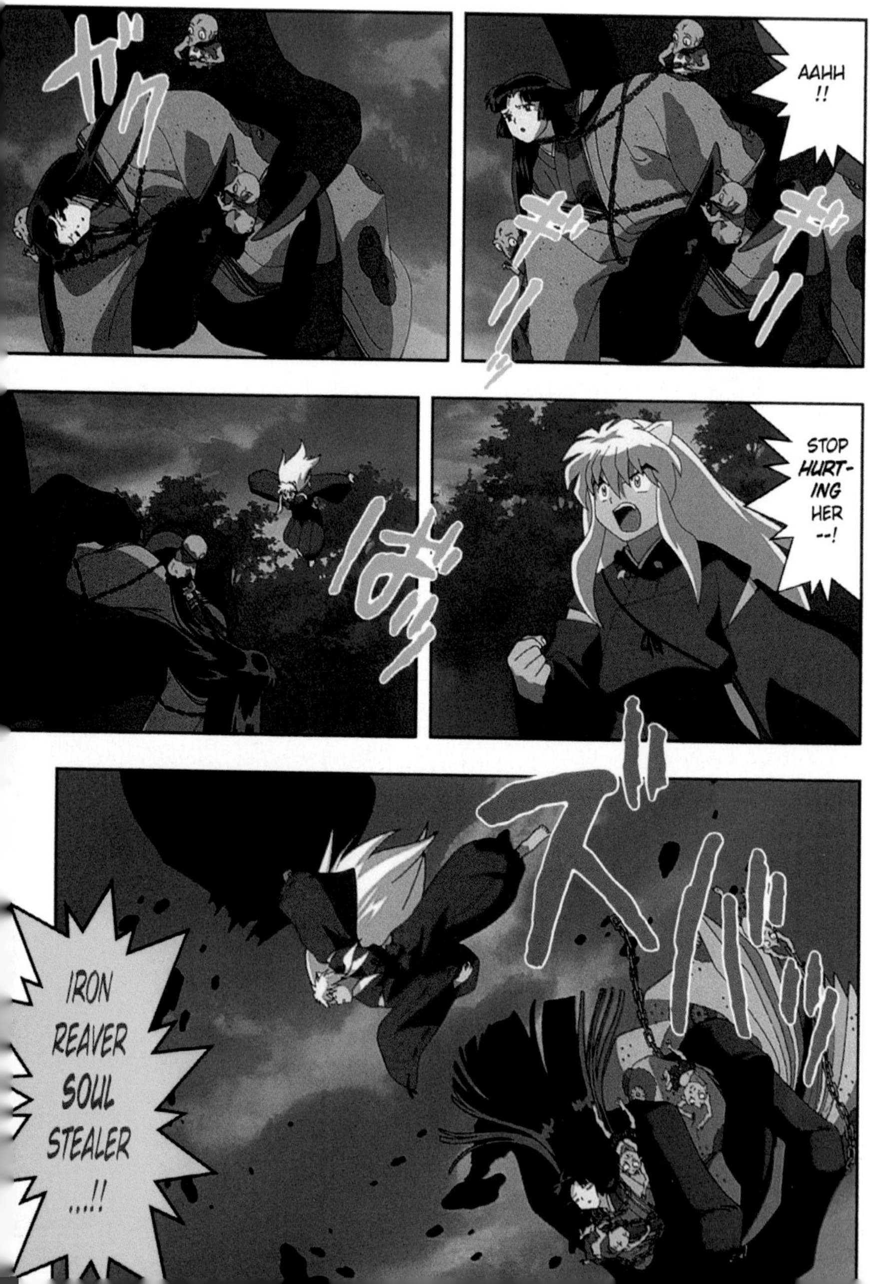
AAHH !!
ギリ
ギリリ
ザク
STOP HURTING HER --!
ばっ
ズバッ
IRON REAVER SOUL STEALER ...!!

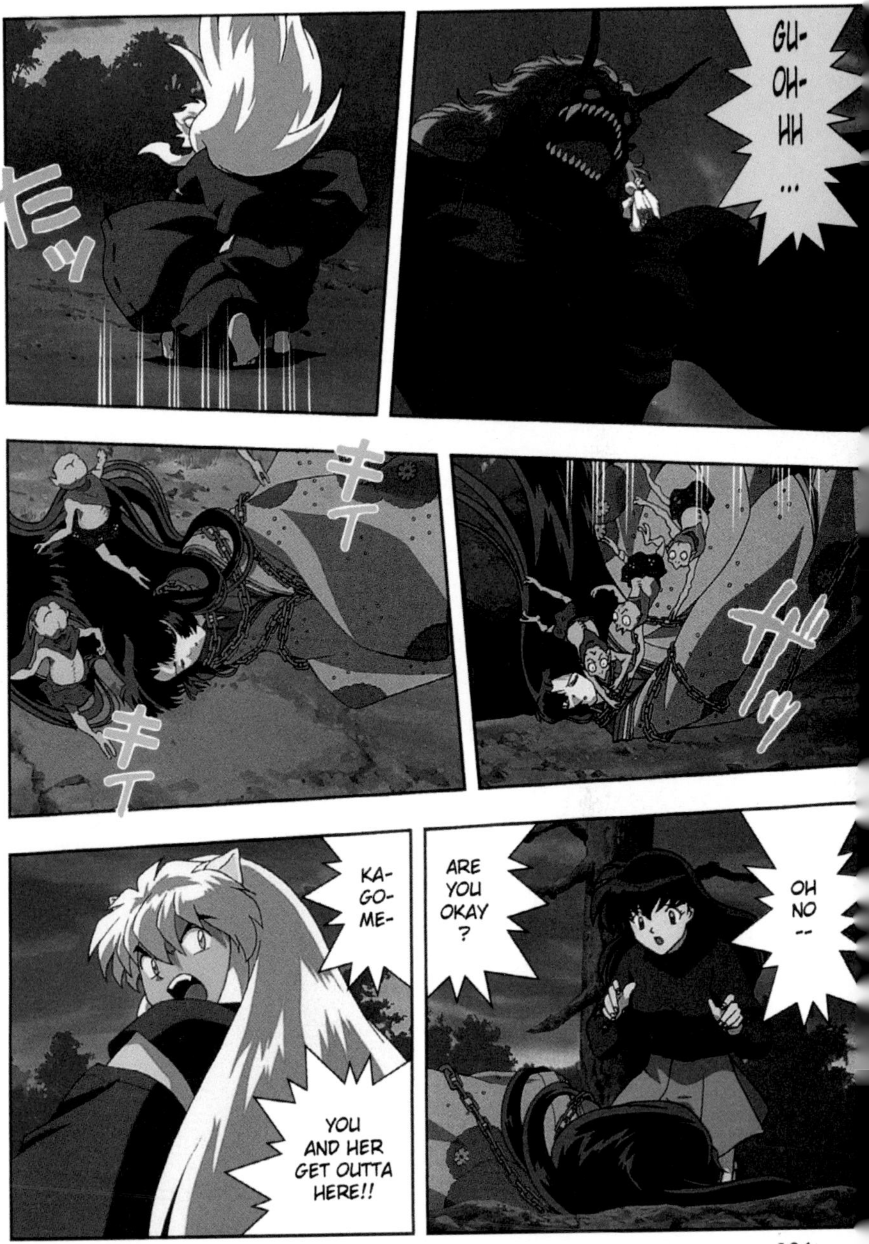
GU-OH-HH...
ザッ
キイ
キイ
OH NO --
ARE YOU OKAY?
KA-GO-ME-
YOU AND HER GET OUTTA HERE!!

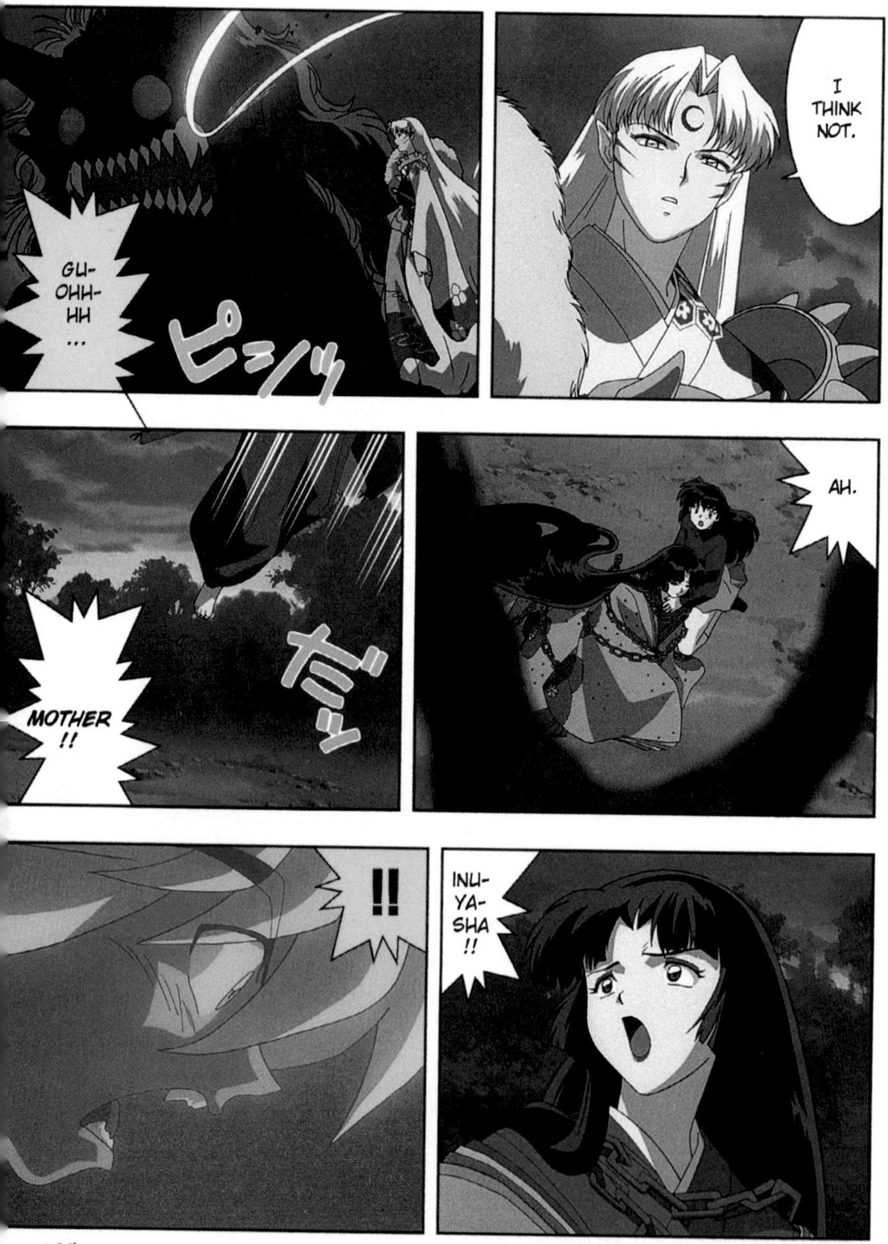
I THINK NOT.
GU-OHHH-HH ...
ピシッ
AH.
MOTHER!!
だッ
INU-YA-SHA!!
!!

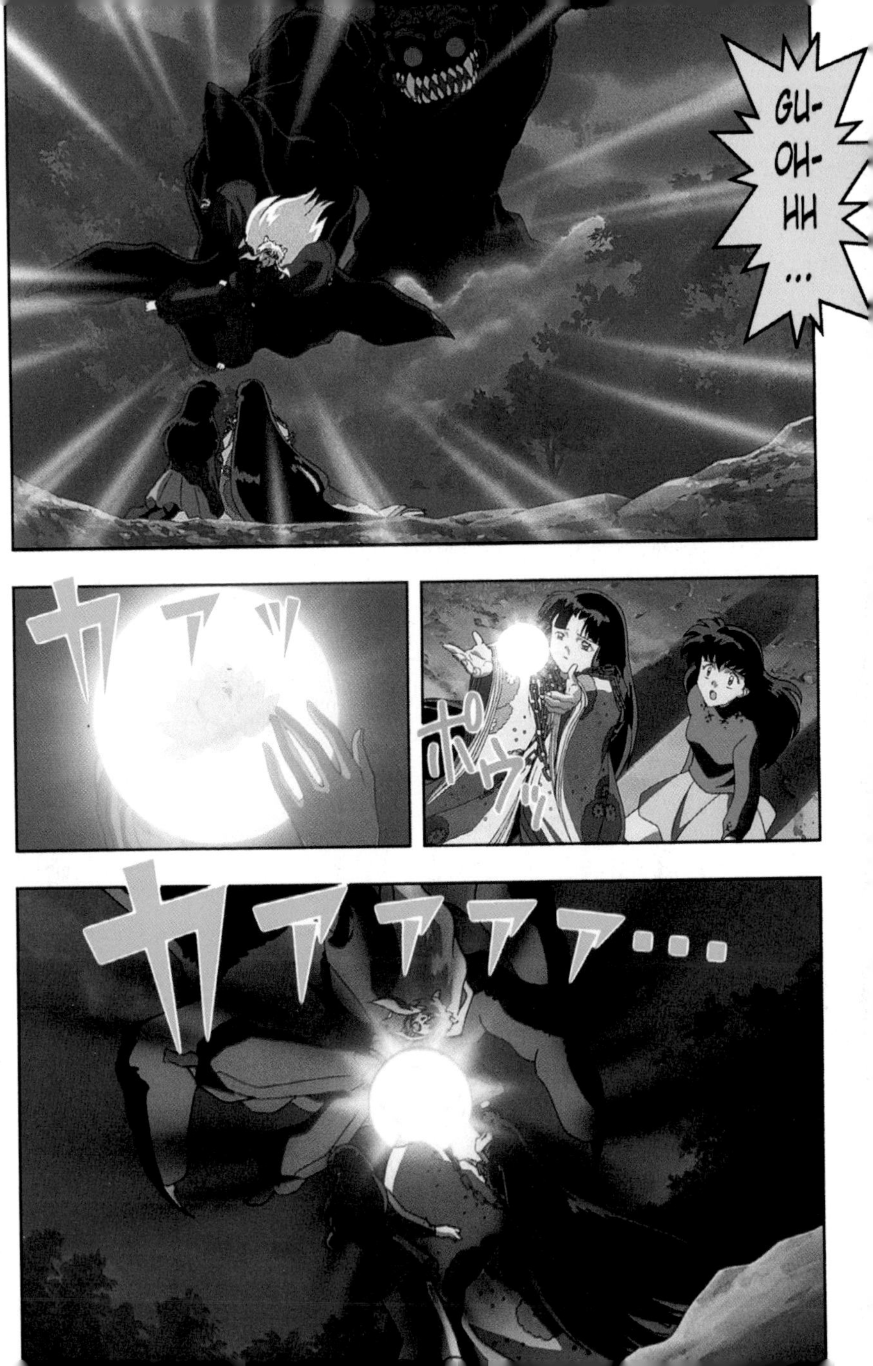
GU-OH-HH...
ポウッ
カアッ
カアアアア...

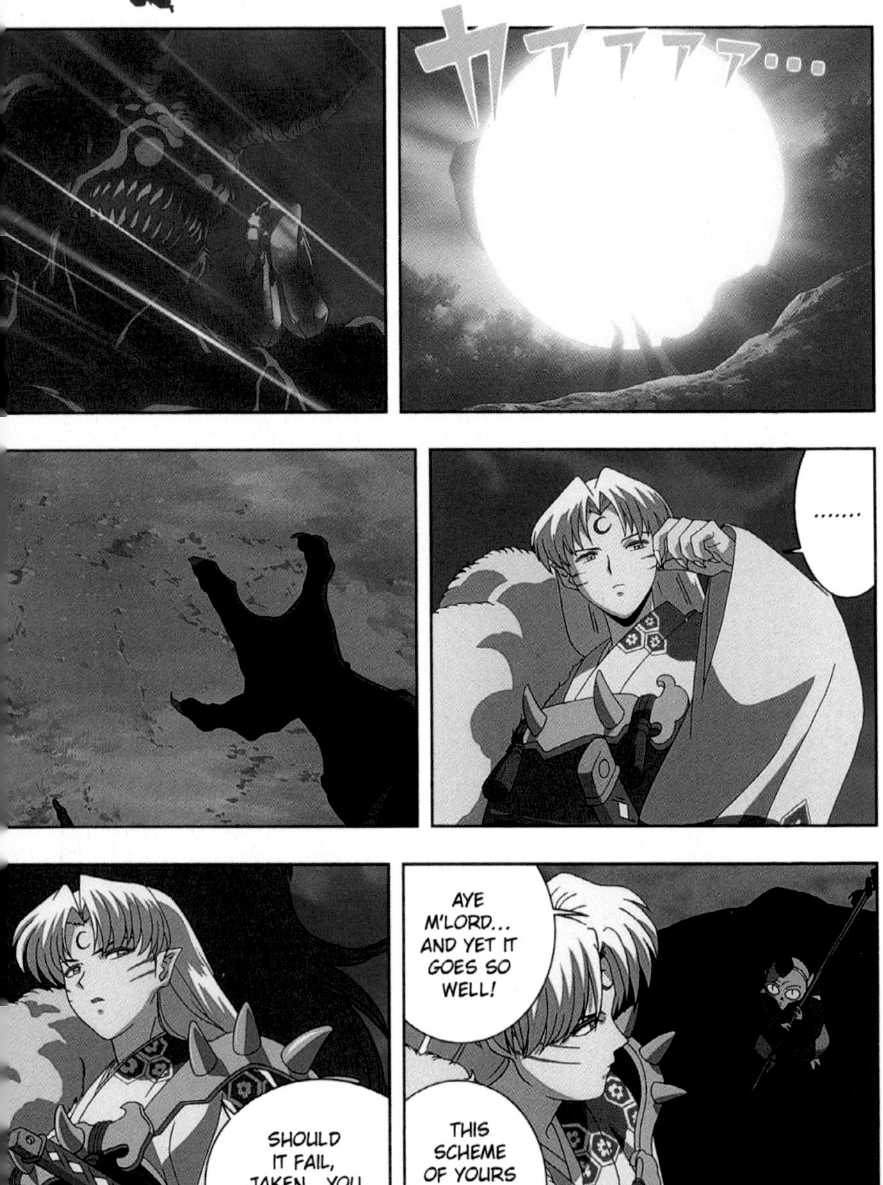
カアアアア...
....
AYE M'LORD... AND YET IT GOES SO WELL!
THIS SCHEME OF YOURS IS BENEATH ME.
SHOULD IT FAIL, JAKEN...YOU WILL DIE.

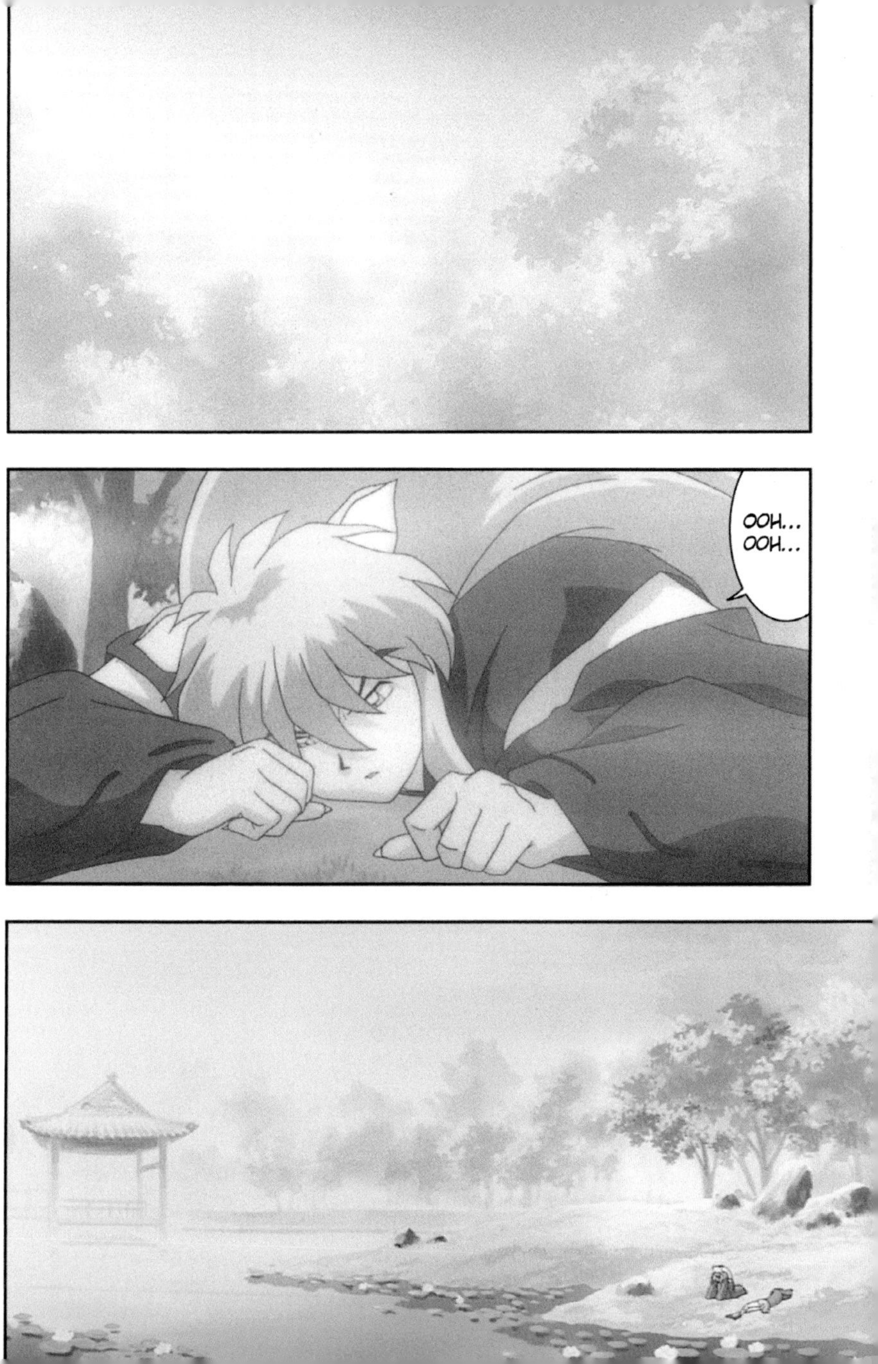
OOH...
OOH...

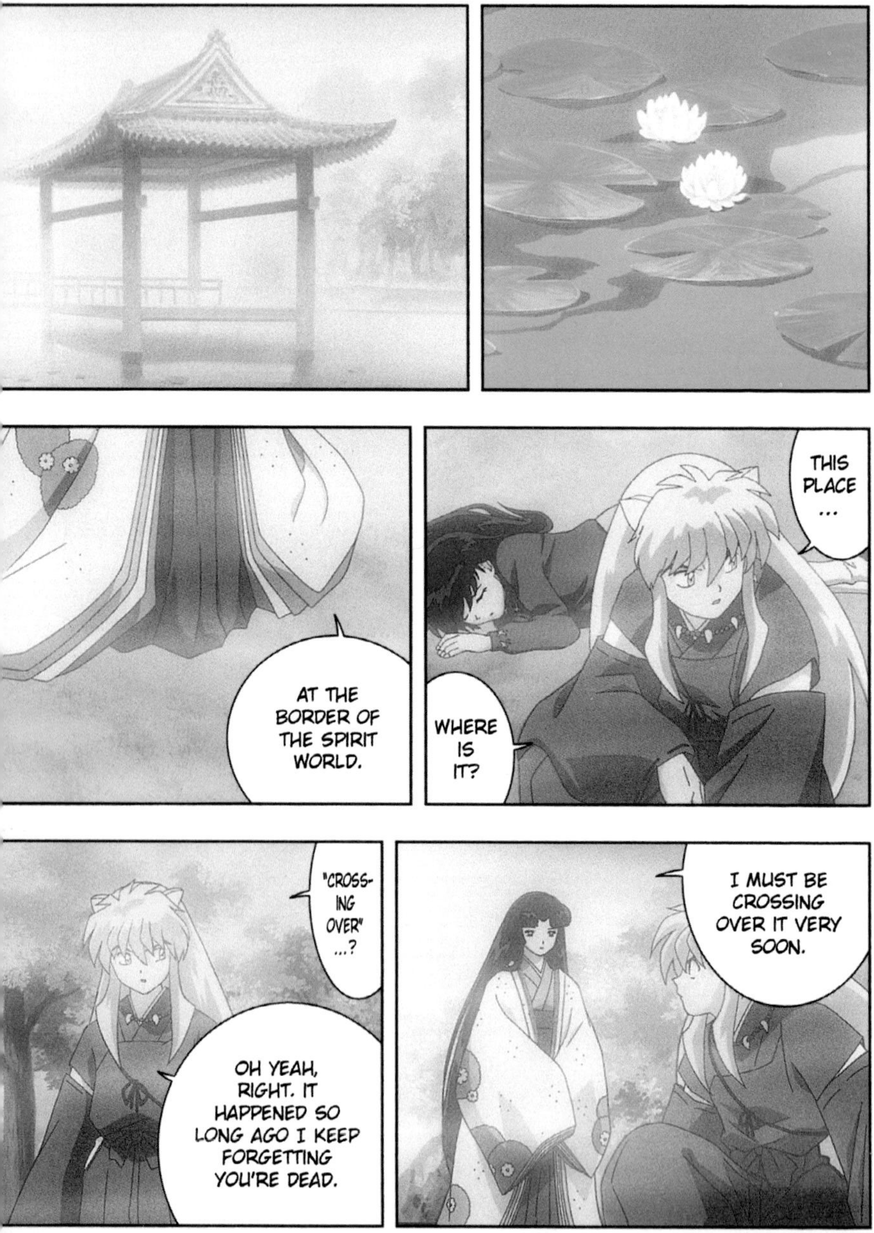
THIS PLACE ...
WHERE IS IT?
AT THE BORDER OF THE SPIRIT WORLD.
I MUST BE CROSSING OVER IT VERY SOON.
"CROSSING OVER" ...?
OH YEAH, RIGHT. IT HAPPENED SO LONG AGO I KEEP FORGETTING YOU'RE DEAD.

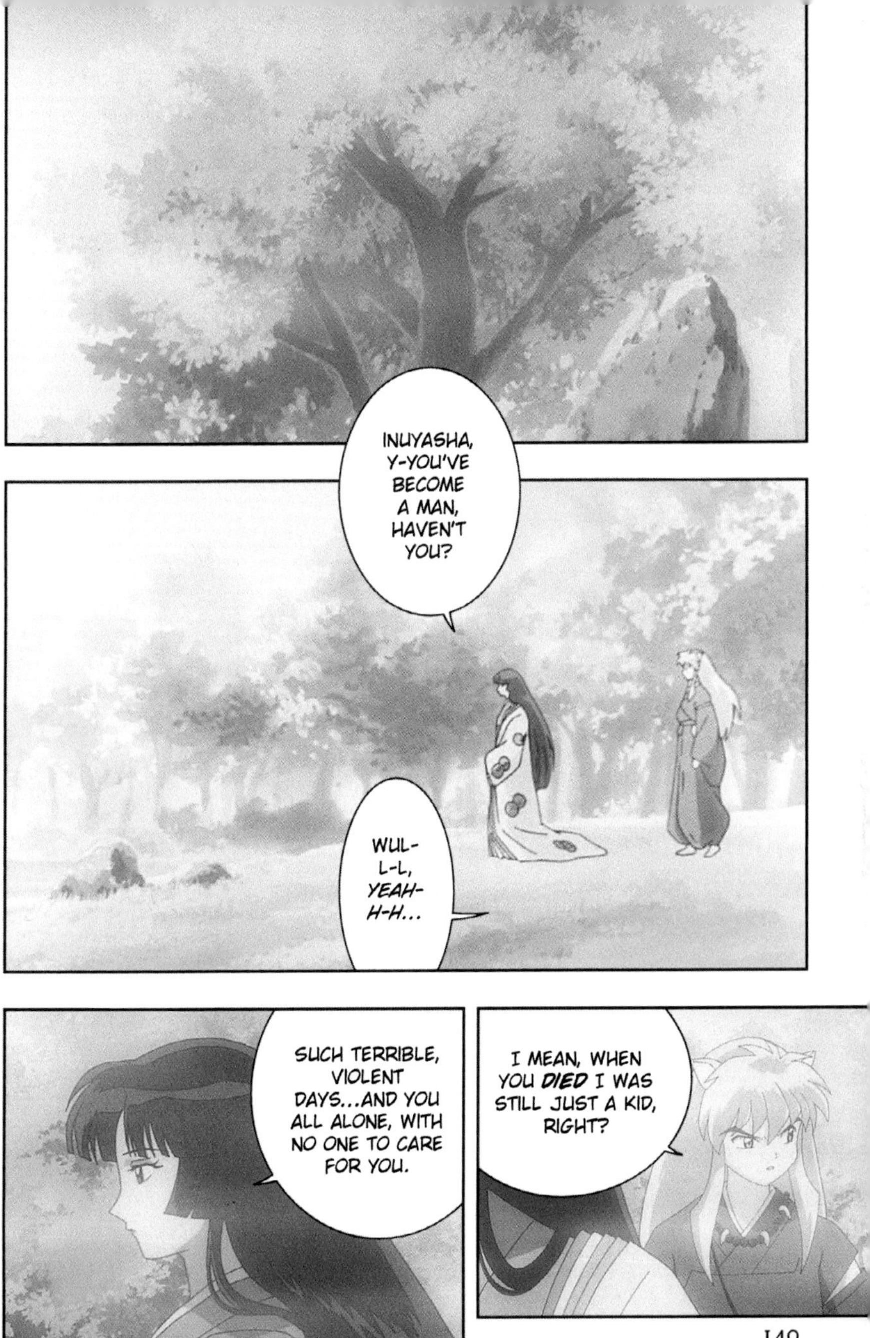
INUYASHA, Y-YOU'VE BECOME A MAN, HAVEN'T YOU?
WUL-L-L, *YEAH-H-H...*
I MEAN, WHEN YOU ***DIED*** I WAS STILL JUST A KID, RIGHT?
SUCH TERRIBLE, VIOLENT DAYS...AND YOU ALL ALONE, WITH NO ONE TO CARE FOR YOU.

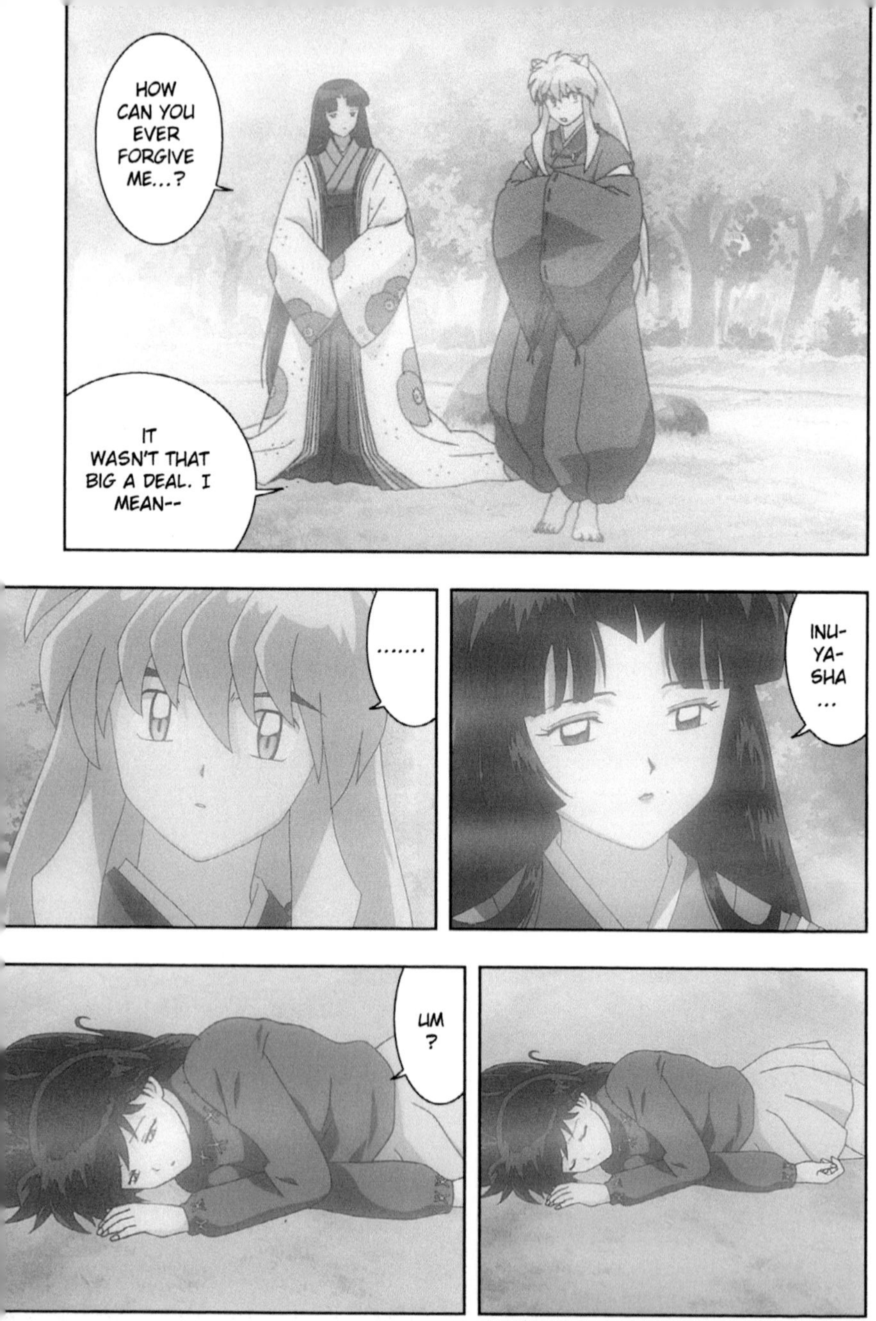
HOW CAN YOU EVER FORGIVE ME...?
IT WASN'T THAT BIG A DEAL. I MEAN--
INU-YA-SHA ...
....
UM ?

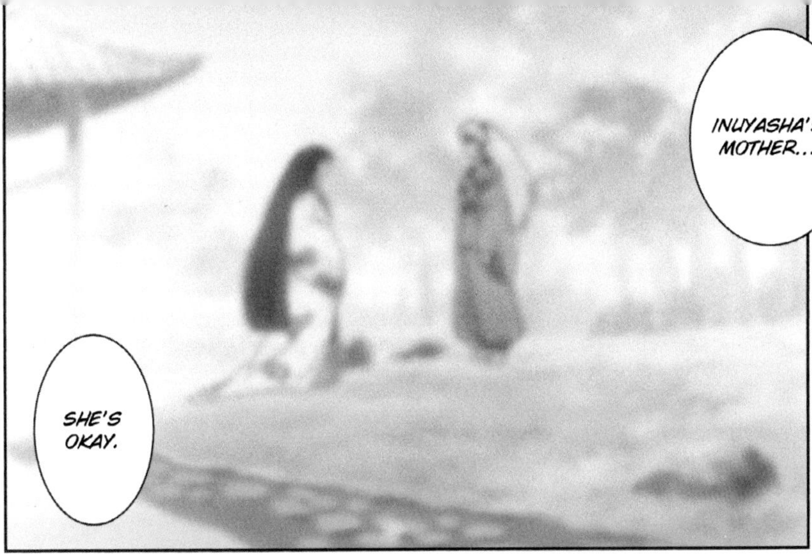
INUYASHA'S MOTHER...
SHE'S OKAY.
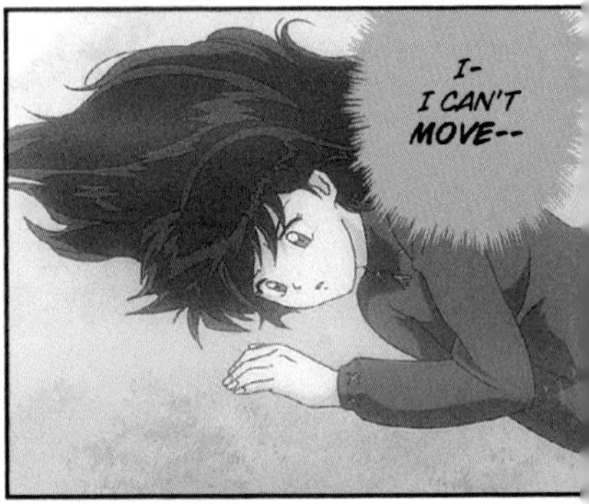
I- I CAN'T MOVE--
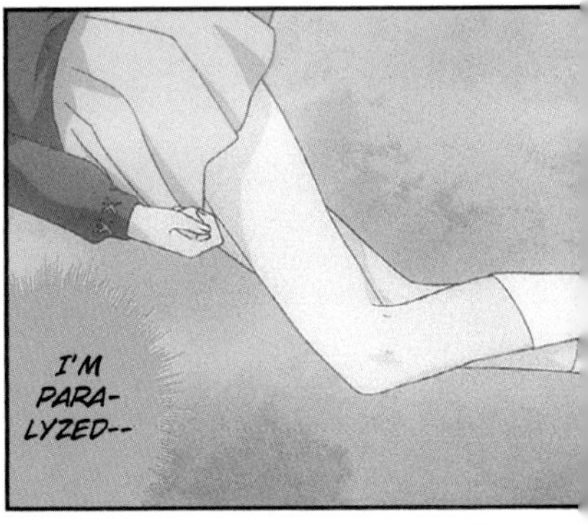
I'M PARA- LYZED--
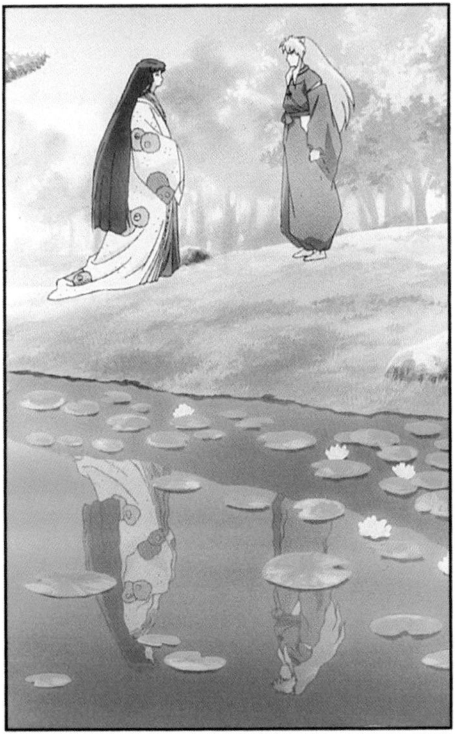

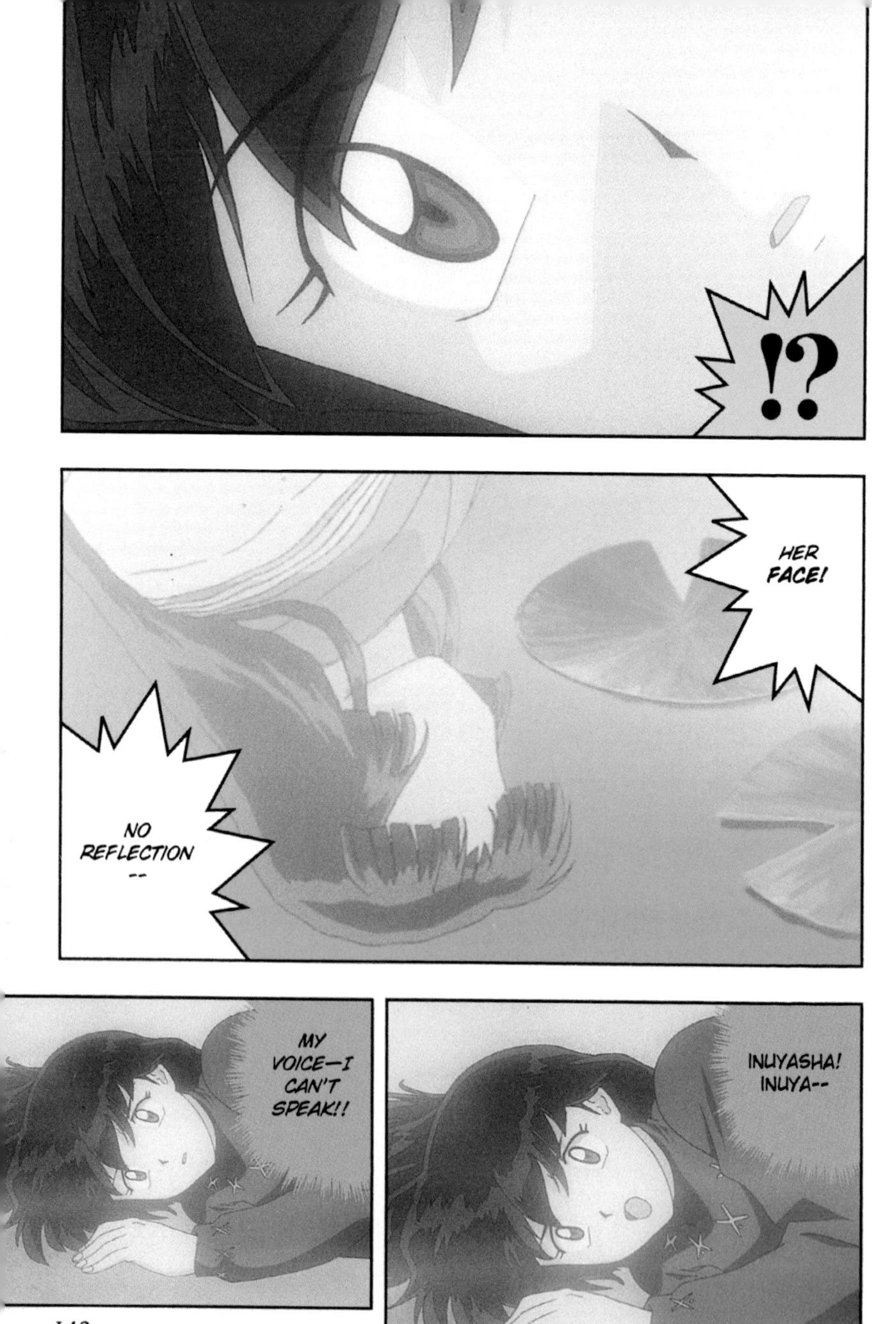
!?
HER FACE!
NO REFLECTION --
INUYASHA! INUYA--
MY VOICE—I CAN'T SPEAK!!

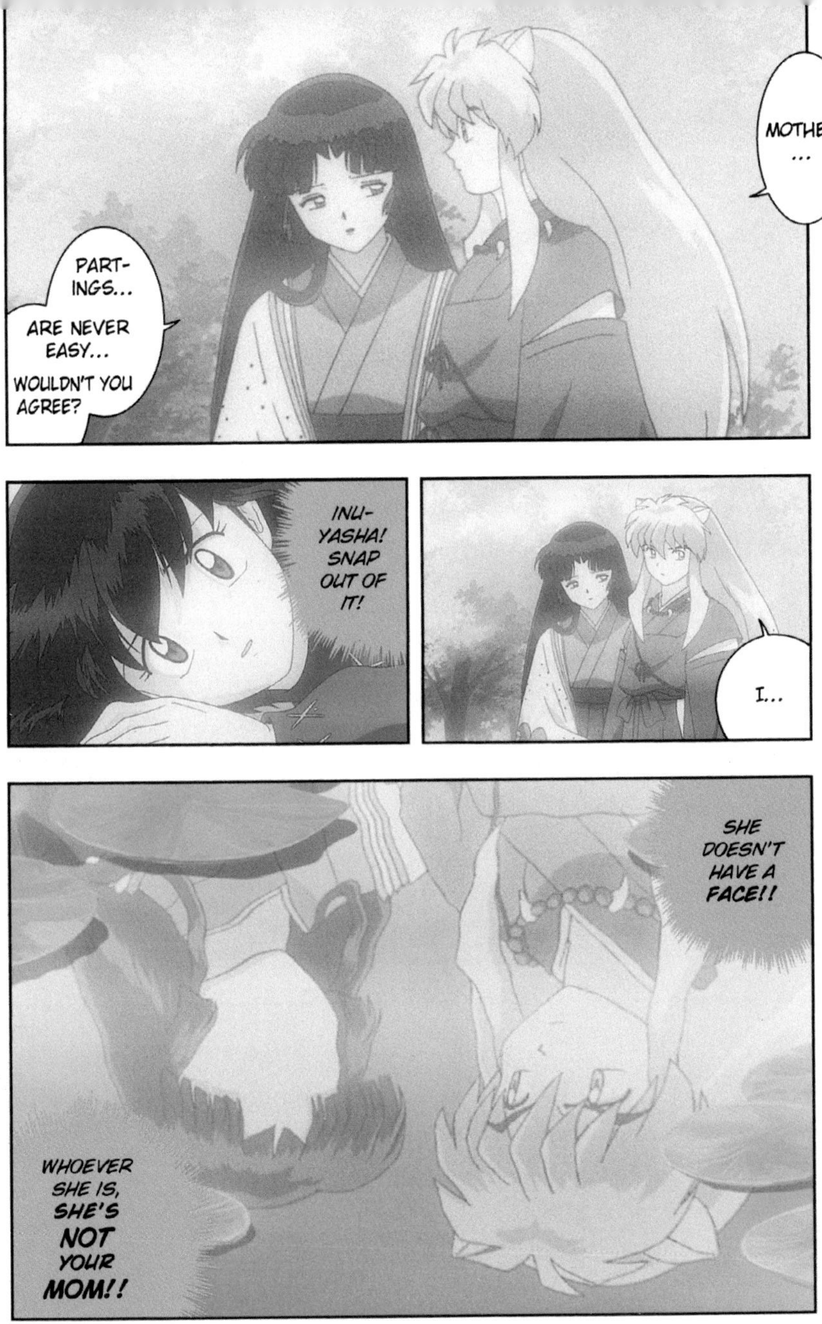
MOTHER ...
PART-INGS...
ARE NEVER EASY...
WOULDN'T YOU AGREE?
I...
INU-YASHA! SNAP OUT OF IT!
SHE DOESN'T HAVE A FACE!!
WHOEVER SHE IS, SHE'S NOT YOUR MOM!!

6
TETSUSAIGA THE PHANTOM SWORD

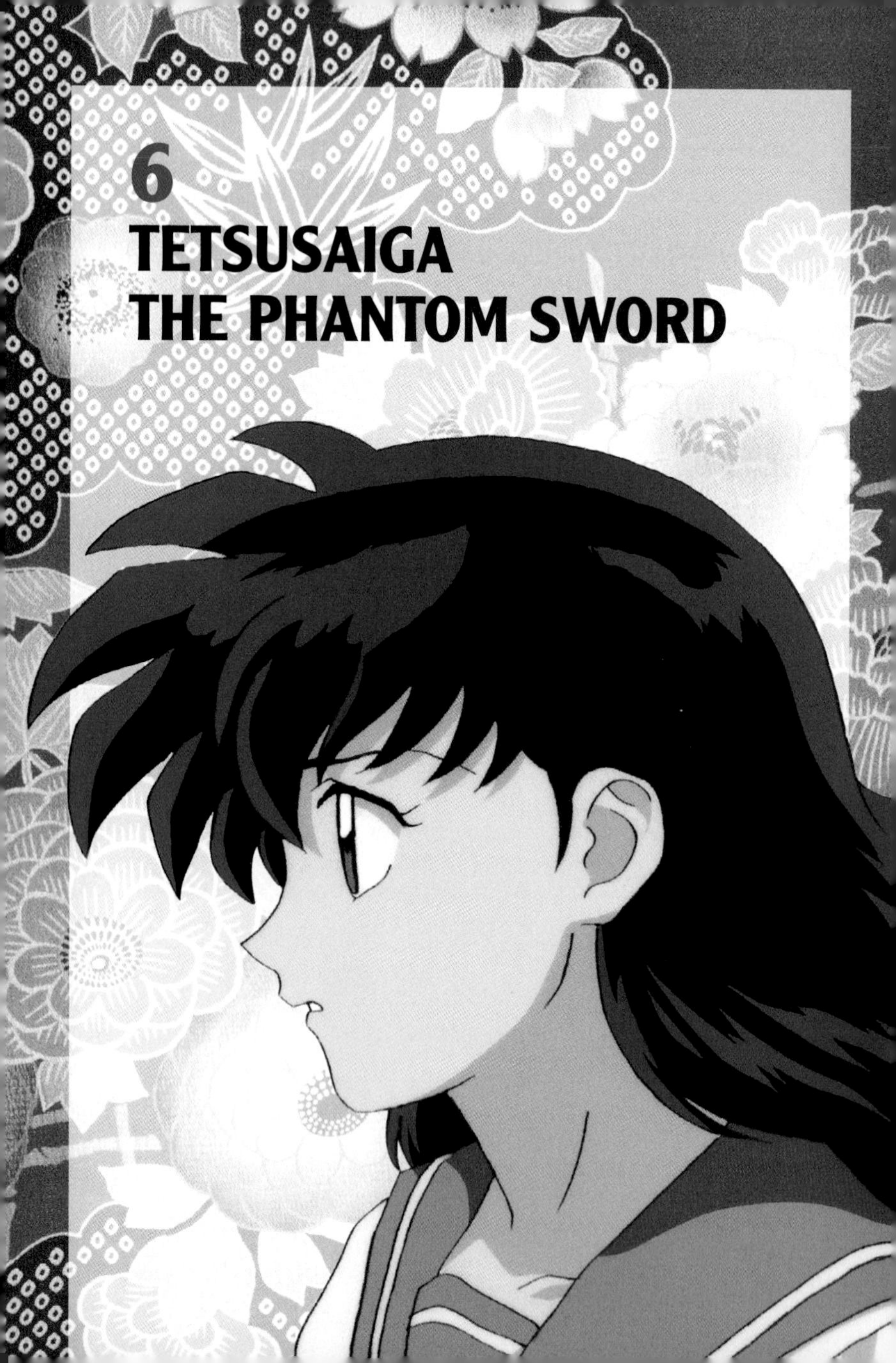

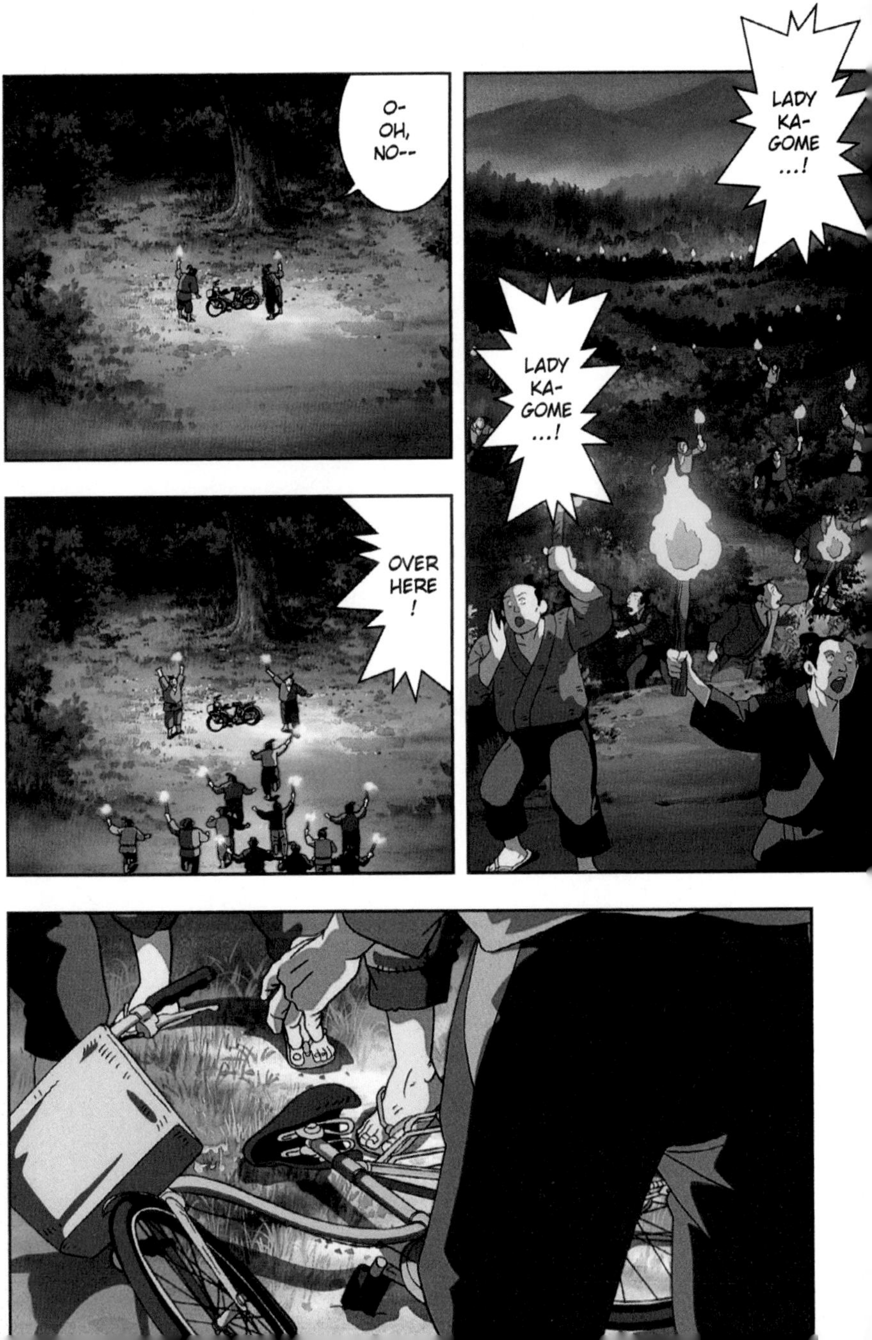
LADY KA-GOME ...!
LADY KA-GOME ...!
O-OH, NO--
OVER HERE !

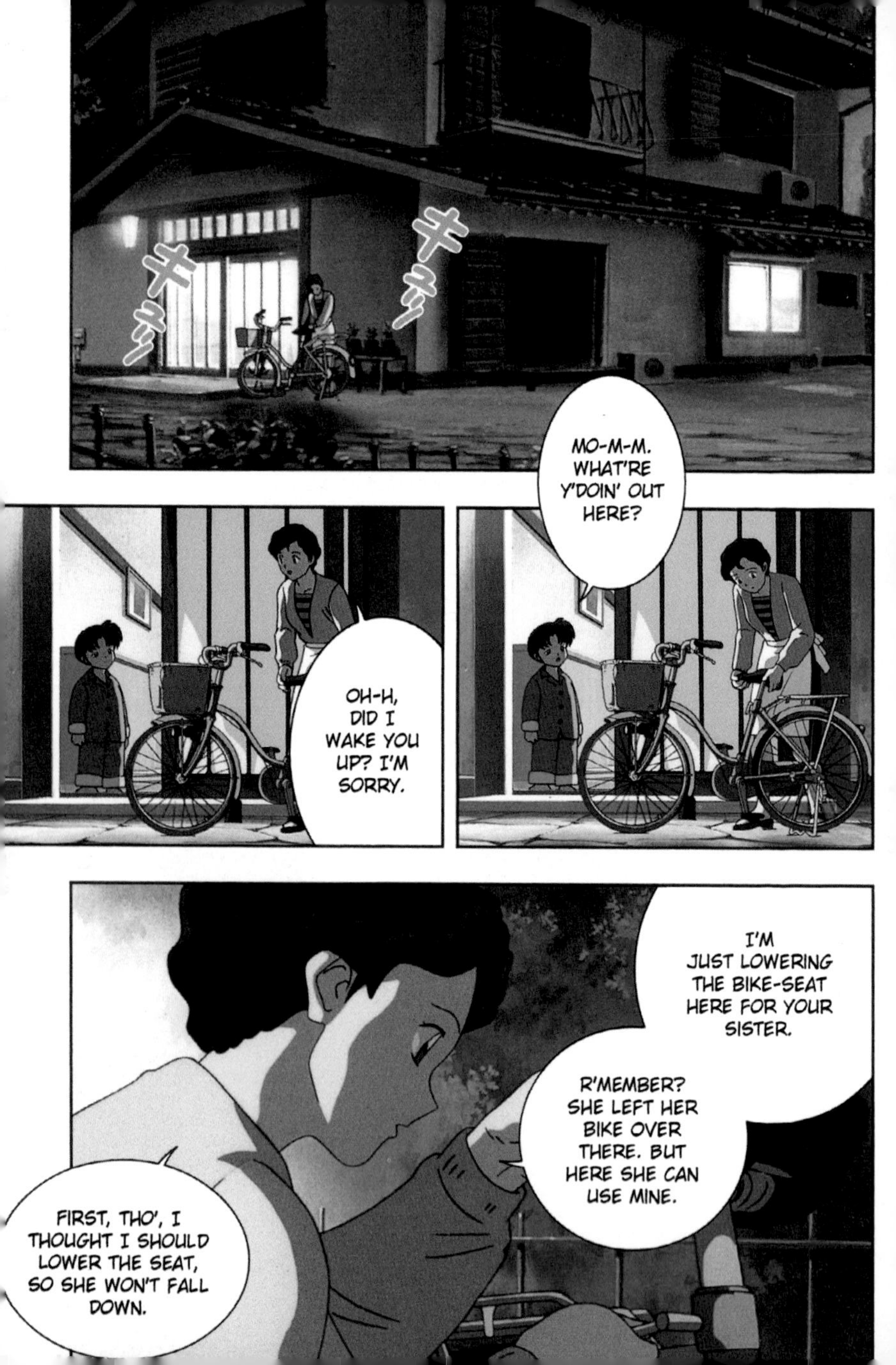
キュッ
キュッ
MO-M-M. WHAT'RE Y'DOIN' OUT HERE?
OH-H, DID I WAKE YOU UP? I'M SORRY.
I'M JUST LOWERING THE BIKE-SEAT HERE FOR YOUR SISTER.
R'MEMBER? SHE LEFT HER BIKE OVER THERE. BUT HERE SHE CAN USE MINE.
FIRST, THO', I THOUGHT I SHOULD LOWER THE SEAT, SO SHE WON'T FALL DOWN.

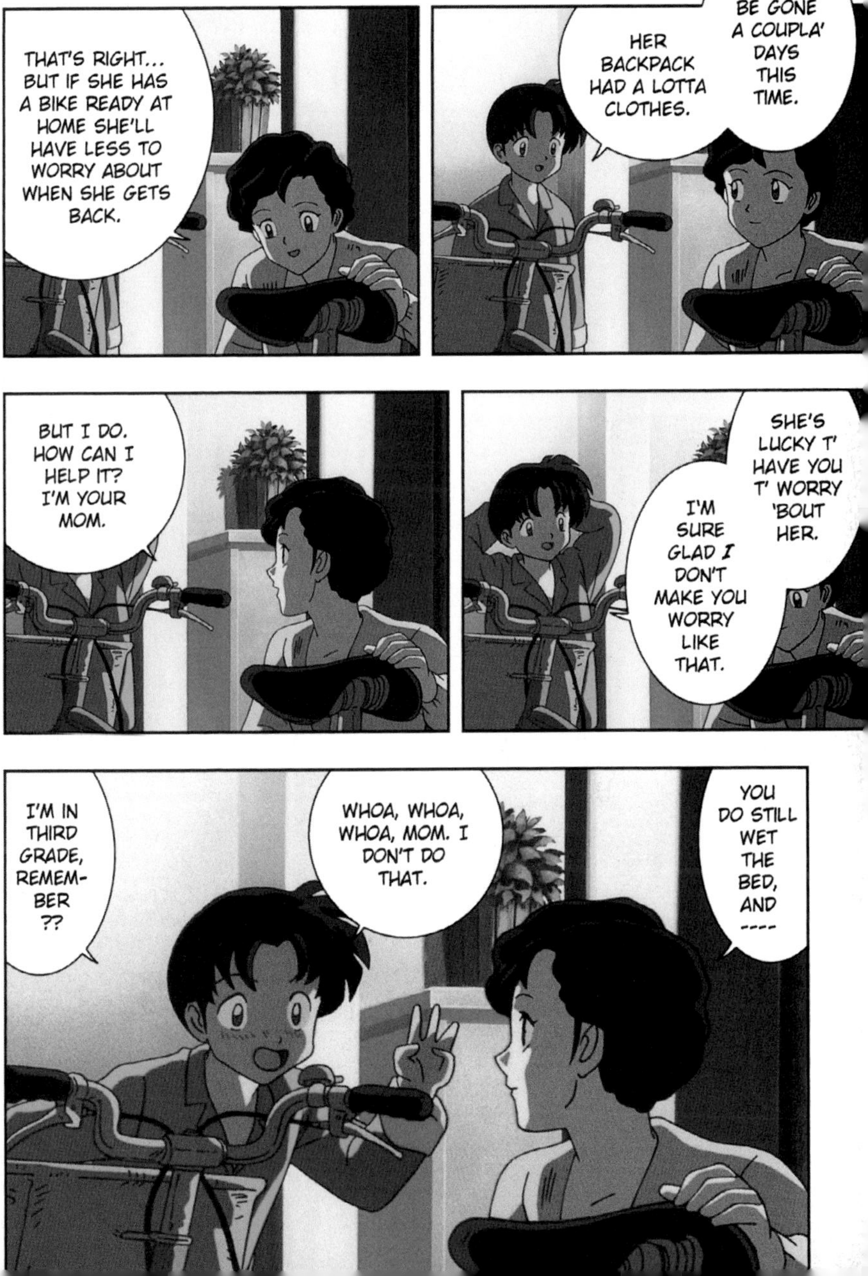
SHE'LL BE GONE A COUPLA' DAYS THIS TIME.
HER BACKPACK HAD A LOTTA CLOTHES.
THAT'S RIGHT... BUT IF SHE HAS A BIKE READY AT HOME SHE'LL HAVE LESS TO WORRY ABOUT WHEN SHE GETS BACK.
SHE'S LUCKY T' HAVE YOU T' WORRY 'BOUT HER.
I'M SURE GLAD *I* DON'T MAKE YOU WORRY LIKE THAT.
BUT I DO. HOW CAN I HELP IT? I'M YOUR MOM.
YOU DO STILL WET THE BED, AND ----
WHOA, WHOA, WHOA, MOM. I DON'T DO THAT.
I'M IN THIRD GRADE, REMEM-BER ??

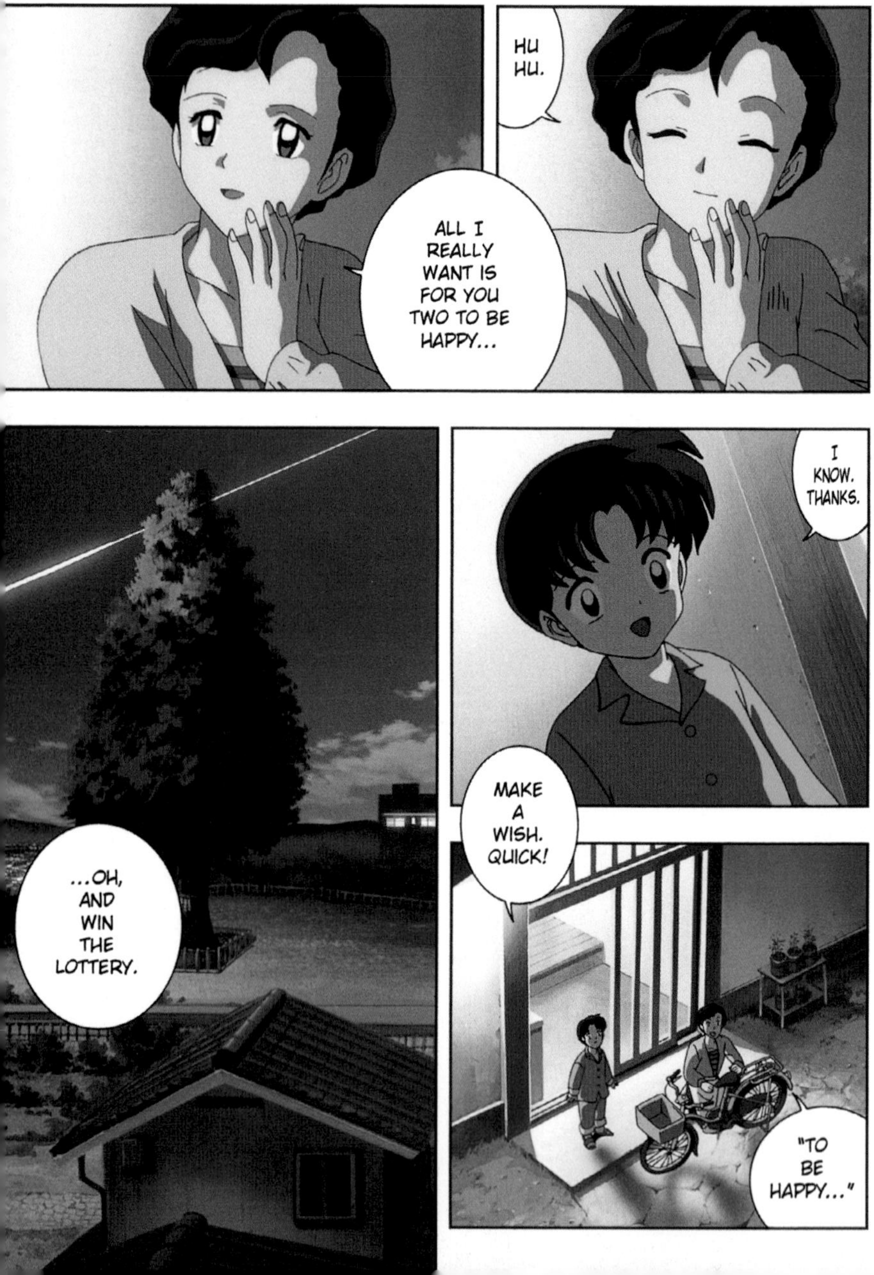
HU HU.
ALL I REALLY WANT IS FOR YOU TWO TO BE HAPPY...
I KNOW. THANKS.
MAKE A WISH. QUICK!
"TO BE HAPPY..."
...OH, AND WIN THE LOTTERY.

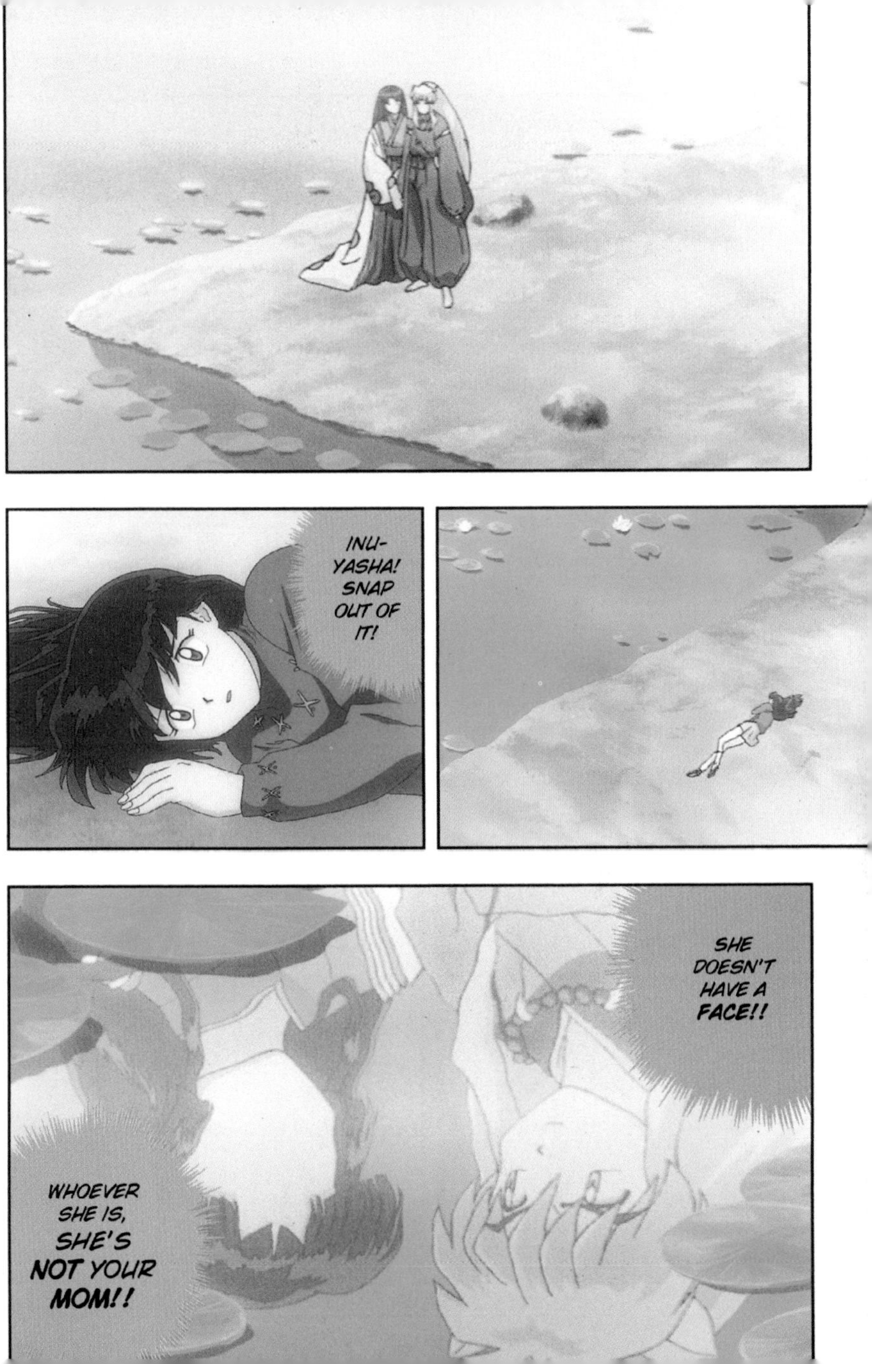
INU-YASHA! SNAP OUT OF IT!
SHE DOESN'T HAVE A FACE!!
WHOEVER SHE IS, SHE'S NOT YOUR MOM!!

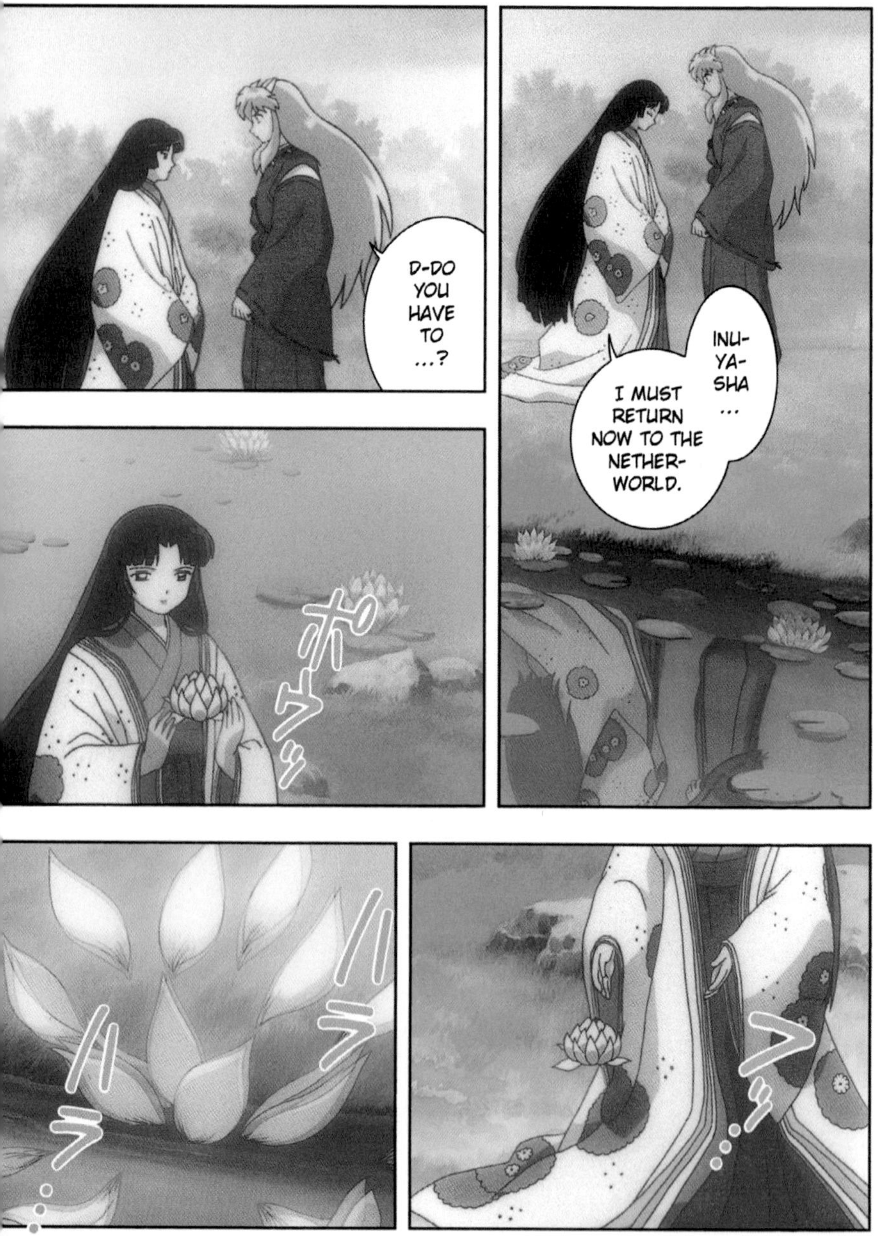
INU-YASHA...
I MUST RETURN NOW TO THE NETHER-WORLD.
D-DO YOU HAVE TO ...?
ポワッ
フッ...
ハラハラ...

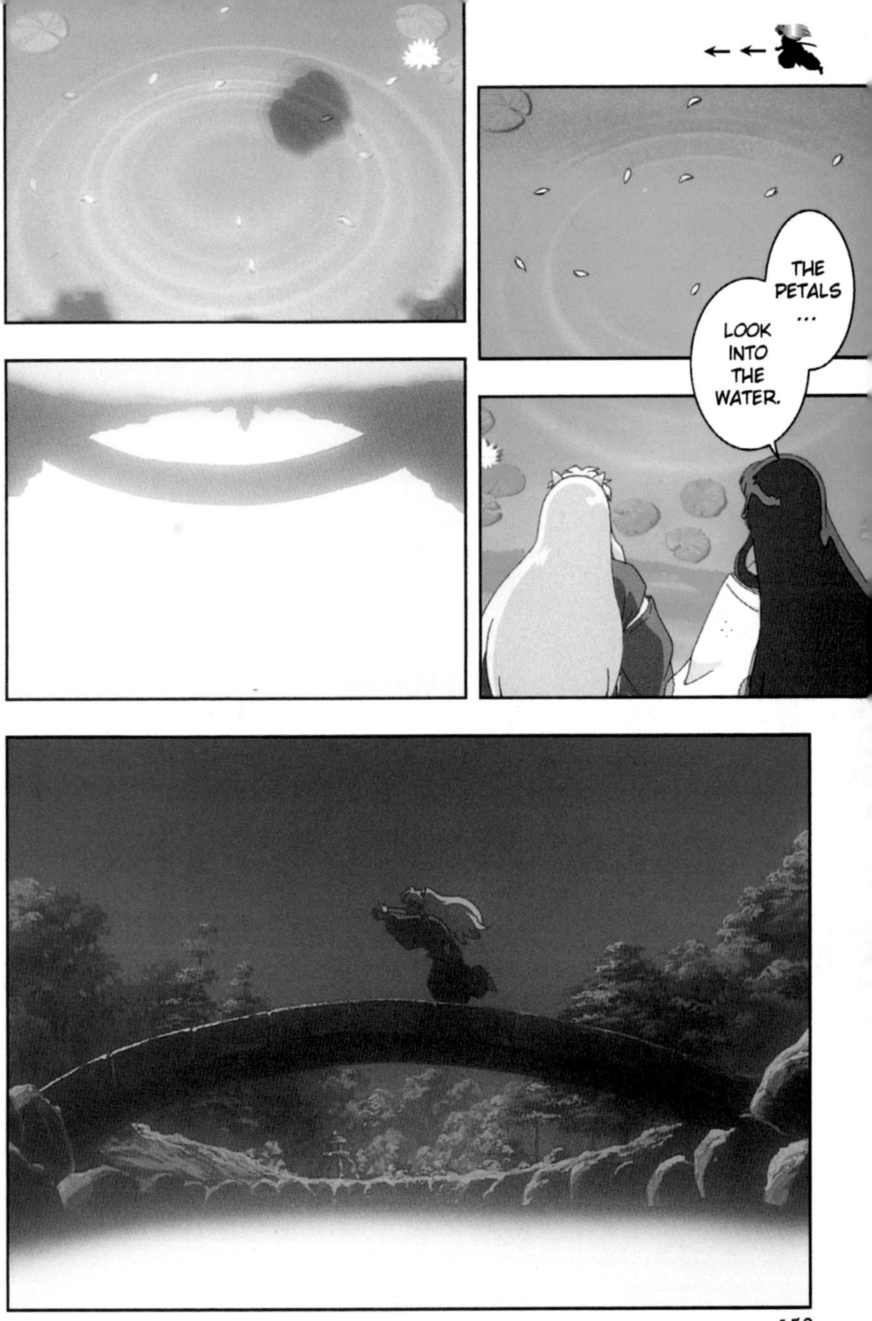
THE PETALS ...
LOOK INTO THE WATER.

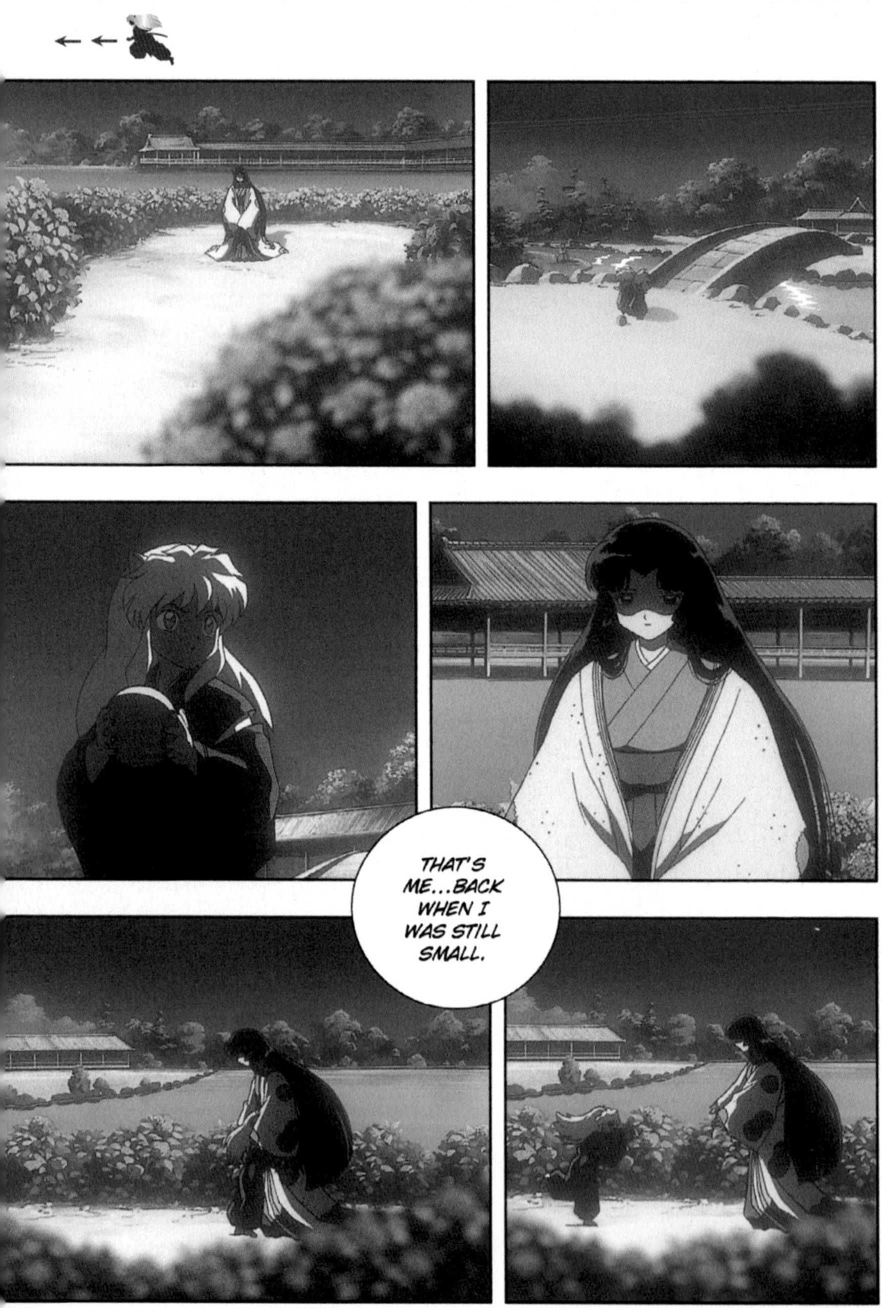
THAT'S ME...BACK WHEN I WAS STILL SMALL.

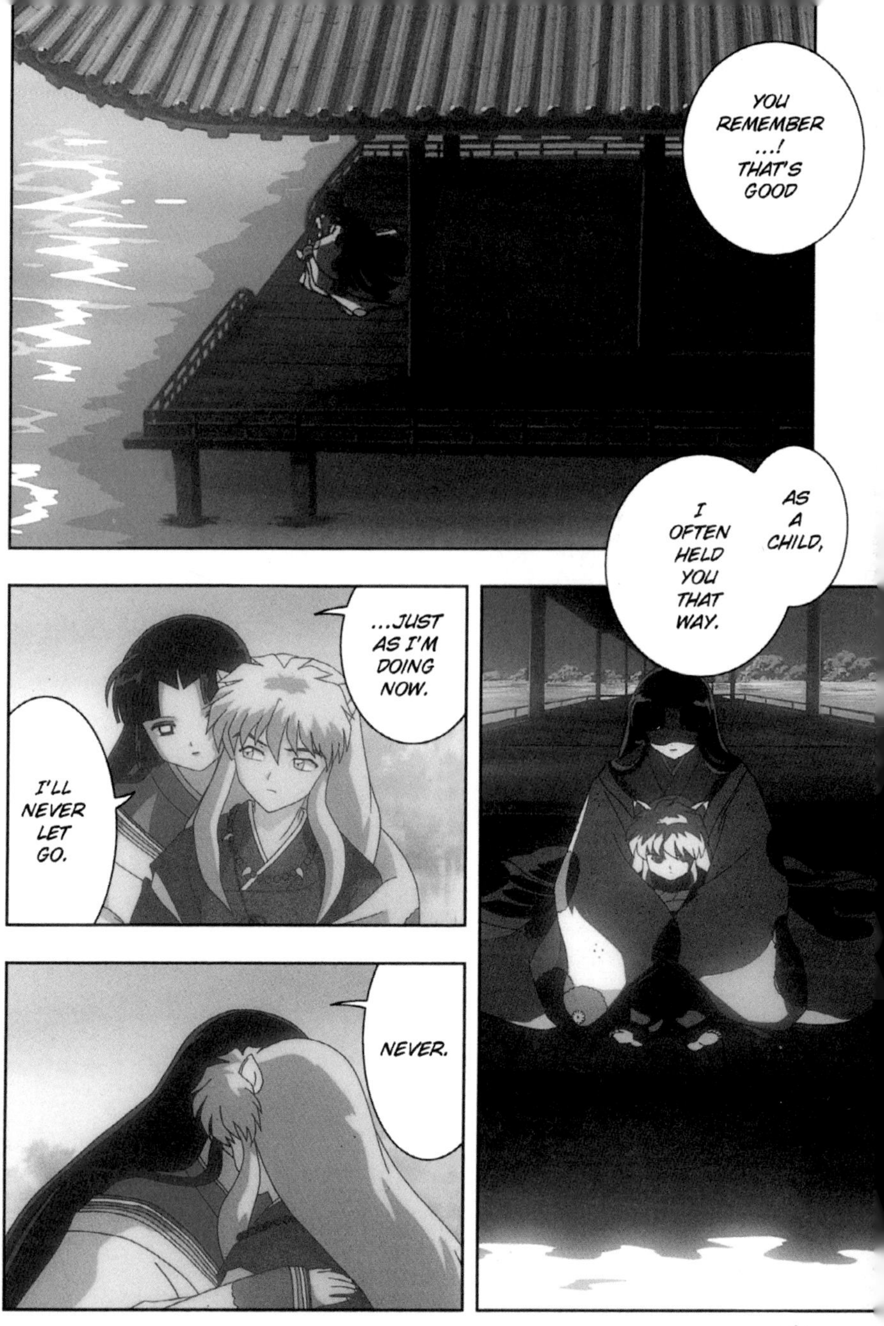
YOU REMEMBER ...! THAT'S GOOD
AS A CHILD, I OFTEN HELD YOU THAT WAY.
...JUST AS I'M DOING NOW.
I'LL NEVER LET GO.
NEVER.

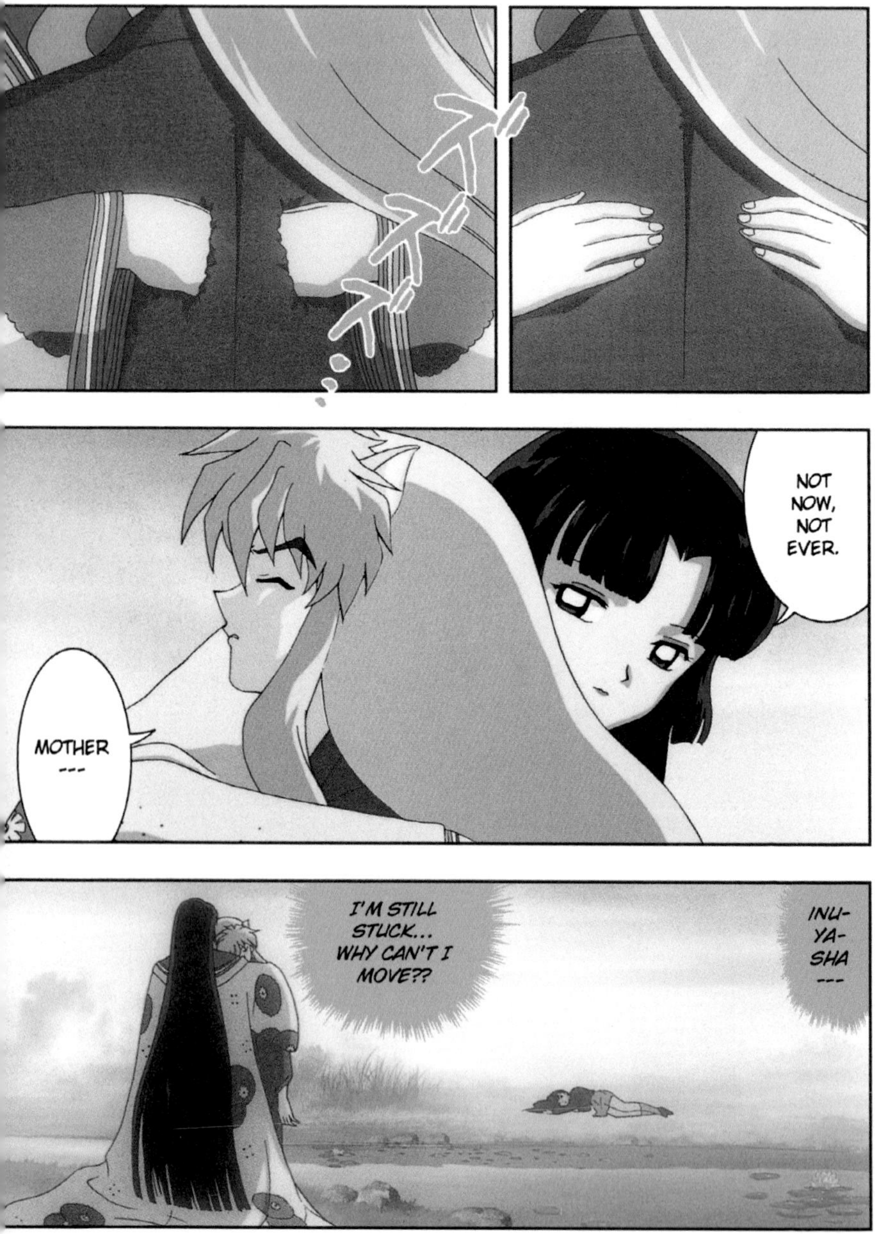
ズズズ…
NOT NOW, NOT EVER.
MOTHER ---
INU-YA-SHA ---
I'M STILL STUCK... WHY CAN'T I MOVE??

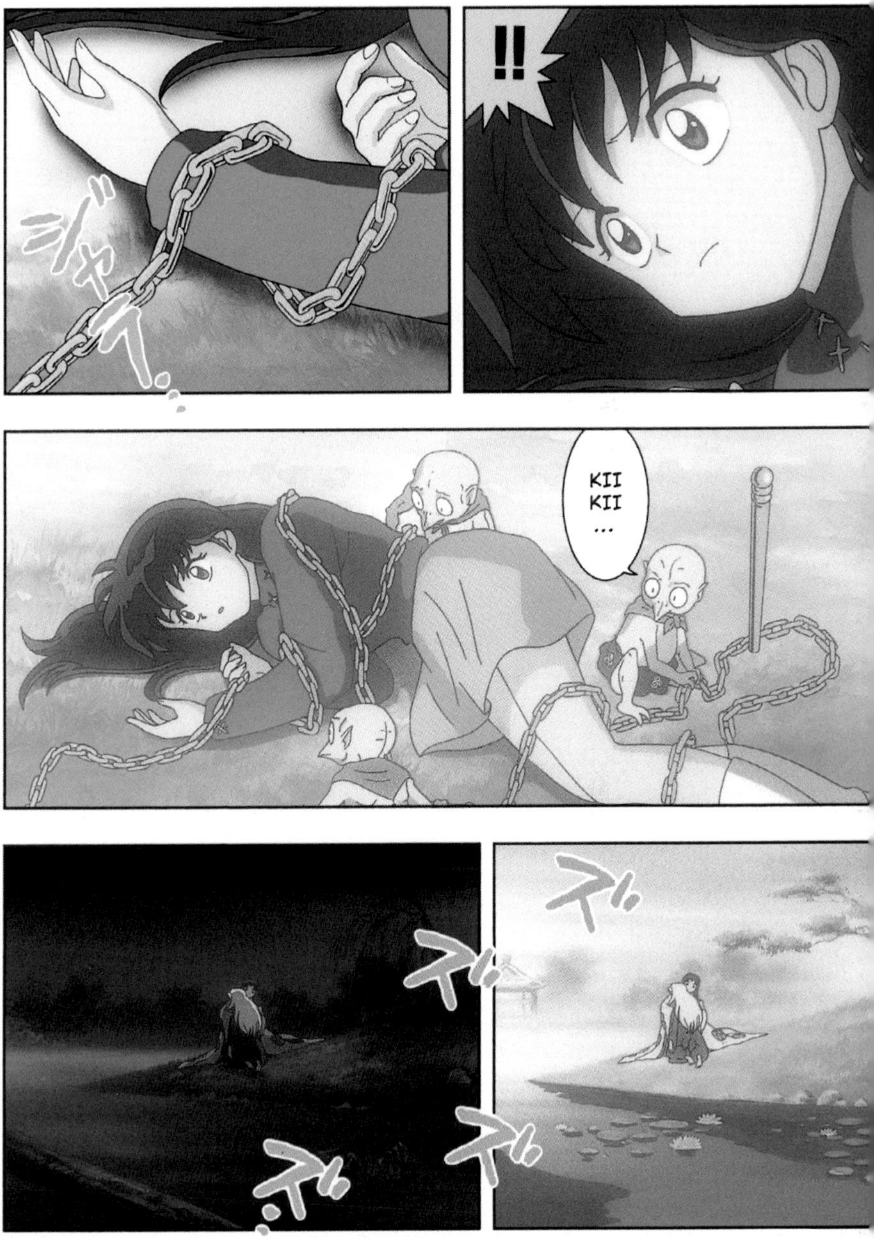
!!
ジャラ…
KII KII ...
ズズズズ…

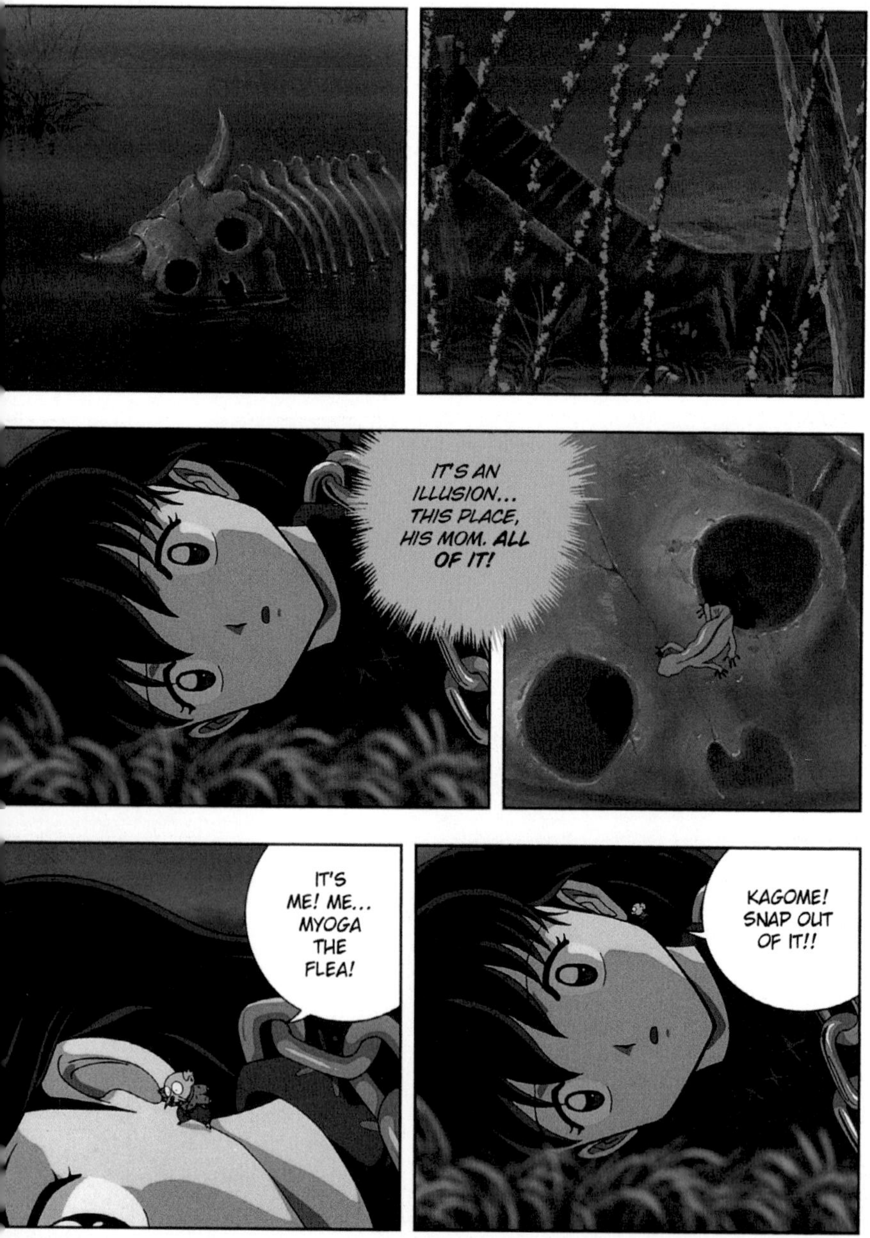
IT'S AN ILLUSION... THIS PLACE, HIS MOM. ALL OF IT!
KAGOME! SNAP OUT OF IT!!
IT'S ME! ME... MYOGA THE FLEA!

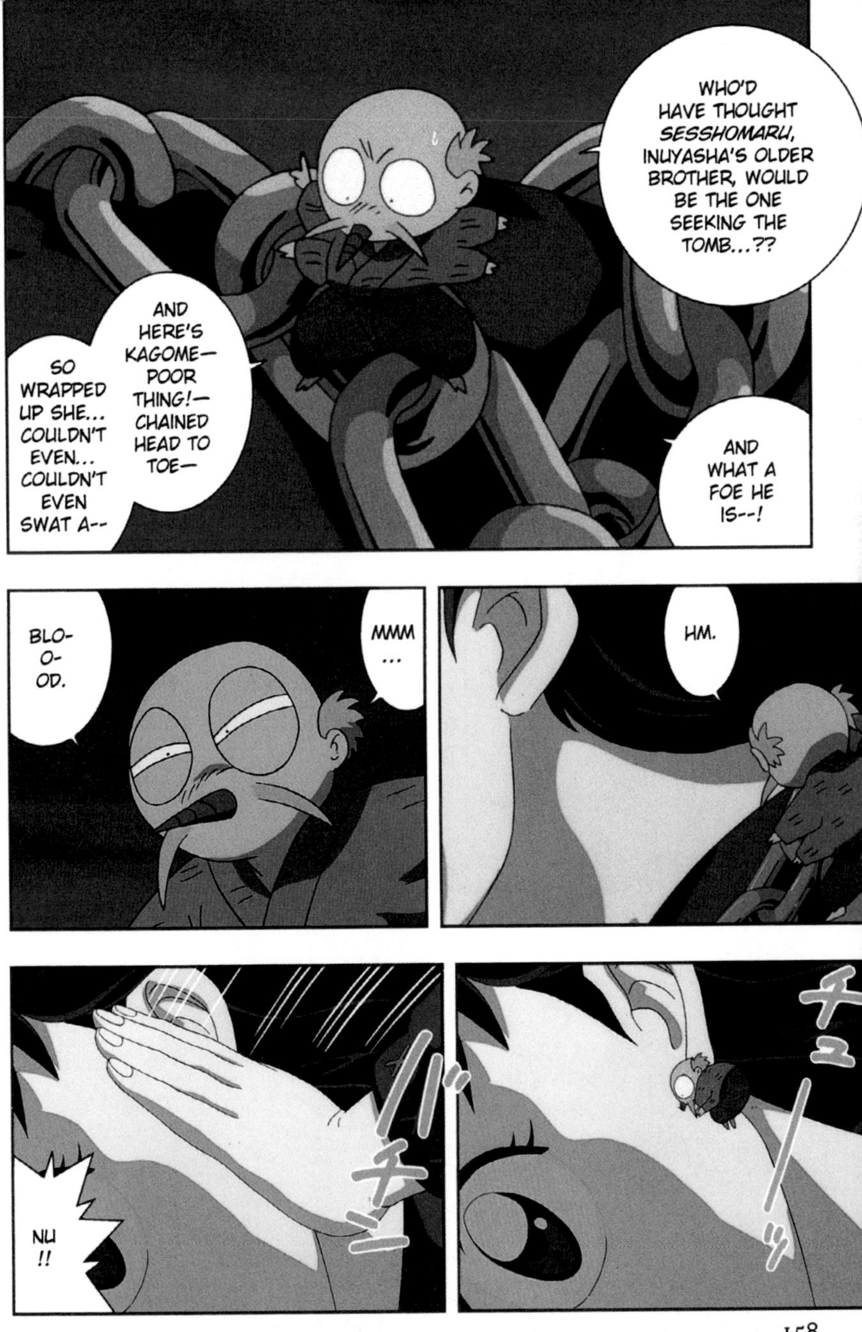
WHO'D HAVE THOUGHT *SESSHOMARU*, INUYASHA'S OLDER BROTHER, WOULD BE THE ONE SEEKING THE TOMB...??
AND WHAT A FOE HE IS--!
AND HERE'S KAGOME— POOR THING!— CHAINED HEAD TO TOE—
SO WRAPPED UP SHE... COULDN'T EVEN... COULDN'T EVEN SWAT A--
HM.
MMM ...
BLO-O-OD.
チュー ッ
NU !!

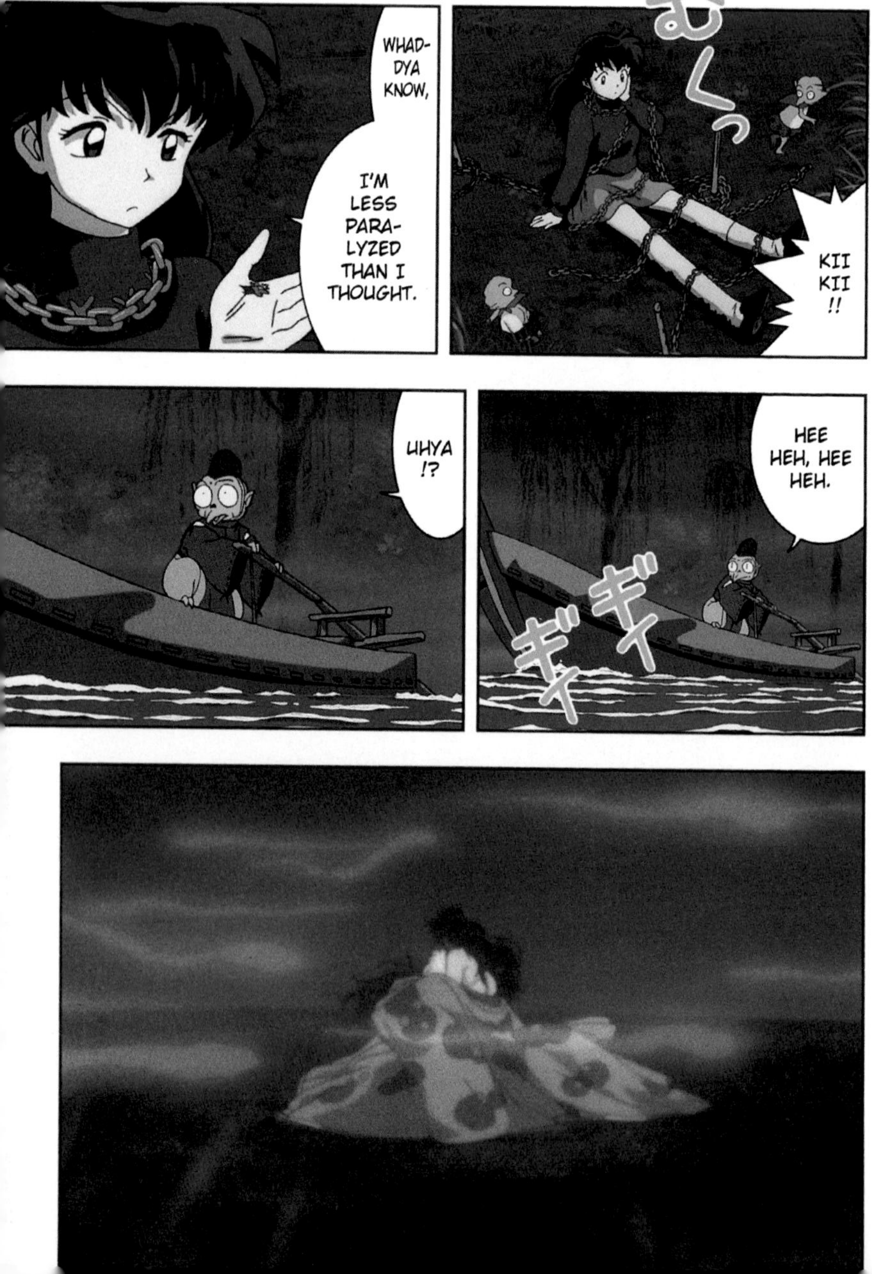

むくっ
KII KII !!
WHAD-DYA KNOW,
I'M LESS PARALYZED THAN I THOUGHT.
HEE HEH, HEE HEH.
ギィ
ギィ
UHYA !?

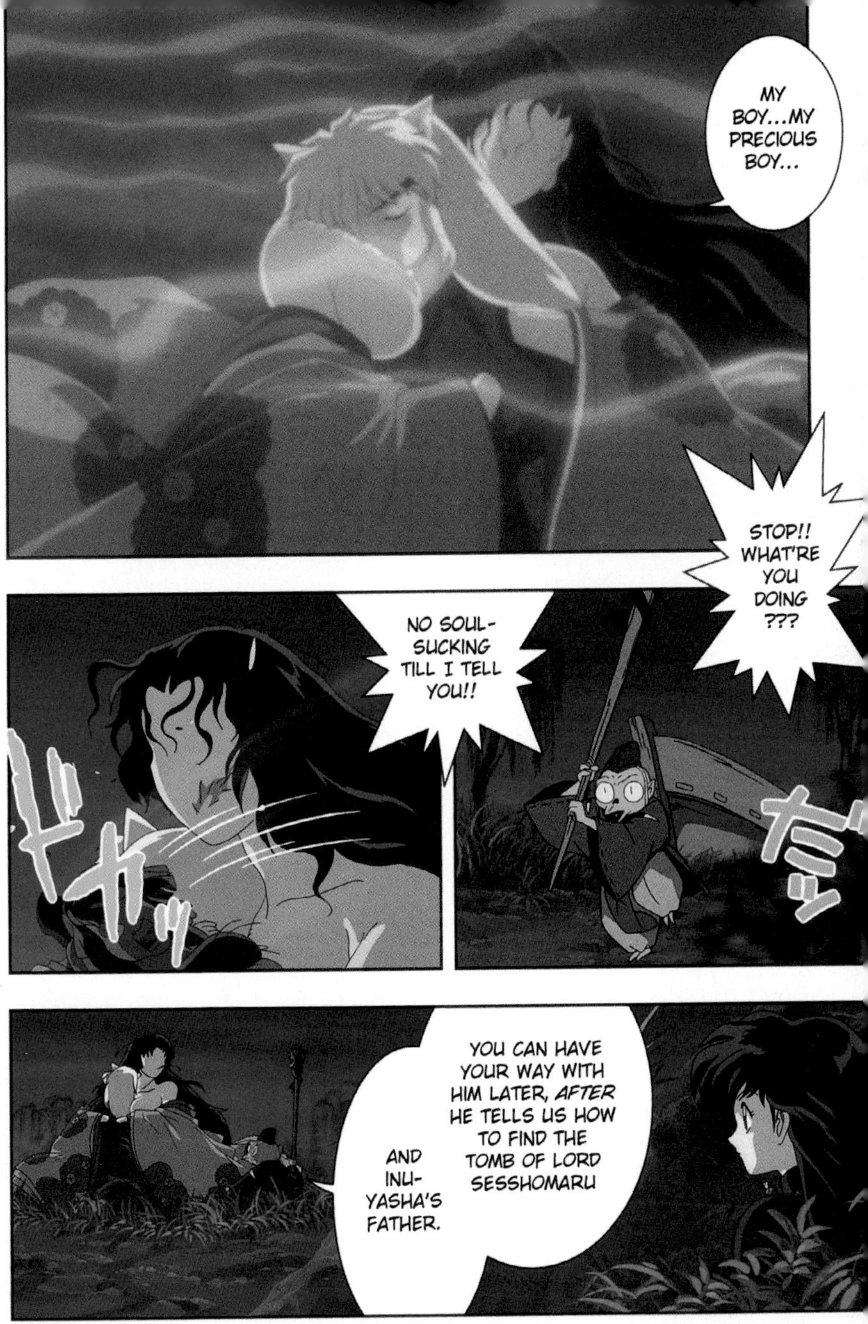
MY BOY...MY PRECIOUS BOY...
STOP!! WHAT'RE YOU DOING???
ダッ
NO SOUL-SUCKING TILL I TELL YOU!!
ドガッ
YOU CAN HAVE YOUR WAY WITH HIM LATER, *AFTER* HE TELLS US HOW TO FIND THE TOMB OF LORD SESSHOMARU
AND INU-YASHA'S FATHER.

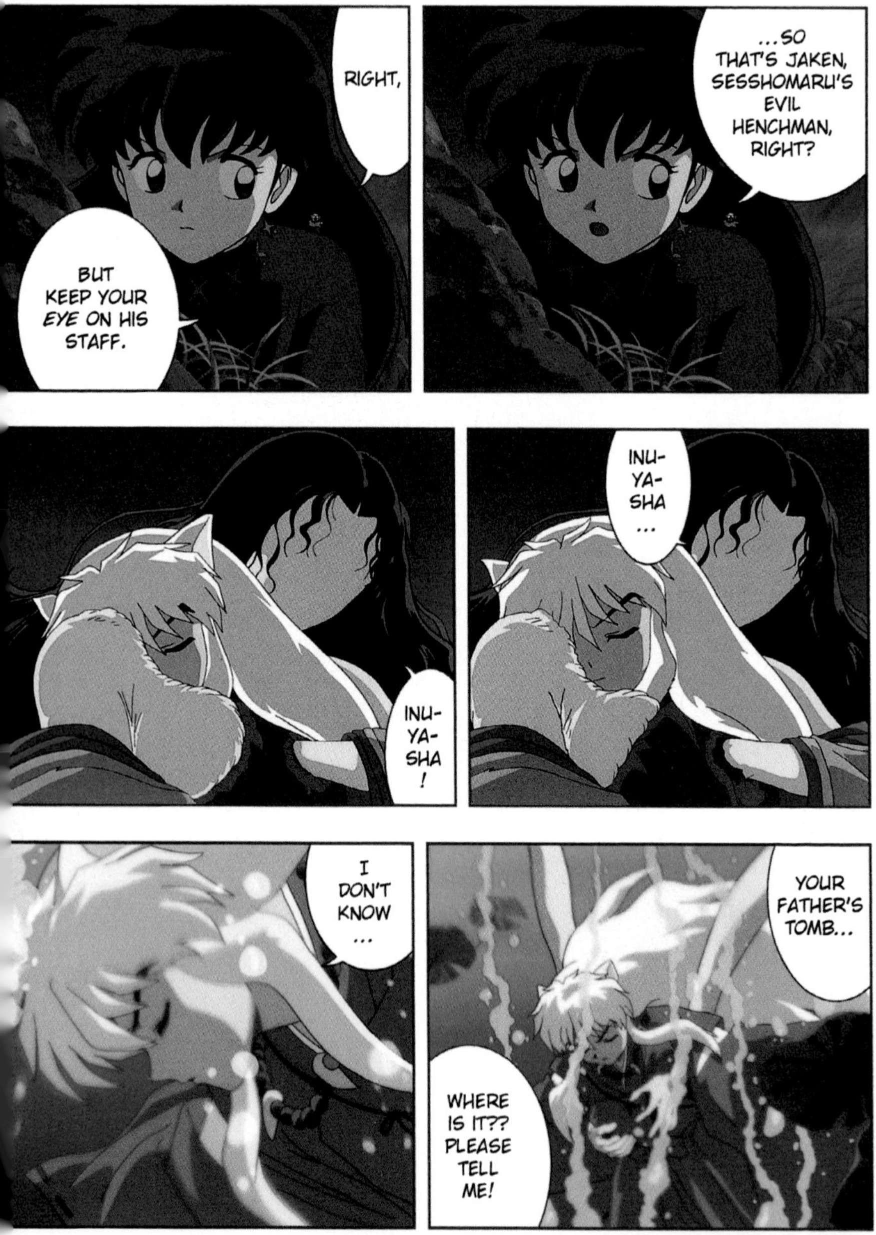
...SO THAT'S JAKEN, SESSHOMARU'S EVIL HENCHMAN, RIGHT?
RIGHT,
BUT KEEP YOUR *EYE* ON HIS STAFF.
INU-YA-SHA...
INU-YA-SHA!
YOUR FATHER'S TOMB...
WHERE IS IT?? PLEASE TELL ME!
I DON'T KNOW...

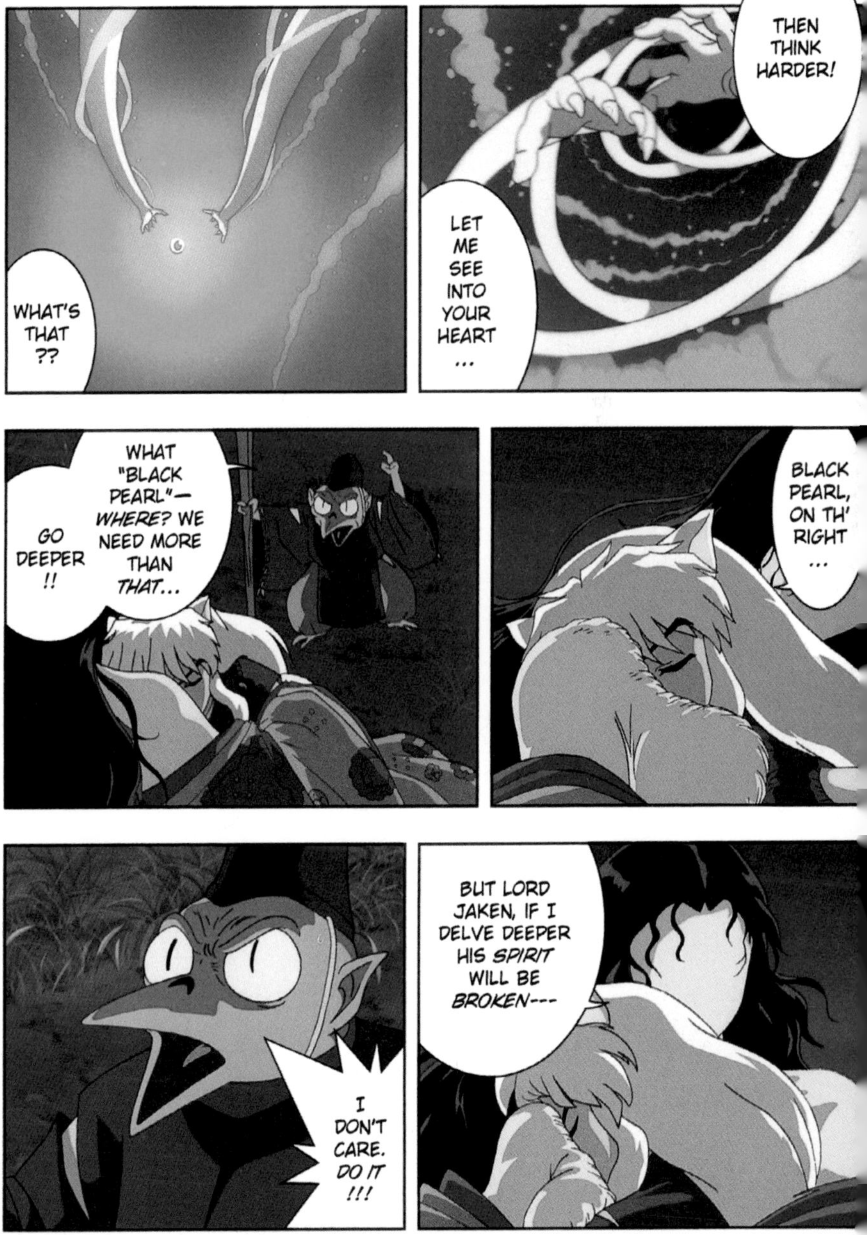
THEN THINK HARDER!
LET ME SEE INTO YOUR HEART ...
WHAT'S THAT ??
BLACK PEARL, ON TH' RIGHT ...
WHAT "BLACK PEARL"—*WHERE?* WE NEED MORE THAN *THAT*...
GO DEEPER !!
BUT LORD JAKEN, IF I DELVE DEEPER HIS *SPIRIT* WILL BE *BROKEN*---
I DON'T CARE. *DO IT* !!!

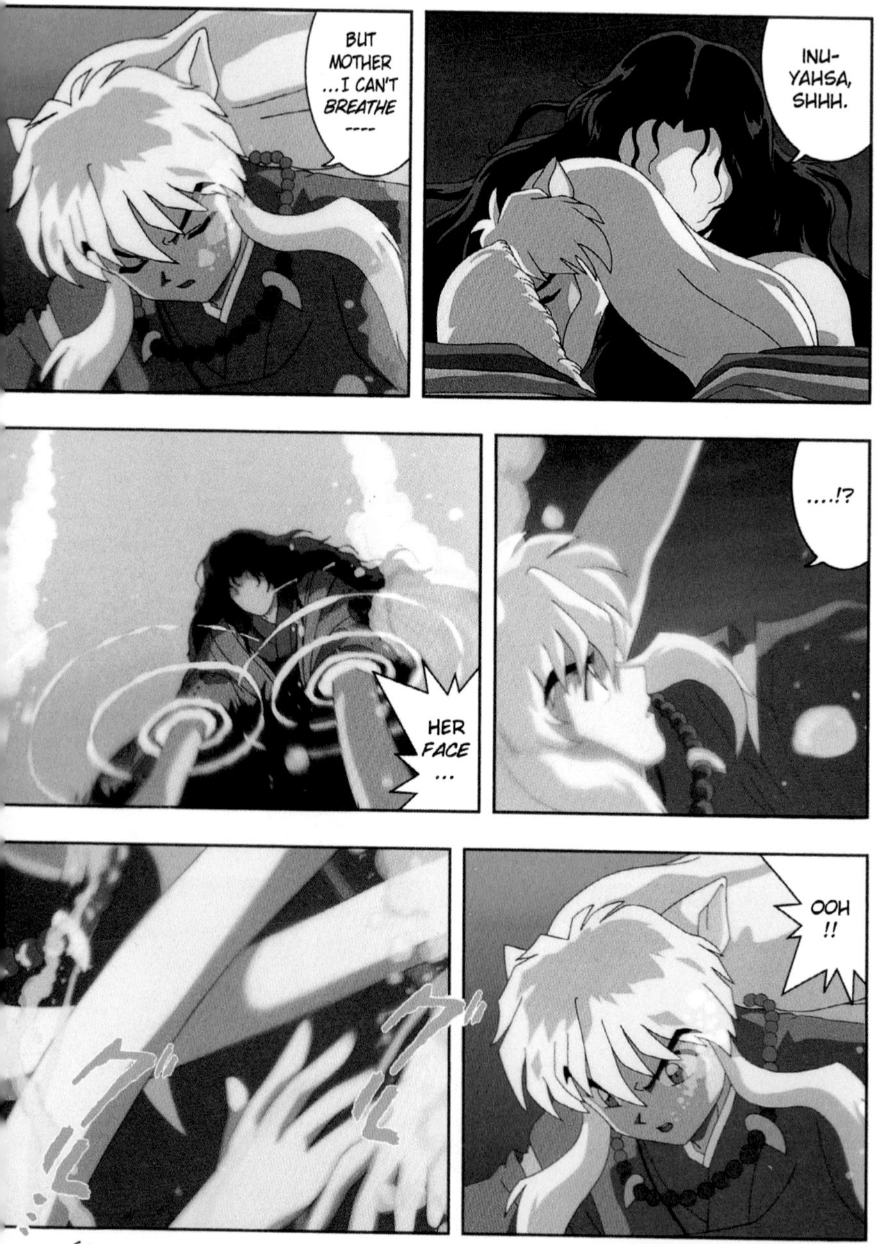
INU-YAHSA, SHHH.
BUT MOTHER ...I CAN'T BREATHE ----
....!?
HER FACE ...
OOH !!

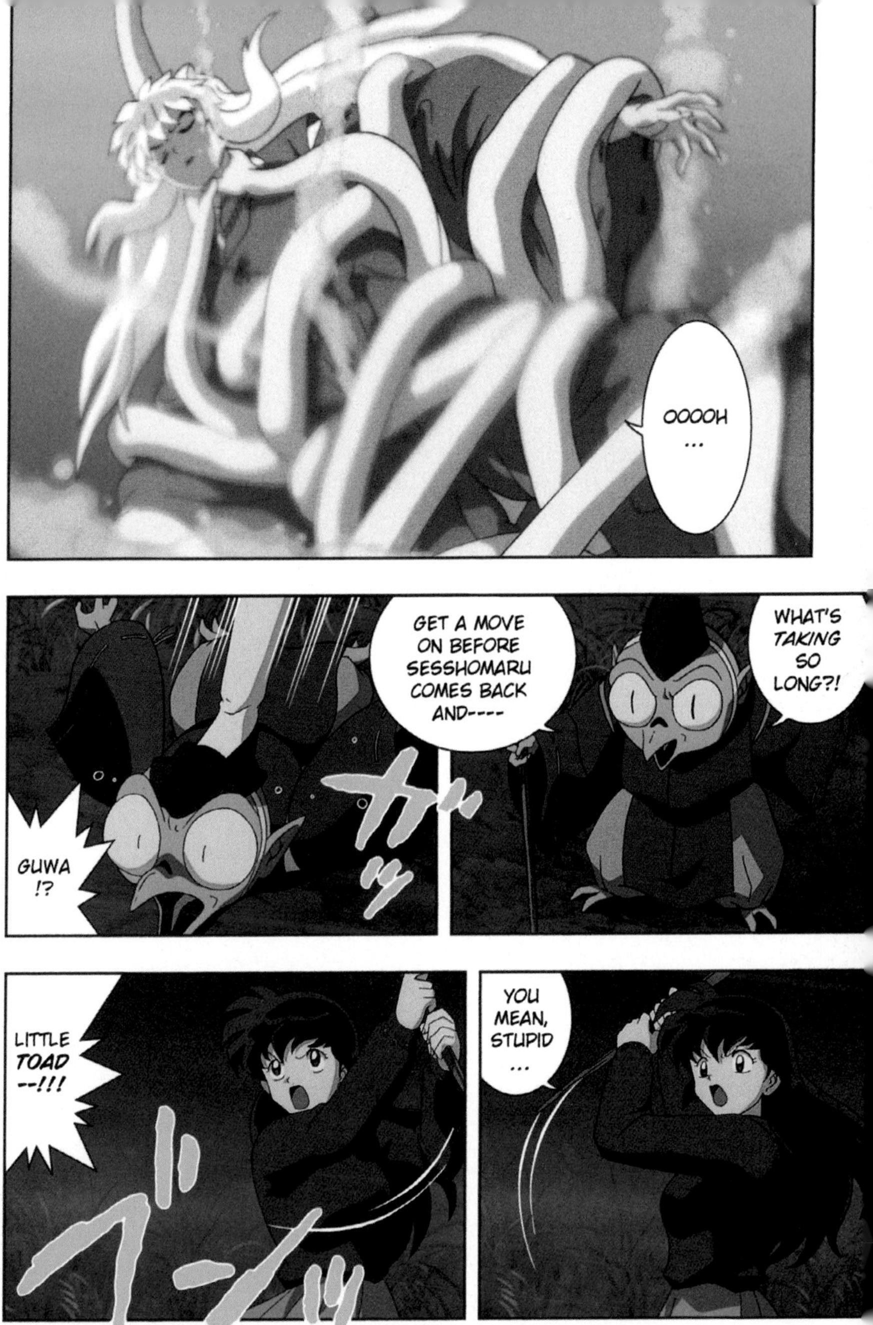
OOOOH ...
WHAT'S TAKING SO LONG?!
GET A MOVE ON BEFORE SESSHOMARU COMES BACK AND----
ガッ
GUWA !?
YOU MEAN, STUPID ...
LITTLE TOAD --!!!
ブーンッ

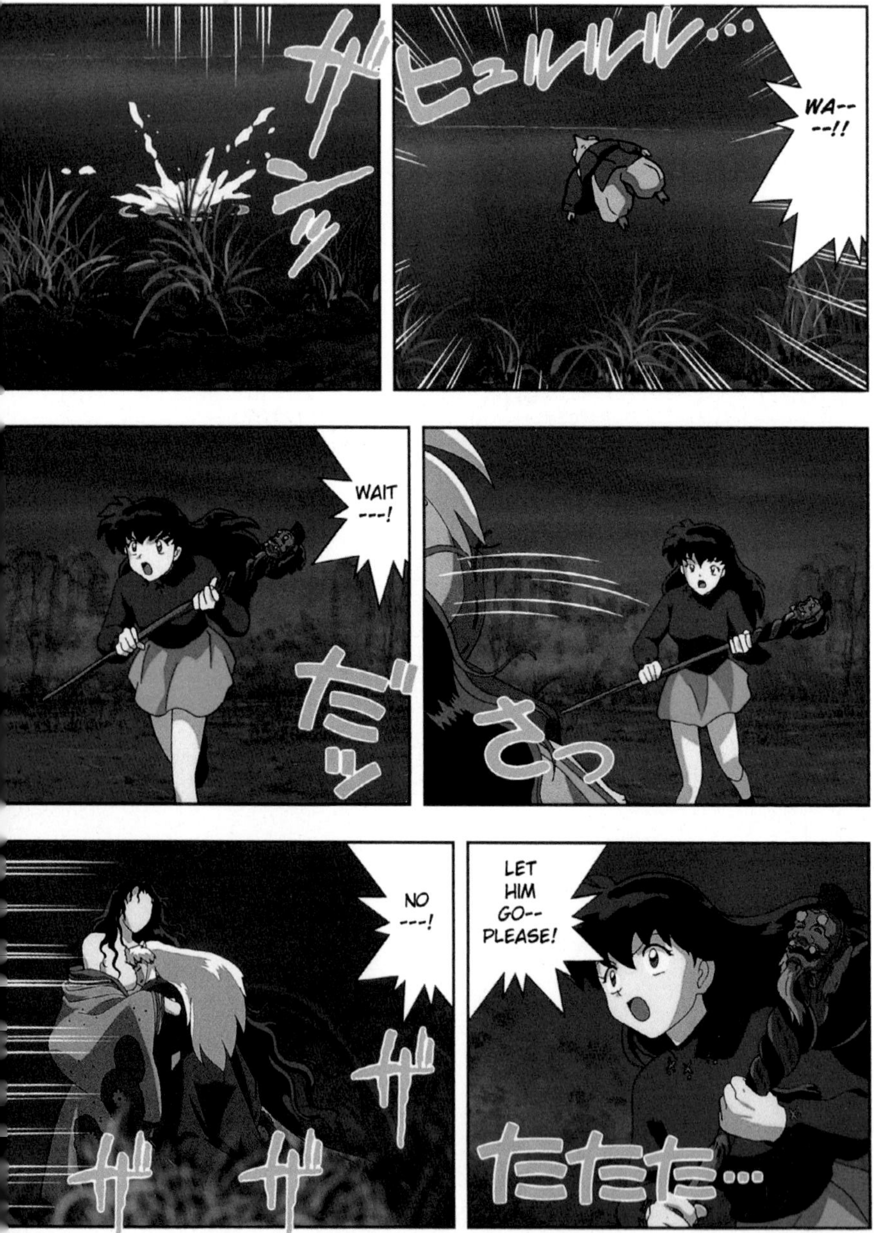
ヒュルルル…
WA----!!
ザシッ
さっ
WAIT---!
だッ
LET HIM GO-- PLEASE!
たたた…
NO---!
ザ
ザ
ザ

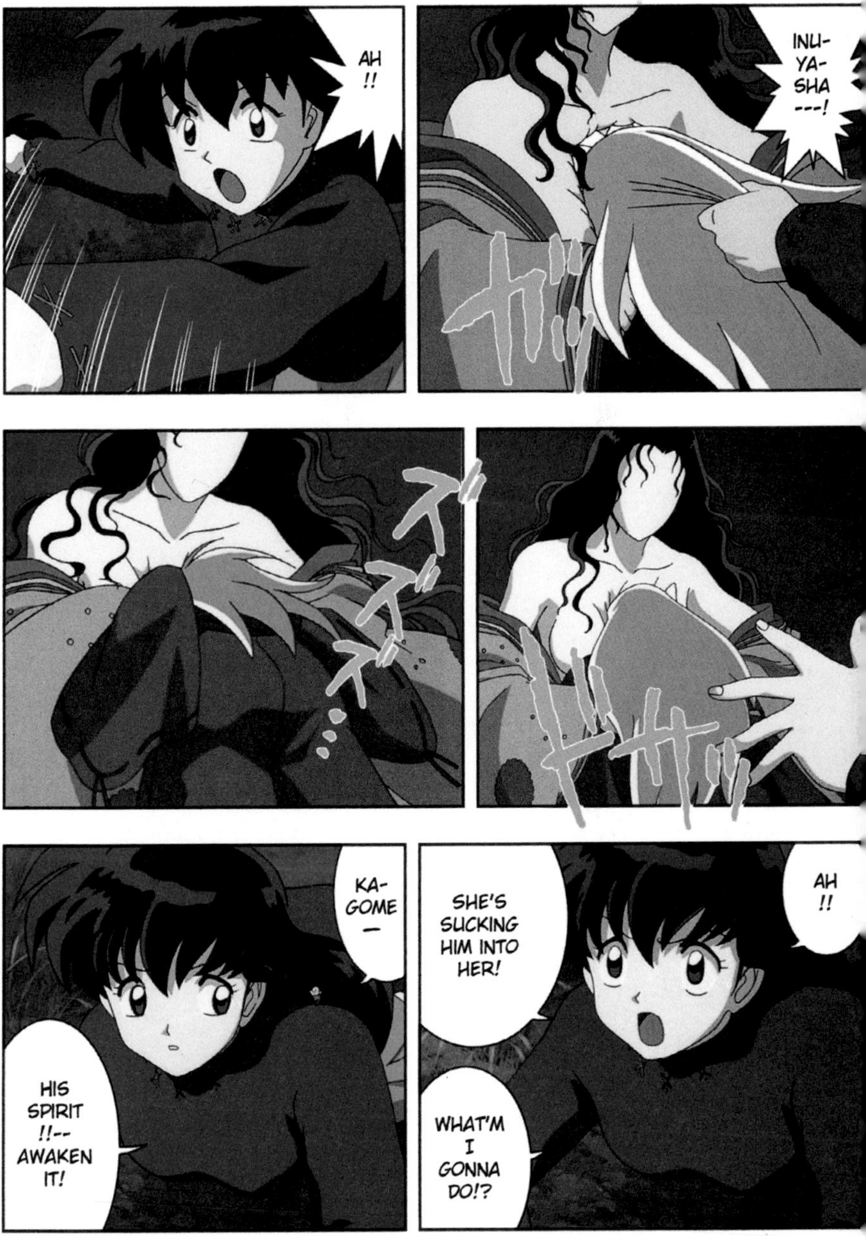
INU-YA-SHA---!
AH !!
AH !!
SHE'S SUCKING HIM INTO HER!
WHAT'M I GONNA DO!?
KA-GOME —
HIS SPIRIT !!-- AWAKEN IT!

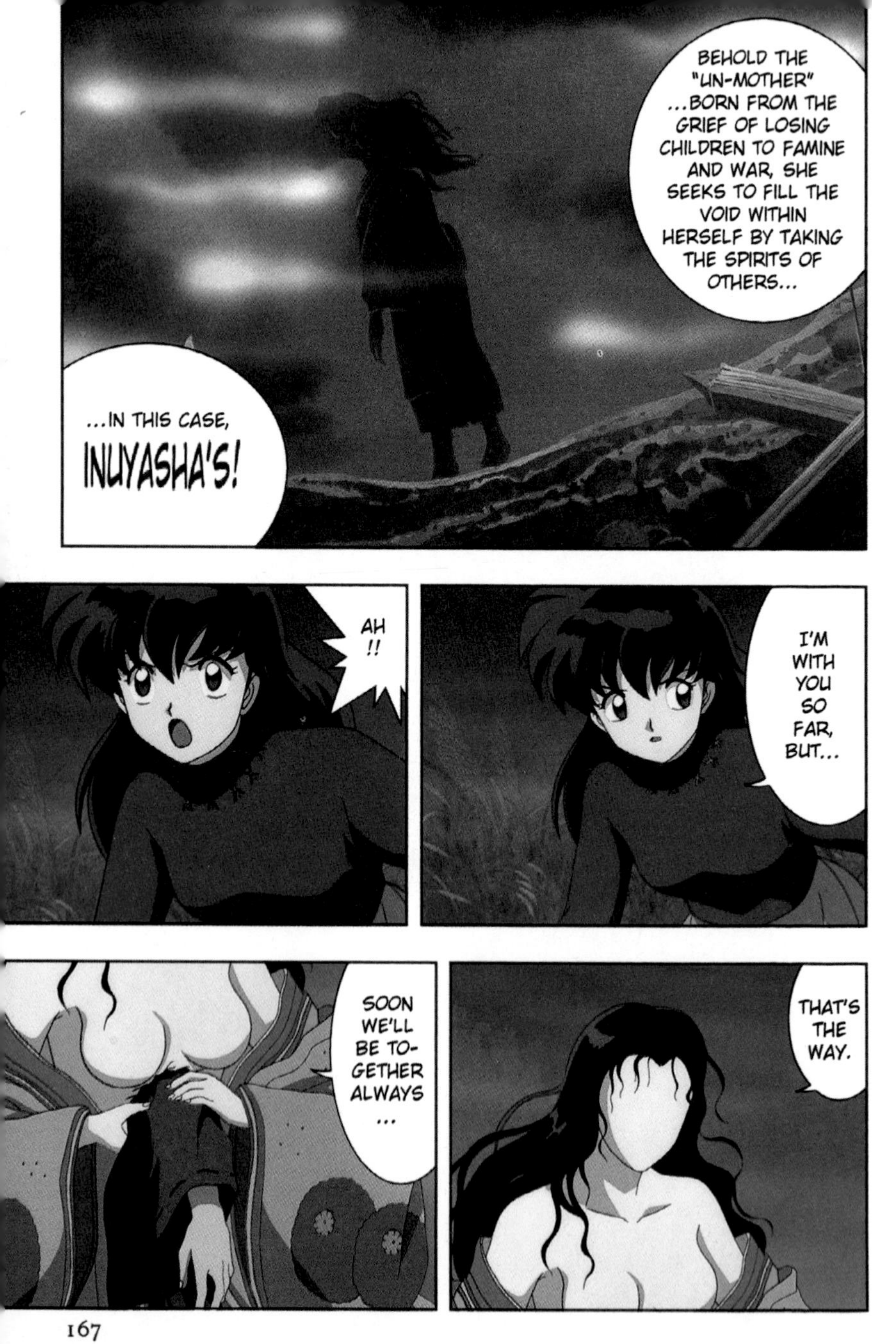
BEHOLD THE "UN-MOTHER" ...BORN FROM THE GRIEF OF LOSING CHILDREN TO FAMINE AND WAR, SHE SEEKS TO FILL THE VOID WITHIN HERSELF BY TAKING THE SPIRITS OF OTHERS...
...IN THIS CASE, INUYASHA'S!
I'M WITH YOU SO FAR, BUT...
AH !!
THAT'S THE WAY.
SOON WE'LL BE TO-GETHER ALWAYS ...

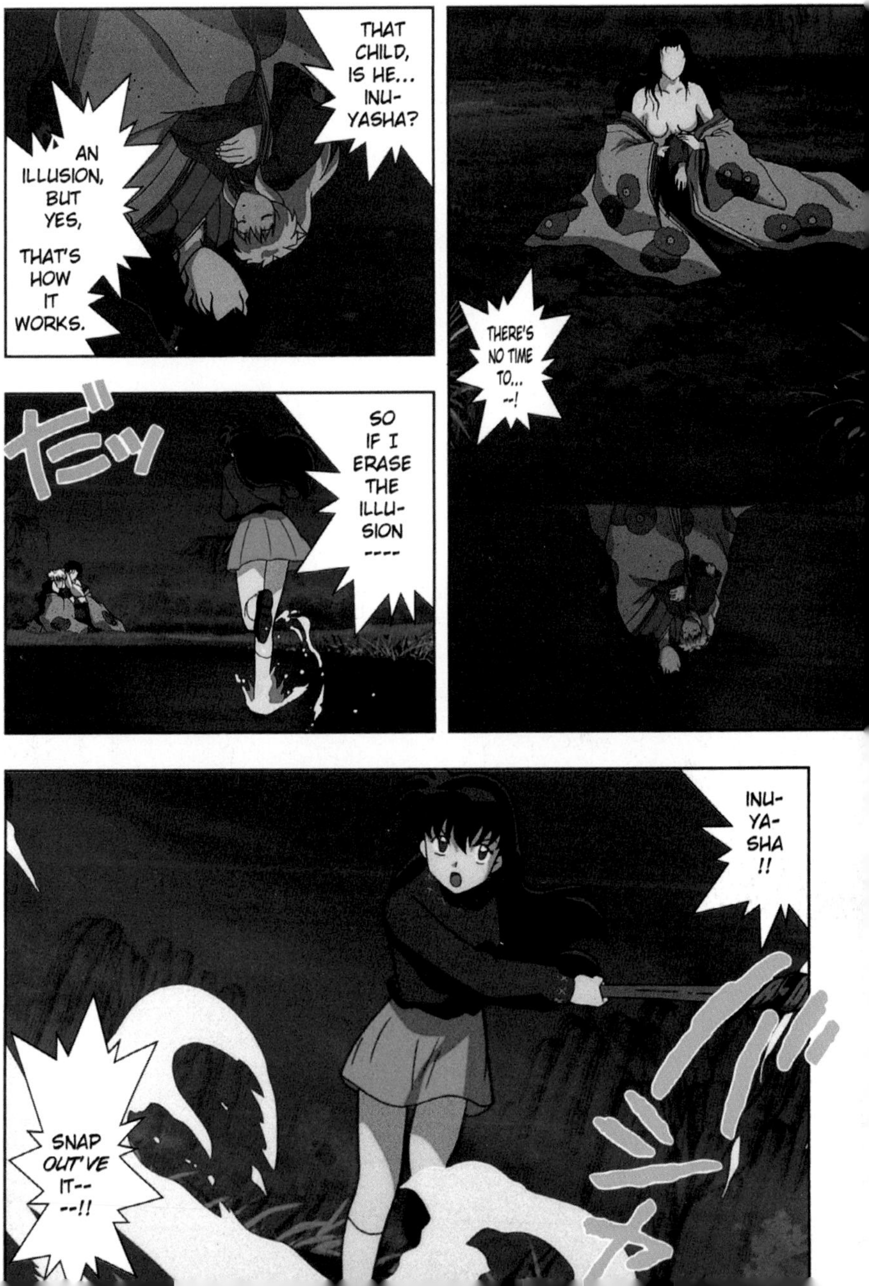
THERE'S NO TIME TO... --!
THAT CHILD, IS HE... INU-YASHA?
AN ILLUSION, BUT YES, THAT'S HOW IT WORKS.
SO IF I ERASE THE ILLUSION ----
INU-YASHA!!
SNAP OUT'VE IT-- --!!

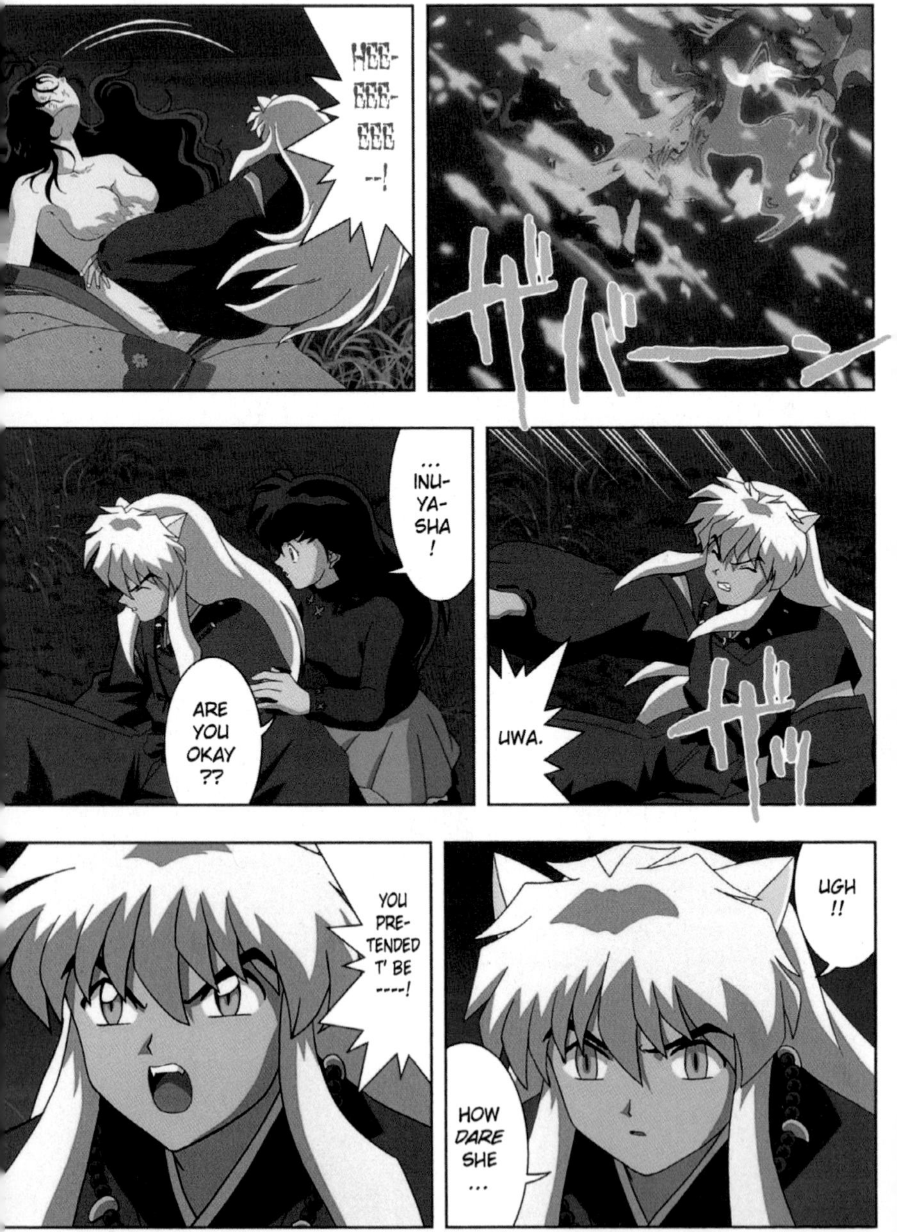
ザバーン
HEE-EEE-EEE--!
ザッ
UWA.
...INU-YA-SHA!
ARE YOU OKAY??
UGH!!
HOW DARE SHE...
YOU PRE-TENDED T' BE ----!

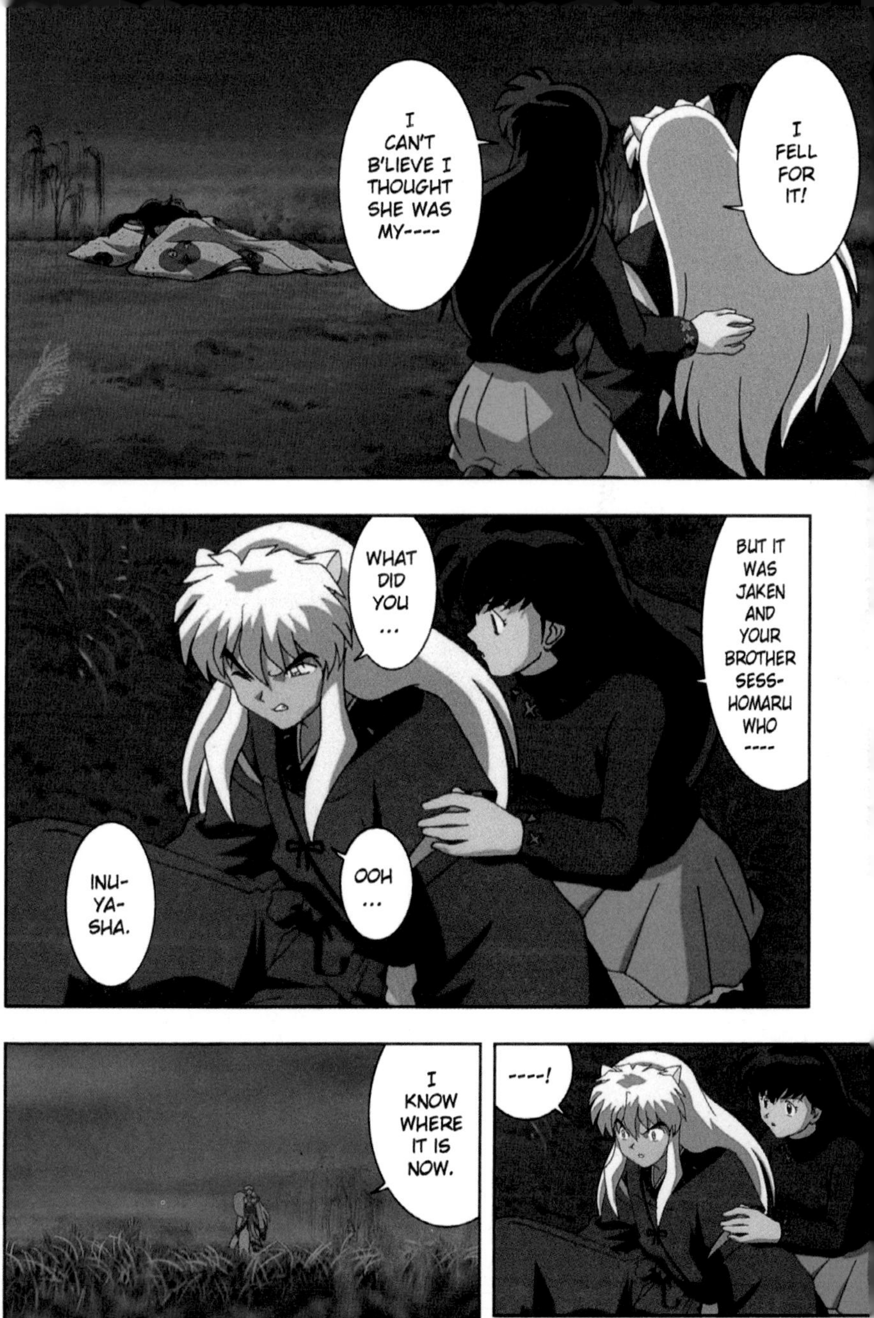
I FELL FOR IT!
I CAN'T B'LIEVE I THOUGHT SHE WAS MY----
BUT IT WAS JAKEN AND YOUR BROTHER SESS-HOMARU WHO ----
WHAT DID YOU ...
OOH ...
INU-YA-SHA.
----!
I KNOW WHERE IT IS NOW.

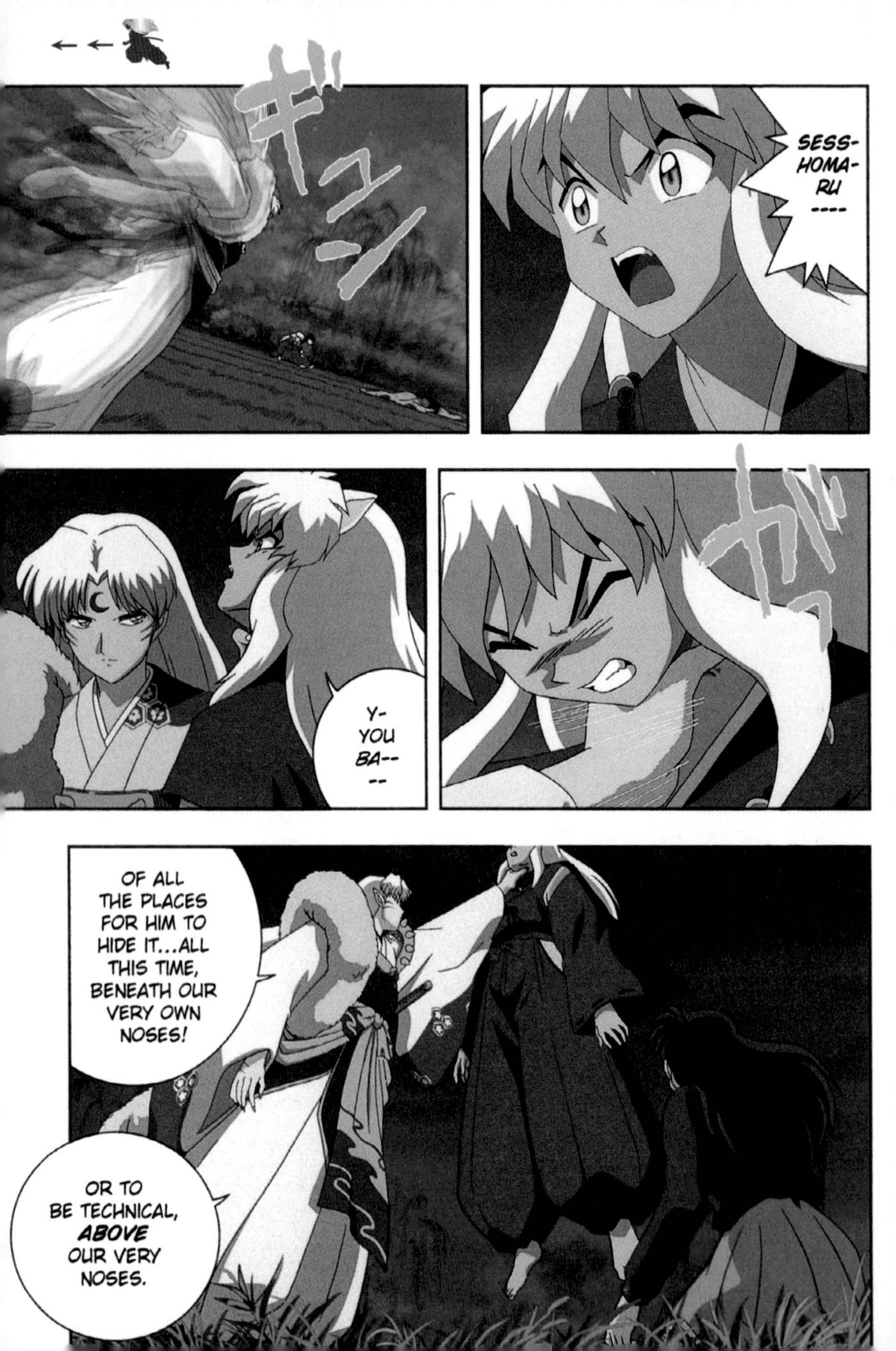
SESS-HOMA-RU ----
ギュン
ガッ
Y- YOU BA-- --
OF ALL THE PLACES FOR HIM TO HIDE IT...ALL THIS TIME, BENEATH OUR VERY OWN NOSES!
OR TO BE TECHNICAL, ***ABOVE*** OUR VERY NOSES.

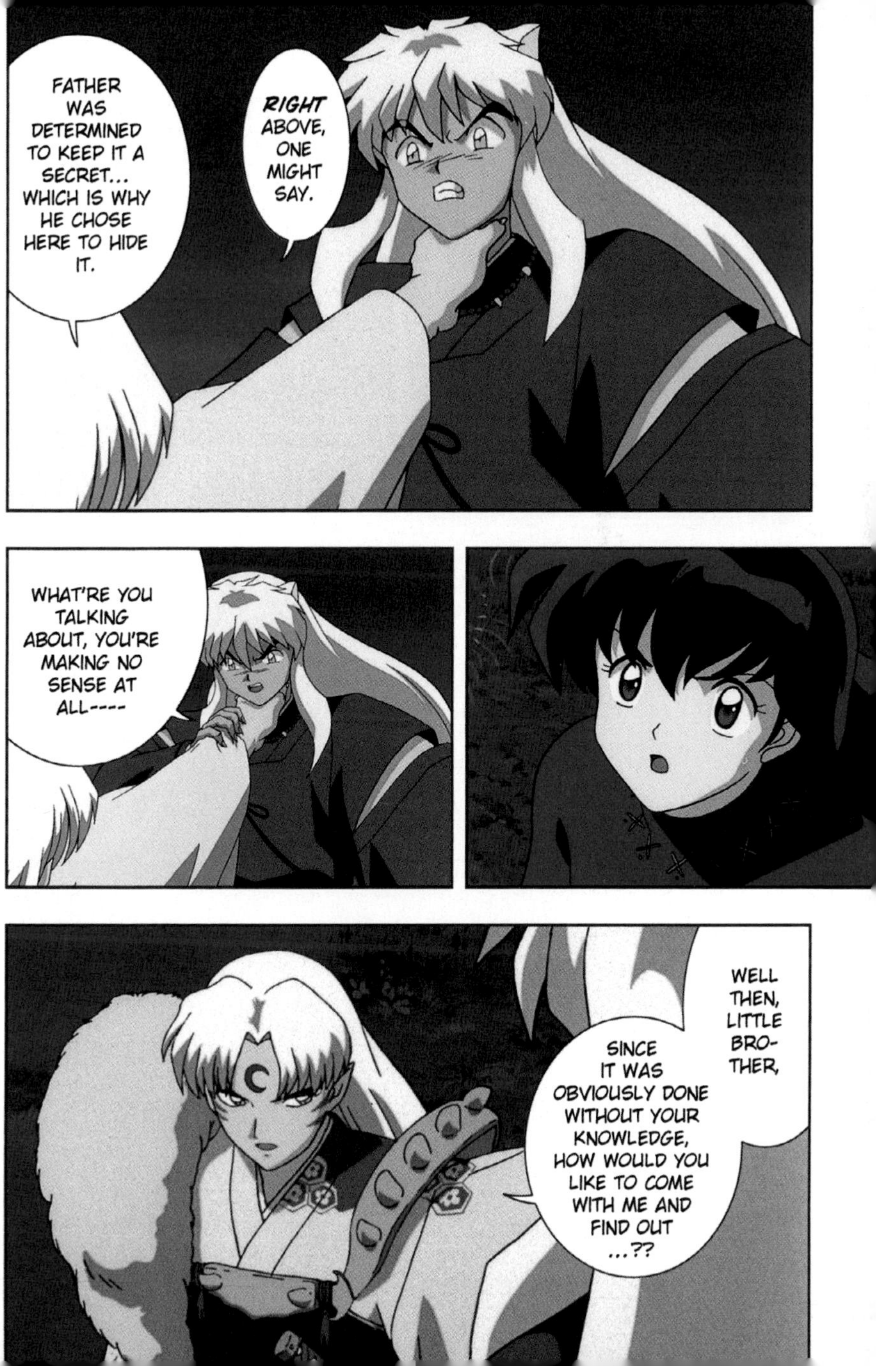
RIGHT ABOVE, ONE MIGHT SAY.
FATHER WAS DETERMINED TO KEEP IT A SECRET... WHICH IS WHY HE CHOSE HERE TO HIDE IT.
WHAT'RE YOU TALKING ABOUT, YOU'RE MAKING NO SENSE AT ALL----
WELL THEN, LITTLE BRO-THER,
SINCE IT WAS OBVIOUSLY DONE WITHOUT YOUR KNOWLEDGE, HOW WOULD YOU LIKE TO COME WITH ME AND FIND OUT ...??

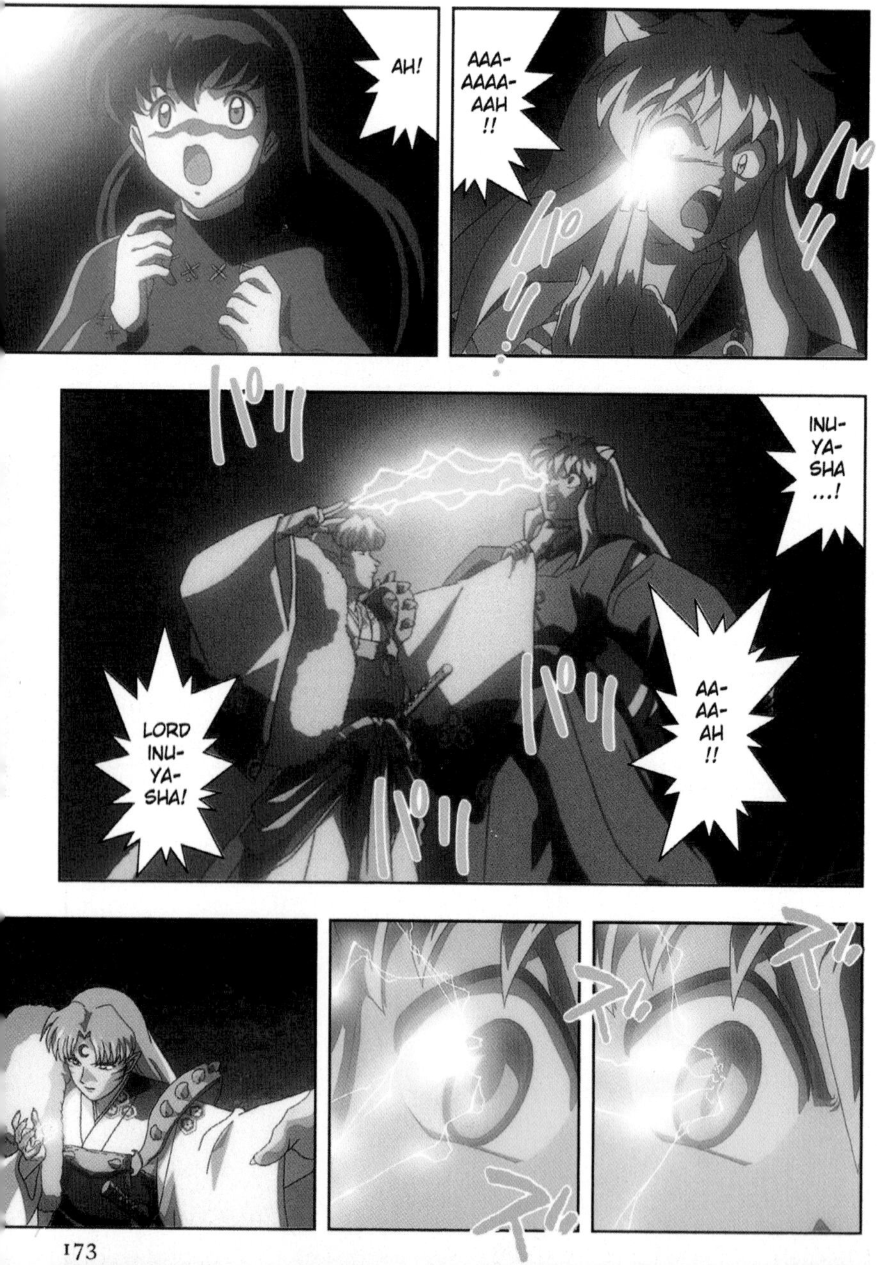
AAA-AAAA-AAH!!
AH!
INU-YA-SHA...!
AA-AA-AH!!
LORD INU-YA-SHA!

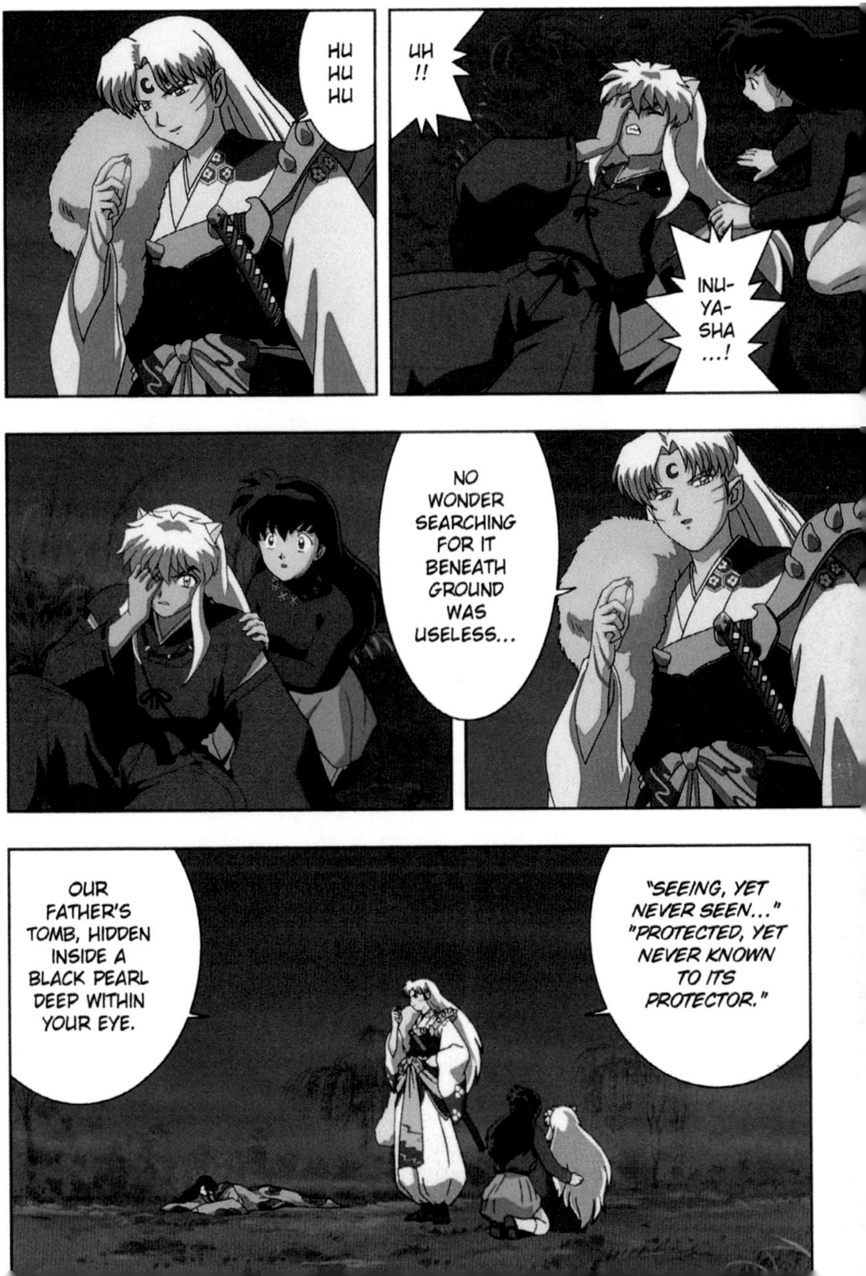
UH !!
INU-YA-SHA ...!
HU HU HU
NO WONDER SEARCHING FOR IT BENEATH GROUND WAS USELESS...
"SEEING, YET NEVER SEEN..." "PROTECTED, YET NEVER KNOWN TO ITS PROTECTOR."
OUR FATHER'S TOMB, HIDDEN INSIDE A BLACK PEARL DEEP WITHIN YOUR EYE.

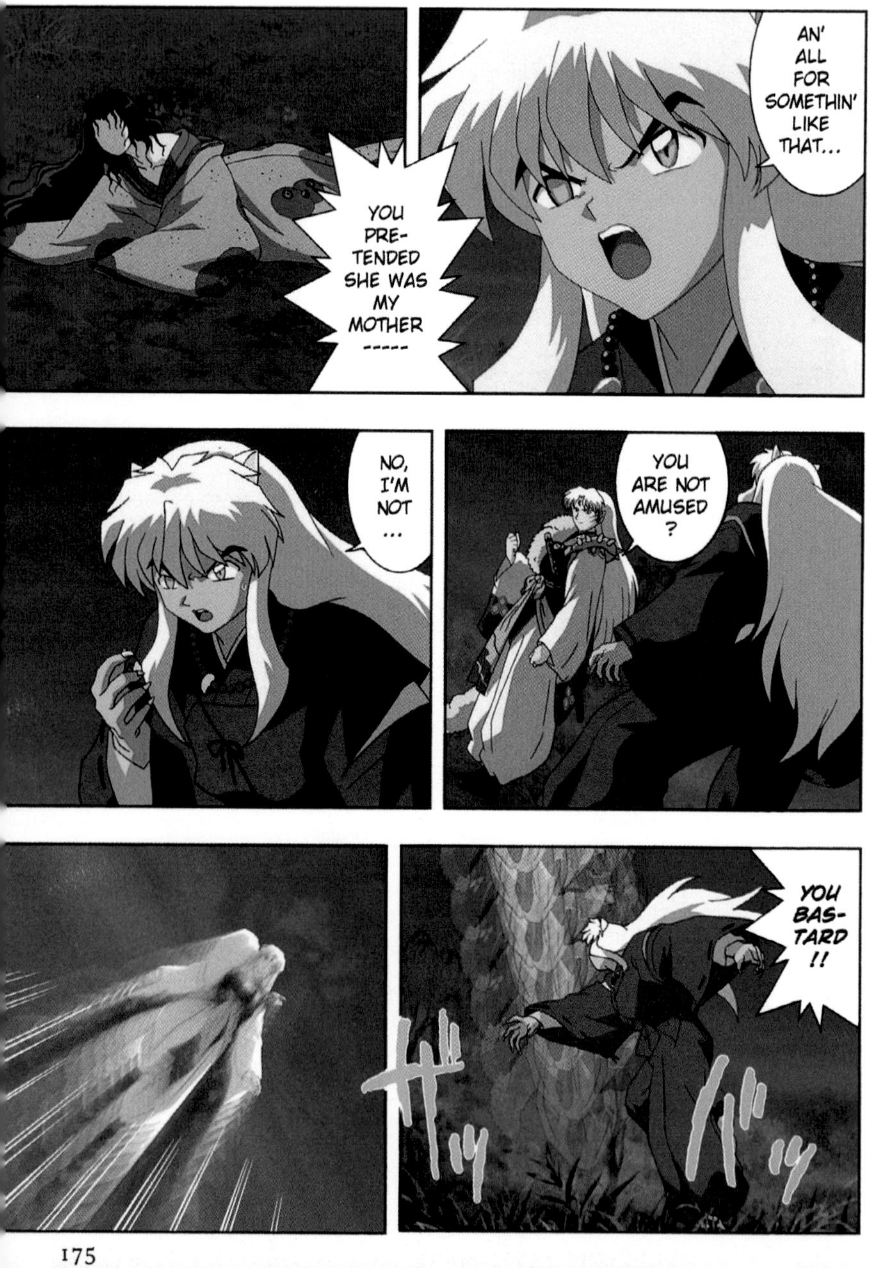
AN' ALL FOR SOMETHIN' LIKE THAT...
YOU PRE-TENDED SHE WAS MY MOTHER -----
YOU ARE NOT AMUSED ?
NO, I'M NOT ...
YOU BAS-TARD !!

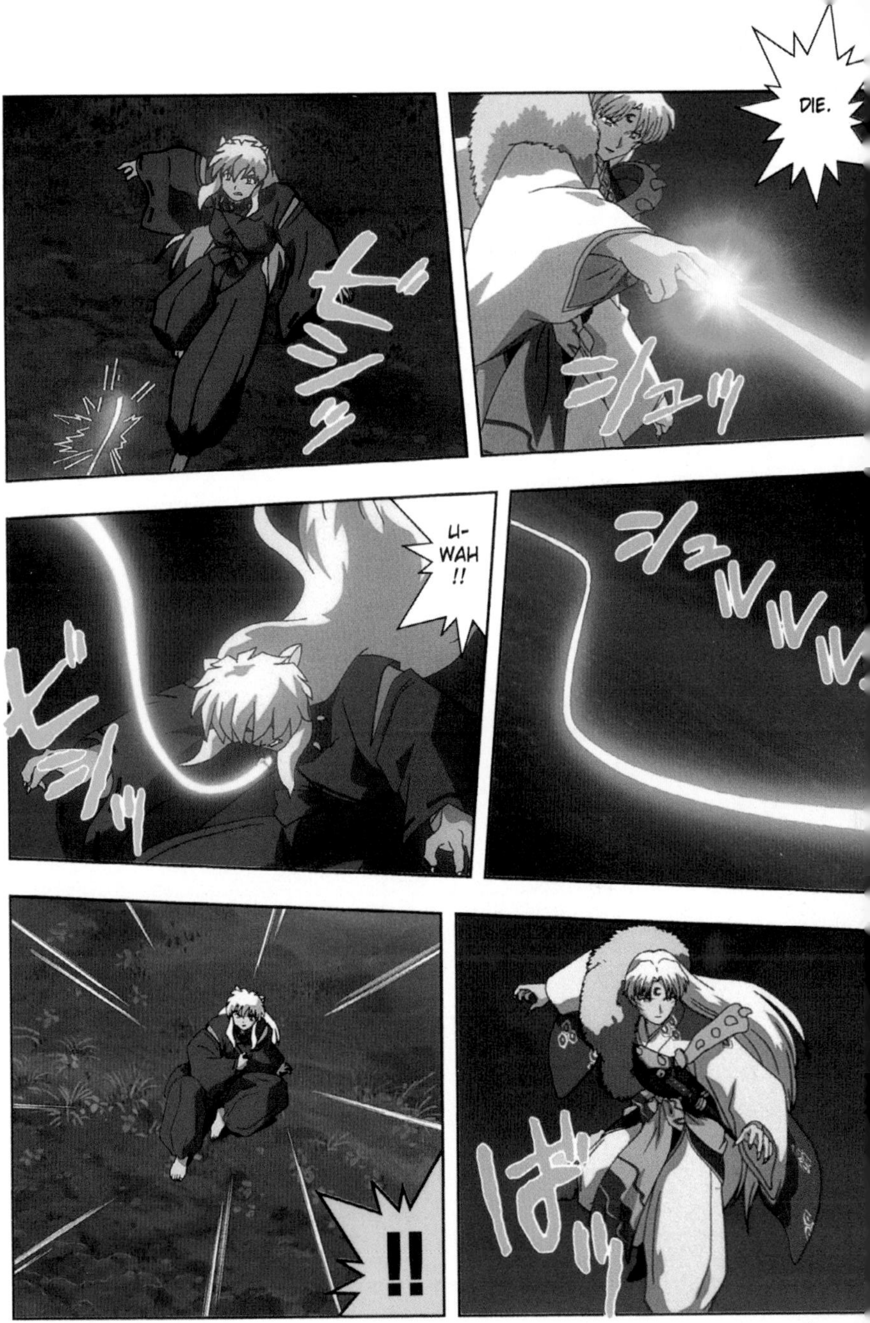
DIE.
シュッ
ビシッ
シュルルル
U-WAH !!
ビシッ
ばっ
!!

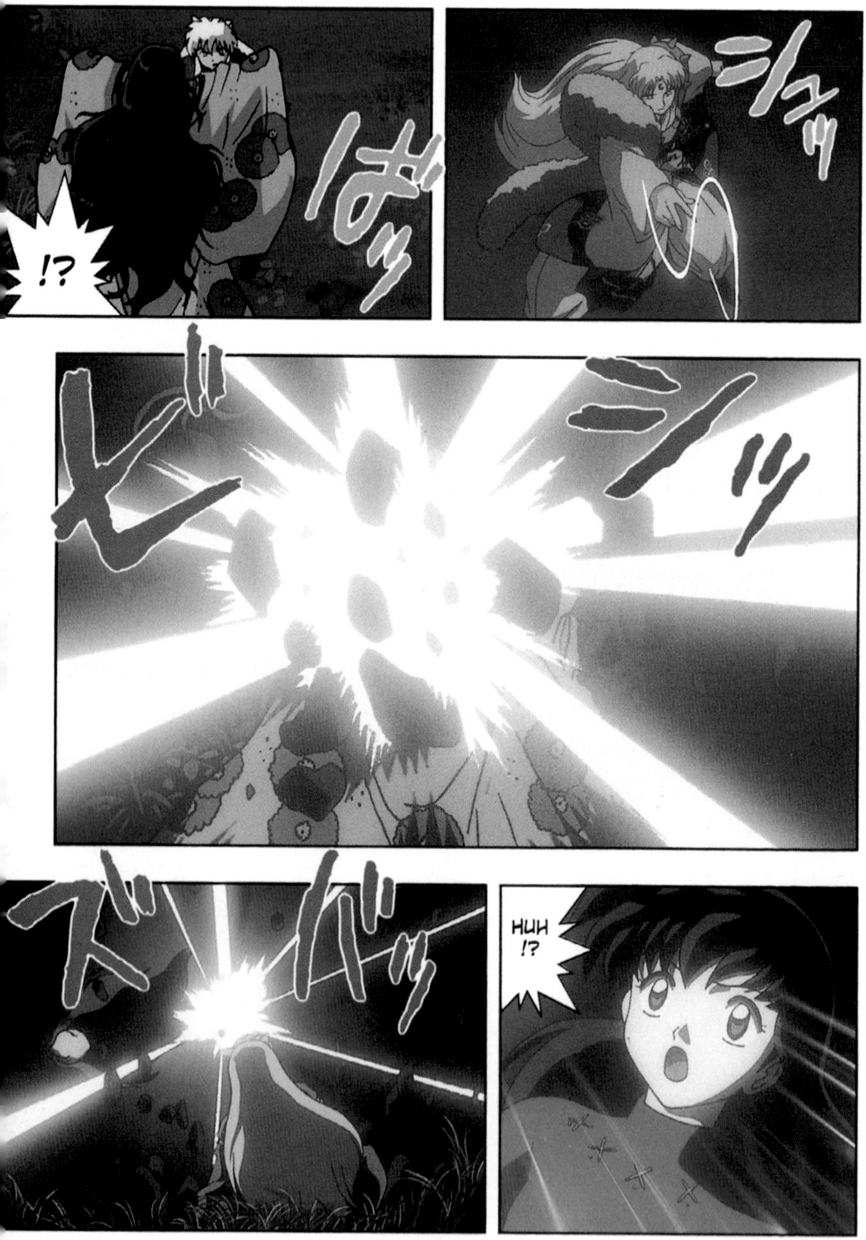
シュッ
ばッ
!?
ビシッ
HUH !?
ズバッ

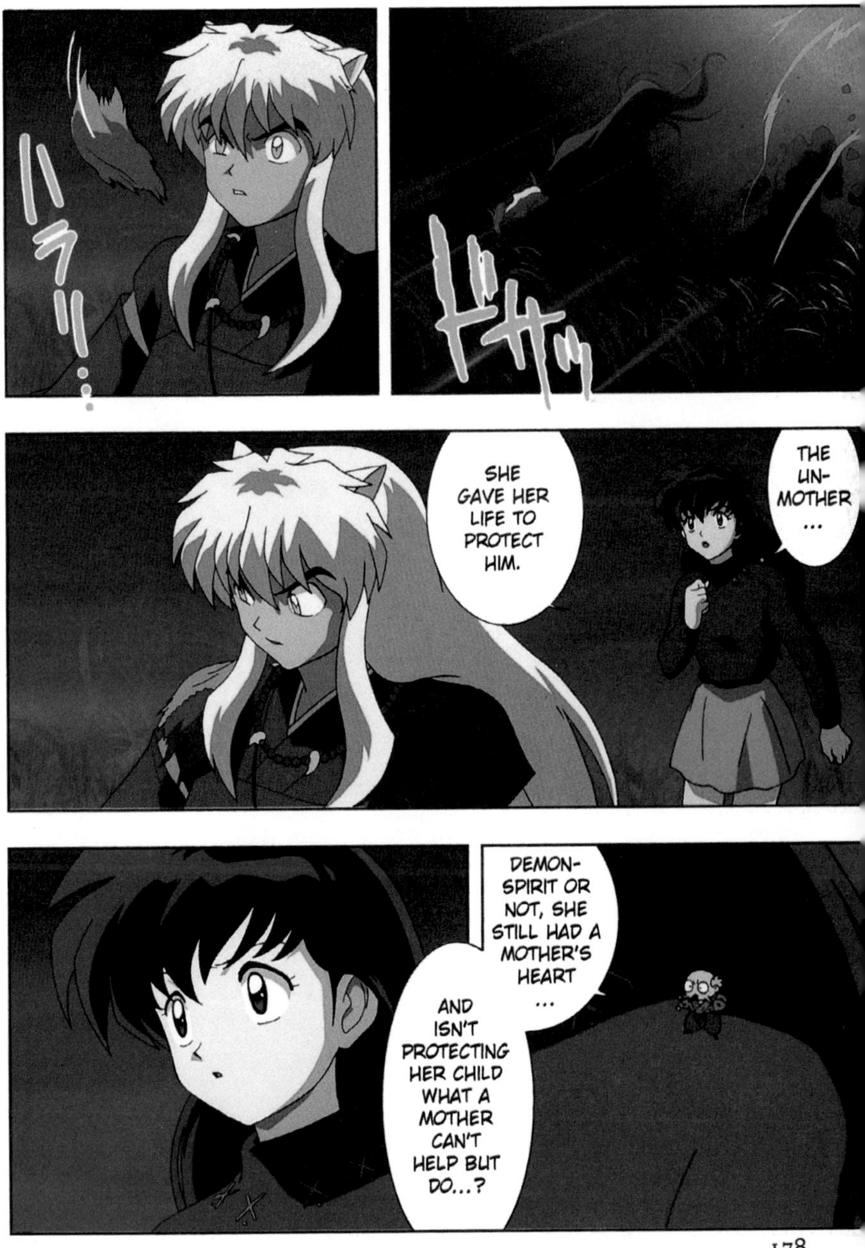
ドサッ
ハラリ…
THE UN-MOTHER …
SHE GAVE HER LIFE TO PROTECT HIM.
DEMON-SPIRIT OR NOT, SHE STILL HAD A MOTHER'S HEART …
AND ISN'T PROTECTING HER CHILD WHAT A MOTHER CAN'T HELP BUT DO…?

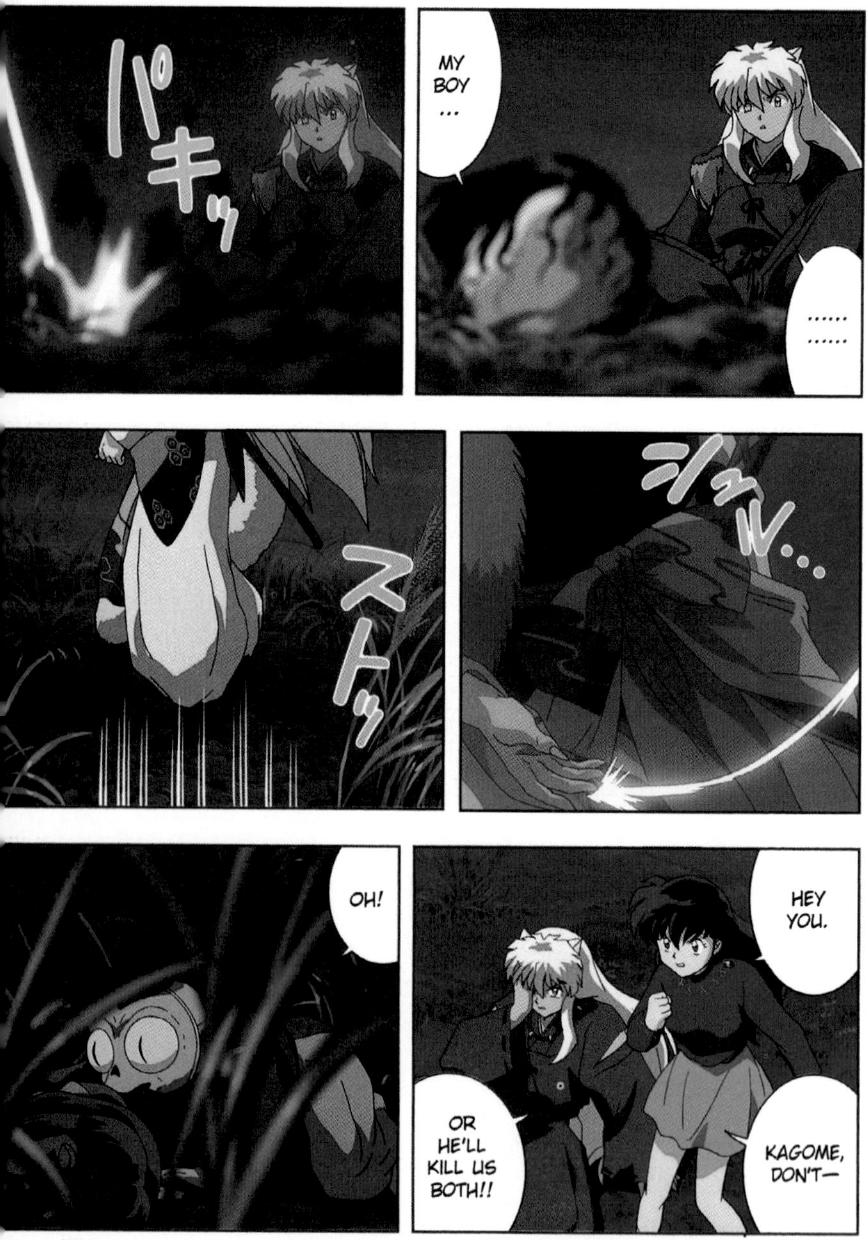
MY BOY ...
......
......
パキッ
シュル...
ストッ
HEY YOU.
KAGOME, DON'T—
OR HE'LL KILL US BOTH!!
OH!

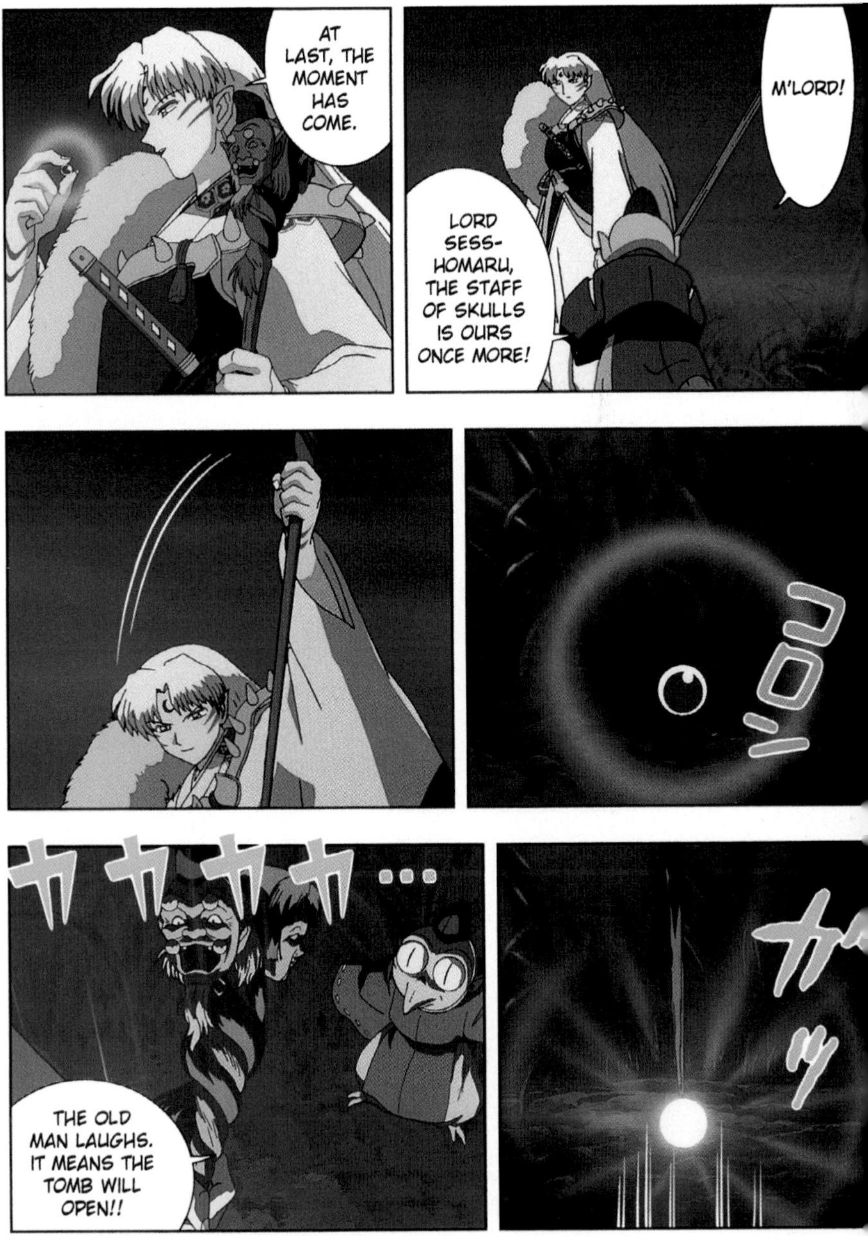
M'LORD!
LORD SESS-HOMARU, THE STAFF OF SKULLS IS OURS ONCE MORE!
AT LAST, THE MOMENT HAS COME.
コロン
カッ
カカカカ...
THE OLD MAN LAUGHS. IT MEANS THE TOMB WILL OPEN!!

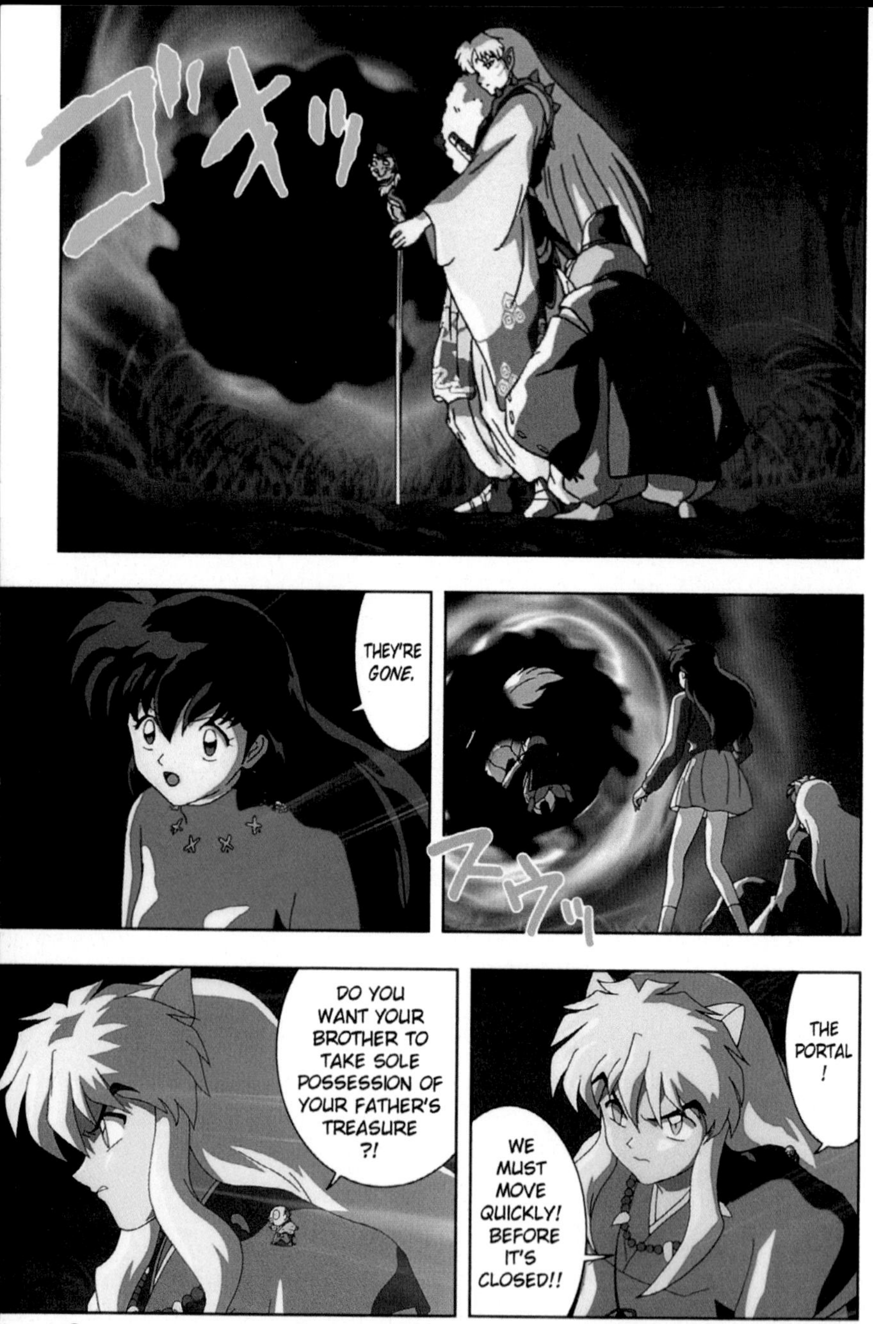
ゴオッ
スウッ
THEY'RE GONE.
THE PORTAL!
WE MUST MOVE QUICKLY! BEFORE IT'S CLOSED!!
DO YOU WANT YOUR BROTHER TO TAKE SOLE POSSESSION OF YOUR FATHER'S TREASURE ?!

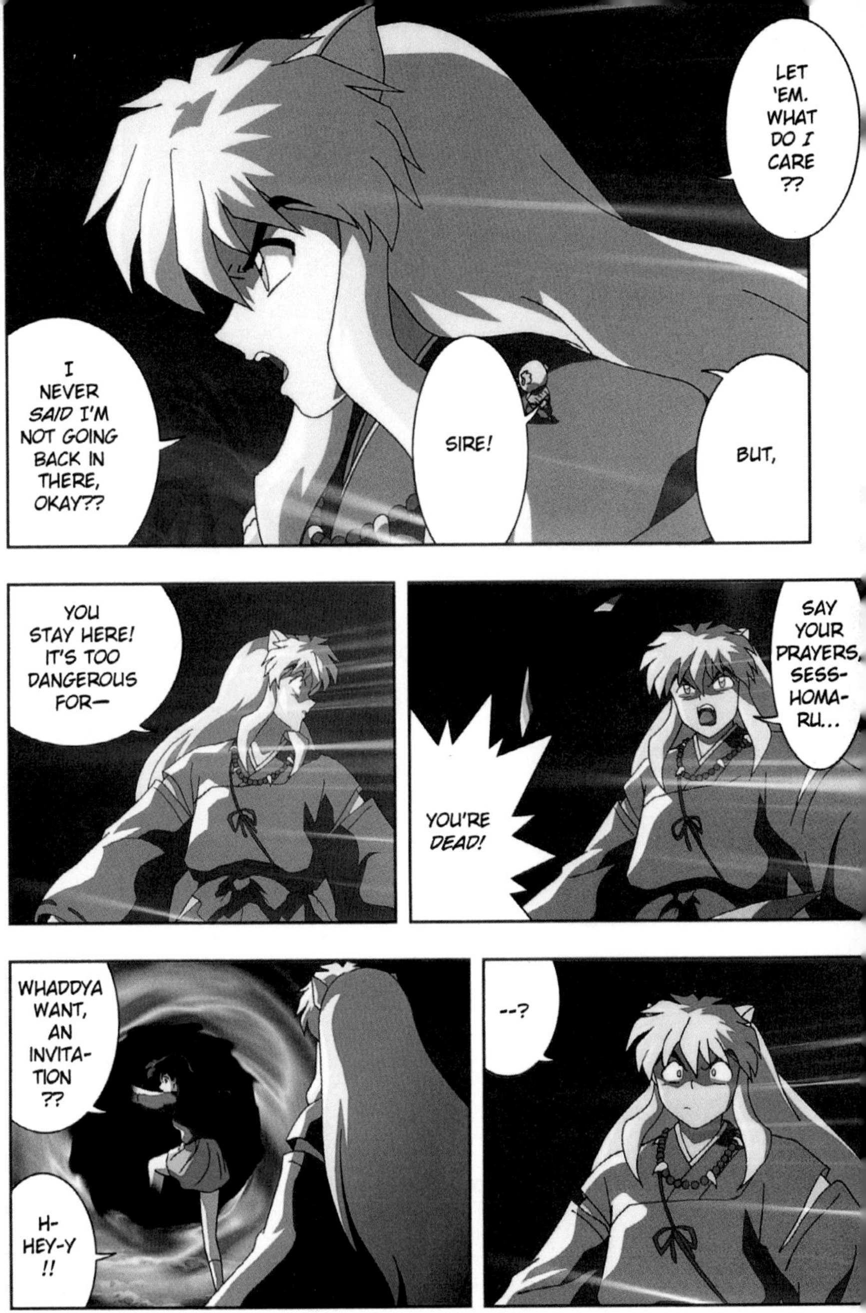
LET 'EM. WHAT DO I CARE ??
BUT,
SIRE!
I NEVER *SAID* I'M NOT GOING BACK IN THERE, OKAY??
SAY YOUR PRAYERS, SESS-HOMA-RU...
YOU'RE *DEAD!*
YOU STAY HERE! IT'S TOO DANGEROUS FOR—
--?
WHADDYA WANT, AN INVITA-TION ??
H-HEY-Y !!

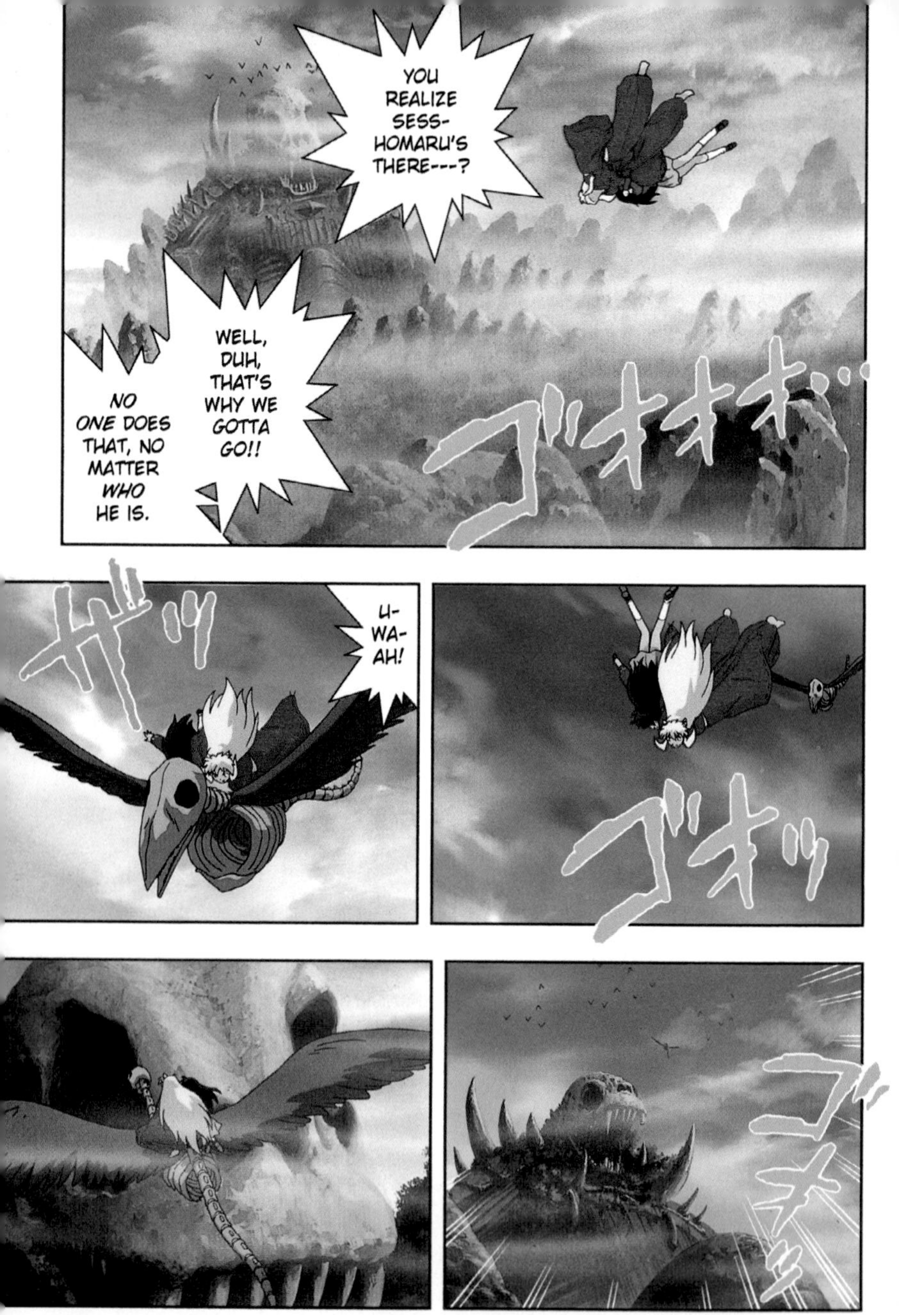
YOU REALIZE SESS-HOMARU'S THERE---?
WELL, DUH, THAT'S WHY WE GOTTA GO!!
NO ONE DOES THAT, NO MATTER WHO *HE IS.*
ゴオオオ…
ゴオッ
ザッ
U-WA-AH!

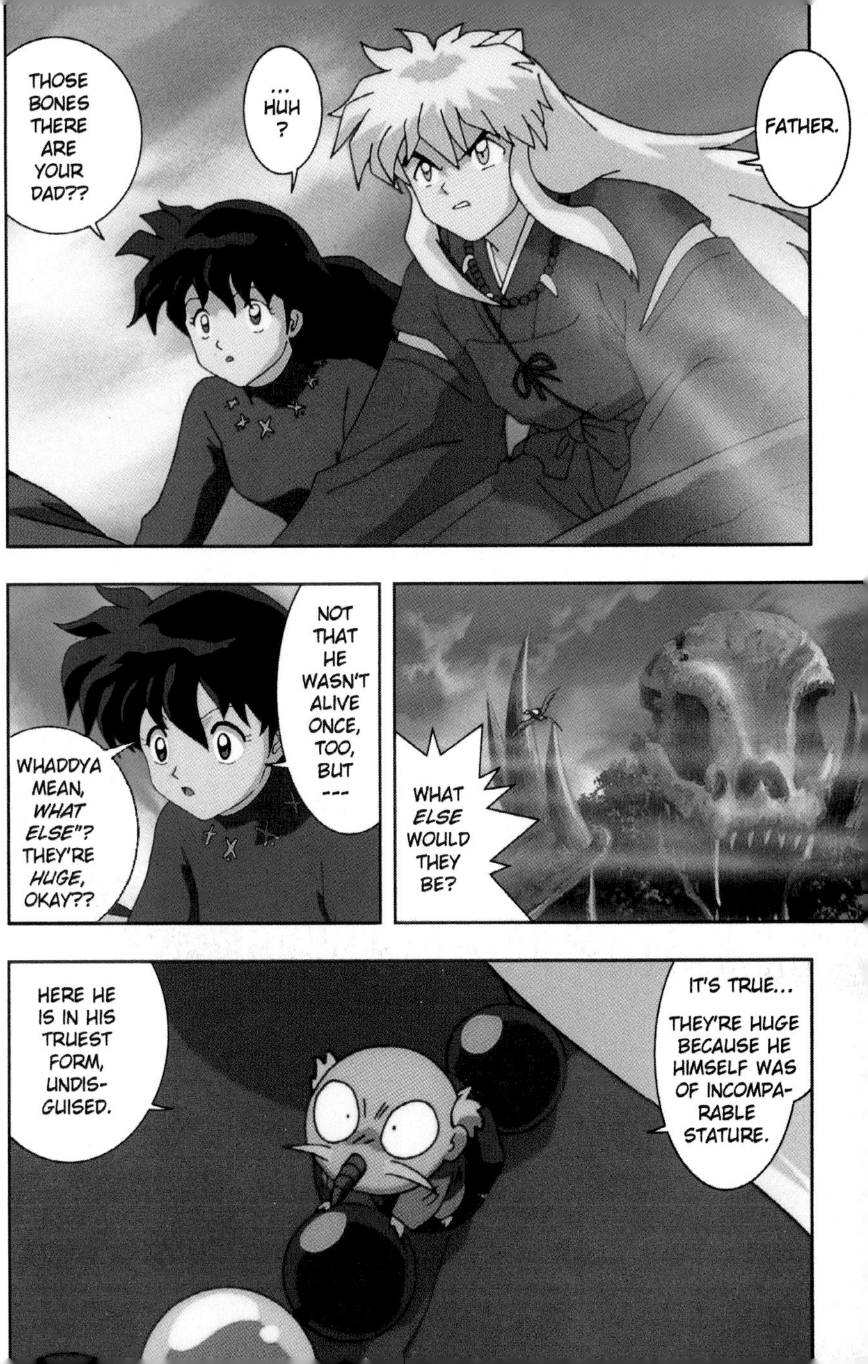
FATHER.
... HUH ?
THOSE BONES THERE ARE YOUR DAD??
WHAT *ELSE* WOULD THEY BE?
NOT THAT HE WASN'T ALIVE ONCE, TOO, BUT ---
WHADDYA MEAN, *WHAT ELSE*"? THEY'RE *HUGE*, OKAY??
IT'S TRUE...
THEY'RE HUGE BECAUSE HE HIMSELF WAS OF INCOMPA-RABLE STATURE.
HERE HE IS IN HIS TRUEST FORM, UNDIS-GUISED.

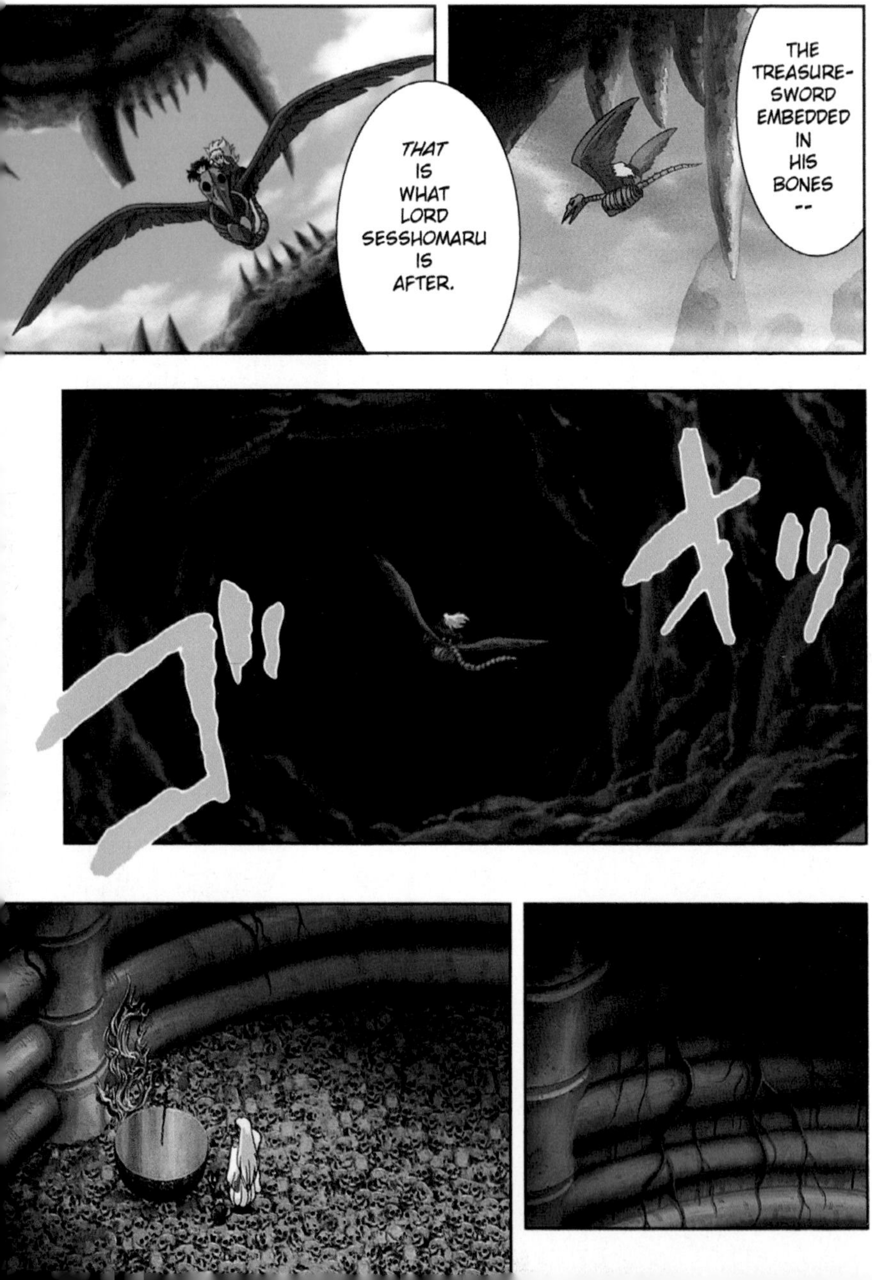
THE TREASURE-SWORD EMBEDDED IN HIS BONES --
THAT IS WHAT LORD SESSHOMARU IS AFTER.
ゴオッ

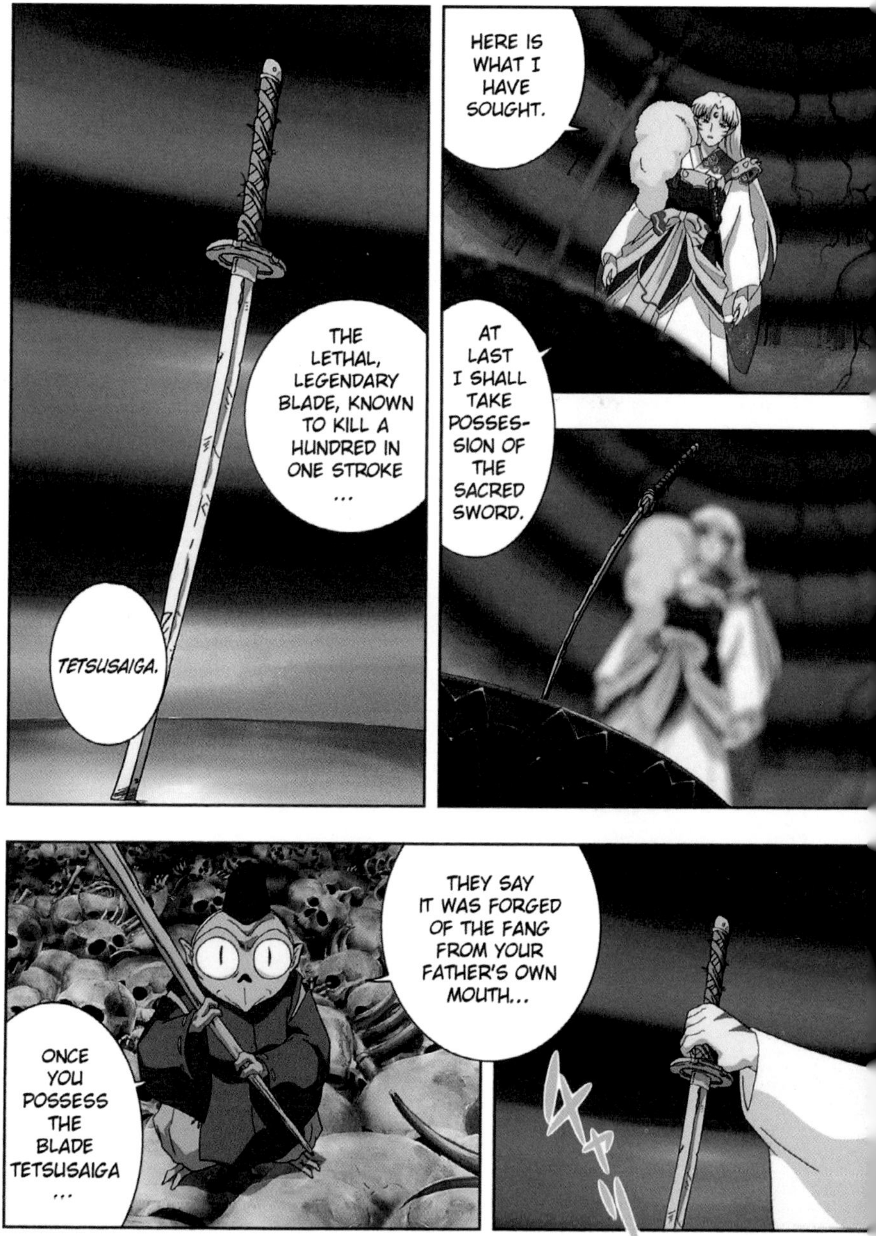
HERE IS WHAT I HAVE SOUGHT.
AT LAST I SHALL TAKE POSSESSION OF THE SACRED SWORD.
THE LETHAL, LEGENDARY BLADE, KNOWN TO KILL A HUNDRED IN ONE STROKE...
TETSUSAIGA.
THEY SAY IT WAS FORGED OF THE FANG FROM YOUR FATHER'S OWN MOUTH...
ONCE YOU POSSESS THE BLADE TETSUSAIGA...

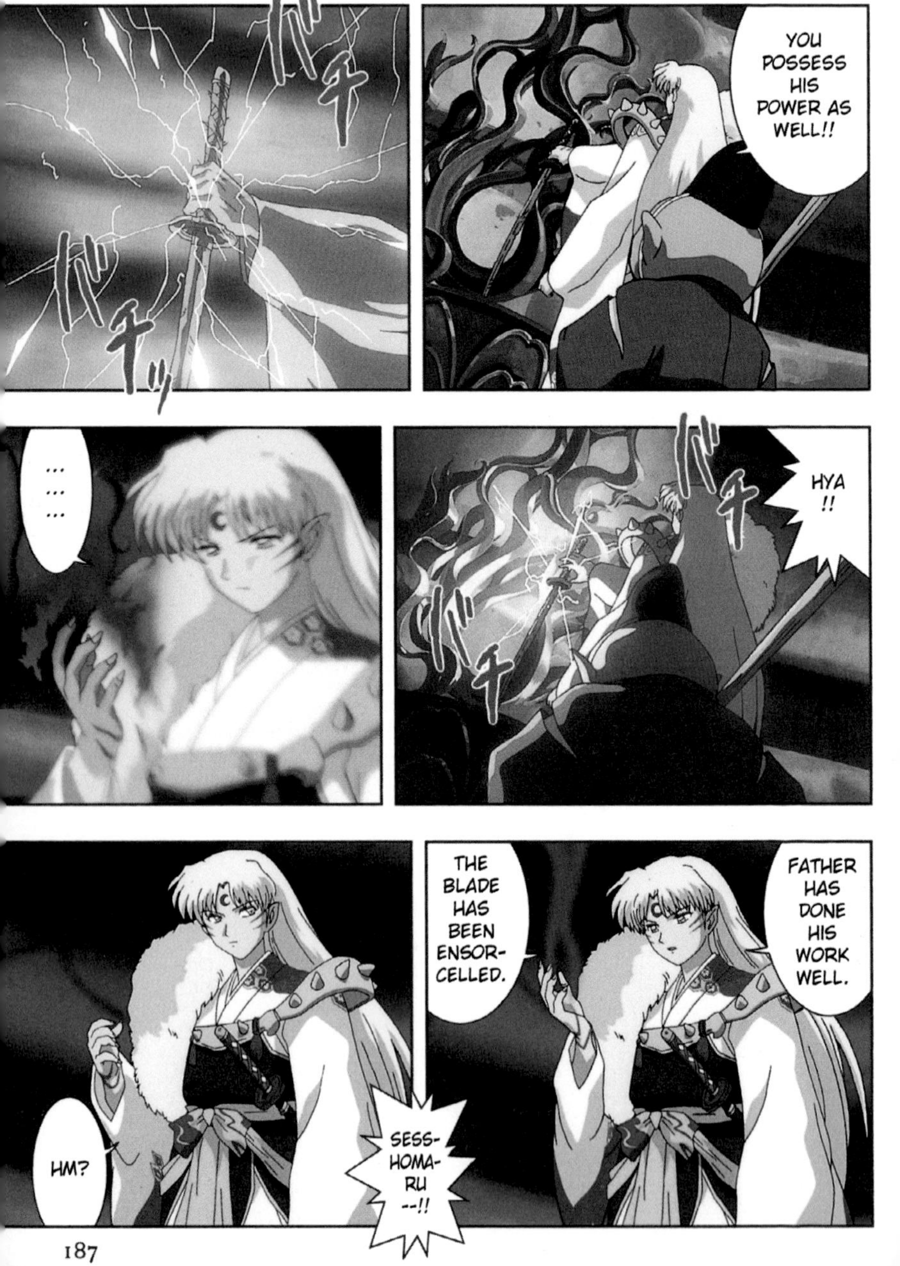
YOU POSSESS HIS POWER AS WELL!!
バチ
バチッ
バチ
HYA !!
バチ
... ...
FATHER HAS DONE HIS WORK WELL.
THE BLADE HAS BEEN ENSORCELLED.
SESS-HOMA-RU --!!
HM?

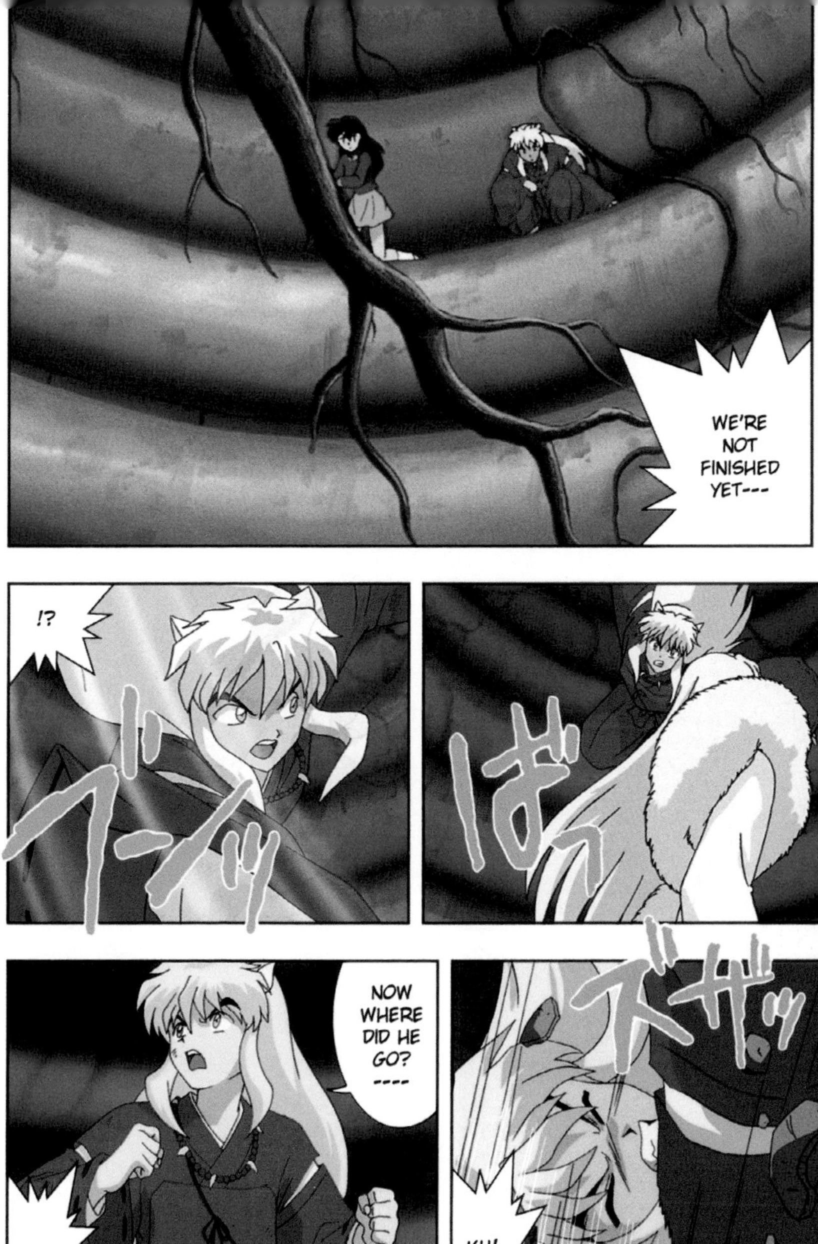
WE'RE NOT FINISHED YET---
ぼっ
!?
ブーンッ
ズザッ
KU!
NOW WHERE DID HE GO? ----
--!

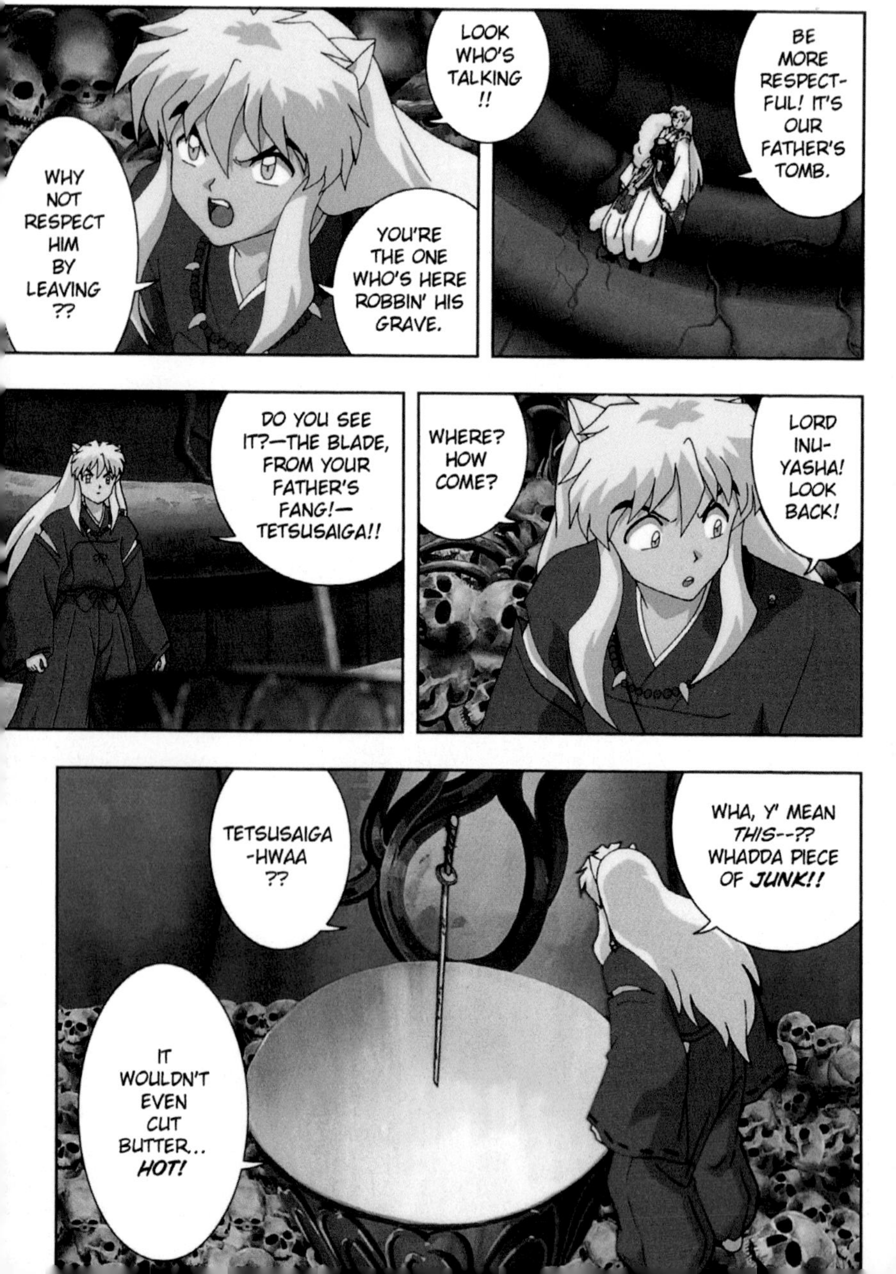
BE MORE RESPECT-FUL! IT'S OUR FATHER'S TOMB.
LOOK WHO'S TALKING!!
YOU'RE THE ONE WHO'S HERE ROBBIN' HIS GRAVE.
WHY NOT RESPECT HIM BY LEAVING??
LORD INU-YASHA! LOOK BACK!
WHERE? HOW COME?
DO YOU SEE IT?—THE BLADE, FROM YOUR FATHER'S FANG!—TETSUSAIGA!!
WHA, Y' MEAN *THIS*--?? WHADDA PIECE OF ***JUNK!!***
TETSUSAIGA-HWAA??
IT WOULDN'T EVEN CUT BUTTER.. ***HOT!***

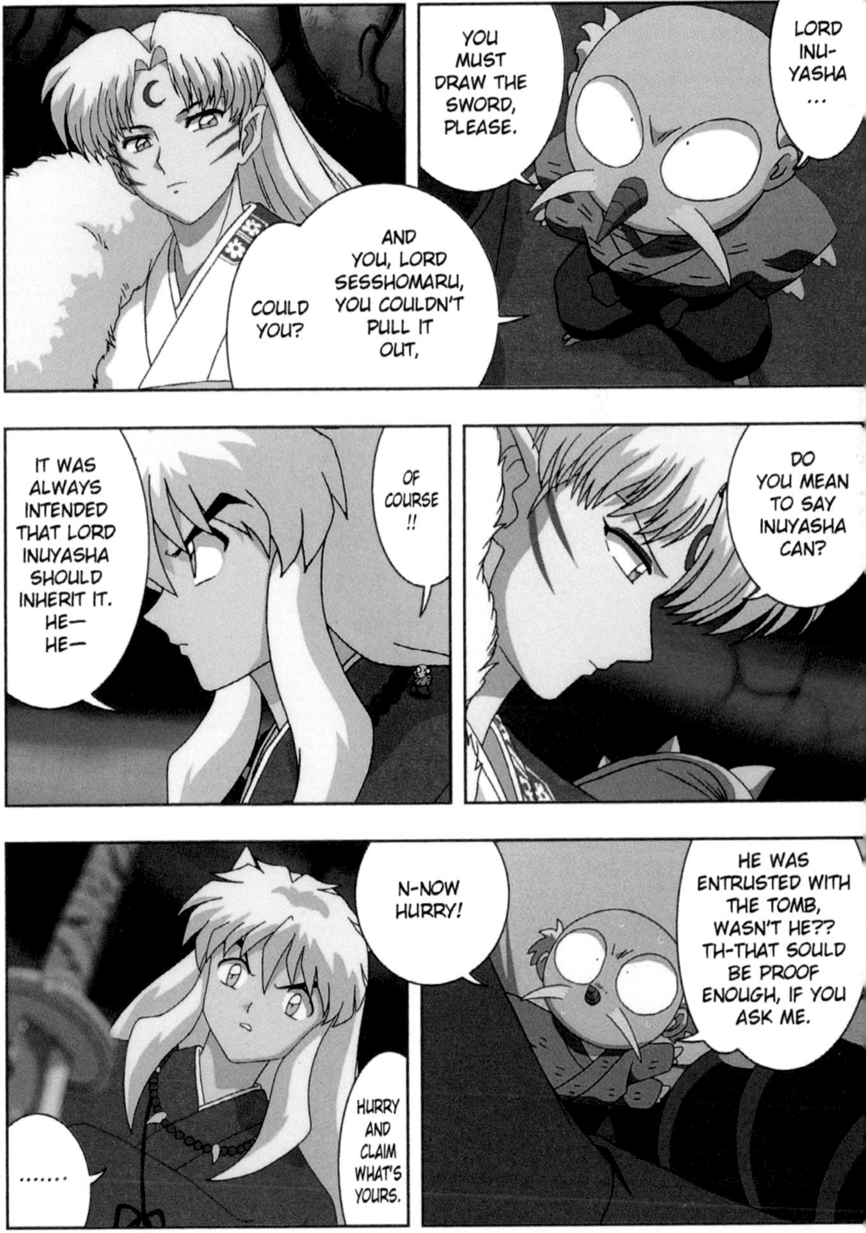
LORD INU-YASHA ...
YOU MUST DRAW THE SWORD, PLEASE.
AND YOU, LORD SESSHOMARU, YOU COULDN'T PULL IT OUT,
COULD YOU?
DO YOU MEAN TO SAY INUYASHA CAN?
OF COURSE !!
IT WAS ALWAYS INTENDED THAT LORD INUYASHA SHOULD INHERIT IT. HE— HE—
HE WAS ENTRUSTED WITH THE TOMB, WASN'T HE?? TH-THAT SOULD BE PROOF ENOUGH, IF YOU ASK ME.
N-NOW HURRY!
HURRY AND CLAIM WHAT'S YOURS.
....

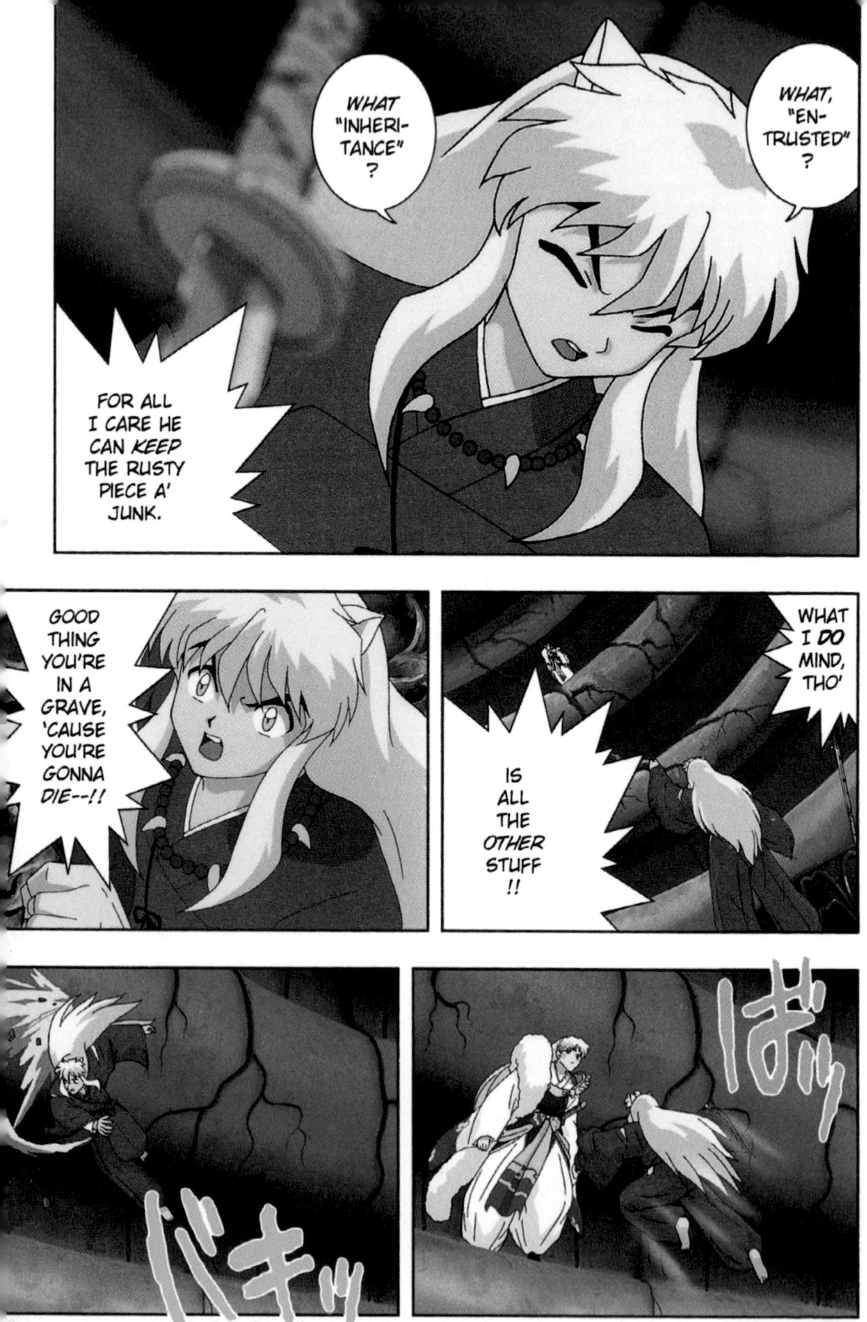
WHAT, "EN-TRUSTED"?
WHAT "INHERITANCE"?
FOR ALL I CARE HE CAN *KEEP* THE RUSTY PIECE A' JUNK.
WHAT I *DO* MIND, THO'
IS ALL THE *OTHER* STUFF!!
GOOD THING YOU'RE IN A GRAVE, 'CAUSE YOU'RE GONNA *DIE*--!!
ぱッ
バキッ

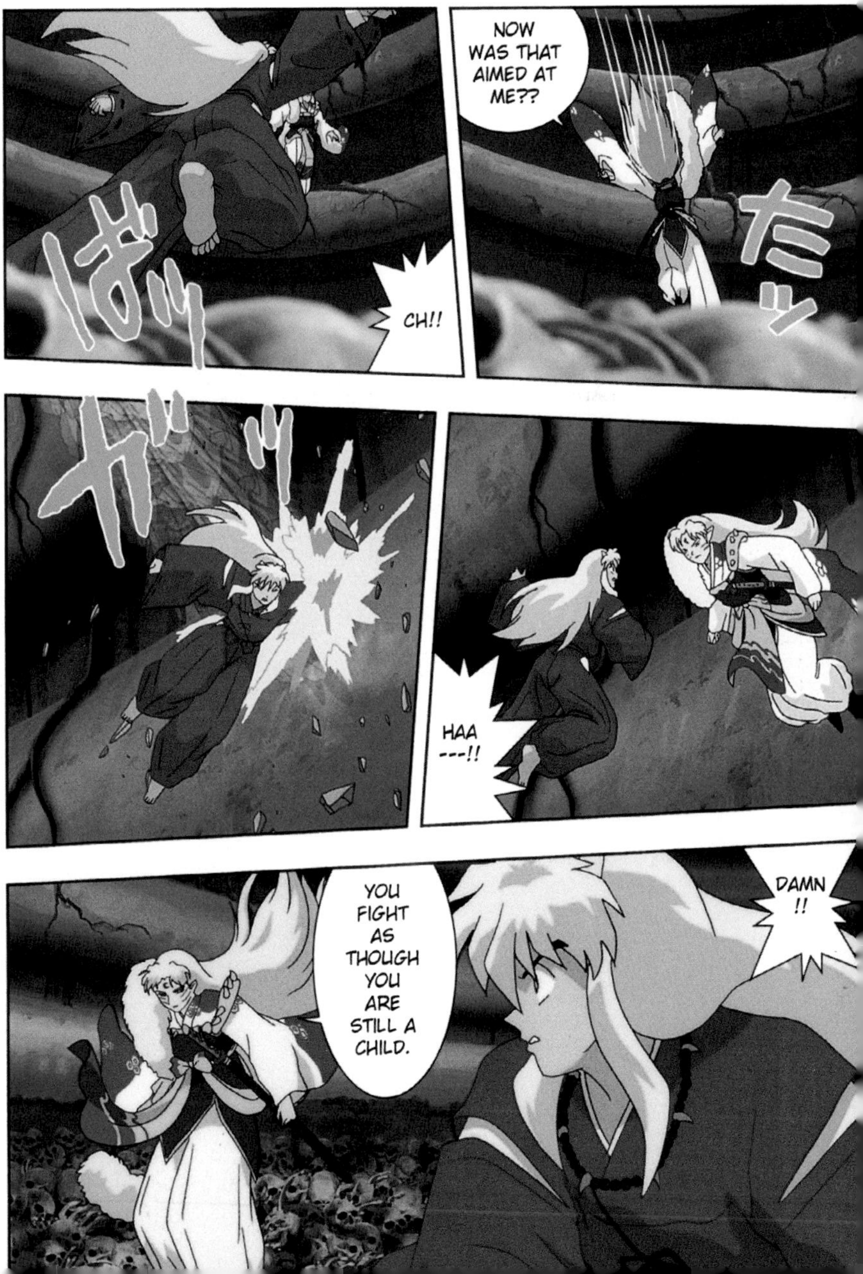
NOW WAS THAT AIMED AT ME??
たッ
ばッ
CH!!
HAA ---!!
ガッ
DAMN !!
YOU FIGHT AS THOUGH YOU ARE STILL A CHILD.

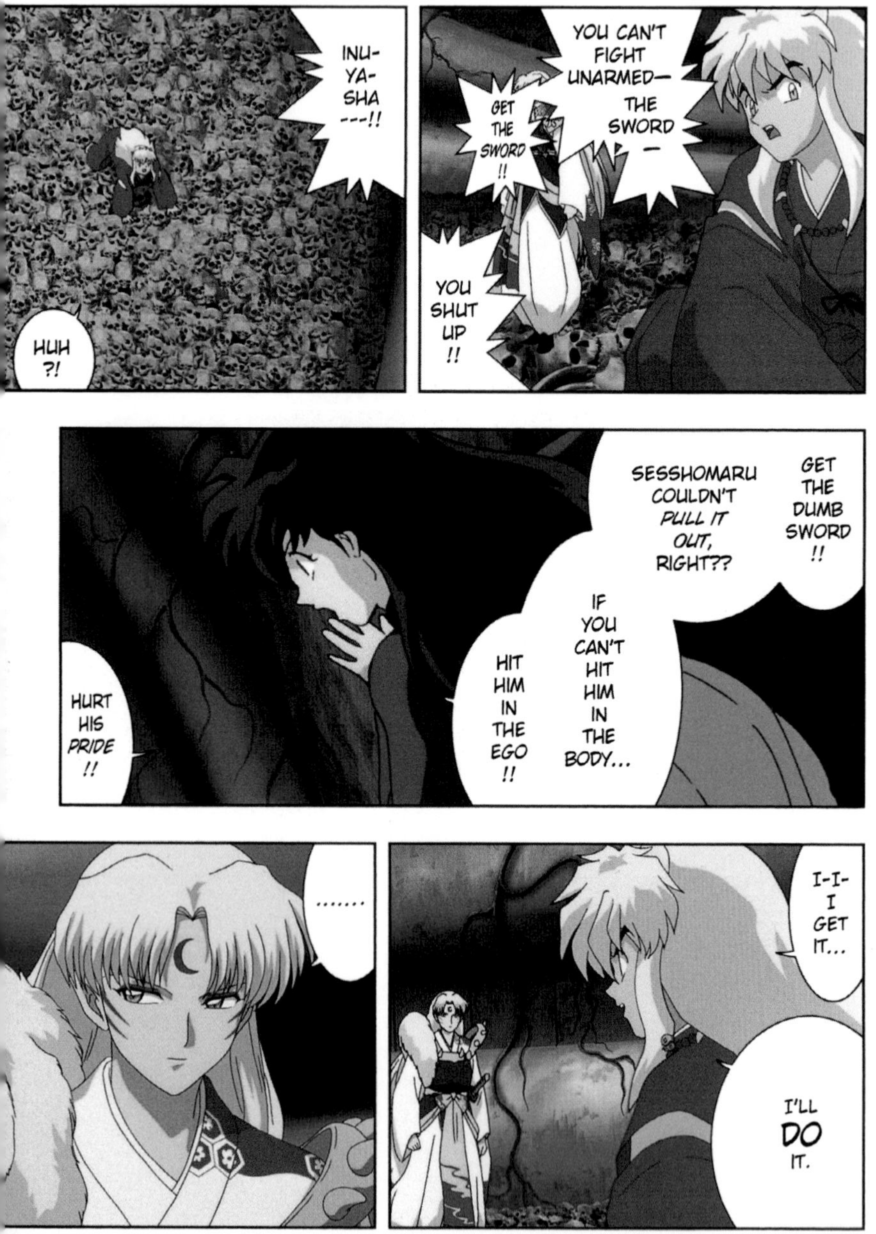
YOU CAN'T FIGHT UNARMED— THE SWORD —
GET THE SWORD !!
YOU SHUT UP !!
INU-YA-SHA ---!!
HUH ?!
GET THE DUMB SWORD !!
SESSHOMARU COULDN'T *PULL IT OUT,* RIGHT??
IF YOU CAN'T HIT HIM IN THE BODY...
HIT HIM IN THE EGO !!
HURT HIS *PRIDE* !!
I-I-I GET IT...
I'LL **DO** IT.
....

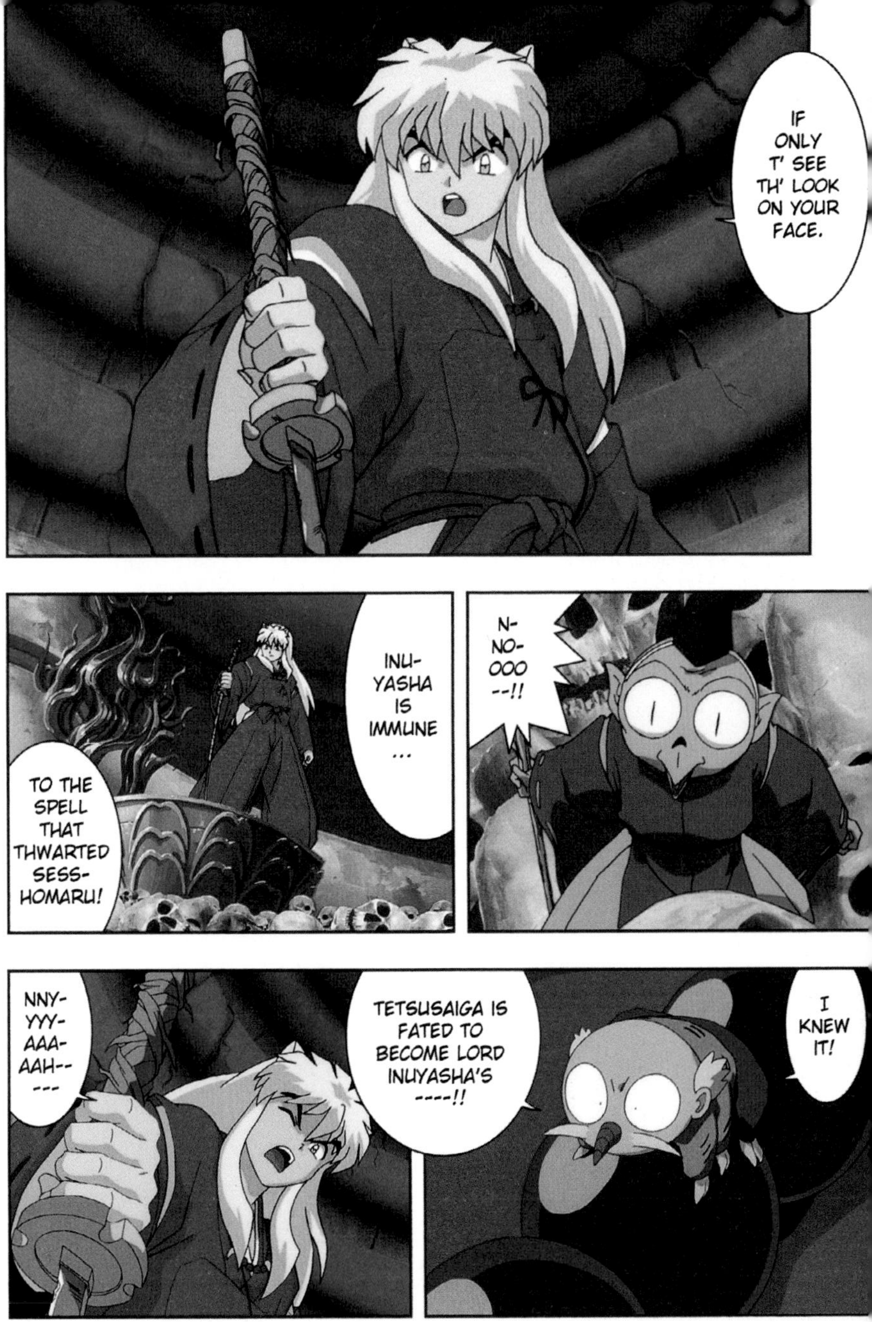
IF ONLY T' SEE TH' LOOK ON YOUR FACE.
N- NO- OOO --!!
INU- YASHA IS IMMUNE ...
TO THE SPELL THAT THWARTED SESS- HOMARU!
I KNEW IT!
TETSUSAIGA IS FATED TO BECOME LORD INUYASHA'S ----!!
NNY- YYY- AAA- AAH-- ---

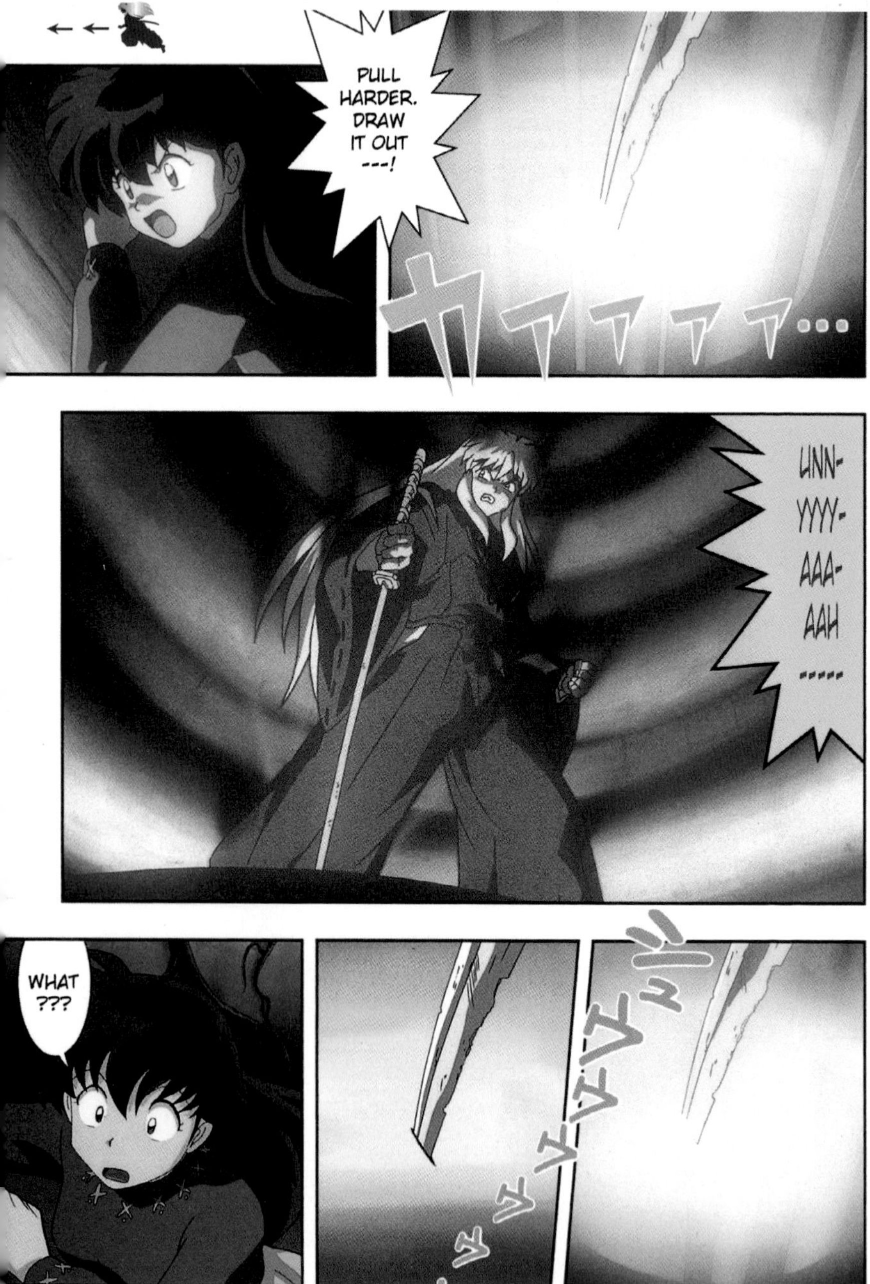
カァァァァ...
PULL HARDER. DRAW IT OUT ---!
UNN-YYYY-AAA-AAH -----
WHAT ???

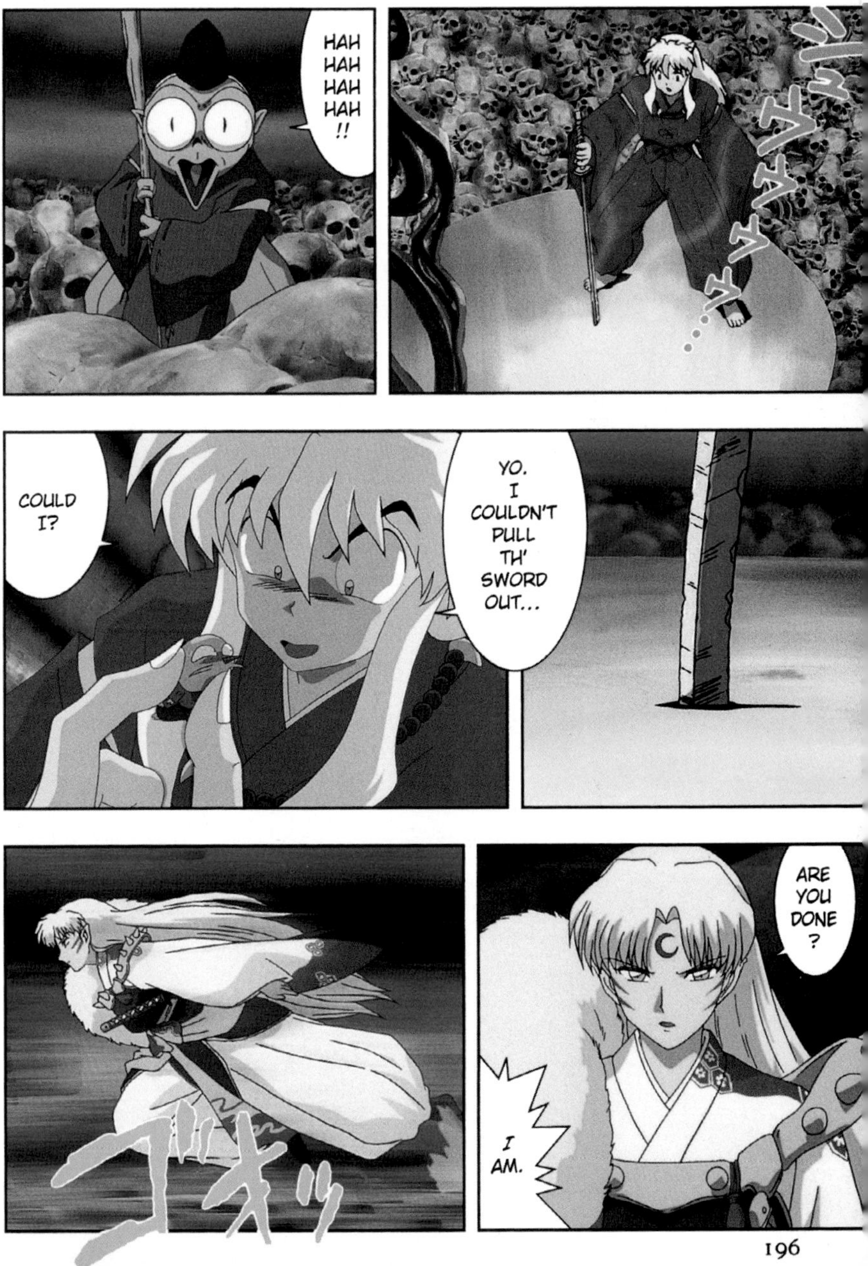
HAH HAH HAH HAH !!
YO. I COULDN'T PULL TH' SWORD OUT...
COULD I?
ARE YOU DONE ?
I AM.

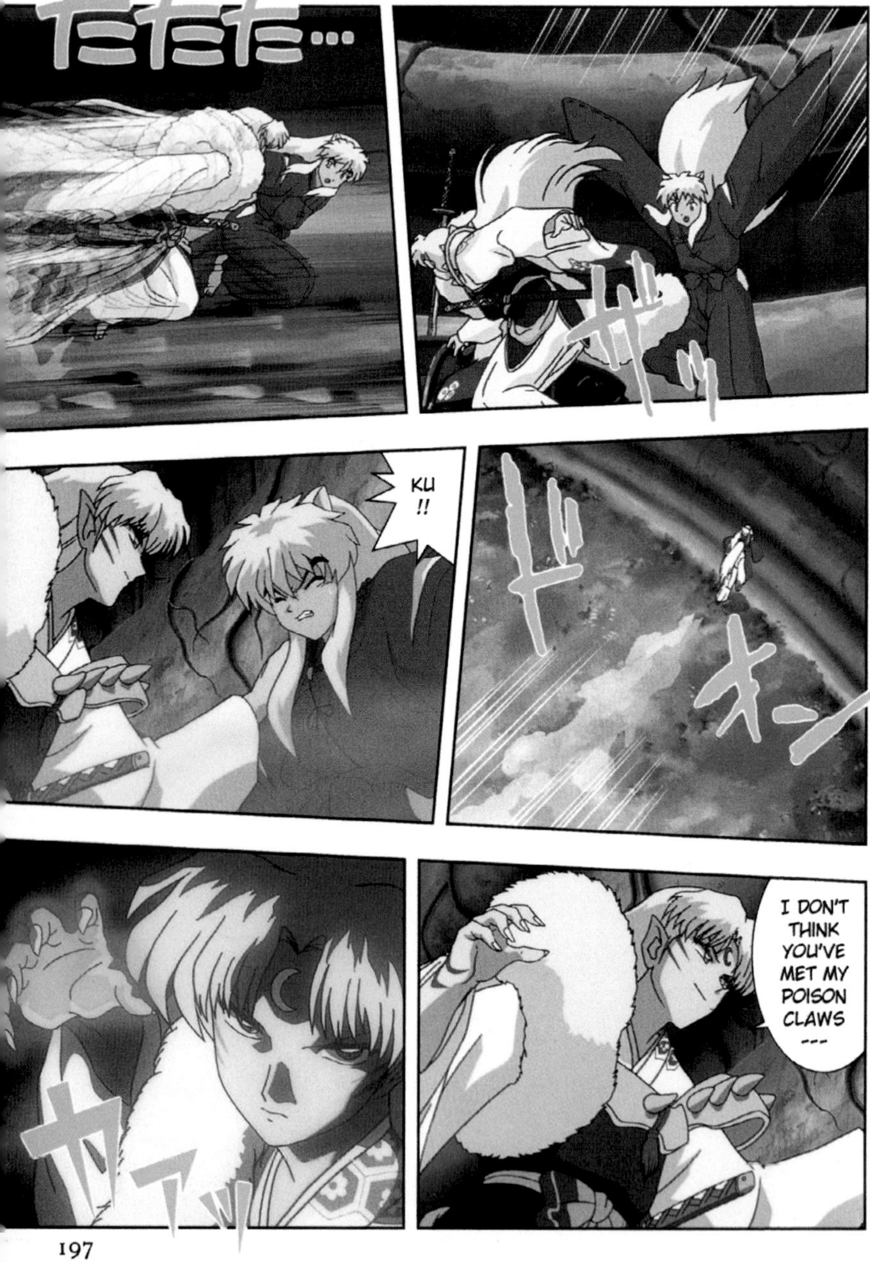
ザッ
たたたた…
ドォーン
KU !!
I DON'T THINK YOU'VE MET MY POISON CLAWS ---
ヤァッ

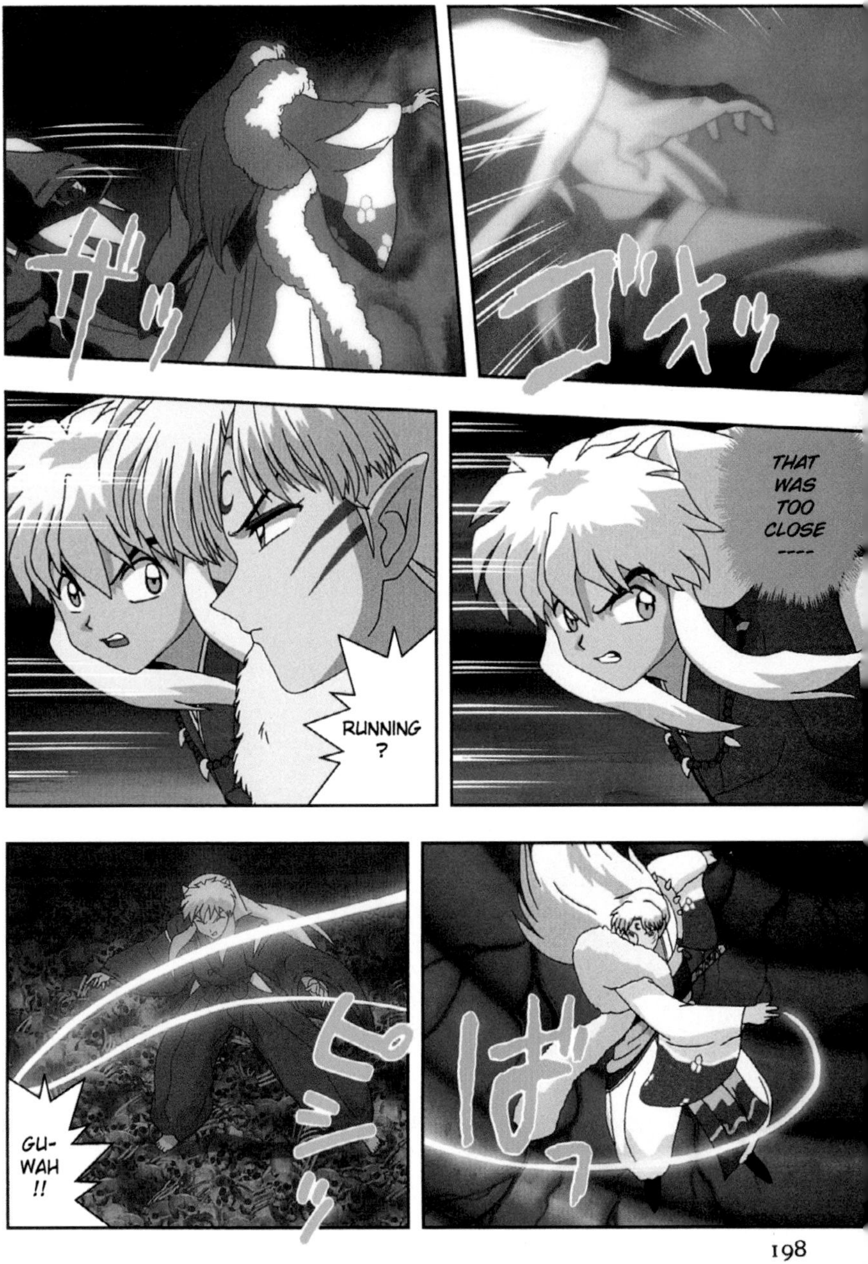
ゴキッ
ザッ
THAT WAS TOO CLOSE ----
RUNNING ?
ぱっ
ピシッ
GU-WAH !!

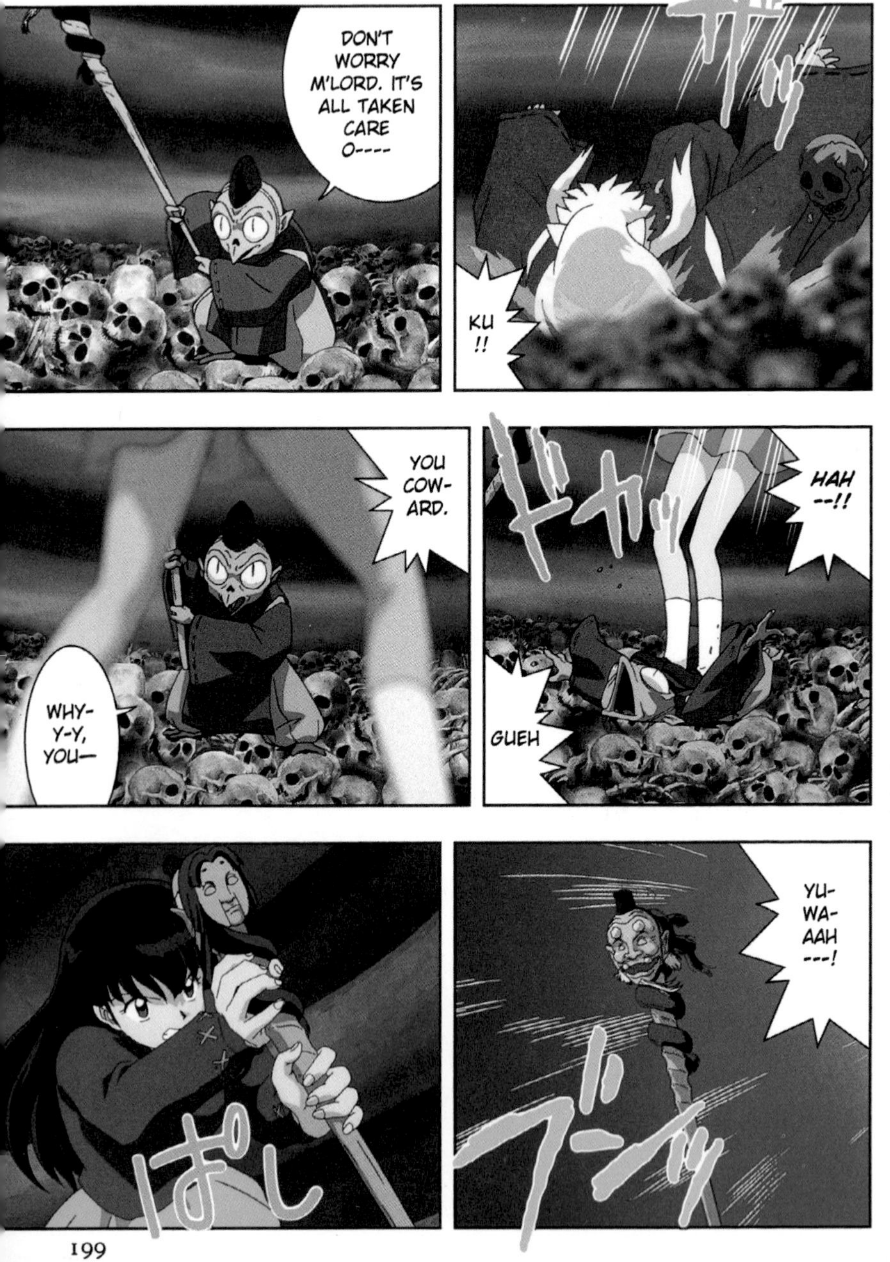
KU !!
DON'T WORRY M'LORD. IT'S ALL TAKEN CARE O----
HAH --!!
GUEH
YOU COW-ARD.
WHY-Y-Y, YOU—
YU-WA-AAH ---!

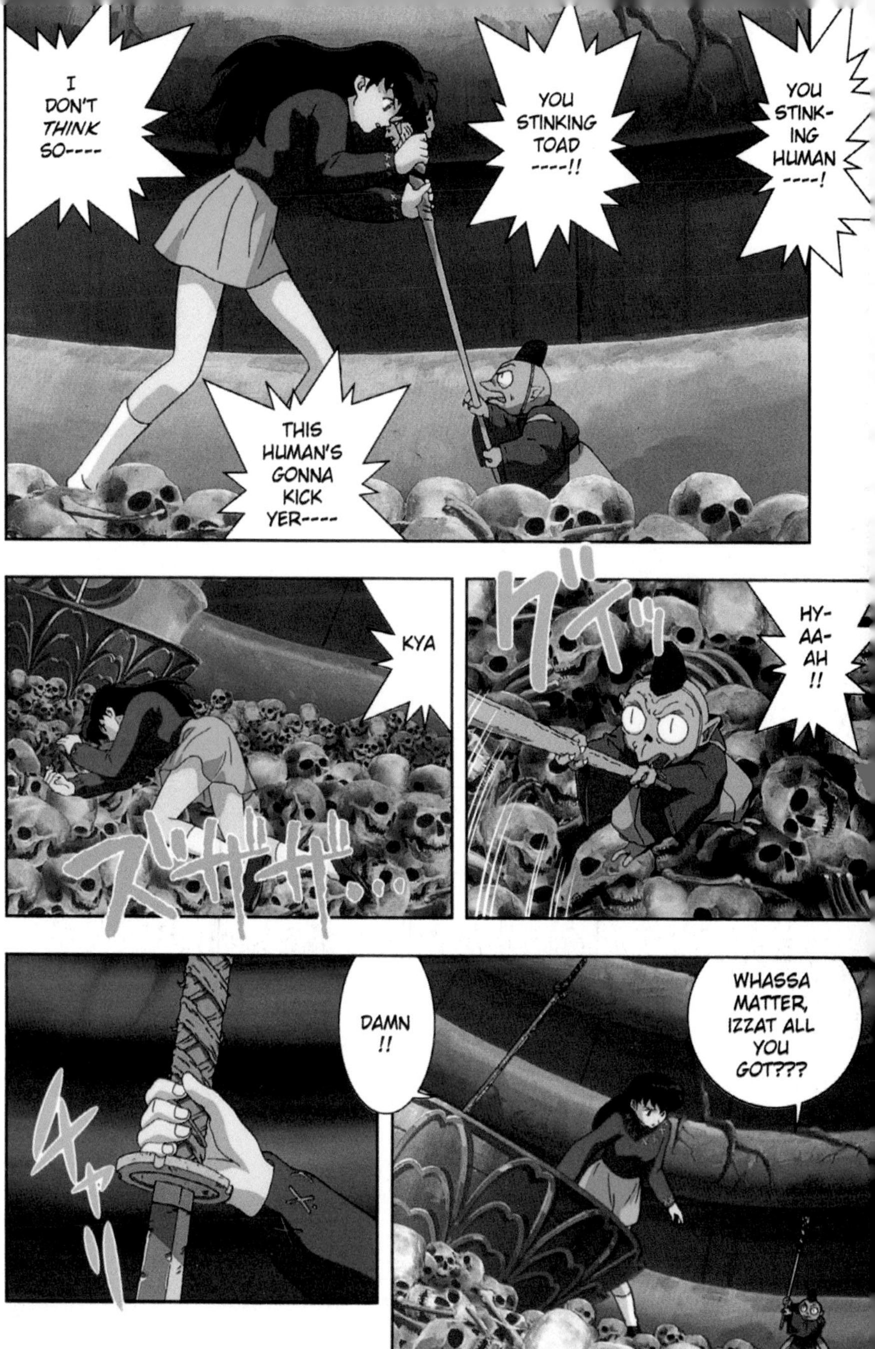
YOU STINK-ING HUMAN----!
YOU STINKING TOAD----!!
I DON'T THINK SO----
THIS HUMAN'S GONNA KICK YER----
HY-AA-AH!!
KYA
WHASSA MATTER, IZZAT ALL YOU GOT???
DAMN!!

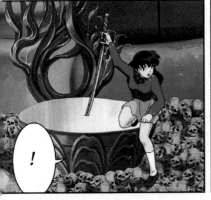

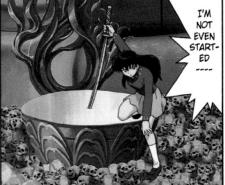

I'M NOT EVEN START-ED ----

!

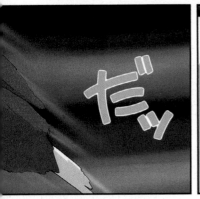

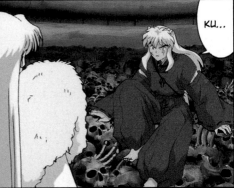

KU...

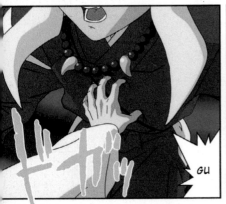

GU

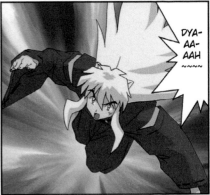

DYA-AA-AAH ~~~~

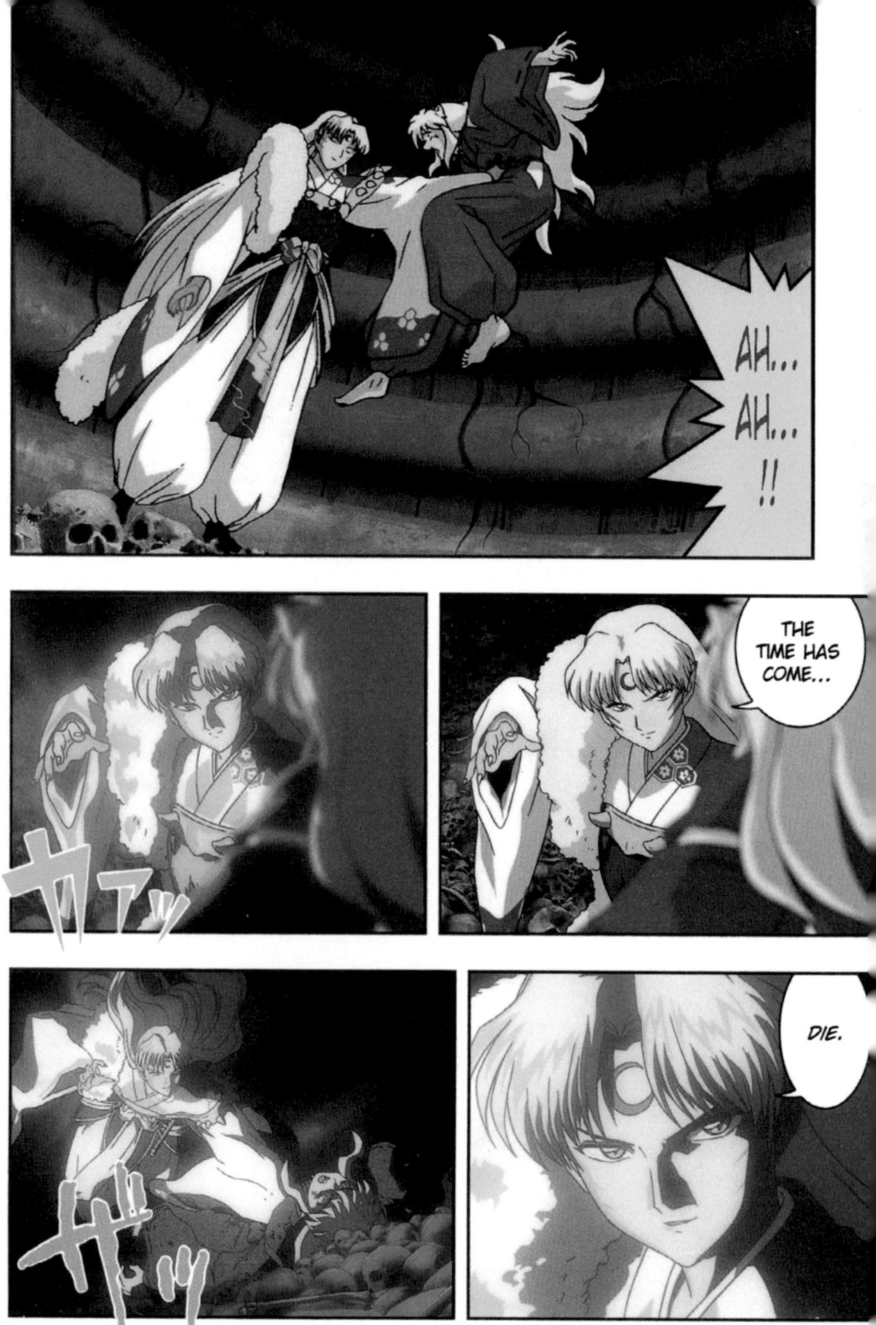
AH... AH... !!
THE TIME HAS COME...
カァッ
DIE.

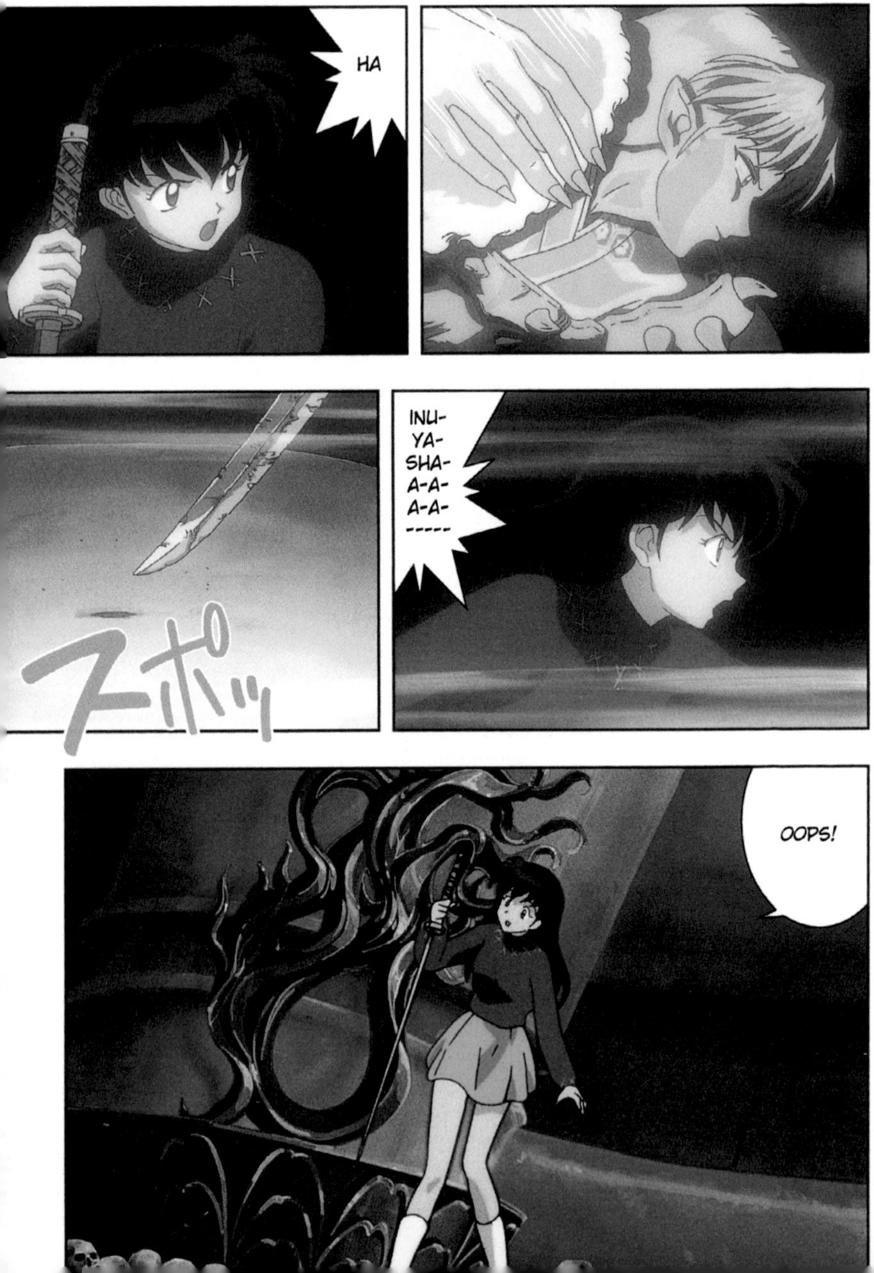
HA
INU-YA-SHA-A-A-A-A------
スポッ
OOPS!

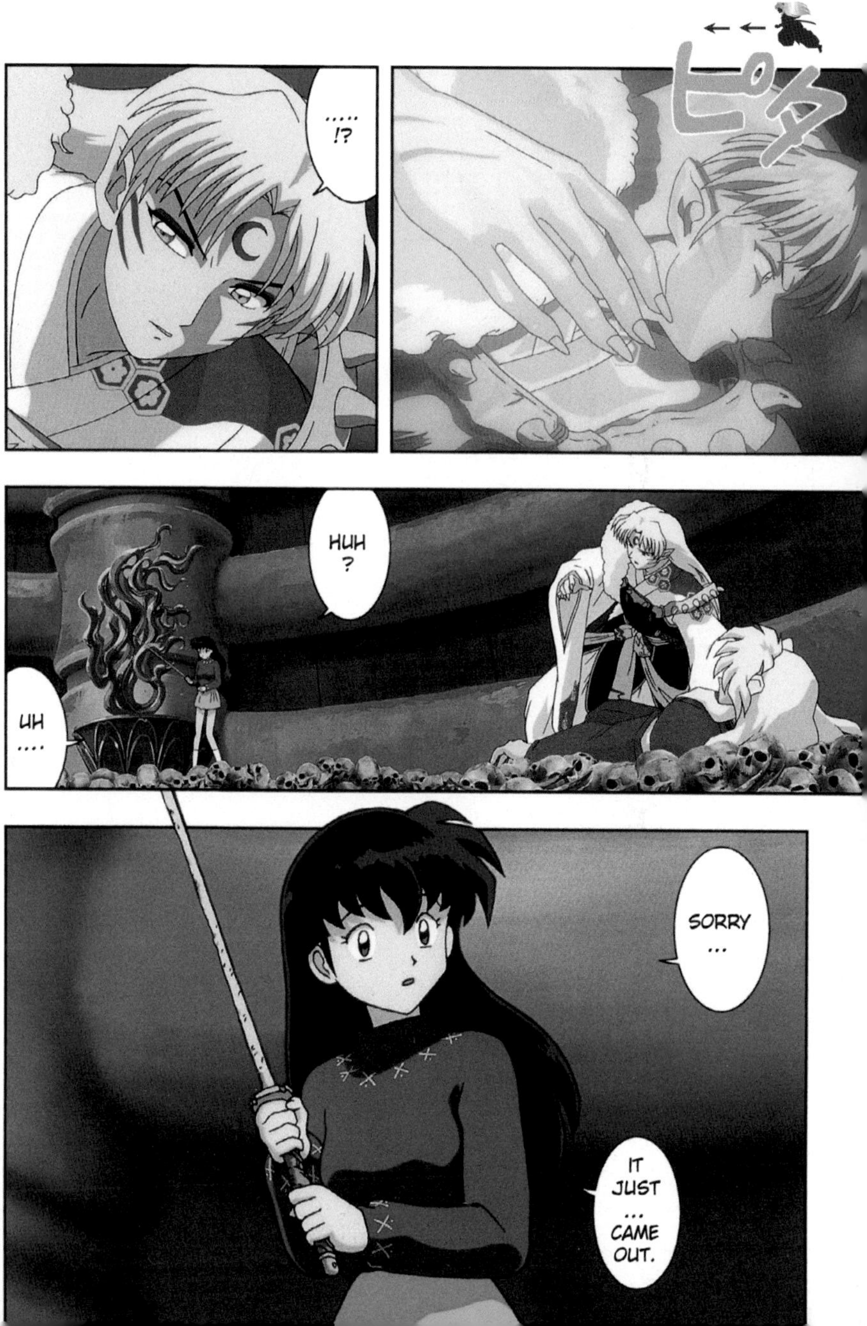
ピタ
..... !?
HUH ?
UH ....
SORRY ...
IT JUST ... CAME OUT.

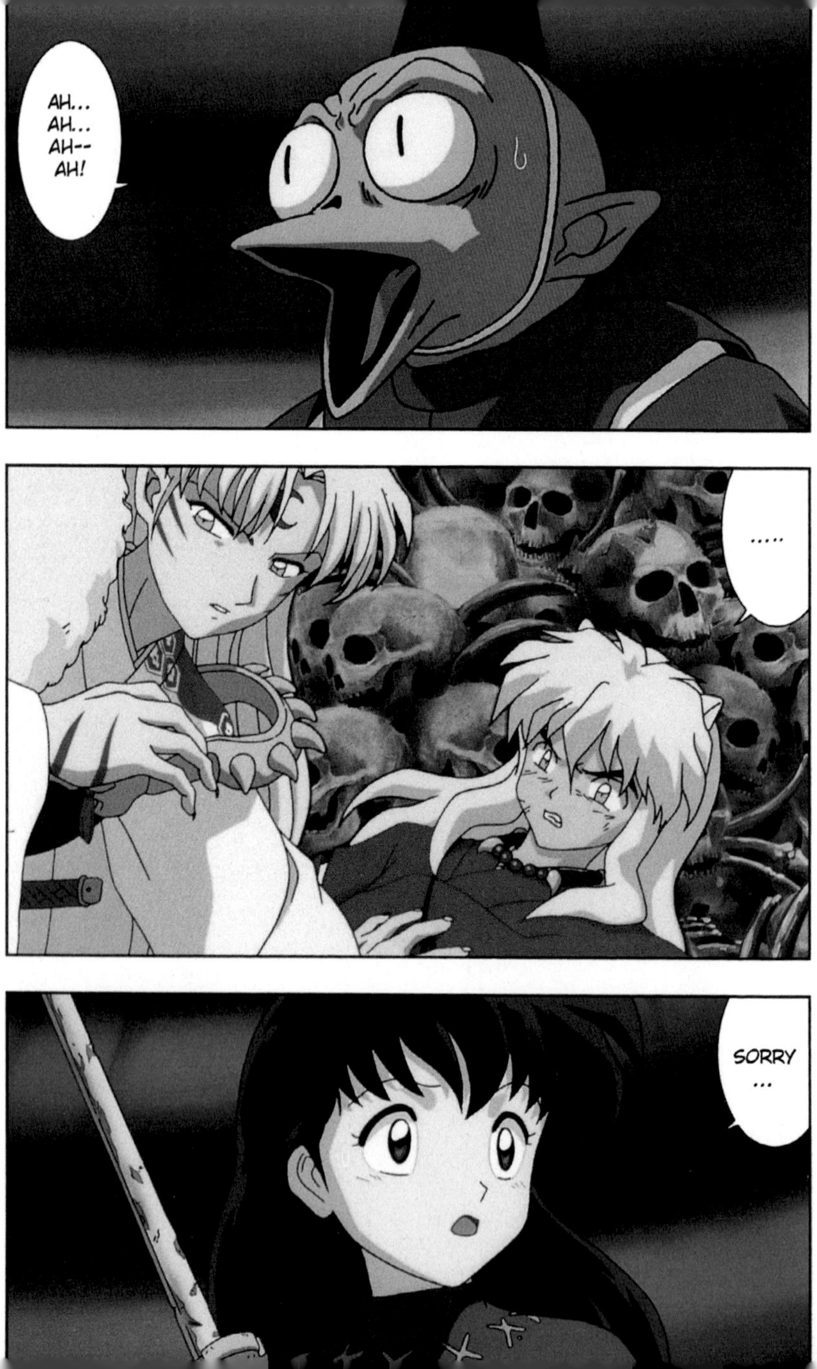
AH... AH... AH-- AH!
......
SORRY ...

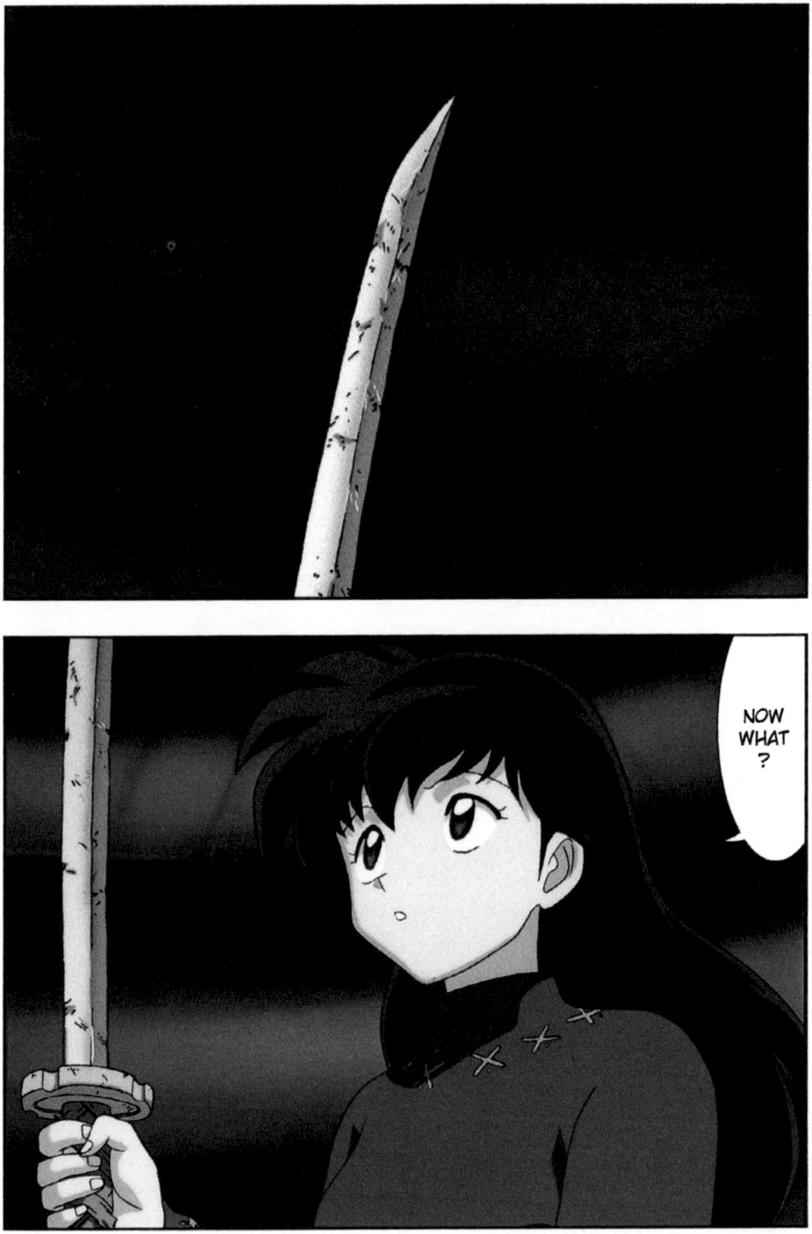
NOW WHAT ?

Glossary of Sound Effects

Each entry includes: the location, indicated by page number and panel number (so 3.1 means page 3, panel number 1); the phonetic romanization of the original Japanese; and our English "translation"—we offer as close an English equivalent as we can.

26.5 FX:Za (hair attackes)
27.1 FX:Shurururu… (hair wraps around Inu)]
27.6 FX:Bun (Inu tries to hit)
28.2 FX:Gui (twang)
28.4 FX:Tsu tsu (sound of blood on hair)
28.6 FX:Zuba (Inu slashes hair)
29.1 FX:Basa basa (dry, sliding away sound)
29.2 FX:Shuuuu.. (windy, misty sound as hair slides?)
30.3 FX:Huasa (mystery rustling gets Kag's attention)
31.4 FX:Ba (jump)
35.4 FX:Za za za (running)
35.5 FX:Za (run and leap)
36.2 FX:Za (landing)
37.4 FX:Za za za (running)
38.3 FX:Kiri kiri (hair slicing)
38.4 FX:Supa (tree sliced, explosion sound)
38.6 FX:Suta (Inu touches down)
39.1 FX:Go go go (hair moving)
39.2 FX:Dohn (Inu jmps)
39.3 FX:Goh (touching down)
40.2 FX:Doh (hair streaks toward our heroes)
40.3 FX:Buo (hair approaching)
40.4 FX:Shururuu… (hair wraps around Inu)
40.5 FX:Zuzaza… (Kag skids in dirt)
41.2 FX:Hyohh… (flying sound)
41.3 FX:Toh (feet land on high-wire hair)
44.3 FX:Buchi (hair attacks)
44.4 FX:Zuba (hair flies by)
44.5 FX:Goh (Inu hitches ride on hair and flies through air)
44.6 FX:Za (whoosh)
FX:Bun (voom)
45.3 FX:Ba (Yura sends out hair)
45.5 FX:Goh (a veritable hair explosion)

Episode 4: "Yura of the Demon Hair"

6.3 FX:Pichon (dripping)
8.2 FX:Gan gan (pound pound)
FX:Peta (sticking stuff on)
9.1 FX:Ga--- (hair dryer sound)
10.1 FX:Za za za (running)
10.2 FX:Za (run and leap)
10.3 FX:Kun kun (sniff sniff)
11.4 FX:Ba (jump)
11.5 FX:Goh (Whoosh. Jumping into magic well)
13.2 FX:Shururuu… (arrow flies)
13.3 FX:Doh (impact)
13.4 FX:Pa—n (bird explodes)
13.5 FX:Pishi (jewel cracks)
13.6 FX:Pa—n (Jewel explodes)
16.3 FX:Gu gu (bubble bubble)
17.4 FX:Dan dan (tromp tromp)
17.5 FX:Gara (abruptly opening door)
19.4 FX:Gui (squeezing arm)
20.4 FX:Hara (sound of shining hair that only Kagome can see)
21.1 FX:Shururuu… (hair twines around hand)
22.5 FX:Ban (sounds of hair approaching?)
23.1 FX:Zawa zawa… (hair making a commotion)
24.3 FX:Buo (hair explodes out)
24.4 FX:Za za za (hair snakes out)
24.5 FX:Zuga (impact as hair attacks and misses Kag)
25.2 FX:Suka (Inu lands)
25.3 FX:Shururuu… (hair unwinding)
25.4 FX:Don don (pounding on door)
25.5/6 FX:Zuba (Inu magic)
26.1 FX:Basa basa (hair rustling)
26.2 FX:Zawa zawa (hair making a commotion)
26.4 FX:Zawa zawa (more of same)

62.5	FX:Za (Yura steps on Inu's hand)
64.5	FX:Gui (twang of hair)
65.1	FX:Zuru (falling)
65.2	FX:Ga (climbing)
65.3	FX:Ba (grab)
65.4	FX:Guo (note: 3 and 4 are generic fight sounds)
65.5/6	FX:Zuba (light)
66.2	FX:Ba ba ba (lots of hair)
66.3	FX:Hu…(fwun)
66.4	FX:Gui ((hair whoosh)
66.5	FX:Don (Inu captured by hair)
67.5	FX:Ta (Yura turns quickly)
68.1	FX:Bari (ripping off hair)
68.2	FX:Da (jump)
68.3	FX:Gui (hair being strung up)
68.6	FX:Ba (Inu parts hair)
69.2	FX:Ba (Yura leaps)
69.3	FX:Gin (slash? sound of metal?)
69.6	FX:Gui (hair twang/whoosh)
69.1	FX:Ba (Yura's move. Whoosh)
69.2	FX:Shurururu… (whizzing thru air)
69.3	FX:Pishi (pulling tight)
69.5	FX:Ba ba ba (Inu's magic)
72.1	FX:Doh doh doh doh (blades pass Yura)
72.2	FX:Pi (blades cut string strangling Kag)
72.3	FX:Shurururu… (whizzing thru air)
72.4	FX:Zu zu zu… (still tied Kag collapsing down onto hair)
73.1	FX:Ta (Inu lands)
73.2	FX:Toh (Inu leaps away)
73.3	FX:Shuta (Inu touches down)
73.4	FX:Doh (Inu stabbed)
74.4	FX:Ba (blade thrown)
74.6	FX:Pita (bade moves toward Inu)
	FX:Ga ga (Kag hammers on skull)
75.1	FX:Ga ga (more hammering on skull)
75.2	FX:Ga ga (more hammering on skull)
76.2	FX:Paki (Kag punctures skull)
76.3	FX:Pita (sword stops abruptly)
76.4	FX:Kaaaaa… (magic released)
77.2	FX:Paki (magic comb breaks)
77.5	FX:Huu… (Yura dissolves)
78.1	FX:Chari (sword clatters down)
46.2	FX:Buo (Inu overcome by hair)
46.4	FX:Su… (hair snakes quickly around ankles)
47.1	FX:Ba (fight sound)
47.2	FX:Hyurururu… (Yura flips as she descends)
47.4	FX:Gishi (sproing! Yura lands on high-wire hair)
47.5	FX:Goh (Yura whooshes back up)
47.6	FX:Zuba (Hair pulls tight)
48.3	FX:Pero (lick)
48.4	FX:Chari (Yura draws sword)
48.6	FX:Goh (Yura whooshes thru air)
49.1	FX:Shu (hair flies past Yura)
49.2	FX:Toh (Yura lights on high-wire hair)
50.6	FX:Shu (nocking arrow)
51.2	FX:Shururu6ru… (arrow flies)
51.5	FX:Hehro hehro (arrows passes past hair)
51.6	FX:Pusu (Pssss. arrow lands in hairball)
52.1	FX:Pohh (magic starts)
52.2	FX:Kaaaaa… (magic spreads)
52.3	FX:Zu zu zu zu (hair comes unbound)
54.1	FX:Gohh (flames)
54.2	FX:Gohhh… (flames)
55.1	FX:Gohhhhh… (flames)
56.2	FX:Ba (Hair encircles wrist)
56.3	FX:Zuba (slash)
56.4	FX:Supa (Yura's hand gets cut off)
57.1	FX:Bura… (hand continues on its merry way)
57.5	FX:Ke ke ke… ku ku ku… (skulls laugh)
58.2	FX:Go go go (Here come the skulls)
58.3	FX:Doga (blow)
	FX:Paki (blow)
58.4	FX:Chari (blade drawn)
58.5	FX:Gohh (sword swipe)
59.1	FX:Bun (vwoom)
59.2	FX:Gin gin (Blades deflected by hair. Ping, ping)
59.4	FX:Gohh (sword swipe)
59.5	FX:Doh (sword cuts thru Inu)
60.1	FX:Dosa (Inu falls)
60.2	FX:Shururuu… (hair goes thru air)
60.3	FX:Pita (hand attaches)
61.3	FX:Bun (slash)
62.1	FX:Doh (punch thru Yura)
62.3	FX:Zuboh (squishy sound as Inu gets hand out of Yura's chest)

114.6 FX:Sukku (Kag stands abruptly)
120.1 FX:Zawa (space) zawa (wind in trees)
120.3 FX:Doh (Inu drops, pushing down Kag)
122.5 FX:Zu zu (space) zu zu (oxcart continues on into clouds)
123.2 FX:Jarra… (clanking of chains)
123.4 FX:Ta ta ta… (running)
124.1 FX:Zu zu zu (demon hand reaches for oxcart)
124.2 FX:Ga (grabs oxcart)
124.3 FX:Bakii (crushes oxcart)
124.5 FX:Guohhhh… (demon roars)
125.1 FX:Guohhhhh… (more roaring)
125.4 FX:Ta (Inu jumps)
126.1 FX:Gohh (flames)
126.3 FX:Toh (Inu touches down)
130.6 FX:Pishi (Sessho's whip)
131.1 FX:Gishi Gishi (chains tugging tighter)
133.1 FX:Giri giri (chains tighten)
133.2 FX:Gaku (Mom falls)
133.4 FX:Ba (Inu leaps)
133.5 FX:Zuba (Inu's magic blow)
134.2 FX:Ta (Inu touches down)
134.3 FX:Za (Mom falls)
134.4 FX:Kii kii (pixie demon voices)
135.2 FX:Pishi (Sessho's whip)
135.4 FX:Da (leap)
136.3 FX:Kaa (Mom's magic)
136.4 FX:Kaaaaa… (magic builds in power)
137.1 FX:Kaaaaa… (magic builds bigger)

Episode 6
Tetsusaiga the Phantom Sword

147.1 FX:Kyu Kyu (seat tightening)
151.3 FX:Po—(sound of Inu mom conjuring flower)
151.4 FX:Fu… (flower drops)
151.5 FX:Hara (pause) hara (flower breaks up)
155.2 FX:zu zu zu (hands sinking into Inu's back)
156. FX:Jyara (chains clanking)
156.4 and 5 FX: Zu zu zu zu… (Inu sinking into mom demon)
158.4 FX:Chu----[!] (slurrrp!)
158.5 FX Bachin (smack)
159.1 FX: Muku (chains disappearing)
159.3 FX:Gii gii (ooars creaking)

81.3 FX:Bashi (Kag whacks Inu on back)
81.4 FX:Dosa (Inu falls)

Episode 5
Aristocratic assassin, Sesshomaru

87.1/2 FX:Grrrr… (growling)
89.1 FX:Ba (wolves charge)
89.2 FX:Shurururururu… (Sessho's magic whip whizzes thru air)
89.3 FX:Zuba (wolves blow up)
90.3 FX:Kiiiii… (staff screams)
91.3 FX:Za za za (wolves running fast)
91.4 FX:Zazaza… (up close sound of running)
94.3 FX:Za (magic at blurring speed)
94.4 FX:Ga (grab to strangle)
95.2 FX:Bun (discarded body falls)
95.3 FX:Zan (stuff blowing up)
97.1 FX:Da (Sessho whizzes past)
97.2 FX:Gohh (roar of flames)
97.3 FX:Gohhhhh… (more flames roaring)
98.3 FX:Shu shu… (sound of smoking ruins)
98.4 FX:Gugu (staff turns head)
99.4 FX:(Jakken gets smakced)
99.5 FX:Zan (splash)
100.1 FX:Zaba (splashing)
100.2 FX:Ga (Sessho pushes Jakken under water again) (note: he really is an awfully nasty guy!)
101.2 FX:Gei (Sessho pushes Jakken under again)
101.5 FX:Goho goho (Jakken coughing/gasping/drowning)
104.1 FX:Pyon (hop)
104.3 FX:Chiri (creaky bicycle sound)
104.4 FX:Guo (Myoga's alarm)
104.5 FX:Puchi (squish)
106.2 FX:Dosa (Inu slams into ground)
110.1 FX:Chu— chu—(slurrrp slurrrp)
110.3 FX:Pachin (Myoga jumps onto Inu's hand)
113.6 FX:Doga (heel lands on Myoga)
114.1 FX:Guri (space) guri (grinding squash for emphasis)
114.1 FX:Gugugu… (Myoga becoming three dimensional again)
114.2 FX:Pon (Pop!)

181.2 FX:Suu (S'maru and Jaken disappear thru hole)
183.1 FX:Gohhhh… (sailing through air)
183.2 FX:Gohhh… (more sailing through air)
183.3 FX:Za (landing on bird)
183.4 FX:Go (roar)
185.3 FX:Goh (they fly off into the vortex)
186.4 FX:Chari (sword being drawn)
188.2 FX:Ba (whoosh)
188.3 FX:Bun (voom)
188.4 FX:Zuza (Inu takes a fall)
191.4 FX:Ba (Inu springs)
191. 5 FX:Baki (crack)
192.1 FX:Ta (S'maru touches down)
192.2 FX:Ba (Inu leaps up)
192.4 FX:Ga (strike)
195.1 FX:Kaaaaah… (sword shining)
195.4/5 FX:Shuuuuuu (sword shining and starting to come out, but…)
196.1 FX:Shuuuuu (light fades away)
196.6 FX:Goh (S'maru strikes)
197.1 FX:Za (Inu come down on S'maru)
197.2 FX:Ta ta ta… (Inu runs)
197.3 FX:Dohhn (jump)
197.6 FX:Kaa (claws approaching Inu)
198.1 FX:Goh (here come the claws)
198.2 FX:Za (Inu dodges)
198.5 FX:Ba (swipe)
198.6 FX:Pishi (whip sound)
199.1 FX:Za (Inu skids to halt)
199.3 FX:Doka (Kag squishes Jaken)
199.5 FX:Bun (Jaken striking with staff)
200.2 FX:Gi (Jalken swings staff)
200.3 FX:Zu zaza… (Kag falling back on crunching skulls)
200.5 FX:Chari (sword is being drawn)
201.4 FX:Da (Inu springs)
201.6 FX:Doga (S'maru's hand slams Inu)
202.3 FX:Kaa (poison claws coming)
202.5 FX:Za (poison claws closer)
203.4 FX:Supo (sword comes loose)
204.1 FX:Pita (S'maru's caws as he gets distracted)

160.2 FX:Da [!] (Jaken landing on ground)
160.3 FX:Da [!] (Jaken landing on ground)
163.6 FX:Guru guru (hands snaking around Inu)
164.3 FX:Ga (wham!)
165.1 FX:Hyurururu… (Jaken flying into pond)
165.2 FX:Zan (little toad-like splash)
165.3 FX:Sa [!] (rustle of cloth)
165.4 FX:Da (footstep)
165.5 FX:Ta ta ta…(Kag's footsteps)
165.6 FX:Za za za (Inu mom moving)
166.1 FX:Ga (Kag grabbing Inu's hair)
166.3 FX:Dosa (falls to breast)
166.4 FX:Zu zu zu… (Inu getting sucked up)
168.3 FX:Da (running)
168.4 FX:Basha (splash)
169.1 FX:Zaba---n (splashing)
171.2 FX:Gyun (S'maru rushing Inu)
171.3 FX:Ga [!] (sound of stranglehold)
173.1 FX:Pari pari (a foreshadowing sound. we find out what this is in frame 3)
173.3 FX:Pari pari pari (zap, zap, zap, sound of magic beam drawing out Jewel)
173.4 FX:Zu (crackly sound of S'maru's magic rays)
173.5 FX:Zu zu (same)
175.5 FX:Ba (Inu's move)
175.5 FX:Za (S'maru's move)
176.1 FX:Shu (beam shooting out)
176.2 FX:Bishi (whip crack)
176.3 FX:Shururuuru (ribbony thing unrolling)
176. 4 FX:Bishi (whip crack)
177.1 FX:Shu (whoosh)
177.2 FX:Ba (sudden appearance)
177.3 FX:Bishi (big whip crack)
177.5 FX:Zuba (light beam flash)
178.1 FX:Dosa (un-mother explodes)
178.2 FX:Harari (Inu's start at kimono scrap)
179.2 FX:Paki (head explodes)
179.3 FX:Shuru… (S'maru's power)
179. 4 FX:Suto (S'maru's movement)
180.3 FX:Koron (Jewel falls)
180.5 FX:Ga (S'maru smashes pearl)
180.6 FX:Ka ka ka ka…. (staff laughs, wuo ho ho ha ha ha in anime)
181.1 FX:Goh (hole opening in clouds)

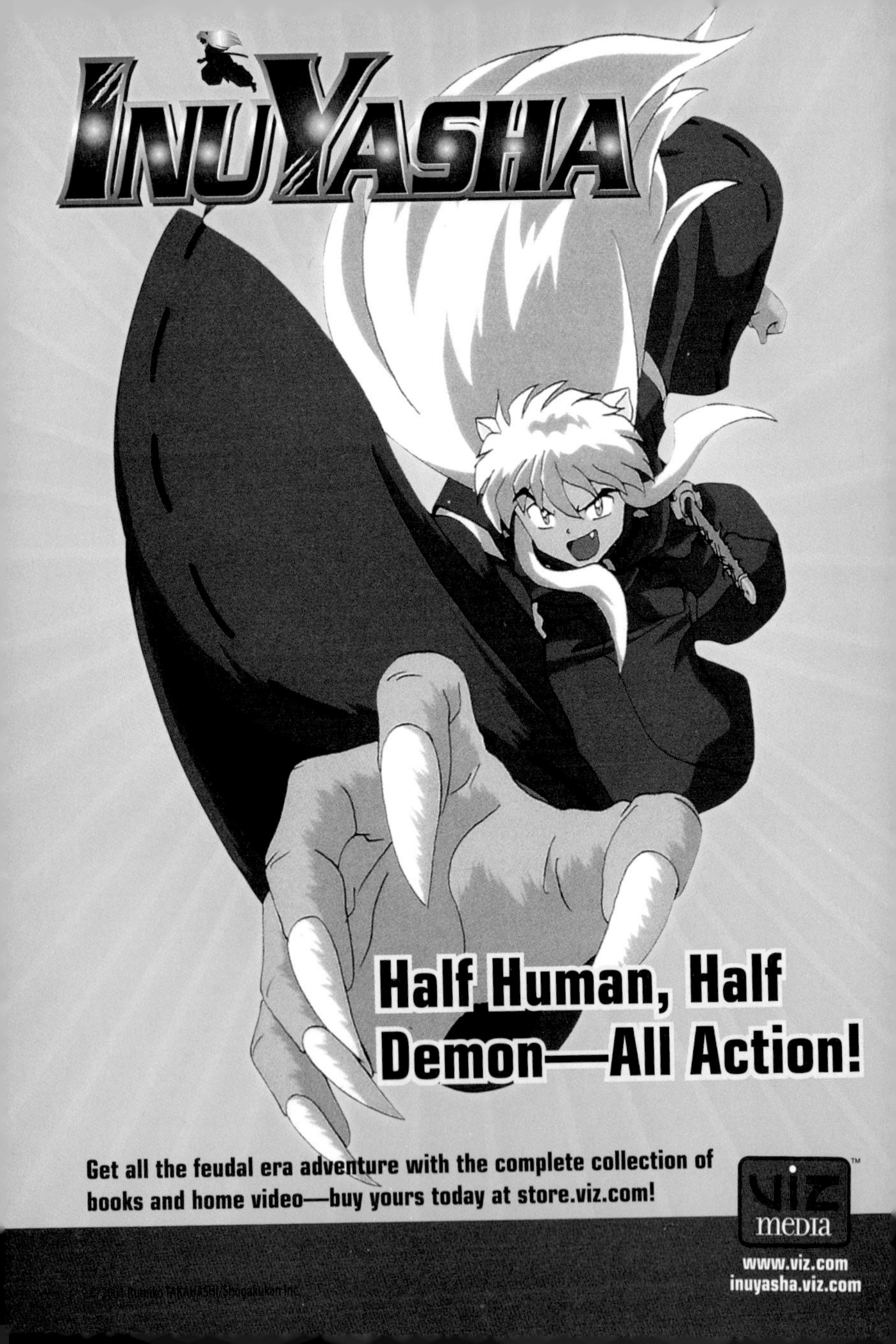
INUYASHA
Half Human, Half Demon—All Action!
Get all the feudal era adventure with the complete collection of books and home video—buy yours today at store.viz.com!
VIZ media
www.viz.com
inuyasha.viz.com
Rumiko TAKAHASHI/Shogakukan Inc.

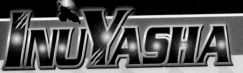

InuYasha

action
viz media
InuYasha
Story and Art by
RUMIKO TAKAHASHI
Vol. 1

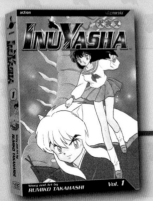

Read the action from the start with the original manga series

action
InuYasha
Ani-Manga
犬夜叉
CREATED BY
RUMIKO TAKAHASHI
1

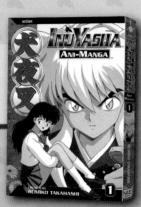

Full color adaptation of the popular TV series

The Art of
InuYasha
犬夜叉
Original illustrations by
Rumiko Takahashi

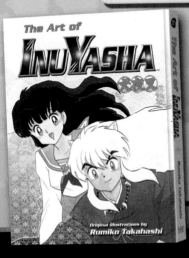

Art book with cel art, paintings, character profiles and more

TV SERIES & MOVIES ON DVD!

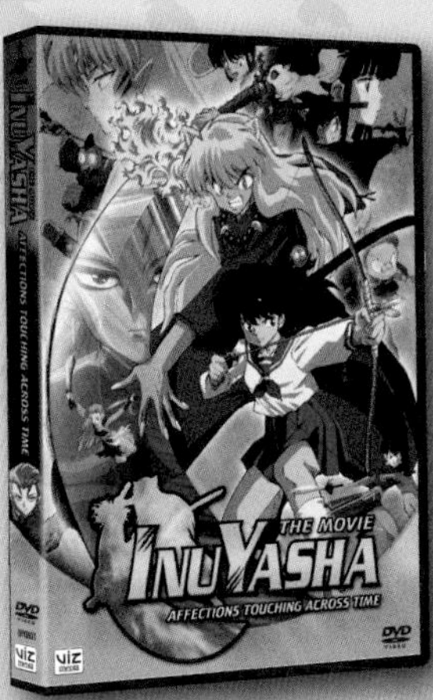
INUYASHA
AFFECTIONS TOUCHING ACROSS TIME
THE MOVIE
INUYASHA
AFFECTIONS TOUCHING ACROSS TIME
DVD
VIZ

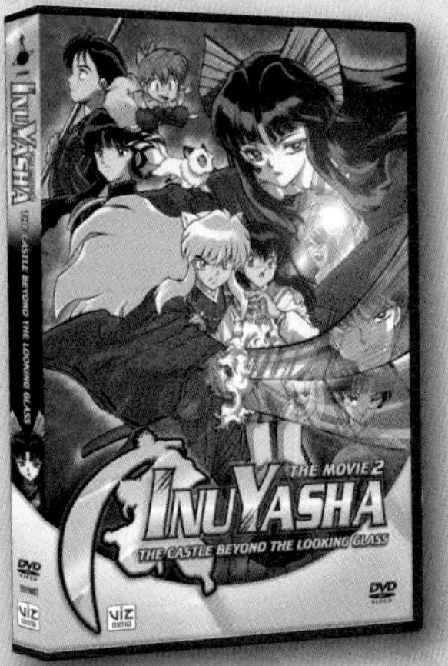
INUYASHA
THE CASTLE BEYOND THE LOOKING GLASS
THE MOVIE 2
INUYASHA
THE CASTLE BEYOND THE LOOKING GLASS
DVD
VIZ

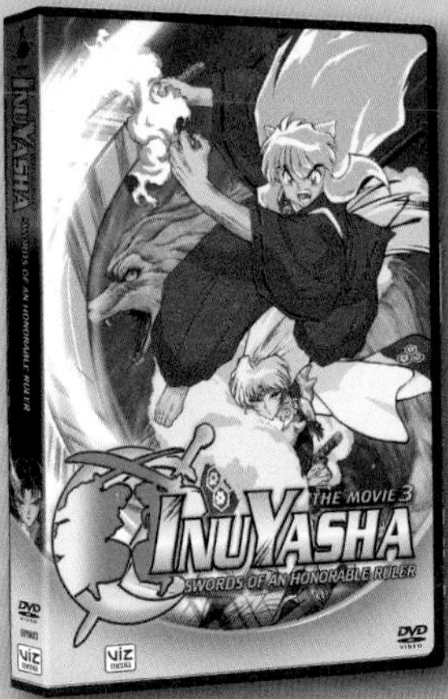
INUYASHA
SWORDS OF AN HONORABLE RULER
THE MOVIE 3
INUYASHA
SWORDS OF AN HONORABLE RULER
DVD
VIZ

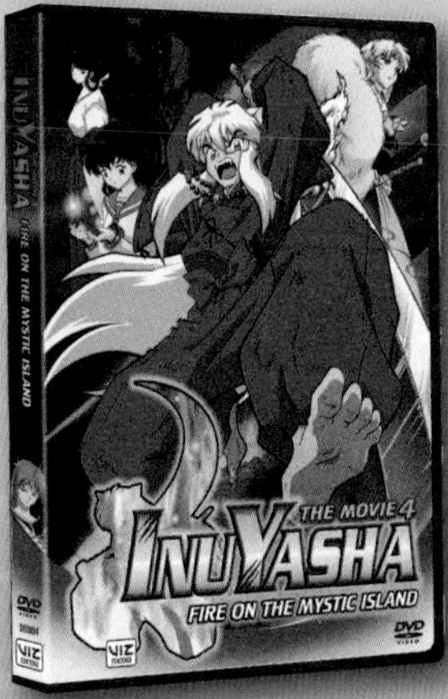
INUYASHA
FIRE ON THE MYSTIC ISLAND
THE MOVIE 4
INUYASHA
FIRE ON THE MYSTIC ISLAND
DVD
VIZ

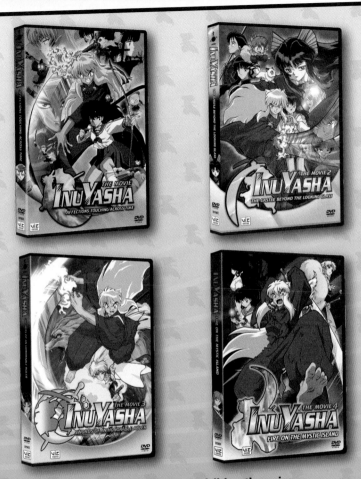

See more of the action in Inuyasha full-length movies

viz media™

www.viz.com
inuyasha.viz.com

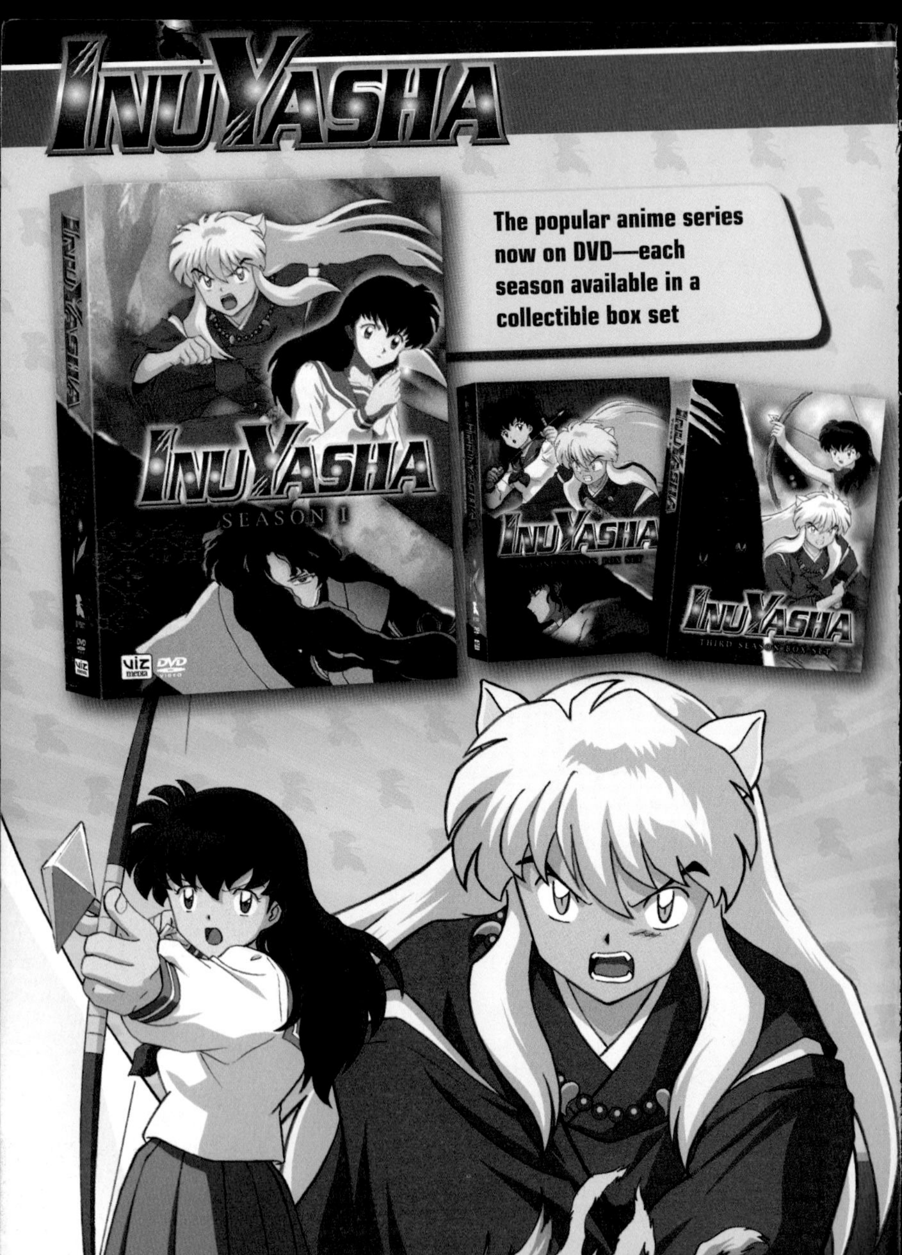
InuYasha
The popular anime series now on DVD—each season available in a collectible box set
InuYasha
Season 1
InuYasha
InuYasha
Third Season Box Set

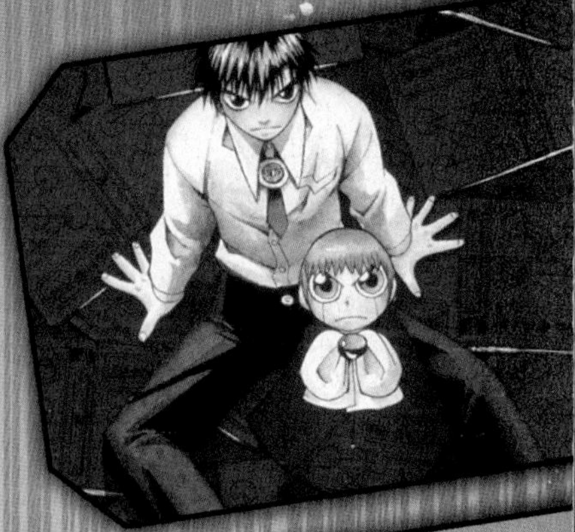
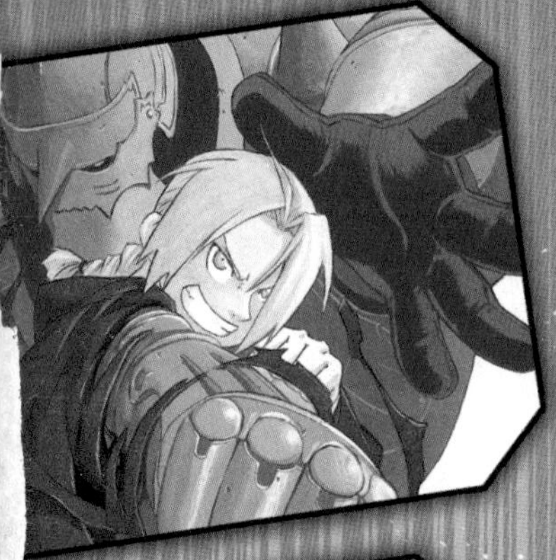
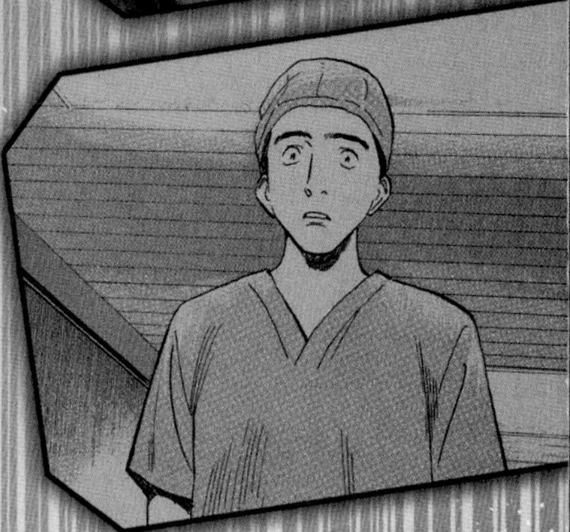
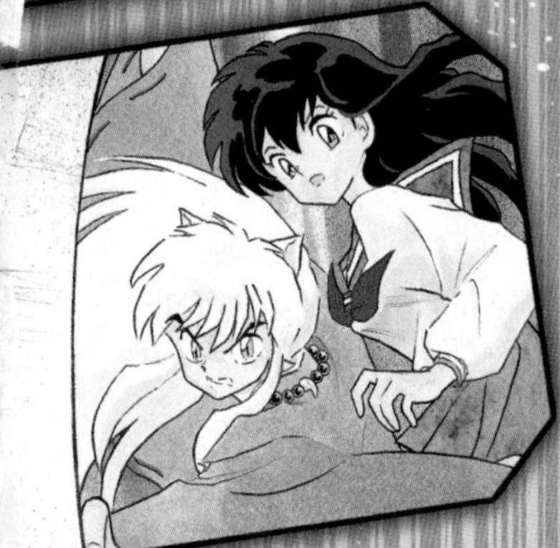